C454556500

City Council
Newcastle Libraries and Information Service

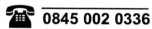 **0845 002 0336**

Due for return	Due for return	Due for return

Please return this item to any of Newcastle's Libraries by the last
date shown above. If not requested by another customer the loan
can be renewed, you can do this by phone, post or in person.
Charges may be made for late returns.

GROWING UP FATHERLESS
IN ANTIQUITY

As the changes in the traditional family accelerated toward the end of the twentieth century, a great deal of attention came to focus on fathers, both modern and ancient. While academics and politicians alike singled out the conspicuous and growing absence of the modern father as a crucial factor affecting contemporary family and social dynamics, ancient historians and classicists have rarely explored ancient father-absence, despite the likelihood that nearly a third of all children in the ancient Mediterranean world were fatherless before they turned fifteen. The proportion of children raised by single mothers, relatives, stepparents, or others was thus at least as high in antiquity as it is today. This book assesses the wide-ranging impact that high levels of chronic father-absence had on the cultures, politics, and families of the ancient world.

SABINE R. HÜBNER is a visiting research scholar at the Institute for the Study of the Ancient World at New York University and an adjunct assistant professor of Ancient History at Columbia University.

DAVID M. RATZAN holds degrees in Classics from Yale and Cambridge Universities. He is currently finishing his doctoral work at Columbia University on the social and economic history of contract in Roman Egypt.

GROWING UP FATHERLESS
IN ANTIQUITY

EDITED BY

SABINE R. HÜBNER

AND

DAVID M. RATZAN

CAMBRIDGE
UNIVERSITY PRESS

CAMBRIDGE UNIVERSITY PRESS
Cambridge, New York, Melbourne, Madrid, Cape Town, Singapore, São Paulo, Delhi

Cambridge University Press
The Edinburgh Building, Cambridge CB2 8RU, UK

Published in the United States of America by Cambridge University Press, New York

www.cambridge.org
Information on this title: www.cambridge.org/9780521490504

First published 2009

Printed in the United Kingdom at the University Press, Cambridge

A catalogue record for this publication is available from the British Library

ISBN 978-0-521-49050-4 hardback

Utriusque patribus,
qui semper nobis affuerunt

Contents

vii

Figures

x

Tables

Contributors

THE EDITORS

SABINE R. HÜBNER is a visiting research scholar at the Institute for the Study of the Ancient World at New York University and an adjunct assistant professor of Ancient History at Columbia University. She studied History and Classics at Münster, Rome, Berlin, Jena, London, Berkeley, and New York, and she has held several fellowships and research grants from the European Union, the German Research Association, and the German Academic Exchange Service. She has published a monograph on the clergy of the later Roman Empire, *Der Klerus in der Gesellschaft des spätantiken Kleinasiens* (2005), as well as various articles on later Roman society, old age in Classical Greece, Greek epigraphy, and marriage patterns in Greco-Roman Egypt. Dr. Hübner's current projects include a monograph on intergenerational relations in the Greco-Roman East, co-editing Blackwell's new *Encyclopedia of Ancient History*, and contributions to the forthcoming *Oxford Handbook on Children in the Ancient World* and the *Blackwell Companion to the Ancient Family*.

DAVID M. RATZAN holds degrees in Classics from Yale University and Clare College, Cambridge. He is currently finishing his doctoral work at Columbia University on the social and economic history of contract in Roman Egypt.

THE CONTRIBUTORS

NEIL W. BERNSTEIN is an assistant professor in the Department of Classics and World Religions at Ohio University. His book, *In the Image of the Ancestors: Narratives of Kinship in Flavian Epic*, was recently published by the University of Toronto Press.

RAFFAELLA CRIBIORE is Professor of Classics at New York University. She has written three books on ancient education, *Writing, Teachers and Students in Graeco-Roman Egypt* (1996), *Gymnastics of the Mind: Greek Education in Hellenistic and Roman Egypt* (2001), and *The School of Libanius in Late Antique Antioch* (2007). She has also co-authored with R. Bagnall *Women's Letters in Ancient Egypt: 300 BC–AD 800* (2006).

MARK GOLDEN is Professor of Classics at the University of Winnipeg. He is the author of *Children and Childhood in Classical Athens* (1990), *Sport and Society in Ancient Greece* (1998), *Sport in the Ancient World from A to Z* (2004), and *Greek Sport and Social Status* (2008). He is also the editor (along with Peter Toohey) of three books on ancient social history.

JUDITH P. HALLETT is Professor of Classics at the University of Maryland, College Park. She received her BA from Wellesley College, and her MA and PhD from Harvard University. She has published widely on Latin language and literature; ancient women writers; gender, sexuality, and the family in ancient Greco-Roman society; and the reception of Classics in the United States.

ANN-CATHRIN HARDERS is a lecturer in Ancient History at the University of Freiburg, Germany. Her research deals with the Roman family, the social history of the Roman Republic, and Hellenistic kingship. Recent articles include studies on Roman prosopography as well as Roman kinship. Her study on Roman kinship, *Suavissima Soror. Zur Bedeutung verwandtschaftlicher Beziehungen in der römischen Republik*, is due to be published in 2008 (Munich).

MYRTO MALOUTA, after completing a DPhil in Papyrology, is a research assistant for the Oxford Roman Economy Project and a junior research fellow at Worcester College, Oxford. Her research lies primarily in papyrology, Roman social and economic history, and history of Greco-Roman Egypt.

SABINE MÜLLER is a lecturer in Ancient History at the University of Hannover. She studied Medieval and Modern History, Art History, and Ancient History in Gießen, where she earned her PhD. She has published articles on Argead Macedonia, the Hellenistic world, gender studies, and art history.

GEOFFREY NATHAN is a lecturer in Roman History in the School of History and Philosophy at the University of New South Wales. He is primarily a social and cultural historian focusing on the late antique and early Byzantine periods. He has written on family life in the late Roman Empire – *The Family in Late Antiquity* (2000) – and his more recent publications include an extensive review article on early Christianity in the *Journal of Religious History* (2008).

DANIEL OGDEN is Professor of Ancient History in the University of Exeter. He is author of, inter alia, *Greek Bastardy* (1996), *The Crooked Kings of Ancient Greece* (1997), *Polygamy, Prostitutes and Death* (1999), *Greek and Roman Necromancy* (2001), *Magic, Witchcraft and Ghosts* (2002), *Aristomenes of Messene* (2004), *In Search of the Sorcerer's Apprentice* (2007), *Perseus* (2008) and *Night's Black Agents* (2008). He is also the editor of *The Hellenistic World: New Perspectives* (2002) and *A Companion to Greek Religion* (2007).

LOUISE PRATT is Associate Professor and Chair of Classics at Emory University. She is the author of *Lying and Poetry from Homer to Pindar: Falsehood and Deception in Archaic Greek Poetics*, as well as of several articles on Homeric and other early Greek poetry. She is currently working on a book provisionally entitled *Representations of Children and Child-rearing in Greek Literature*.

WALTER SCHEIDEL is Professor of Classics and, by courtesy, History and Chair of the Department of Classics at Stanford University. His research focuses on ancient social and economic history, pre-modern demography, and comparative and trans-disciplinary world history. His most recent publications include *The Cambridge Economic History of the Greco-Roman World* (2007, with I. Morris and R. Saller) and *The Dynamics of Ancient Empires* (2008, with I. Morris).

MARCUS SIGISMUND is a lecturer in Early Christian History and New Testament Exegesis at the Bergisch University, Wuppertal. He received his PhD in ancient history in 2002 (Bergisch University, Wuppertal) and is currently a post-doctoral researcher in the GRF-project "Septuaginta-Zitate im Neuen Testament" located at the Barmen School of Theology.

GEORG WÖHRLE is Professor of Classics at Trier University. His research focuses on ancient natural philosophy, medicine, rhetoric, and the reception of ancient literature. Among his many publications are *Hypnos, der Allbezwinger. Eine Studie zum literarischen Bild des Schlafes in der griechischen Antike* (1995) and *Telemachs Reise. Väter und Söhne in Ilias und Odyssee oder ein Beitrag zur Erforschung der Männlichkeitsideologie in der homerischen Welt* (1999).

Acknowledgments

No project like this comes to completion without a great deal of work by a host of people, many of whose names never appear in any library catalogue. We would therefore like to express our debt of gratitude first to the contributors whose commitment and enthusiasm for this project never flagged and who were both exceptionally generous with their advice and profoundly professional in their willingness to work with us as the manuscript moved through each stage of the editorial process. The volume as a whole was peer-reviewed by anonymous readers for Cambridge University Press and we are immensely grateful for their insightful comments. Many thanks also go to all those who read drafts of our Introduction. In particular, we want to thank Roger S. Bagnall, Beryl Rawson, and Richard P. Saller for their general advice. Jane F. Gardner pointed out several invaluable corrections with respect to some of the legal aspects of fatherlessness and guardianship. Rebecca Winers clarified many important elements of comparison that we had missed. We benefited greatly from the careful and exacting reading of both Giovanni Ruffini and Katharina Volk. Last but not least, we wish to thank Michael Sharp, his publishing assistant at Cambridge University Press, Petra Michalkova, and our indefatigable copy-editor, Jan Chapman, for all their help in shepherding this volume through to publication.

Note on abbreviations

Abbreviated references to ancient authors and works conform to the conventions of the *Oxford Classical Dictionary* (3rd edn.). A key to abbreviated papyrological references may be found in *Checklist of Greek, Latin, Demotic and Coptic Papyri, Ostraca and Tablets* (ed. [Oates,] Bagnall *et al.*; http://scriptorium.lib.duke.edu/papyrus/texts/clist.html).

Introduction

Fatherless antiquity? Perspectives on "fatherlessness" in the ancient Mediterranean

Sabine R. Hübner and David M. Ratzan

The modern study of the family was born in crisis, a response to the unmistakable and disturbing changes in family life precipitated by the Industrial Revolution. Although research into the family has changed profoundly in aim and method since the early nineteenth century, the original, underlying sense of crisis has persisted, reinterpreted with every succeeding generation.[1] In the 1990s the crisis in the family was articulated and popularized as a crisis of "fatherlessness." In the United States one critic thus decried the rise of a "culture of fatherlessness," fearful that fatherhood itself was close to extinction in a newly "fatherless America."[2] Fatherlessness, however, is not a uniquely American condition: similar concerns have recently been raised in Western Europe.[3]

Any discussion of fatherlessness fundamentally resolves into a debate over the importance of household form and composition. Household form greatly affects family relations and the interdependency of kin members, helping to define the roles each member plays in the family. The sudden disappearance of any family member necessarily results in multiple dislocations and readjustments, particularly when that member is as central to a family as the father. Father-absence was, in fact, the point of departure for much of the twentieth-century study of the father, a field that blossomed in recent decades with studies of fathers and fatherhood from

---

[1] For quick discussions on the intellectual and historical background to family studies, see Bridenthal 1982; Casey 1989; and Collier, Rosaldo, and Yanagisako 1992.

[2] Blankenhorn 1995; cf. Horn, Blankenhorn, and Pearlstein 1999.

[3] Although the idea may be traced back beyond the psychoanalytic and critical theory traditions, these are the most influential traditions informing the modern concept of fatherlessness. See Nobus 2003; cf. Horkheimer's "Autorität und Familie" (first published in 1936, now collected in Schmidt 1985; translation available in Horkheimer 1982); Mitscherlich 1963 (now available in translation: Mitscherlich 1993); Trowell and Etchgoyen 2002. For concerns about fatherlessness in Europe, see, e.g., Matussek 1998; 1999; 2006; and Nobus 2003.

4 SABINE R. HÜBNER AND DAVID M. RATZAN

a variety of perspectives, multidisciplinary and multicultural.[4] Indeed, for
many scholars the absence of the father remains an important, even defining,
aspect driving contemporary family dynamics.

The second part of the twentieth century also witnessed a renewed
interest in the ancient family, with great attention paid to the ancient father
in particular.[5] Much of this work concentrated on the ideology of patriarchy
and fatherhood, or alternatively on the effects of a father's presence, including his relationship to, and power over, his family, and the sentimental
ideals of conflict and concord in ancient family life. It is remarkable,
however, that despite a perennially high rate of father-absence in all ancient
societies (as we shall see below), ancient fatherlessness has not been investigated in its own right, leaving us no true counterpart to the modern
research on fathers and father-absence.[6]

This volume neither offers a complete overview of the experience of all
fatherless children in antiquity nor traces a history of fatherlessness over the
centuries. Rather, in bringing together into one place for the first time a
cross-section of thematic and methodological approaches to ancient father-
absence, it seeks to lay a foundation for an initial approach to fatherlessness
in the ancient Mediterranean world. Broadly speaking, the chapters herein
explore the various disturbances associated with a father's absence and the
coping strategies employed to alleviate the effects of those disturbances. It is
therefore not a book about orphans or even children per se, but rather more
generally about family dynamics and the ways in which ancient people
compensated for the loss of a father. The contributors discuss marriage
patterns, child-rearing, surrogate fathers, the position of women and children in ancient societies, and the personal, emotional, economic, and social
consequences of father-absence. At another level, the combination of persistent father-absence and patriarchy in the ancient world ensured that the
ramifications of father-absence went beyond individuals and their families

---

[4] See the review of the literature and the various chapters in Marsiglio *et al.* 2000 and Lamb 2004. On
early studies of fathers and father-absence, see Lamb 2000 and Lamb and Lewis 2004.
[5] The secondary literature on the ancient family is vast. The most recent views and bibliography can be
gleaned from the following: Wiedemann 1989; Golden 1990; Rawson 1991a; Dixon 1992; Cohen 1993;
Perdue 1997; Pomeroy 1997; Rawson and Weaver 1997; Gardner 1998; Nevett 1999; Nathan 2000;
Neils and Oakley 2003 and Rawson 2003. For the ancient father generally, see J. Martin 1984. For the
Greek world, see Finlay 1980; Strauss 1993; French 1999; Wöhrle 1999 and Shapiro 2003. For the
Roman world, see Lee 1979; Hallett 1984; W. V. Harris 1986; Lacey 1986; Thomas 1986; Eyben 1991;
LeMoine 1991; Stevenson 1992; Arjava 1998; Shaw 2001; and Cantarella 2003.
[6] The notable exception is the work of Richard Saller. Otherwise, such scholarship as there is on ancient
father-absence is scattered and technical. More recently fatherlessness has been considered indirectly
as the background for work done on widows and orphans, e.g. Weiler 1980; Krause 1994–5; McGinn
1999; and Hanson 2005. Cf. discussions of replacement strategies, e.g. Bremmer 1976; 1983; and 1999.

to involve whole communities and sometimes even the state, ultimately finding expression in literature and politics, as several of the contributors show.

In exploring ancient fatherlessness, however, we must be on our guard against mechanically importing assumptions implicit or latent in the concept into a social and historical context where they may be inappropriate or misleading. The masterful discussions of Beryl Rawson, Keith Bradley, Richard Saller, and Suzanne Dixon of what it means (and has meant) to study the ancient "family" all stand as clear warnings in this regard: language is implicated in method and prescribes the limits of historical inquiry.[7] It is therefore important to recognize that "fatherlessness" is not a neutral term: it is a category born of rhetorical art, not sociological science, a watchword for a movement that advocates the importance of fathers per se – not just the number of "parents" in the home, but the presence of biological fathers.[8] As such, "fatherless" is a label that has been applied to an array of different family forms in recent years with the purpose of organizing them into a single phenomenon seen as inherently detrimental to the children who experience it and to society as a whole. In this formulation, fatherless families include families headed by divorced, widowed, or single mothers by choice, as well as those headed by lesbian couples and mothers raising children with the help of stepfathers, boyfriends, or relatives. In other words, "fatherlessness" is a consciously polemical interpretation of the rise of the single-mother family and the concomitant expansion of economic and social freedoms women have gained over the last century in the United States and Western Europe.[9]

The number of children now growing up in such homes is indeed striking. To take the United States as one particularly well-researched example, in 2001 there were approximately 18.5 million children, or a quarter of all American

---

[7] Rawson 1986; Bradley 1991a: 1–12; Saller 1994: 74–101 (cf. Saller 1984); and Dixon 1992: 1–35.
[8] For an excellent collection of the major viewpoints involved in this movement, see Daniels 1998; cf. Nobus 2003; Pleck 2004. At its core, the intellectual underpinnings of the contemporary fatherhood movement are rooted at least as much in concerns about the meaning and future of marriage as in the fate of fathers. Thus it has not been surprising to see the ground shift once again in the last decade in the United States to the issue of same-sex marriage and domestic partnerships (anticipated by Siverstein and Auerbach 1999). For the evolving academic and political interest in marriage both in the United States and elsewhere, see the *Journal of Marriage and Family* 66.4 (2004), which contains the proceedings of the 2003 National Council on Family Relations Conference in Vancouver, "The Future of Marriage" (Amato 2004 offers an introduction to the papers), as well as the recent additions of Amato 2007 and Blankenhorn 2007.
[9] On the rise of the single-mother household, see, e.g., McLanahan and Sandefur 1994 and McLanahan and Carlson 2004; cf. Bradshaw *et al.* 1999 and Lerman and Sorenson 2000 on the associated rise of the nonresidential father.

children, growing up in homes with only one biological parent, and the overwhelming majority of these parents were mothers (78 percent).[10] Many, if not most, of these children knew who their fathers were, but the extent to which their fathers participated in their lives and contributed to their upbringing varied greatly.[11] Most of these families are the products of divorce, but increasingly also of the separation of unmarried couples.[12] In fact, over 30 percent of all births in the United States at the turn of the millennium were out of wedlock, up from 6 percent in 1960. Such families have been called "fragile families," because they are significantly less stable than families in similar circumstances headed by married couples.[13] As of 2001, 2.1 million children (or 3 percent of the total population of children) lived in "fragile families," but given the typical rate of dissolution, a great number of them will have subsequently joined the ranks of those living in single-parent homes. All together then, there were at least 23 million children in 2001, or nearly one-third of the children in the United States at the time, already living apart from their fathers or at risk of doing so in the near future.

These numbers are of particular and immediate concern because there appears to be a relationship between being raised in single-mother homes and certain negative outcomes, such as increased risks of lower academic achievement, teen pregnancy, criminal behavior, and idleness as young adults as compared with children raised by continuously married parents.[14] Perhaps more surprising is the fact that this correlation has been shown to hold true even for children raised with the aid of surrogates such as grandparents, stepfathers, or unmarried partners, while it is much weaker for

[10] Unless otherwise noted, the following statistics come from Kreider and Fields 2005. It is important to note that the Survey of Income and Program Participation (SIPP) does not take into account marital status when tabulating "two-parent" homes, while the Current Population Survey (CPS) does. Hence, there are more children in two-parent households in SIPP than in CPS (see Fields 2003). As we are primarily concerned with the living arrangements of children rather than the parents' marital status per se, we shall rely on the SIPP numbers. For Europe, see O'Brien 2004.

[11] Cherlin 1992: 79–80; McLanahan and Sandefur 1994: 96–8; Bradshaw et al. 1999; Lerman and Sorenson 2000; McLanahan and Carlson 2004: 376; and Amato and Sobolewski 2004. But see the recent methodological critique of Pasley and Braver 2004 with regard to measuring involvement of nonresident fathers.

[12] The divorce rate in the United States appears to have held steady in the 1990s after climbing precipitously between 1950 and 1970. The nature and relationship of divorce, marriage, and cohabitation is changing in both the United States and Europe. See Cherlin 1992; Bramlett and Mosher 2002; and Amato 2007.

[13] McLanahan and Carlson 2004. This stands in distinct contrast to much of Western Europe, where cohabitation is more common and stable, and has seen much higher rates of out-of-wedlock births than the United States for much of the twentieth century. See Seltzer 2000; Smock 2000; Simmons and O'Connell 2003; S. Brown 2004; Heuveline and Timberlake 2004; Seltzer 2004.

[14] Angel and Angel 1993; McLanahan and Sandefur 1994; Amato 1994; Hoffmann and Johnson 1998; cf. Amato and Sobolewski 2004.

children raised by widows.[15] Finally, this relationship has been observed to operate, though varying in degree, in families of every race and socio-economic stratum.[16] To this extent modern "fatherlessness" is a sociological phenomenon with a measurable impact on children and their mothers that even those who celebrate the new freedom that single-motherhood represents for women must confront. On the other hand, most sociologists do not believe that what is being detected in this correlation is necessarily the absence of the father per se (and therefore only remediable by his return in his "traditional" capacity), but rather a host of associated effects connected to his absence (and so remediable by other means). The relationship between poverty and father-absence, for instance, remains a particularly controversial matter.[17] Again, there is no evidence to suggest that the children of same-sex couples are at any disadvantage purely on the basis of not having two parents of different sexes or two parents to whom they are biologically related.[18] For these reasons and others, many have seen the popular and politicized formulation of "fatherlessness" as essentializing and overinclusive, and most sociologists prefer to speak in terms of father-absence instead of fatherlessness.[19]

In rejecting the idea of fathering as a natural role based on sex, most sociologists do not deny that there is a biological component to fathering, but instead emphasize the ways in which this biological relationship is mediated by culture, often resulting in strikingly different ways of being a father. Michael Lamb, the foremost authority on contemporary fathering, has consistently maintained this position, gathering over the last thirty years numerous studies of fathers from different cultural milieus.[20] For Lamb,

---

[15] McLanahan and Sandefur 1994: 64–78; cf. Biblarz and Gottainer 2000 and Hofferth and Anderson 2003. There are a significant number of children in these categories in the United States: 4.5 million children (or 6 percent of the total population of children) live with their mother and partner, step or adoptive, married and unmarried. 2.5 million (3 percent) live with a single mother and at least one grandparent. Widows, however, have been a declining percentage of mothers over the last century. This is a finding that conservative critics tend to point up, e.g. Popenoe 1996: 151–2.

[16] McLanahan and Sandefur 1994: esp. 56–63.

[17] See, e.g., McLanahan and Sandefur 1994: 79–94 and the responses of Crowder and Teachman 2004 and Gupta, Smock, and Manning 2004. Cf. Knoester and Haynie 2005 on the relationship between family structure and youth violence, and Pong, Dronkers, and Hampden-Thompson 2003 on the relationship of family structure to educational attainment. Some researchers even find family structure to be relatively unimportant in predicting well-being, e.g. Lansford *et al.* 2001.

[18] Tasker and Golombok 1997; Silverstein and Auerbach 1999; Stacey 2003. This is a finding that conservative critics have typically ignored or discounted, e.g. Blankenhorn 1995: 171–84 and Popenoe 1996: 147.

[19] See the criticism of Stacey 1998 and Silverstein and Auerbach 1999 (but see also the debate engendered by Silverstein and Auerbach's criticism in the subsequent volume (55) of *American Psychologist*: 678–84).

[20] Lamb 1987; cf. relevant chapters on fathering in different cultures in Lamb 2004.

what most fathers across different cultures share is not an essential nature, but three vital familial functions, namely the provision of economic, social, and emotional support for the mother and her children.[21] These are, in fact, the three main areas in which most researchers see the effects of father-absence, and the correlated negative outcomes of father-absence mentioned above have generally been interpreted as owing to deficits of paternal economic, social, and emotional support.[22] For instance, with respect to economic impact, the influential analysis of McLanahan and Sandefur found that families typically lose about half of their income when fathers leave.[23] As for paternal social support, these same authors related it to the idea of "social capital," or the store of useful knowledge contained in human relations.[24] In other words, when fathers leave, they take with them not only their money, but also their personal skills, knowledge, and connections. Finally, they found that without the emotional and parenting support of a father, single mothers raising a family alone often become stressed and that this stress sometimes translates into worse outcomes for the children.[25]

While both sides of this debate over the meaning and implications of the rise of the single-mother household have often defended their positions by placing them in a historical context, few if any have reached back beyond the nineteenth century. Yet, as we mentioned above, there is one very good reason to do so: demographic studies strongly suggest that the proportion of children raised by a mix of relatives, stepparents, and single mothers was at least as high, if not higher, in every pre-modern society before the so-called "demographic transition" than it is today.[26] The last twenty-five years of work on the demography of the Roman world in particular has resulted in a consensus with respect to certain structural features of its population, such as an average life expectancy in the ancient Mediterranean at birth of approximately twenty to thirty years and the tendency of non-elite males to marry comparatively late in life, at twenty-five to thirty years of age.[27] Men

[21] Lamb and Tamis-Lemonda 2004. Cf. Downey, Ainsworth-Darnell, and Dufur 1998 and Stolz, Barber, and Olsen 2005.
[22] McLanahan and Sandefur 1994.
[23] McLanahan and Sandefur 1994: 79–94; cf. McLanahan and Carlson 2004. See n. 17 above for critical responses to these correlations.
[24] McLanahan and Sandefur 1994: 3–4, cf. 116–33; Amato and Sobolewski 2004, 342–4; cf. J. Coleman 1988.
[25] McLanahan and Sandefur 1994: 98–115 (note that argument over the importance and role of divorce in child welfare is particularly contentious).
[26] On the "demographic transition," see Parkin 1992: 71–2; cf. Friedlander, Okun, and Segal 1999.
[27] The bibliography on ancient demography has grown tremendously in this period. Some of the most important works are the following: Hopkins 1966; Saller and Shaw 1984; Shaw 1984; 1987; 1996; Hansen 1986; Saller 1987; 1994; Parkin 1992; Bagnall and Frier 2006 (1st edn. published in 1994); Scheidel 1996; 2001a; 2001b; 2001c.

thus became fathers for the first time relatively late in life, and this resulted in a comparatively large generation gap between fathers and their children. The combination of high mortality and late marriage meant that a striking number of fathers died before their children reached adulthood.[28] In fact, model life tables suggest that perhaps as many as one-third of all children in every social and economic stratum over the entire ancient Mediterranean would have lost their fathers before they reached age fifteen. Another third lost their fathers before they reached age twenty-five. Therefore, unlike modern fatherlessness, which is the product of parental separation, ancient fatherlessness was rooted in paternal death, which was pervasive and endemic, not merely the occasional or exceptional by-product of environmental catastrophe or war.[29]

While the causes of modern and ancient father-absence are radically different, the rough similarity of scale of the two phenomena suggests that a comparative approach might produce interesting results. Before proceeding, however, it must be acknowledged that the above description is in both cases a simplification: in the ancient and modern worlds multiple demographic regimes may be detected at work in different socio-economic strata and geographic regions.[30] This in turn results in different rates of fatherlessness between the various sectors of society. But our point here is, first, that in both cases there is no sector or strata or class that does not experience some significant level of fatherlessness and, second, that, given the causes, the experience of fatherlessness is likely to be fundamentally similar at all levels, though again its effects probably varied in degree according to wealth and status (as indeed has been shown in the modern context by McLanahan and Sandefur). The first comparative insight, then, comes in the simple recognition of fatherlessness in antiquity as a phenomenon. If we follow most sociologists and dismiss the overly broad definition of fatherlessness based on some essential, timeless paternal role, we are left with a more limited version of the phenomenon based on the basic

[28] Cf. the Denis, Desjardins, and Légaré 1997 and Légaré and Naud 2001 studies of the effects of similar rates of paternal death in sixteenth- to eighteenth-century Canada.

[29] Saller 1994: esp. 181; cf. Saller 1987. On the relationship of war to ancient demography and society, see J. K. Evans 1991; Rosenstein 2004; and Scheidel 2007a; cf. Scheidel 1996: 117–24. Fatherlessness in the twentieth century has been intimately associated with war, see Griswold 1993: 161–84 and Blankenhorn 1995: 50–60; cf. Lamb 2000: 28–9. Fatherlessness by divorce or separation surpassed fatherlessness by death in the United States only in the 1970s (Cherlin 1992: 25). Divorce also separated some children from their parents in antiquity, but the children usually continued to live with their fathers (Rawson 1986: 32–7; Rawson 2003: 225–32).

[30] Scholars of both periods have been sensitive to this fact, though of course the ability to differentiate between regimes is obviously much greater and more precise in the modern context. On the importance of status to ancient demography, see, e.g., Parkin 1992; Saller 1994; McGinn 1999; on regional mortality patterns in ancient Italy see Sallares 2002.

functions that most fathers play in the life of the family, economically, socially, and emotionally as spouses and parents. As discussed above, the research into this more limited version of fatherlessness tends to show that having biological fathers around to perform these functions matters, even if the exact nature of the relationship is debated. The combination of a structural father-absence based in demography and the generally patriarchal cultures of the ancient Mediterranean almost certainly meant that most societies would have experienced at least this limited form of fatherlessness as a phenomenon with a measureable impact on families and children.

Such a recognition recommends to us a convenient framework for thinking about the effects of ancient father-absence: routine paternal death meant that ancient families regularly suffered and compensated for the loss of a father's economic, social, and emotional support. Although affective relationships, such as that between a father and his children, have a history in themselves, we should not find it surprising to discover that ancient fathers cared for their children and that it was this love that in part drove them to take an active role in the moral, vocational, intellectual, and religious development of their children.[31] When they were gone, the mother thus missed an important partner and support when it came to parenting. Unfortunately, our sources only occasionally allow us to hear of the emotional strain that widowed mothers must have routinely experienced as a result.[32] Most ancient fathers in the Mediterranean also typically acted as heads of household, representing an important connection between the family and the rest of the community. As a consequence of the father's social role in such cultures, the social capital that families lost with his death was particularly important. Finally, the loss of a father in antiquity necessarily entailed some economic disruption, and those children who could not rely on an inheritance or family support faced considerable economic challenges with social repercussions. Destitute fatherless boys who were not lucky enough to be adopted or taken in by relatives would have had to resort to work from an even earlier age than might otherwise have been the case.[33] Moreover, time and money for even a rudimentary education would be

---

[31] Hallett 1984: 99–149; Golden 1990: 94–7; Eyben 1991; Saller 1994: 102–32, 100–14; but see Bradley 1991a (esp. 125–55) on the strength of emotional and affective ties in the Roman family.

[32] See Hübner (this volume).

[33] On adoption, see Corbier 1999; cf. Marsman 2003: 322 for the ancient Near East. In most ancient families children were important producers even while their parents were alive. Child labor contributed to the home economy as well as providing training for the child in preparation for his or her adult life. In the Roman world the normal age of apprenticeship seems to have been between twelve and fourteen years of age (see Bradley 1991a: 103–24). For the relatively recent change in the child's role in the family economy, see de Regt 2004.

tight to non-existent.[34] The situation for destitute orphaned girls, however, could be even worse. They too had to earn a living, and if they could not continue in the family trade, they might have to find work as a domestic servant or, in the worst-case scenario, as a prostitute. Their poverty would also be a barrier to the respectability conferred by an honorable marriage, as they would have difficulty in raising the required dowry. Without a dowry the chances of finding a willing husband were negligible.

As a functionalist account, this limited version of fatherlessness allows for the expression and mix of paternal roles to be defined by culture. Thus, while all three of these basic paternal functions were inevitably disrupted by death, the extent of disruption depended greatly on the composition of the household, itself the product of particular family circumstances and the prevailing cultural patterns of family formation.[35] For instance, among the aristocratic families of the later Roman Republic neolocality upon marriage seems to have been the norm (i.e. when the newly wed couple moved out of their parents' households in order to set up their own), so such households appear to have consisted of conjugal units with their children, so-called "nuclear" families.[36] In light of their epigraphic study, Saller and Shaw extended this conclusion from the city of Rome to the Western half of the Roman Empire, at least among the levels of society that participated in the epigraphic culture.[37] In nuclear households the father usually held the position of head of household; in the absence of adult sons still in the home, his death usually turned life for his family upside down. In Classical Greece, on the other hand, Gallant has seen the joint family type as predominant.[38] In this type of family the father usually is either subordinated to his own father if the latter is still alive, or if he has died, then the father is on equal rank with his brothers, perhaps living with several of them and their wives in a joint household. In joint families there is thus the potential for several "fathers" in the home in the form of uncles or adult cousins, so a fatherless child could probably rely on other adult male household members to mitigate the disruption caused by a father's death. For instance, economic provision might not be as completely interrupted as it was for those living in

---

[34] This was not the case for the wealthy, who found various ways to finance their educations to the highest levels even after the death of a father. See Cribiore (this volume).

[35] See, e.g., Bradley 1991a: 125–55; cf. Dixon 1999: esp. 218. Some scholars suggest that losing a father might even impact on a child's survival rate to different degrees depending on the family type, social structure, and remarriage. See Van Poppel 2000 and Gullickson and Hammel 2004.

[36] Veyne 1978; Saller and Shaw 1984; cf. Dixon 1992: 1–35. This is not undisputed: see Bradley 1991a; 1991b; D. Martin 1996; and the discussion of McGinn 1999: 625–30.

[37] Saller and Shaw 1984; cf. Saller 1984 and Shaw 1984.

[38] Gallant 1991: 27–30; cf. Cox 1998: 141–3.

a nuclear family, and resident uncles might be available to take over some aspects of the late father's emotional, educational, and social roles.[39]

But this may be approaching the question of family type too schematically: even in societies where the joint family is the ideal, often the majority of households experience a series of different forms over the life cycle because of certain demographic and socioeconomic forces. For instance, as Bagnall and Frier have shown for Roman Egypt, the early death of fathers and the failure to produce a male heir meant that more than two-thirds of all households were at any one time de facto nuclear households.[40] By the same token, economic and social background mattered: in Roman Egypt urban families were far more likely to be "nuclear" than were village families. Finally, as Benigno has stressed, the walls of a household need not correspond precisely to "the boundaries of mutual rights and duties" between members of the wider family. In other words, households are not merely residential units but groups defined by reciprocal obligations and rights as to provision of economic and emotional support, independent of common residence.[41] So, even after the death of a father in a nuclear family, his children and widow might have found help from relatives living next door.[42]

The second insight we may draw from the modern debate is more provocative. Again, while we may dismiss the essentialist premise of the broad definition of fatherlessness, the suggestion that different ways of missing fathers can be experienced as a shared or single phenomenon is intriguing in itself. In other words, were there forms of fatherlessness in antiquity not based in paternal death? If so, what were they? How were they experienced and by whom? And what, if any, connection might they have had to the experience of demographic fatherlessness? Just as today, so in the past we find that there was more than one way for a child to grow up "fatherless." As the contributors who deal in these alternative forms of fatherlessness show, they reveal important aspects of ancient society and the ways in which families were dynamically related to larger cultural, economic, and political forces. Demographic fatherlessness must remain the major focus because it was by far the dominant form of fatherlessness in antiquity, but other forms of fatherlessness, such as that experienced by slave or illegitimate children, act

---

[39] Such relatives, however, would be unlikely to support the widow indefinitely. Younger widows who were more able to find a willing husband therefore often remarried. See Gardner 1986: 50–6; Bradley 1991b; Bagnall and Frier 2006: 126–7; 153–5; and Hübner (this volume); cf. Dupâquier *et al.* 1981.

[40] Bagnall and Frier 2006: 56–7; cf. Clarysse and Thompson 2006 (Ptolemaic period) and Cox 1998: 141–3 (Athens).

[41] Benigno 1989: 186. Benigno in his study emphasizes that support from more distant kin most likely decreased as one travelled down the socioeconomic ladder.

[42] Cf. Davis 1977: 174–5.

as useful counterpoints in this volume, spurring us to think more laterally and expansively about the ways in which ancient fathers could be absent and what this might have meant for both their families and their communities.

Several chapters in this volume deal directly or indirectly with an ancient institution of fundamental importance to fatherless children, namely guardianship. Many ancient Mediterranean cultures shared the conception of the orphan as a vulnerable figure and a person in need of special support. Orphans are, in fact, paradigmatic examples of weakness in many ancient societies, as they were usually unable to defend themselves and therefore open to oppression and exploitation.[43] One response was to see them as enjoying the special protection of the gods and thereby casting their defense as a religious duty. The kings of the ancient Near East, for instance, boasted of the number of orphans they supported, thereby giving proof of their piety and virtue as rulers.[44] Judaism, Christianity, and Islam all inherited this tradition and in all three the protection of orphans is set down as a religious obligation, while the neglect of orphans is seen as an indicator of social and moral decay.[45] In the Greek and Roman worlds, however, the protection of fatherless children was couched in legal rather than religious terms.[46]

Unlike the tradition emanating from the Near East, the Greeks and Romans did not generally see the support of orphans and their widowed mothers as a public duty, but rather as a private obligation deserving public protection. In this respect, the law merely reflected the concerns of those who drafted it: the citizens of ancient city-states who aimed at the maintenance and protection of their personal property and dependants. The most famous exception proves the rule: the Athenian democracy at one time took an active interest in supporting orphans at public expense, but the concern here was ideological and based on status: the orphans were the sons of Athenian citizens who had fallen in battle for the city.[47] The majority of children who grew up without fathers in Athens received no regular support from any public source. This was true of the Greek or Roman worlds until

---

[43] See Wöhrle (this volume) and Sigismund (this volume).

[44] Fensham 1962; Weiler 1980: esp. 193; Kämmerer 1994; Feucht 1995: 384; Marsman 2003: 321–4.

[45] E.g. Job 24; cf. Prov. 23:10–11. See Sigismund (this volume). Compare with these the *spoliator pupilli* as a type indicative of a corrupt society (Saller 1994: 191–2).

[46] Mention of orphans in explicitly religious contexts is comparatively rare in the Greek and Roman worlds. In fact, it may be that we should even read Hesiod's description of them as under the protection of Zeus (*Op.* 320–34) in light of the connections it has with the Wisdom literature of the Near East (cf. West 1978: 3–60 and West 1997). Although it was not the product of divine revelation, Greek and Roman law should nevertheless not be entirely dissociated from religion. For instance, it is instructive to recall that a Roman often interpreted his legal duty to his ward as a sacred duty (Saller 1994: 190–1).

[47] See Stroud 1971; cf. Arist. *Pol.* 1268a8–11. See also Golden (this volume): 44–5.

the Christianization of the Mediterranean in the fourth and fifth centuries CE.[48] Given the demographic reality of the ancient world, guardianship was a common institution, familiar to nearly everyone. It was also, therefore, an institution that must have had an appreciable effect on the disposition of property. For these reasons among others, Saller suggested more than a decade ago that "the *pupillus* and the *tutor* ought to loom much larger in our social (and economic) histories of the Roman world."[49] Indeed, guardianship permeates much of this book and in order to familiarize the reader with its basic features we give a brief summary of it here before turning to a description of the contents of the chapters themselves.

For the Classical or Hellenistic Greek world we are best informed about the workings of guardianship as an institution from Athens through the law court speeches of Demosthenes, Isaeus, Lysias, and the like, as well as from further allusions to it in comedy, philosophy, and history.[50] Legally, every Athenian citizen child who lost his or her father before reaching the age of majority was supposed to have one or more guardians, or *epitropoi*, appointed. Formally, these guardians were responsible for the management of the ward's estate, the provision of daily maintenance, and legal representation in business transactions until he or she came of age at eighteen. Their primary function was thus to manage and preserve the property for the heir.[51] Usually, the father prearranged a guardian during his lifetime or by will; if he failed to do so, the duty seems to have fallen automatically to the nearest male agnate. However, making close relatives the guardians of an orphaned child could be risky: the guardian would then be next in line to inherit, creating a potentially fatal conflict of interest.[52] If no close relative was available, it was the duty of

---

[48] Even then, the impact of such charity was uneven, on which see below. The well-known *alimenta* programs of the Roman Empire do not seem to have been designed to help fatherless children per se, but rather aimed at promoting the birth-rate in Italy (although inevitably, some of these children became fatherless during the course of receiving aid from the foundation). See Duncan-Jones 1982: 288–319; cf. Wiedemann 1989: 38–9.

[49] Saller 1991: 46.

[50] For other city-states our knowledge is much more impressionistic. For instance, Diodorus Siculus (12.12–15) reports that similar laws were laid down by Charondas in Sicily, and we know of provisions treating the guardianship of fatherless children from Gortyn (*IC* IV.72, cols. 3.45–4.23). The following account generally relies on Harrison 1968–71: I, 99–108. For earlier discussions, see Schulthess 1886 and Lipsius *et al.* 1905: II, 520–37. See also Golden's discussion (this volume): 44–6.

[51] Plato goes so far as to describe an orphan's receiving guardians after his father's death as experiencing a "second birth" (*Leg.* 926e).

[52] Thus Charondas recommended dividing guardianship and custody: the patrimony would then be administered by the paternal relatives, while the mother's side (which was not in the line of succession) cared for the orphan (Diod. Sic. 12.15). Plato may have also recognized this problem when he provides in the *Laws* for the appointment of five guardians, two each from the paternal and maternal sides and a close, but unrelated friend (924b; cf. Schulthess 1886: 86).

the eponymous archon to appoint a guardian. The allied institution of the epiclerate for daughters had a similar aim to guardianship proper: not to protect the welfare of an orphaned girl so much as to secure the continuation of the *oikos* by having her marry a close paternal relative in the hope that she might bear a son who would thus continue her father's line.[53] Typically, orphans stayed in their paternal homes, where they were raised by their mothers (unless they remarried), while the guardian distributed a daily allowance (*trophē* or *sitos*) out of the child's patrimony.[54] The only time we hear of orphans living in the households of their guardians is when the latter married their wards' mothers and became their stepfathers.[55] Finally, when the orphan came of age, the guardian was required to turn over his patrimony and render an account.[56] In cases of mismanagement (a constant complaint in the Athenian courts), the young man could bring an action against his former guardian.[57]

Guardianship under Roman law operated in a broadly similar fashion. As in the Greek world, the Roman state allocated no direct support to orphans but rather helped to enforce the wishes of fathers by supporting and policing the appointment and performance of guardians, who were known as *tutores*.[58] Although historically *tutores* appear to have been concerned primarily with estate management and preservation, they were later held responsible for the moral development of their wards, not just their physical well-being.[59] Fathers therefore naturally attempted to assign guardianship to trusted persons, such as adult sons, brothers, or close friends, usually designating them in wills, and in the matter of selection the father's choice was rarely questioned.[60] If the father failed to appoint a guardian, however, the duty automatically fell to the closest agnate, who thereby became the *tutor legitimus*, or the statutory guardian. If no close male agnate was available, after the *lex Atilia* (*c.* 210 BCE) a third type of *tutor* could be appointed by the urban praetor at the request of the child's mother or relatives (or in the provinces, by

---

[53] Harrison 1968–71: I, 149–52; cf. Karabélias 1982 and Golden (this volume): 46.
[54] The guardian either managed his ward's estate himself or leased parts of it until he or she came of age. See Harrison 1968–71: I, 104–5.; cf. Schulthess, *RE*, s.v. μίσθωσις: 2111–12.
[55] Harrison 1968–71: I, 105; cf. Schulthess 1886: 94–5. MacDowell assumes that the ward regularly moved into his guardian's household but fails to bring any evidence for it (1986: 94). For co-residence with guardians who were also stepfathers, see Hübner (this volume): 73–4; cf. 65–6.
[56] Harrison 1968–71: I, 105. For the arrangements made for female orphans after they came of age, see Harrison 1968–71: I, 108–15.
[57] Harrison 1968–71: I, 115–21, 247; cf. Davies 1971: 113–59 and Hunter 1989b.
[58] For a more complete account, see the relevant chapters in Kaser 1971 or Borkowski and du Plessis 2005; cf. Saller 1994: 181–203.
[59] Crook 1967: 113–24; Rawson 2003: 71–3.　　[60] E.g. *Dig.* 26.3.3–4, 6.

the governor under the much later *lex Iulia et Titia*.[61] In each case the office
was the same; only the route to becoming *tutor* differed. It was not until late
in the Roman period that mothers were legally allowed to perform this office,
and even then it was subject to certain restrictions.[62] Yet, although the *tutor*
had legal authority over the property, mothers throughout the Roman period
remained the primary caregivers for their children.[63] While it seems that
guardians and mothers (or other relatives) were generally able to cooperate
in the raising of the child, sometimes conflicts arose between them over the
division or performance of responsibilities. One of the most common disputes was over the size of the maintenance allowance, an amount determined
subjectively according to the family's rank and means (and thus open to
differences of interpretation).[64]

Unlike in the Greek system, the degree of a Roman guardian's involvement in his ward's financial transactions depended on the latter's age.
Fatherless children under the age of seven did not have any say at all in
property and business matters, while those between the ages of seven and
fourteen could make business decisions, but the guardian had the last word.
Attaining the age of majority, however, did not confer total independence
on the child, and it is also at this point that we begin to find gender
distinctions in the law. Girls came of age at twelve, at which time they
received a *tutor mulieris*; for boys the age was fourteen, and technically they
were then free from supervision.[65] Yet, in the Republic, young men between
the ages of fourteen and twenty-five were often assigned *curatores*, who in
the beginning were no more than occasional advisors, assisting them in
financial transactions and providing security on an ad hoc basis for those
who wanted to do business with fatherless young men.[66] In the imperial
period, however, the *curator*'s role became more important, with the result
that by the late second century CE minors could apply to the praetor in
Rome (or to the governor in the provinces) for regular *curatores* for the

[61] Gai. *Inst.* 1.185. Sometimes a local *curia* or council would take on this responsibility: see Saller 1994:
184 and more recently Chiusi 2005: 106–18. Cf. Scheidel (this volume) on the potential availability of
adult sons or surviving brothers.
[62] Arjava 1996: 76–110, esp. 89–94; Gardner 1998: 247–52; and Hübner (this volume): 67–9.
[63] On child-rearing after death or divorce, see Rawson 1986: 32–7 and Rawson 2003: 225–32; cf. *Codex
Iustinianus* 5.49.1,pr. (223 CE); *Novellae Iustiniani* 22.38 (sixth century CE); Saller 1994: 193–5.
[64] E.g. *Dig.* 26.7.12.3 (Paul) and 27.2.3 (Ulpian); cf. Saller 1994: 193–6 and Hanson 2005.
[65] For the *tutor mulieris*, see Dixon 1984; 2001: 73–88; Gardner 1986: 14–22; 1993: 85–109; cf. Arjava
1997.
[66] Women could also ask for or be given *curatores* in certain circumstances, and it seems that by the third
century there was little difference between the sexes when it came to the appointment of *curatores*: see
the *Fragmenta Vaticana* §110 (Paul); §§ 201–2 (Ulpian) = Riccobono, *FIRA* II: 490, 504; *Dig.* 26.5.7
(Ulpian), 26.5.13.2 (Papinian); cf. *Dig.* 4.4.3.5 (Ulpian).

whole of their minority.[67] By late antiquity the appointment of a *curator* was compulsory and "regularized in a way effectively to extend guardianship from puberty to age twenty-five."[68] Technically, *curatores* could not be appointed by will but occasionally this happened and it is likely that a father's wishes in this regard were given due weight.[69]

Had the Roman law of guardianship been obligatory for all fatherless minors under the age of fourteen in the empire (i.e. after 212 CE), then at least one in every three living adult males in the Roman world would have been pressed into service as a *tutor* for a fatherless child, regardless of his ability or willingness to be one.[70] But the law did not specify this: in the event that the father left no will and there was no statutory guardian (a real possibility as Scheidel shows in his chapter), there may have been certain cases in which children had no guardian appointed, for the reality was that many families in the ancient world did not bother with formal guardianship at all because their property was not worth arguing about, at least not legally.[71] This was a reality the law occasionally recognized: "A father gives a *tutor* in vain to a natural son to whom nothing has been left, nor can he be confirmed without inquiry."[72] Furthermore, as Hübner discusses, the documents from Roman Egypt disclose a striking number of widowed mothers acting as guardians for their orphaned children despite the express prohibition of the law.[73] While this might be attributed to pre-Hellenistic

---

[67] Kaser 1971: § 90; cf. *Dig.* 4.4.1.3 (Ulpian).   [68] Saller 1994: 188.

[69] E.g. *Dig.* 26.3.1.3 (Modestinus); cf. the similar situation with mothers appointing testamentary *tutores*, again legally irregular, e.g. *Dig.* 26.3.2 (Neratius).

[70] According to the Coale–Demeny model life tables, the group of men over the age of twenty-five (i.e. those able to serve as guardians) constituted approximately 20 percent of the total population, while nearly 40 percent of the total population was under the age of fourteen. If we multiply the percentage of each segment of the population pyramid for those under fourteen by the percentage of those who had already lost their fathers and add these figures together, we find that 17 percent of these minors were fatherless, or 7 percent of the total population. This leaves us with a ratio of eligible guardians to fatherless minors of 3:1 (cf. Scheidel, this volume). This rough estimate intentionally does not take into account a host of complicating and important factors, such as the proportion of the population who were slaves (so would either not need or be ineligible to serve as tutors), the need for men to act as guardians to unmarried women, and the legal exceptions from service, among them old age, poor health, number of children, public office, and military service. For these exceptions, see the various rulings collected in *Dig.* 27.1; cf. Saller 1994: 187–9. There are many petitions in the papyri aiming to secure such exceptions, e.g. *P.Oxy.* 3.487 = *M.Chres.* 322 (note the age of the ward and the fact that he has no relatives on either side able to take on the guardianship).

[71] Cf. Daube 1966: 71–5; Cherry 1996; Rawson 2003: 71.

[72] *Dig.* 26.3.7.pr. (Hermogenian); cf. *Dig.* 38.17.2.26 (Ulpian).

[73] Such women appear in the documents as *epitropoi* (*P.Oxy.* 6.898 [123 CE]), *phrontistriai* (*BGU* 1662 [182 CE]), *prodikousai* (*P.Lond.* 2.196 [first or second cent. CE]), or *epakolouthēriai* (*BGU* 1070 [218 CE]). We also find grandmothers (*P.Fuad.* 35 [48 CE], *SB* v.7558 [173 CE], and *P.Lond.* 3.1164 [212 CE]) and a sister (*P.Ath. 7* [first century CE]) serving as orphans' guardians. For basic treatments of the relationship of Roman law of guardianship to the papyri, see Mitteis 1912: 243–56 and Taubenschlag 1955: 157–81. For a recent collection of documents on papyrus dealing with guardianship, see Krause 1994–5: III, 88, n. 15.

Egyptian practice, as Wolff has suggested, or might even represent a wider custom of the ancient Eastern Mediterranean, it is also likely that in many cases the mother was the best placed to look after the interests of her children, whatever the law prescribed.[74]

Given the range of material, periods, and cultures covered by the contributors, we thought it best to group the chapters into four thematic parts. Each part will emphasize a particular aspect of ancient fatherlessness. The chapters of Part I, "Coping with demographic realities," trace the basic demographic, economic, and social dimensions of fatherlessness in the ancient world and glance at some of the ways in which individuals and communities responded. The introductory chapter by Walter Scheidel sets the stage for those that follow by reviewing the state of current research into the demography of ancient fatherlessness. In the process he not only assesses the number of children who would have been without fathers, but goes a step further and attempts to gauge the impact of the demographic regime established by Saller on the population of adults who were potentially available to take over the paternal role for fatherless children. Scheidel's conclusions are rather bleak: not only was there a shortage of paternal uncles and grandfathers to fill the gap, but children born to older men were also at severe risk of having no male relatives at all, including brothers, of the requisite age to assume guardianship.[75]

Next we turn to Mark Golden's review of the social responses to fatherlessness in Classical Greece and Rome. In effect, Golden adds interpretive color and texture to the bare-bones demographic sketch drawn by Scheidel. Using an impressive array of literary sources, he begins by exploring the mythological and cultural associations of fathers and fatherlessness before turning his attention to the social, political, and emotional responses to the phenomenon. In many ways, Golden's study functions as an overture for the rest of the volume, introducing many key motifs that subsequent chapters develop, such as guardianship and adoption, the spectrum of more informal

---

[74] Wolff 1978: 78, n. 31; 91, n. 96. We find a similar situation in Asia Minor, see Krause 1994–5, esp. vol. III; Hübner (this volume): 67–8; 74. Cf. n. 75 below.

[75] We occasionally hear exactly this situation being alluded to in the papyri, e.g. *P. Harr.* 68 (cf. *P. Diog.* 18), where in 225 CE M. Lucretius Diogenes petitions to be made guardian of two of his dead sister's children, since one, Lucretius, was an *apatōr* (see below and Malouta [this volume]) and the father of the other, Rufus, was dead. According to Diogenes, he was their "closest relative" left, so unless we attribute to him some unsavory motive, we must presume that there were no available male agnates interested in the children or their inheritance (note that the *apatōr* bears the same *nomen* as his mother and the petitioner). Besides the complicated family relations (there was a third child, but he was in his father's power), this papyrus is remarkable also for what it implies, namely that the sister, Octavia Lucretia, not only retained custody of Lucretius and Rufus, but must have exercised tutelary powers over them while alive (see Hübner [this volume]: 67–70). Cf. *P.Oxy.* 3.487 (n. 70 above).

practices, such as fosterage, the roles of uncles and stepfathers, and the relationship of politics, ideology, and society to fatherless children. Two ideas in particular find fuller expression in later chapters. First, despite what Scheidel's modeling would lead one to expect, fatherlessness might not always have represented an unmitigated disaster for the children left behind: there were institutions beyond guardianship, both familial and social, that often helped to lessen the impact and disruption of a father's death. As he reminds us, simply by virtue of its frequency, losing a father at a young age "stood in the midrange of life's tragedies." Secondly, Golden also points out that a father's death may have occasionally opened up opportunities for children in antiquity (though mostly for wealthy young men).

Sabine Hübner then provides us with an overview of remarriage in the ancient Eastern Mediterranean from Classical Athens to late antique Egypt. She addresses in detail the various pressures and choices that a widow faced in the aftermath of her husband's death, such as remaining a widow or remarrying, and what impact this decision would have on her children's upbringing and inheritance. Hübner also redresses a long-standing imbalance in the scholarship on the ancient family by collecting the evidence for stepfathers. Unlike stepmothers in antiquity, stepfathers did not have a reputation for malice and abuse. Hübner explains this difference by showing that stepfathers were unlikely to be living with their stepchildren under the same roof, since marriage patterns in the Greek East resulted in many more co-residential stepmothers than co-residential stepfathers.

The final chapter in this part, by Marcus Sigismund, moves beyond the confines of the Greco-Roman sphere and investigates the concept and reality of the fatherless child in the Old and New Testaments. Sigismund describes how widows and fatherless children were conceptualized in the Old Testament as being at the margins of Jewish society, but also how they were supported by the Jewish community, particularly by the organization of the tithing system in the Second Temple period. He then goes on to show how the first generations of Christians interpreted the Jewish Scriptures they inherited by extending the charitable practices associated with the Second Temple to all fatherless children in their communities. Although his sources do not allow for a clear picture of how the early Christians went about fulfilling their mission, his discussion invites us to reflect on the differences between the more universalizing Christian attitude towards fatherless children per se and the more narrow focus of Greek and Roman society on particular orphans as described in Golden's chapter.

The next part, "Virtual fatherlessness," is dedicated to exploring forms of fatherlessness not caused by paternal death, the alternative types of fatherlessness we alluded to above. One way in which different forms of fatherlessness were marked off was by language, as each type had something of its own vocabulary. Given the manner in which most children lost their fathers, the most common words for fatherless children signified the deprivation of death: *orphanos* in Greek and *orbus* in Latin both come from a common Indo-European root meaning "bereft," either from the point of view of either children who had lost their parents or conversely parents who had lost a child.[76] When used of children, both words could describe those who had lost a father or a mother or both, but the specific meaning of "fatherless" was not uncommon. In Greek, *orphanos* remained the most common word for a fatherless child regardless of the context. In Latin, however, there was another word which applied only to fatherless children, *pupillus*, denoting a child's status as one under the care of a legal guardian.

Some children, however, were socially or legally fatherless. Fathers in antiquity could in certain cases suffer "social" death as a civic penalty. This loss of civil status sometimes resulted in their children becoming "fatherless" (and thus in need of a guardian).[77] In a similar fashion, children born to free mothers were free, but legally fatherless if their mothers were not married to their fathers. In the Greek-speaking East, such children were usually known as *nothoi*, as opposed to the legitimate *gnēsioi*. In the Archaic and Classical periods, they were also sometimes ominously referred to as *skotioi*, "born in the dark," or ironically as *parthenioi*, the "virgin-born."[78]

Legitimacy in the Roman world had a different complexion because it was less important socially or ideologically than in the Greek world, remaining above all a legal concept attached to citizenship.[79] Roman "bastards" were technically children born to parents who lacked merely the civic capacity to marry legally (the right of *conubium*). As a consequence, such "illegitimate" children in turn lacked certain legal capacities under Roman law. This legal status, however, did not overlap with any sense of social illegitimacy except

[76] *Orphanos*: Chantraine 1984: s.v. ὀρφανός (p. 829); with reference specifically to the loss of fathers, e.g. Hom. *Il.* 6.432. *Orbus*: Ernout and Meillet 1960: s.v. *orbus* (pp. 466–7); cf. Treggiari 1991a: 72–3 and Nathan (this volume): 277. Compare both with the Hebrew tradition, e.g. Psalm 10; cf. Sigismund (this volume): 84; 86–7.

[77] Such was the case in both Athens (see Harrison 1968–71: I, 99) and Rome (see Gai. *Inst.* 1.128; cf. 1.158–63, 170).

[78] On Greek bastardy, see Patterson 1990; Ogden 1996; and Ogden (this volume). As Ogden has shown, these terms confuse notions of naturalness of birth and legitimacy of status. We see the same confusion when it comes to adoption: natural sons are referred to as *gennētos* ("begotten") or *alēthinos* ("true" or "real"), whereas adopted sons are *poiētos* (or *eispoiētos*), literally "made" or "created," or *thetos* (or *thesei*), "established," both of which are opposed to *phusei*, "by nature."

[79] For Roman illegitimacy, see Rawson 1989; Gardner 1997; and Phang 2002.

coincidentally, and in fact many such children may have even lived with their fathers in stable relationships.[80] For Romans, therefore, illegitimacy was neither a barrier to natural family ties (which the law recognized in certain contexts) nor carried much of a social stigma. For this reason it is unsurprising that the Romans had no word corresponding precisely to the Greek *nothus*; in fact, they borrowed it whenever they felt the need, and this was not very often.[81] Illegitimate children in the Roman world were instead more likely to be called (or call themselves) *spurii*, which may have been translated as *apatōr* in the Greek East.[82]

Finally, there was one type of ancient fatherless child for whom we have no word except "slave": slaves legally had no fathers (or mothers or brothers or sisters, for that matter) and so technically could not be "fatherless," but of course this did not mean that slaves did not form emotional attachments within their biological families. In fact, slave children were in even greater danger of losing their fathers early in life because owners routinely broke up slave families.[83]

Our first view of virtual fatherlessness is presented by Daniel Ogden, who gives us a view of bastardy in Classical Athens. He describes how notions of illegitimacy resulted in the systemic and systematic separation of a father from his child in thought, language, and law, a separation which aimed at breaking the reciprocal bonds of responsibility that traditionally character-ized the parent–child relationship in the ancient Mediterranean.[84] The proximate cause of this distancing was the ideology of citizenship, which led naturally to a preoccupation with policing the boundaries of legitimacy. Ogden, however, goes on to show how this ideology was itself supported by deep structures in Greek thought generally. Thus, he moves from cultural and political practices to a discussion of language and myth in the second section of his study, exploring the ways in which the Greeks sought to

[80] Generally, see Rawson 1989. This was particularly likely in certain special cases, such as the children of imperial soldiers (who were not allowed to marry, see Phang 2001; cf. Phang 2002), freed slaves and Junian Latins (who had certain legal disabilities, see Weaver 1997: 55–72), and the so-called *apatores* (see below).

[81] Cf. Quint. *Inst.* 3.6.97: *nothum qui non sit legitimus Graeci vocant: latinum rei nomen … non habemus, ideoque utimur peregrine* ("The Greeks call illegitimate children *nothi*. We do not have a Latin word for this … and so we use the foreign word").

[82] Gaius' proposed etymology of *spurius* (*Inst.* 1.64) is as illuminating about a certain Roman view of "fatherlessness" as it is false (cf. Plut. *Mor.* 288e–f). The word may be of Etruscan origin and related to *spurcus*, or "impure" (Ernout and Meillet 1960: s.v. *spurius* [p. 645]). On the self-identification of *spurii*, see Rawson 1989: 29–39. For *apatores* (and their possible relationship to *spurii*), see Youtie 1975; cf. van Minnen 1994; Phang 2001, *passim*; and Malouta (this volume).

[83] Bradley 1987: 47–80. For more recent discussion and bibliography, see Rawson 1989; Dixon 1992: 127–30; Phang 2002: 361, n. 44.

[84] E.g. Parkin 1997: 124–6 and Saller 1991.

understand their attitude toward children who threatened the sociopolitical order.

The second version of virtual fatherlessness, described by Myrto Malouta, leads in the opposite direction: she discusses a legal fiction of the Roman Empire imposed on fathers and their children by the state for reasons still unclear to us. Malouta's study represents a return to a problem famously discussed by Herbert Youtie more than thirty years ago.[85] There are from imperial Egypt many attestations of free people, both men and women, who did not have the legal right to a patronymic from birth, but instead were referred to in documents as *apatōr* ("fatherless"), or alternatively *chrēmatizōn mētros* ("[officially] using [the name of his/her] mother"). Unlike Ogden's *nothoi*, these children often had fathers who were not only intimately involved in their lives but even solicitous about their welfare and can be found arguing with the authorities about the status of their children. Practicing a careful source criticism, Malouta attempts to define the *apatores* of Roman Egypt more precisely than her predecessors by taking advantage of the additional documentation and technological advances that have emerged in the intervening years.

From the definitions and descriptions offered in the first two parts, we move to the ways in which fatherlessness was represented and manipulated in Greek and Roman literature, rhetoric, and politics. Part III, "Roles without models," explores the ways in which father-absence and the lack of this culturally important role model were represented in literature. We begin, appropriately enough, with the Homeric epics. Georg Wöhrle in his study of the social aspects of fatherlessness in Homer paints a picture that corresponds to the situation Sigismund describes for the Old Testament: in Homer's world, the loss of a father often translated into the loss of status, rights, property, and protection for the child. Wöhrle also takes pains to highlight the discourse of fatherlessness in Homer, particularly in the *Odyssey*. Fatherlessness, as he demonstrates, develops beyond the unfortunate, almost tragic consequence of the Iliadic heroic code to become one of the central preoccupations and poetic themes of the *Odyssey*. Importantly, we can see Wöhrle addressing, albeit indirectly, the idea of social capital alluded to above: Telemachus' position of weakness as an orphan is in part related to the loss of his father as the mediator between the *oikos* and the community. Telemachus' journey of exploration in the first four books of the *Odyssey* may thus be understood as a son's quest to build up his own store of social capital by reestablishing and reactivating his father's personal connections.

---

[85] Youtie 1975.

The second chapter in this part treats another of Homer's fatherless children, Diomedes. Louise Pratt illustrates the manner in which father-lessness can be seen as central to Homer's conception of this hero and what this can tell us about Homer's view of the relationship between heroism and fathers and sons. Pratt's main point is that we must see Diomedes as a warrior defined by the memory of a father he never knew. The result, she argues, is the peculiarly inhuman and static heroism for which he is known. Though fatherlessness is not as central to the *Iliad* as it is to the *Odyssey*, Pratt successfully demonstrates the ways in which Homer uses fatherlessness as a paradigmatic structuring device for the character of Diomedes in order to create an effective foil to Achilles, a hero who is represented as experiencing a dynamic relationship to fatherhood.

From Homer we leap to the ambitious attempt by Judith Hallett to recover something of a woman's perspective on fatherlessness in her read-ings of two influential Roman women, Cornelia, the powerful and cultured mother of the Gracchi, and Sulpicia, the refined elegist of the Augustan age. She argues that we must not understand these women as mechanically filling men's roles in their writings, but rather as co-opting the authority of their absent fathers, each to her own literary end. Hallett begins by describing what she sees as Cornelia's clever manipulation of her father's image and career in order to influence her own fatherless boys. She then turns to Sulpicia and shows how the poet deployed her poetic gifts in service of a role tradi-tionally played by her father, the public praise for the dead of her *familia*. Hallett ends with a suggestion advanced by Golden: in both cases she sees paternal death not so much as a tragedy, but rather as an opportunity for a form of self-expression that would have otherwise been denied.

This brings us to our final part, the "Rhetoric of loss." Our interest here is the rhetoric of fatherlessness, broadly construed. There were, as it turns out, several rhetorics of fatherlessness in antiquity. At different times and places and for different ends we see writers, politicians, and professional rhetori-cians alternately promoting, excusing, condemning, down-playing, and ostentatiously overcoming either their own fatherlessness or that of others. We begin with Sabine Müller's discussion of the perennially ambiguous and enigmatic figure of Sulla, who was left fatherless at a relatively tender age. However, unlike most of the other fatherless people investigated in the book, he embraced this identity, creating an image of himself as a self-made man "in no need of a father." In an age that Cicero thought inimical to history itself for the freedoms aristocrats took in padding their ancestries,[86]

---

[86] Cf. Cic. *Brut.* §62.

Müller contends that Sulla took the radical decision to obscure his patrician lineage. He did so in order to avail himself of a particular strain of Eastern and Hellenistic political rhetoric that emphasized a ruler's divine election. Sulla's use of fatherlessness is thus an exploration of the limits of the idea broached by Golden and elaborated by Hallett that fatherlessness could sometimes be a source of opportunity.

From the age of Sulla we move to the *domus* of Augustus with Ann-Cathrin Harders. It is commonly known that Augustus used his family as a public platform for his politics. Harders revisits this theme, but with a view to exploring a particular aspect of Augustus' paternalism: his treatment of the fatherless sons of his archenemy and one-time brother-in-law, Marcus Antonius. Specifically, Harders returns to a debate over the social roles of Roman uncles (*avunculi*) and argues that Augustus framed his relationship to these children in terms of the traditional role of the *avunculus* (i.e. acting as an informal guardian to one's sister's children) in order to exploit it for his own political and dynastic ends. For Harders, this role allowed Augustus to advertise both his personal *pietas* as a "family man" and his commitment to political reconciliation, all the while affording him greater control over the lines of succession to his position.

Next, Neil Bernstein widens the scope by looking at the rhetoric of fatherlessness not just in the pursuit of personal power but as integral to the system of imperial politics. Bernstein examines the writings of two authors, Statius and Pliny the Younger. He begins with Statius, showing how the poet confronts and overcomes the latent criticism of the fatherlessness of the young Crispinus, the subject of one of his encomia, by praising the boy's precocious maturity and superior virtue. This conveniently affords Statius the opportunity to advertise the most excellent guardianship of the emperor Domitian (the exact nature of this "guardianship" is left ambiguous). Bernstein then turns to the career and writings of Pliny, who was himself left fatherless and as a consequence depended on and subsequently pro-moted a system of elite surrogacy. Together, both cases document the extent to which surrogacy had become an important practice among the Roman elite and part of the very fabric and ideology of imperial politics. Bernstein's discussion thus allows us to see the ways in which elite "fathers" and "sons" overcame biological fatherlessness and used the rhetoric of surrogacy to perpetuate elite rule.

From the construction of the rhetoric of fatherlessness we move to the teaching of rhetoric in late antique Antioch as Raffaella Cribiore considers the education of fatherless boys through the letters of Libanius. As we should by now expect, she finds that fatherlessness was a common experience in the rhetor's school. More surprising, however, is her determination that such a loss had little effect on the average students' educational career, at least insofar as its impact can be seen in their length of attendance or academic success. As she suggests, wealthy families in the late antique East had long since developed networks and strategies to support their sons and daughters after the loss of a father. In other words, as in Bernstein's chapter above, we are here seeing various forms of social capital being put to work. Also as above, these networks extend beyond the family. For instance, Libanius himself interceded on behalf of some of his orphaned students, a natural office for him to provide, since he, like Pliny, had grown up fatherless. In his capacity as someone who experienced fatherlessness at an early age, Libanius gives voice to the suggestion made by Golden, Hallett, and Müller, that in the right circumstances losing a father was tantamount to new freedom: "I would have been so glad to see my father in his old age, but I know this for certain, that if my father had reached a ripe old age, I would now be engaged upon a different life path."[87]

Finally, Geoffrey Nathan's study examines the issue of surrogate fatherhood in the late antique West, with specific attention to any effect that Christianity might have had. Through his examination of three case histories, he argues that certain cultural expectations surrounding guardians that stretch back into Classical times continued until the end of the ancient world and beyond. He sees the rise of Christianity not as something that radically altered surrogacy but rather provided a new avenue for articulating "traditional" concerns for the fatherless.

In conclusion, we offer some thoughts as to the limits and purpose of studying ancient fatherlessness. As we have seen, fatherlessness was endemic to family life in the ancient world and has lately reemerged as a basic structural feature of modern family life in much of the industrialized West for the foreseeable future. Then as now nearly a third of children spent a significant part of their childhood away from their biological fathers. Again, then as now a significant number of fatherless children were raised primarily by their mothers. Given the structural similarity of the phenomena and the demonstrable impact that modern fatherlessness has been shown to have on the lives of children, the idea that fatherless children in antiquity suffered from some of the same root problems as their modern counterparts deserves to be taken seriously. Between the two, however, there are crucial differences and these differences help to define the limits of comparison.

---

[87] *Or.* 1.6. See Cribiore (this volume): 257.

Fatherlessness in antiquity was for the most part the unhappy product of short life expectancy, typical of all pre-modern societies, and the relatively late age at marriage for men. The effects of ancient fatherlessness were exacerbated by the grim economic realities of the pre-industrial world. Although the situation was often clearly different for many children from the highest strata of society, they represented but a small proportion of all the fatherless children in the ancient world. The vast majority of ancient peoples lived out their lives in villages under the shadow of famine, without anything like the freedom of movement or opportunity for employment that now exist, particularly for women. It was this reality that reinforced the importance of family and shaped the contours of the various social responses we see in this volume, formal and informal, to the fatherless. Thus, in this world, defined by tightly knit, traditional communities, even widowed mothers who stayed single were probably not so alone in their efforts, or so far from their relatives, as many of the single mothers raising children today in America or Europe. Then again, these families were confronted with the total loss of their fathers, as opposed to the spectrum of loss characteristic of contemporary divorce or separation, and as we have seen there may have been no other living relatives to fill the gap. In all cases, it is clear that there was a harsh reality behind the cliché of the fatherless child as poverty-stricken, oppressed, and miserable.

This reality was also the reason why the wider family remained the most important support for fatherless children throughout antiquity. Only extraordinarily did the state intervene, usually when the sense of group identity was strong enough to reinterpret the political community as a sort of family. This happened for a time in Athens, as Golden describes, where the city in effect became a surrogate father to the young boys whose biological fathers had died for the good of the democracy. Again, as Bernstein and Cribiore show, social networks developed based on identities that transcended family and on which we see the fatherless children of the elite relying in order to maintain their positions in society. In the main, however, Greeks and Romans saw fatherless children only in terms of whose children they were. Since the family was the basic political, economic, and religious unit of ancient life, it was only when the family itself was threatened that the state intruded, ensuring that those charged with safeguarding its continued existence vis-à-vis fatherless heirs lived up to their obligations.

Jews and Christians, on the other hand, understood their responsibility to have been to all fatherless children in their group simply by virtue of their being fatherless, or at least this was the ideal as we see in Sigismund's discussion. Yet even this widened sense of responsibility ended at the boundaries of the group:

Christian help for widows and orphans was first and foremost Christian help for Christian widows and orphans.[88] With the Christianization of the Roman state there was suddenly both motive and means for a truly institutional response to fatherlessness in the Mediterranean world. And indeed, for a time the various charitable foundations of the late antique and Byzantine worlds offered not only food and shelter to fatherless children, but often education for boys and sometimes dowries for the girls as well.[89] The structural limitations of the ancient economy, however, kept these and similar efforts by smaller, poorer parishes or individuals from helping more than a minority of fatherless children. Also, and perhaps more importantly, as we see in Nathan's chapter, Christian values only slowly, and then only partially, transformed older, underlying social attitudes and responses to fatherlessness.[90] Therefore, despite the sea change that Christian charity appears to represent, the extended family necessarily remained the first and last resort for the majority of fatherless children in antiquity.

Finally, the adoption of a comparative approach does not commit us to the assumption that the ancient experiences and responses to fatherlessness studied in this volume necessarily bear directly on the fatherlessness of our increasingly globalized, post-industrial, multi-cultural world.[91] Indeed, the important differences described above illuminate how systemically different the two phenomena are, and thus the fact that any solution to the modern problem of fatherlessness will have to take into account the particular historical nexus of cultural and economic forces that have produced it, in the process balancing the freedom of women with the idea that begetting children creates a responsibility to raise them. A more directly comparable situation to ancient fatherlessness is the tragic orphan crisis in Africa precipitated by the HIV/AIDS epidemic, where extended family members, in most cases grandparents, aunts, and uncles, somehow manage despite their own dwindling ranks to absorb and care for over 90 percent of the now millions of children who have outlived their parents.[92] Then again, the experiences and solutions of the past may help to contextualize and clarify

---

[88] Finn 2006: 67–73; cf. 222–31 on Basil's charitable/euergetic actions on behalf of the whole of Caesarea during a famine.

[89] See Krause 1994–5: IV, 5–51; T. S. Miller 2003; and Nathan (this volume).

[90] For a succinct characterization of the limits and failings of late antique charity for the widows and orphans, see Krause 1994–5: IV, 49–51.

[91] T. S. Miller (2003: 13–15), for instance, goes too far in this direction in his defense of the relevance of the history of Byzantine orphanages to contemporary policy debates.

[92] Foster *et al.* 1997; Foster 2000; Hunter 2003: esp. 45–7; and Heymann *et al.* 2007. See also www.avert.org/aidsorphans.htm.

some of the key points in our understanding of or approach to the type of fatherlessness we experience today. In this regard, perhaps the most important lesson the studies in this book collectively teach is about the ways in which broader conceptions of the "family," – such as one finds among the Jews of the Second Temple, the early Christians, the Roman political elite, or even the far-flung network of the Eastern elites that came together in Libanius' school – led to wider zones of accountability, with whole communities shouldering responsibility for their members' children; but here we see the idea of family itself being stretched to its effective limit.[93] In looking at why and how some cultures or societies take responsibility for the fatherless perhaps we may begin to see a set of possible responses to modern fatherlessness beyond a return to the "traditional" family or reliance on bureaucratic government intervention. It is true that fathers no longer define families, but it is also true that some of the most successful attempts at ameliorating the effects of fatherlessness seen in this book represent the extension of lines of responsibility beyond the boundaries of the patriarchal family.

[93] Compare the attitudes and responses to fatherlessness of the Jewish community in medieval Cairo richly documented by Goitein (1967–93: III, 292–312; cf. II, 91–142). He found that despite the efforts made on behalf of such children by the community not only were the economy too weak and the juridical and communal organizations too loose for them to be widely effective, but also there remained a "host of conceptual shortcomings, religious and social" that contributed to the basic failure of the community to alleviate the suffering caused by early paternal death, among them the fact that in this "male-oriented society … when the father died, his dependents became, as it were, outsiders; they had no rights, only a claim to charity. But human charity, as a prayer has it, 'is scarce in providing, but plentiful in causing shame'" (III, 312).

PART I

Coping with demographic realities

CHAPTER 2

The demographic background

Walter Scheidel

The severe mortality regime of the ancient world caused many minors to lose their fathers. In Classical Athens men attained legal maturity at the age of eighteen while women commonly married in their mid-teens and passed under the control of their husbands.[1] In Roman society, males entered legal adulthood at the age of fourteen and assumed unqualified competence at twenty-five.[2] Women were considered mature at twelve and often appear to have begun marrying in their late teens.[3] In Roman Egypt men started paying poll tax at fourteen and the majority of women found husbands in their mid-to-late teens.[4] According to the Old Testament, Jewish men became liable to conscription and taxation at the age of twenty, whereas the later rabbinic tradition set the age of majority at twelve years for women and thirteen years for men.[5] Under these circumstances the loss of fathers during the first fifteen to twenty years of life mattered most and merits our attention here.

The average scale of loss was a function both of the overall age structure of the population and of male marriage practices. With the help of a computer simulation of the Roman kinship universe, Richard Saller established the basic parameters.[6] In his own words, this exercise "generates a model population by simulating the basic events of birth, death and marriage, month by month, in accordance with the age-specific probabilities of those events as established by the demographic parameters."[7] Saller devised three different scenarios to capture the probable range of life experiences in Roman society. The default model, labeled "Ordinary," aims to represent the general population by positing a mean age of first marriage of twenty

---

[1] E.g. Garland 1990: 180, 211; Pomeroy 1997: 23; 196, n. 10.
[2] E.g. Saller 1994: 185, 188; Gardner 1998: 146–8.   [3] Saller 1994: 25–41, 185. See also below.
[4] Bagnall and Frier 2006: 27, 113.   [5] Num. 1:2–3; Exod. 30:13–14; *Niddah* 5.6.
[6] Saller 1994: 43–69, superseding Saller 1987. His model was generated by the CAMSIM program developed by James Smith.
[7] Saller 1994: 44.

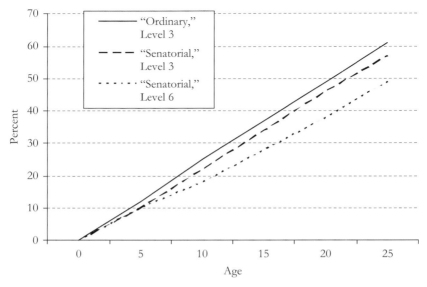

Figure 1 Proportion of fatherless individuals according to different scenarios of paternal marriage age and life expectancy (source: Saller 1994: 48–65).

years for women and thirty years for men, and an age structure consistent with a standard model life table based on a mean female life expectancy at birth of twenty-five years. The other two ("Senatorial") options envision marriage at younger ages as documented for elite circles, with means of fifteen years for women and twenty-five years for men, and a mean life expectancy at birth of either twenty-five or thirty-two and a half years, to allow for the (arguably remote) possibility of significantly lower elite mortality.[8]

In terms of the average risk of losing one's father, these three scenarios differ to a limited degree but ultimately generate fairly similar outcomes (Fig. 1). Depending on our choice of demographic conditions, between 28 and 37 percent of all individuals would have lost their fathers by age fifteen, and between 49 and 61 percent by age twenty-five. Thus, broadly speaking, about one-third of all Romans would have lost their fathers before they attained maturity (for men) or were married (for women). Closer to four in

---

[8] Saller 1994: 45–6; Coale and Demeny 1983: 43–4 (Model West Levels 3 and 6 Females). For elite mortality, cf. Scheidel 1999.

ten male Athenians became fatherless before they entered the *ephēbeia*, and over half of Romans did so prior to the *aetas perfecta* of twenty-five, the age of legal majority at which time one had complete freedom from curatorial oversight.[9]

These reconstructions critically depend on two variables, male age at first marriage and age-specific mortality levels. This raises the question of whether these starting assumptions are sufficiently well established to support these models, and to what extent historically plausible modifications might alter the predicted outcomes.

In the most general terms, as the annual odds of death gradually increase with age from the mid-teens onwards, delays in male marriage raise the proportion of minors who grow up fatherless. With regard to classical Greek society, late male marriage – around age thirty – seems largely uncontroversial.[10] By contrast, Saller's thesis of relatively late first marriage among Roman men has recently been challenged by Arnold Lelis, William Percy, and Beert Verstraete.[11] They not only – correctly – emphasize that literary evidence for Roman aristocratic marriage customs suggests lower male marriage ages even than Saller's "Senatorial" model, of closer to twenty years rather than twenty-five, but less convincingly reject Saller's reconstruction of non-elite marriage practices derived from shifts in commemorative preferences in funerary inscriptions from the western parts of the Roman Empire. Saller takes the age at which deceased men began to be primarily commemorated by wives rather than parents – of around thirty years in most samples – as indicative of the customary age of male first marriage.[12] As I have argued elsewhere, this reading is more readily consistent with the available data than is the rival claim of Lelis, Percy, and Verstraete that commemorative shifts for men were largely determined by the presence or absence of living fathers.[13] At the same time, however, it deserves notice that this finding of late male marriage is limited to those elements of the population that are represented in the epigraphic record, that is, predominantly "Romanized" and urban groups. Comparative evidence from late medieval Tuscany suggests that male marriage age in villages could be much lower than in cities: unfortunately, we have no way of ascertaining whether or not this was also true of Roman populations.[14]

This leaves us with an ambiguous result: while Saller's projections are likely to approximate the experience of urban populations in the western Roman

---

[9] See the Introduction to this volume for a brief overview of guardianship in the Greco-Roman world.
[10] E.g. Pomeroy 1997: 23.   [11] Lelis, Percy, and Verstraete 2003.   [12] Saller 1987 and 1994: 25–41.
[13] Scheidel 2007b.   [14] Herlihy and Klapisch-Zuber 1985: 203–11.

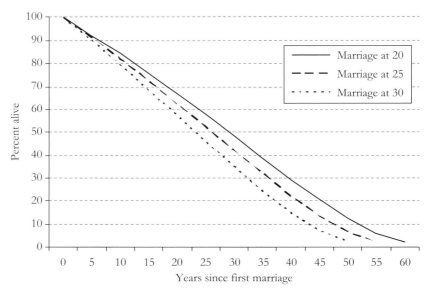

Figure 2 Probability of male survival according to paternal age at first marriage
(Model West Level 3 Males) (source: Coale and Demeny 1983: 43).

Empire, we must allow for the possibility that thanks to male marriage at younger ages, the rural majority may conceivably have witnessed a lower incidence of fatherlessness. Even so, any such difference was bound to be modest (Fig. 2). For children born to fathers soon after their first marriage, the difference was fairly negligible: a person born to a thirty-year-old man was only 10 percent more likely to lose that father within the first fifteen years of life than someone born to a twenty-year-old man. The offspring of older men were more heavily affected by paternal marriage age: for instance, a person born fifteen years after the father's first marriage at age thirty faced a chance of losing that father within the first fifteen years of life that was one-third higher than for someone born fifteen years after a father's first marriage at age twenty (viz. 48 versus 36 percent). On average, however, the overall incidence of paternal loss among minors was only moderately sensitive to male age at first marriage.[15]

Mortality, the other principal variable, also merits further scrutiny. Saller's simulation is based on standard model life tables that rigidly

---

[15] The impact of birth order is explored in greater detail below.

extrapolate from (known) low-to-medium-mortality regimes to (unknown) high-mortality regimes with scant regard for the peculiarities of archaic disease environments. Critics have charged that at very low levels of life expectancy – that is, at those levels that are relevant for ancient historians – these models may well exaggerate the scale of infant mortality and under-estimate death rates among adolescents and young and middle-aged adults.[16] If correct, the latter suggests that ancient rates of fatherlessness might have been (even) higher than predicted by standard model life tables. Once again, however, any reasonable amount of adjustment has only a limited effect on the overall likelihood of paternal loss. Woods' new alter-native high-mortality life tables for southern European populations consis-tently posit higher age-specific mortality risks for teenagers and young and middle-aged adults than existing models: in his estimate, compared with Coale and Demeny's predictions, the odds of dying in a population with a mean life expectancy at birth of twenty-five years (for women) were higher by 39 percent from ages twenty to twenty-five, by 44 percent from ages twenty-five to thirty, by 35 percent from ages thirty to thirty-five, by 30 percent from ages thirty-five to forty, by 25 percent from ages forty to fifty, and by 8 percent from ages fifty to fifty-five.[17] In this scenario children born to men in their twenties, thirties, and forties – that is, the great majority of all children – would more often have lost their fathers as minors than previously thought.

The extent of this divergence is impossible to quantify in detail without rerunning the entire simulation of the Roman kinship universe with new mortality rates. Nevertheless, the differences in the mean probability of parental death are relatively modest overall: in the case of women – while Woods' life table deals only with women, we may reckon with similarly sized differences for male life tables – the odds of dying in any given five-year period between ages twenty and fifty rise from 9 to 12 percent in the standard model to 12 to 15 percent in the new projections. Thus, the resultant rates of paternal loss were by no means dramatically higher than in existing reconstructions. Figure 3 illustrates the difference in the survival chances of mothers: the corresponding curves for fathers (which are unavail-able for the Woods model) may assume a somewhat different shape but the average degree of divergence would presumably be similar.

---

[16] See Coale and Demeny 1983: 3–36 for the data and methodology underlying conventional model life tables. For criticism, compare Woods 1993; Scheidel 2001c; Woods 2007.

[17] Woods 2007: 379, table 2.

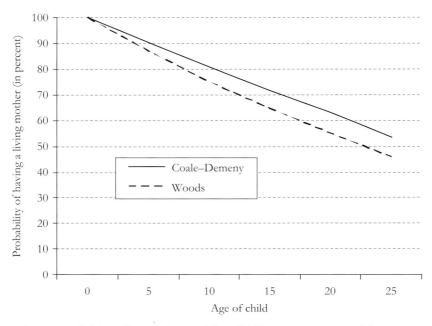

Figure 3 Probability of maternal survival for a child born to a woman aged thirty in a population with a mean life expectancy at birth of twenty-five years (source: Coale and Demeny 1983: 43; Woods 2007: 379).

All in all, we may conclude that Saller's projections are fairly robust in the sense that they are only mildly sensitive to historically plausible changes in our assumptions concerning male age at first marriage and adult mortality rates. In a further step, we may compare the average likelihood of the death of a father to that of the loss of other adult male relatives who were suitable guardians of minors, most notably paternal uncles and grandfathers. Figure 4 suggests that the presence or absence of a living father was the single most important indicator of the level of protection enjoyed by a minor. In the majority of cases the loss of a father could not have been offset by the appointment of a paternal uncle or grandfather as guardian simply because no such relatives were still alive and able to serve in this capacity.

At the same time, brothers who were old enough to serve as guardians (that is, twenty-five years old under Roman law) must have been rare except among children born to older fathers, but such children were disproportionately prone to losing their fathers as minors and even less likely to benefit from the presence of paternal uncles or grandfathers. In order to illustrate the probable

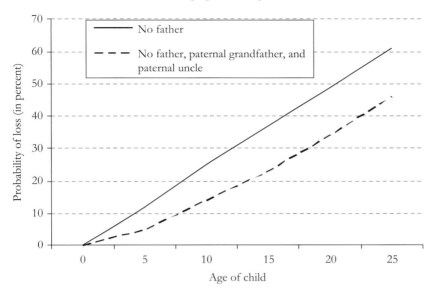

Figure 4 Probability of loss of father and of loss of father, paternal grandfather, and any paternal uncles ("Ordinary," Level 3) (source: Saller 1994: 52).

shifts in the identity of adult male caregivers depending on paternal age, I consider two bounding scenarios: the experience of a child born to a father aged twenty-five and that of a child born to a father twice as old.

Figures 5 and 6 show that a child born to a twenty-five-year-old man was relatively well buffered against risk. While he or she would not be able to draw on the services of an older brother – unless an older male had been adopted by one's own father – the risk of ending up without a mature male paternal relative who was suitable as a guardian was fairly low: only one in seven by age fourteen, and one in three by the less important threshold of age twenty-five. Conversely, the corresponding odds were much worse for a child born to a fifty-year-old man: close to one-half by age fourteen, and five in six by age twenty-five. In other words, risk was more than three times as high by age fourteen, and two-and-a-half times as high by age twenty-five.[18]

To what extent would the presence of adult brothers mitigate the deficit of other mature male relatives among children born to older men? This

[18] Despite frequent paternal remarriage, children born to older men were also on average more likely to have older mothers and hence fewer mature maternal relatives who could serve as guardians: cf. Saller 1994: 52–3.

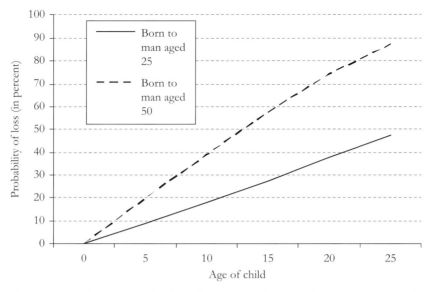

Figure 5 Mean risk of loss of father depending on paternal age at birth of child (source: Coale and Demeny 1983: 43).

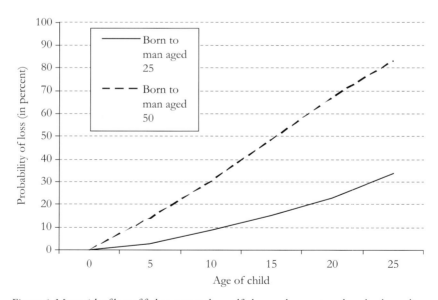

Figure 6 Mean risk of loss of father, paternal grandfather, and any paternal uncles depending on paternal age at birth of child (source: Coale and Demeny 1983: 43; Saller 1994: 52).

question is difficult to answer precisely without recourse to Saller's simulation program but can nonetheless be addressed with some confidence. If we schematically envision a scenario in which two brothers were born twenty and ten years prior to the birth of a child fathered by a fifty-year-old man, their mean chances of being alive at the time of the birth of the third child were 43.6 and 48 percent, respectively.[19] By the time that that child reached age fourteen, his or her chance of having a twenty-five-year-old brother who could act as a *tutor* or *curator* had already dropped to one in three. At that age, the average cumulative risk of lacking a living father, paternal grandfather, paternal uncle or mature brother was one in three, and hence more than twice as high as the odds that a coeval individual born to a twenty-five-year-old man might find him- or herself in the same situation. While the presence of mature brothers increased the availability of close-kin guardians for the offspring of older men, it could not fully compensate for the higher rates of loss associated with high paternal age.

It is true that some minors must have had at least one adult (paternal) cousin who could have provided tutelage. Recourse to this type of relative was a function of two unrelated variables, paternal birth order and paternal age at one's own birth: children of late-born fathers were more likely to have adult cousins (who had been born to older uncles) who might serve as guardians, as were late-born children of any fathers with brothers who had produced male issue. In the Egyptian census returns several individuals lived in the households of (older?) cousins, which indicates that this need not have been an uncommon arrangement.[20] Unfortunately, although this option may on average have been more readily available to the children of older fathers, existing simulations do not allow us to quantify its potential significance.

With this caveat, and all other things being equal, it nevertheless appears likely that the children of younger fathers were better off than the progeny of older men. Not only were the former less likely to lose their fathers as minors, they also had a much better chance of being cared for by mature close paternal relatives in the event of their father's death than were the children of older men.

[19] Incidentally, this chimes with Saller's estimate that a notional average fifty-year-old man had a 69 percent chance of having any living sons (1994: 52), although his simulation does not allow for the birth of an additional child at that age. Thus, my example overstates actual reproductive success, and thereby also the likelihood of the presence of surviving older brothers.

[20] See Bagnall and Frier 2006: 145-Ar-20 (co-resident cousins of declarant are minors), 159-Ar-10 (age difference unknown), 173-Ar-11 (age difference unknown), and perhaps also 159-Ar-13 (possible co-resident underage cousin). I owe these references to Sabine Hübner.

Taken together, the growing risk of fatherlessness associated with rising paternal age, the concurrently growing paucity of other mature male relatives, and the relative scarcity of mature brothers indicate that birth order was an important determinant of a child's security and well-being. The census records of Roman Egypt show that men customarily continued to father children well into their fifties: the median age of paternity appears to have been around 37–8 years.[21] We can only surmise that Greeks and Romans more generally displayed similar habits, with the result that a substantial share of all children would have been fathered by men in their forties and fifties.

In conclusion, we may distinguish among three ideal-typical categories:

- Children of relatively young men whose fathers lived on and continued to father more children. They would grow up under the care of their fathers and might later be called upon to assume responsibility for their younger siblings once their father had finally died.
- Children of relatively young men whose fathers died young and who subsequently grew up under the tutelage of mature male relatives of the deceased father, and who did not have to assume responsibility for younger siblings later on.
- Children of older men who more frequently lost their fathers as minors and were more likely to grow up under the care of others and to come under the control of guardians who were not close paternal relatives.

In practice, the boundaries between these ideal types were fluid, and intermediate experiences must have been common. Even so, these scenarios arguably represent the most typical outcomes and provide a rough demographic template that helps historians to structure the experience of growing up fatherless in antiquity.

---

[21] Bagnall and Frier 2006: 146.

CHAPTER 3

Oedipal complexities

Mark Golden

It was King Cecrops who first founded marriage at Athens. As a result (according to Charax of Pergamum) he was called *diphyēs*, "two-natured," because through him humans recognized that they were born of two beings.[1] Charax, a historian who may have lived in the second century CE, knows another explanation for Cecrops' epithet, and there were more besides – that he was bilingual, that his temperament changed over time, that he was half-serpent and half-man – but the invention of so fundamental an institution as paternity is in line with his other associations.[2] Cecrops is variously credited with being Athens' first king, with choosing Athena as his city's patron, with recognizing Zeus as the supreme god, with (less successfully) ending the sacrifice of living victims.[3] We might regard him (as writers from at least the fourth century BCE did) as a culture hero.[4] Or even as the father of his country. After all, in one version of Athena's struggle with Poseidon to be recognized as the tutelary deity of Athens, Cecrops arranged a vote of the citizens. The women voted in a bloc for Athena and, more numerous as they were, narrowly carried the day.[5] The men responded in a manner not unknown in respect to modern elections: they removed women's right to vote or to be called Athenians and, more pertinently here, decreed that children must be known by their father's name alone. Cecrops, it seems, discovered paternity as a biological fact and then presided over its establishment as a prime marker of social identity. Fathers not only mattered, they mattered more.

If Cecrops found fathers, many in antiquity lost them. (In both Greek and Latin, they were termed orphans – *orphanoi/ai, orbi/ae* – even if their

Thanks to the editors for their invitation to contribute to this volume and to Jan Bremmer, Scott Forbes, Karen Hunt, Pauline Ripat, and Michael Wahn for subsequent encouragement and advice.

[1] Charax, *FGrH* 103 F 38–9; Clearchus, *Ath.* 13.555d; cf. *Suda* s.v. *Kekrops*; schol. Ar. *Plut.* 773.
[2] Gourmelen 2005: 97–112.   [3] Apollod. *Bibl.* 3.14.1–2; Paus. 8.2.2–3, cf. 1.26.5.
[4] Vidal-Naquet 1981b: 198–9; R. C. T. Parker 1987: 193–8.   [5] August. *De civ. D.* 18.9.

mothers still survived; I will use this term here.)[6] Homer provides a particularly moving testament to the effects of a father's loss. Toward the end of Book 22 of the *Iliad*, Andromache climbs the walls of Troy to see the corpse of her husband, Hector, as it is dragged behind Achilles' chariot. She faints and, when she comes to, makes a long speech of lamentation, dwelling not on her own fate but on that of their infant son Astyanax:

> Our son is still a baby,
> The one we bore, you and I, ill-fated as we are. You will not be a help to
> Him, Hector, since you have died, nor he to you,
> For, even if he escapes the war with the Greeks and its many tears,
> There will always be toil and care for him
> In the future. For others will take away his land.
> The day of orphanhood makes a child friendless.
> He always hangs down his head, his cheeks run with tears,
> He goes in need to his father's companions,
> Tugging one by his cloak, another by his tunic.
> Someone pities him and gives him a cup for a short while,
> But he moistens only his lips, not his palate.
> And a boy whose parents are both alive thrusts him from the feast,
> Striking him with his hands and attacking him with abuse:
> "Go away, you! Your father isn't dining with us."
> And the boy returns in tears to his widowed mother,
> Astyanax, who before on his father's knees
> Used to eat only the marrow or the rich fat of sheep …
> Now he will suffer many things, having lost his dear father.   (22.484–507)

In the end, of course, Astyanax, deprived of his father's protection, is dashed to death on the Trojan plains where Hector is being dragged.[7]

There is much here to resonate today, as we recall the photographs of the young John-John Kennedy at his father's funeral or watch the images of AIDS orphans flicker and die on our television screens. And the orphan's plight is a staple of ancient culture, too, from the appeals of litigants in Athenian courts to the depictions of foreign children in scenes of triumph and war in Roman public art.[8] (These are often shown with women only, while paternal figures accompany citizen children.)[9] Some may reflect on the sad-eyed consequences of being deprived of a father less finally. Canada

---

[6] This would be the place for a pun on "orphan" and "often," but I will defer to those in Gilbert and Sullivan's *The Pirates of Penzance*. They do not work very well in North American English anyway.
[7] For a longer discussion of this passage and orphans in Homeric culture, see Wöhrle (this volume): 164–6.
[8] Litigants: Andoc. 1.148; Lys. 3.6–7; 13.45; 20.34–6; Isae. 5.10–11; Dem. 19.310; 38.19–20; 53.29; Pl. *Ap.* 41e; cf. Cic. *Verr.* 2.1.59.15.
[9] Uzzi 2005: 164–6.

long took native children from their families and educated them in residential schools, generally Church-run institutions which worked to eradicate their language and culture before returning them to a society in which they were now strangers. Fatherless as they were, many of these children later proved to be poor parents, contributing to a cycle of dependency and abuse.[10]

However, even a cursory review of ancient epic reveals that boys might respond to a father's absence or loss in different ways; not every outcome is as dire as Astyanax's.[11] Achilles' son, Pyrrhus or Neoptolemus – "Young War" – never knows him; he grows up to be a near match for his father as a fighter, nonetheless. But whereas Achilles releases Hector's body to the suppliant King Priam, Neoptolemus – "the first great war criminal of Greek cultural history" – cuts down Priam's son Polites before his father's eyes.[12] "Achilles, the man whose son you falsely claim to be, was not like this towards his enemy," the old man rebukes him. "You will go as a messenger to Peleus' son," replies Neoptolemus. "Remember to tell him of my dismal doings and of my unworthiness of him (*degenerem*). Now die."[13] Achilles was fated to surpass his father, the gift of his goddess mother; Neoptolemus' youthful cruelty must strike us as all too human, in need of a father's discipline or example.[14] Elsewhere in the *Aeneid* both Aeneas and Ascanius are deprived of their fathers in the course of the poem, Aeneas by the death of Anchises (at the end of Book 3) and Ascanius by Aeneas' journey to the court of Evander and the future site of Rome (in Book 8). In these cases too the son must do without a father's guidance at a time of crisis. Aeneas forms a new attachment, with Queen Dido of Carthage, and loses sight of his own mission and the responsibilities it requires; Ascanius spurs on Nisus and Euryalus to the nighttime raid which ends in their deaths.[15] In all three instances a father's absence presents a challenge that sons are not yet able to meet. Telemachus, however, takes a different trajectory. Left alone for the twenty years of Odysseus' Trojan war and travels – his name means "distant battler" – Telemachus sets out on a journey of his own, one on which he discovers something of his father and his world and begins to learn how to be like him. When the two finally meet back in Ithaca they are able to stand side by side to

[10] The most authoritative account may be found in the *Report of the Royal Commission on Aboriginal Peoples*, vol. I: *Looking Forward, Looking Back* (Ottawa, 1996): 333–409.
[11] Lee 1979; Wöhrle 1999; cf. Wöhrle (this volume).
[12] Quotation: Most 1985: 160. But for a different reading of the early evidence, see Burnett 2005: 188–91.
[13] Virg. *Aen.* 2.540–50.
[14] See the contributions of Pratt, Müller, and Bernstein (this volume) for discussions of the relationship of fatherlessness to the moral education or state of sons.
[15] Merriam 2002.

slay the suitors and reclaim the home and kingdom rightfully theirs. At the
end of the *Odyssey* they are joined by another missing father, old Laertes, long
exiled to a plot of land far from the city. All three unite for a final battle,
fathers and sons who find themselves to be worthy equals despite their many
years apart.[16]

Alan Shapiro has emphasized the variety of treatments of this "absent
father syndrome" in Greek myth.[17] In real life too outcomes might depend
on a host of factors. Citizens (my focus in this chapter) would likely fare
differently than other free children or slaves, the rich than the poor, boys
than girls, infants than their older siblings. The cause of fatherlessness might
matter too: was a father dead or divorced or merely away for a while? Had
he rejected a child, failed to acknowledge it, or disinherited it? If dead – how
did he die? Public and private provisions for orphans must have been
exceptionally important: the support of the community, the availability of
mothers and other kin, the kindness of strangers. In addition, we should
be aware of the distinction between the norm – most Greeks and Romans
could expect to lose their fathers, just as we do now – and unexpected crises.
Finally, we should admit (as I think the *Odyssey* does) that the absence of
a father could offer opportunity as well as hardship and grief. In what
follows I will touch on a few of these issues, however impressionistically.
My comments will be most directly relevant to Classical Athens and to the
Rome of the late Republic and early Empire.

PUBLIC PROVISIONS FOR THE FATHERLESS

Zeus watched over Greek orphans.[18] Fatherless Athenian children were under
the further protection of an annual magistrate, the eponymous archon, who
supervised auctions for leases of their land and presided over lawsuits brought
against those who did them or their property harm.[19] These lawsuits could
be brought by any adult male citizen and such a plaintiff was exempt from
the usual grave sanctions imposed on those who withdrew their cases or failed
to persuade at lease one-fifth of the jurors. Other laws protected orphans'
property by forbidding guardians to risk it through bottomry loans and by
exempting them from public services for a year after they came of age.[20] Boys
whose fathers had died in war were supported by the state until they came of

---

[16] Felson 1999. See also Wöhrle (this volume) on Telemachus' fatherlessness.
[17] Shapiro 2003.   [18] Plut. *fr.* 40 Sandbach = schol. Hes. *Op.* 327–34.
[19] *Ath. Pol.* 56.6–7. See discussion and bibliography for guardianship generally in the ancient world in
      the Introduction (13–18).
[20] Lys. 32.24–5.

age;[21] at some time before the mid-fourth century they were then presented to the audience at the Greater Dionysia, decked out in the panoply of war as if to replace their fallen fathers.[22] In the meantime their fellow citizens were to show them the affection their fathers would: this is not a matter of money alone.[23] In special cases fathers might be honored posthumously by provisions made (or allegedly made) for their children. The fifth-century statesman and commander Aristides is said (implausibly) to have died poor, so the community dowered and paid for the weddings of his daughters and gave his son land on the island of Euboea, a cash gift, and a daily pension.[24] The daughters (Plutarch says) were given in marriage from the Prytaneion, a building which housed the city's hearth fire and was somehow linked to the arrangements for war orphans. It also served as the site for murder trials of animals and inanimate objects, defendants with no citizen kin to support them. In all this, the city is to be thought of as taking over the duty of a household's head.[25]

In Roman law, minors whose fathers had died – *pupilli/ae* – had to have a guardian, *tutor*.[26] Some *tutores* will have been appointed by will or, if the father had died intestate, served by virtue of their relationship to him (as one of his agnates). Others might be nominated by the mother or another family member but in any case needed to be confirmed in office by a magistrate (at Rome itself, a praetor). The emperor Marcus Aurelius created a special officer, the praetor *tutelaris*, with oversight over *tutores*.[27] Suitability would be an important criterion for *tutores*, willingness less so, since only exceptional circumstances could give rise to an exemption. In theory this law applied to all, but it is unlikely that fatherless children had the protection – or the inconvenience – of a *tutor* unless there was significant property or their education was at stake.[28] Nor were girls and boys treated alike: boys were free from *tutela* at fourteen; *tutores* had girls under their protection until just twelve, the age at which they could make a will or marry; the

---

[21] Thuc. 2.46.1; Arist. *Pol.* 2.1268a8–11; *Ath. pol.* 24.3. According to the *Politics*, this was true at Miletus and other *poleis*, too.

[22] Isoc. 6.82; Aeschin. 3.154.

[23] Lys. 2.75. Some families may have tried to get the money at least for their sons by arranging for posthumous adoptions into the families of the fallen at the end of the Peloponnesian War (Slater 1993).

[24] Dem. 20.115; Aeschin. 3.258; Plut. *Arist.* 27.1–3, with the skeptical comments of Davies 1971: 51–2.

[25] S. G. Miller 1978: 13–20; Katz 1993: 176.

[26] See also the Introduction (15–18) for additional discussion and bibliography on Roman guardianship.

[27] *SHA, Marc.* 10.11; Rawson 2003: 73. Roman authorities in Egypt made the guardians of underage orphans submit annual accounts from at least the early third century CE (*P. Oxy.* 58.3921).

[28] Rawson 2003: 71, 187.

praetor, however, might make allocations from an estate for the education
of both boys and girls as late as their twentieth year.[29]

At Athens too orphaned girls and boys experienced different treatment, as
signaled already by the arrangements made for the sons (only) of the war dead.
An Athenian girl who had neither father nor brother – an *epiklēros* – might be
betrothed by her father's will. Otherwise, a near relation, a member of the
anchisteia, was required to marry her himself or to see to a marriage with an
appropriate dowry, pegged to her family's income and census class. (This too
came under the purview of the eponymous archon.) Such girls would have
little or no input into the choice of a husband; in fact, even those who were
already married when their father died might find themselves subject to a
claim by one of the *anchisteia*, though perhaps only if they had not yet
borne a son.[30] On the other hand, a law attributed to Solon stipulated that
the husband of an *epiklēros* had to have intercourse with her at least three
times a month.[31] Plutarch says this attention is a mark of affection and
regard which prevents bad feeling and estrangement. No doubt he is right,
but it is likely that the intention of the lawgiver was to ensure that the
husband had not claimed his wife only in order to gain access to her
father's property. Still, other Athenian women had no such guarantee.
Epiklēroi who were daughters of state debtors also benefited from slightly
different rules than those affecting sons. Sons inherited a father's obligation to the community along with his property; if unable to pay in full,
they too suffered their father's *atimia*, or loss of citizen rights. This would
hardly affect daughters, whose civic scope was so much more restricted.
But what of their husbands? The man who married an *epiklēros* did not
share his bride's father's *atimia* as long as the property was enough to pay
even a portion of the debt.[32]

FATHER FIGURES, SUBSTITUTES, SURROGATES

The Roman *tutor* was frequently envisaged as a father figure. The jurist
Callistratus, writing in the third century CE, thought that the *pupillus*
deserved the same care from his *tutor* as a child from his father and Pliny
the Younger testifies that his *tutor* Verginius Rufus "showed him the

---

[29] *Dig.* 27.2.2.pr. (Ulpian). After age twelve, Roman girls usually exchanged one sort of *tutor* for another
in that they were then subject to *tutela mulierum*. Roman boys, however, were throughout the
imperial period increasingly under the protection of *curatores* from ages fourteen to twenty-five.
[30] Isae. 3.64; Schaps 1979: 28–9.   [31] Plut. *Sol.* 20.3.   [32] Isae. 10.16–17; Kapparis 1994.

affection of a parent."[33] Were there other ways for a child to acquire a substitute or surrogate father? One main modern means, adoption, had other ends in antiquity. At Athens "adoption was primarily construed as benefiting the adoptee, providing for his need of a descendant," to provide support in old age and continue the family line afterwards;[34] Roman adoption "had nothing to do with the welfare of children."[35] In both societies adoptees were usually adults; different as it was in detail and in design, this was true of adoption on Hellenistic Rhodes as well.[36] Private adoption, *adoptio*, at Rome required that the adoptee be *in potestate*, still under the control of the *paterfamilias*; those adopted by *adrogatio* – through the curiate assembly or later by a rescript of the emperor – needed to give consent. Minors were therefore ineligible until the second century CE and their adoption by *adrogatio* was hedged by restrictions even afterwards.[37] Clearly, all this can have done little for fatherless children.

How about foundlings? Roman tombstones include surprisingly numerous references to *alumni/ae*, usually translated as "nurslings, foster-children"; these make up 3 percent of all persons commemorated with a term of relation on the epitaphs collected in *CIL* vi (from imperial Rome) as compared with the 15 percent who were sons and daughters.[38] Roman fathers reserved the right to accept or reject children born into their house-holds, a prerogative exercised by the *kyrios*, or head, of an Athenian *oikos* as well. (The head of a Spartan household, in contrast, had to defer to the judgment of "the elders of the tribesmen.")[39] These were exposed, as were many illegitimate infants whose fathers declined to acknowledge them or were unknown.[40] Most died. Some, however, especially those set out in a place customarily used for this purpose (as seems to have been the case at Athens), might be rescued and raised. Is it possible that some *alumni/ae* were children who became fatherless in this way? Certainly it is: but far from all and they may have made up only a minority, a small one at that.[41]

Societies throughout Europe and western Eurasia have developed a number of institutions which allow children to circulate outside their

---

[33] *Dig.* 26.7.33.pr.; Plin. *Ep.* 2.1.8. Cf. Bernstein's discussion (this volume) of Pliny and his relationship to his surrogate and adoptive fathers.

[34] Rubinstein 1993: 13; cf. 1999: 52.   [35] Crook 1967: 111.

[36] Gabrielsen 1997: 113.   [37] Gardner 1998: 165–75.

[38] Nielsen 1999.   [39] Plut. *Lyc.* 16.1; Link 1998.

[40] There is no agreement on the extent of this practice; for references to recent studies, see Arjava 1996: 81, n. 12 and Golden 2000: 39, n. 38, and add Scheidel 1997; W. V. Harris 1994; 1999; Rousselle 2001; E. Scott 2001; and Ingalls 2002.

[41] Compare the rather different views on the overlap between foundlings and *alumni/ae* in Bradley 1991a: 62; Dixon 1999: 223; Nielsen 1999: 250; Rawson 2003: 251–2.

birth families and so to gain access to father substitutes if they need them: godparenthood, milk kinship, apprenticeship, fosterage.[42] Christian godparenthood is obviously irrelevant to pagan antiquity; milk kinship – despite the use of the term *homogalaktes*, "milk-sharers," by Aristotle in his discussion of partnerships in the introduction to *Politics* – is probably of little importance at most.[43] Apprenticeship is poorly attested for Classical Athens. Thanks to a recent discovery, however, we now know of one fourth-century apprentice by name, a young man named Lesis, not a citizen, who wrote a letter complaining about his treatment in a foundry. The letter is addressed to Lesis' mother and a certain Xenocles, who is apparently not his father.[44] Documents on papyrus leave us better informed on apprenticeship in Greco-Roman Egypt.[45] These concern boys and girls, slave as well as free, apprenticed, mostly to weavers, from the age of twelve or thirteen. Sometimes it is the mother who makes the contract on behalf of her child or (in one instance) approves of terms he had negotiated for himself – these children may be fatherless. However, fathers too appear in these contracts, even fathers who are themselves weavers but seem to have preferred to let someone else teach their children the trade. Similarly, in second-century CE Syria, Lucian's father apprenticed him to learn the family business from one of his uncles, a sculptor.[46] Lucian broke a slab of stone, was punished and (much like Lesis five hundred years before) complained to his mother. Other masters were more lenient – the epitaph for an apprentice named Florentius claims that his master loved him more than a son[47] – but their paternal feelings obviously do not guarantee that their charges had no father of their own.

There is more to say about fosterage. Specialists in this area distinguish two types, kinship and alliance fosterage, "a patron–client bond expressed in terms of quasi-kinship."[48] A special form of alliance fosterage, allegiance fosterage, is used for political purposes.[49] It sometimes involves the fostering of high-status children by their social inferiors ("cliental fosterage") and sometimes the movement of children of lower status to the homes of the elite ("patronal fosterage"). In general, cliental fosterage includes infants and their nursing; patronal fosterage, older children. We find an example of patronal fosterage in ancient Macedon, where (likely from the fifth century at least) teenage boys attended the royal court, waiting on the king's table,

[42] Parkes 2003; 2004; 2006. For *erastai* as surrogate fathers to their young *erōmenoi* at Sparta, see Plut. *Lyc.* 18.4; Cartledge 2001: 97.
[43] Arist. *Pol.* 1.1251b18; Derks 1995.   [44] E. Harris 2004.
[45] Bradley 1991a: 107–16.   [46] Lucian, *Somn.* 1–4.   [47] *CIL* vi.10013.
[48] Goody 1982: 114.   [49] Parkes 2003: 742–5; 2006: 359–70.

accompanying him on the hunt, and, toward the end of their stay, serving as his bodyguard.[50] The fathers are usually styled "the most respected men of Macedonia," "Macedonians in office," or "the king's friends."[51] We may think of these boys (usually called "royal pages" in modern scholarship) either as means to strengthen ties between the king and the Macedonians who ranked beneath only him or as thinly disguised hostages; either way, the institution makes most sense if their fathers are alive, and indeed Diodorus says they were sent by their fathers. Alexander the Great extended the custom when he directed some ten thousand soldiers returning home to Macedon to leave in his charge the children they had had by foreign women.[52]

Kinship fostering is both better attested and more directly relevant, since it is often a response to a family crisis, such as a father's death. Whereas alliance fostering results in a child's being raised apart from the father, it is his unavailability which often motivates kinship fostering. In legend Neoptolemus was raised by his maternal grandfather in Achilles' absence, as Theseus was raised by his after King Aegeus returned to Athens. On the Athenian comic stage, the young Pheidippides says he will turn to his uncle (as he calls his mother's uncle) if his father will not let him race his chariot.[53] Mothers' brothers were a resource in real life too: Charmides was raised by his (Andocides' father), as were Isaeus' clients in a lawsuit over the estate of Cleonymus.[54] In addition, sisters' sons (or other descendants) are much more common among adoptees than paternal kin.[55] No one has done more than Jan Bremmer to bring out the prominence of the mother's father and brother in fostering, which he regards as an Indo-European characteristic.[56] Some have been skeptical.[57] But a passage in the life of Demosthenes included with the works of Plutarch offers some support, for Greece anyway.[58] After his father's death, reports the anonymous biographer, Demosthenes was cheated by his guardians. When he reached majority and brought suit against them, he leveled his accusations against his mother's brother above all. In fact, this is wrong: the extant speeches – available to the biographer as well – reveal that it was his cousin and prospective stepfather, Aphobus, who bore the brunt of Demosthenes' blame. It was surely the biographer's assumption that the

---

[50] Hammond 1990; Heckel 1992: 237–44.   [51] Ael. *VH* 14.48; Arr. *Anab.* 4.13.1; Diod. Sic. 17.65.1.
[52] Arr. *Anab.* 7.12.2, cf. Diod. Sic. 17.110.3, Plut. *Alex.* 47.6.   [53] Ar. *Nub.* 124–5.
[54] Andoc. 1.48–50; Isae. 1.1–15.   [55] Cox 1988: 389–90.
[56] Bremmer 1976; 1983; 1999; cf. Bettini 1991: 39–66. Cf. Harders (this volume) on this role and the career of Augustus.
[57] Parkes 2006: 363–4, cf. Treggiari 1993: 275–6 (on Bettini).   [58] [Plut.] *Mor.* 844cd.

Table 3.1. *Percentage of men (Male, "Ordinary," West Level 3)*
at various ages with living kin

	0 yrs	5 yrs	10 yrs	15 yrs	20 yrs	25 yrs	30 yrs
Mother's father	34%	24%	15%	8%	4%	1%	0%
Father's father	17%	10%	5%	2%	0%	0%	0%
Mother's brother	54%	51%	48%	44%	39%	34%	29%
Father's brother	49%	45%	41%	36%	30%	25%	19%

Table 3.2. *Percentage of men (Male, "Senatorial," West Level 3)*
at various ages with living kin

	0 yrs	5 yrs	10 yrs	15 yrs	20 yrs	25 yrs	30 yrs
Mother's father	46%	35%	25%	17%	10%	5%	2%
Father's father	27%	19%	11%	6%	3%	1%	0%
Mother's brother	54%	51%	48%	44%	40%	35%	30%
Father's brother	50%	46%	41%	37%	32%	27%	21%

mother's brother would carry most of the responsibility or be most liable to an accusation of treachery that caused this slip.

Bremmer rejects one explanation for preferring a mother's kin, the influence of matrilineality or matriarchy, and suggests a series of alternatives: the closeness of brothers and sisters (as compared with other sibling relationships), the absence of *patriapotestas* in the maternal line (for Rome), the disinclination of men to keep a close watch on their children's upbringing (for Greece). Not all of these are beyond dispute: the lack of interest our elite-male literary sources show in young children needs to be balanced by the glimpses they give of fatherly affection among Greeks.[59] Whatever their force, however, demographic realities may have had more impact than any on a tendency toward entrusting fatherless children to maternal kin.[60] I present in Tables 3.1 and 3.2 the percentages of males of various ages (at five-year intervals) for whom kin of different degrees of relationship may have survived. These are drawn from Richard Saller's computer-generated life tables based on both male "Ordinary" Level 3 West (with male age of

---

[59] French 1999.   [60] Cox 1998: 116, n. 39.

marriage at 30) and male "Senatorial" Level 3 West (with male age of marriage at 25).[61]

At all ages, it is much more likely that a mother's father is alive (and available as a fosterer) than a paternal grandfather. The spread in survivability favors a mother's brother less strikingly, but it is still noticeable, varying from something over 10 percent for a five-year-old to about 30 percent for a young man of twenty. (The paternal uncle of Isaeus' clients died before their mother's brother took them in.) These results are quite insensitive to the age of marriage: the differences are nearly as great when men wed five years younger.

From mothers' kin to mothers. They provided the most effective mode of replacing a father, through remarriage.[62] We are not concerned with the aftermath of divorce: at both Athens and Rome children remained in their fathers' custody, though of course this need not involve their fathers in looking after them any more than it does now.[63] Typically, stepfathers came on the scene only after a father's death. Though children remained in their father's *oikos* at his death under Athenian law, mothers might take them into their new husband's household on remarriage nonetheless.[64] And the ten-to fifteen-year difference in the customary age of first marriage for men and women at both Athens and Rome produced many widows. One study estimates that 558 Athenian wives in every thousand lost their husbands at some time after their marriage and that there were 200 more widows than widowers;[65] another, that 40 percent of Roman women between the ages of forty and fifty were widows.[66] Widows and orphans made up a separate census class at Rome. Remarriage was encouraged, certainly for those young enough to have or bear small children, and was even arranged by an Athenian husband in his will;[67] Augustus' laws imposed financial penalties on (most) widows who failed to remarry within a specified time. As a result, many orphaned children had stepfathers. It is curious, therefore, that sources display so little interest in them.[68] Compare the abundant and often bloodstained traces of stepmothers in the mythic imagination. Amphitryon raises Zeus's son Heracles even though he has one of his own; Hera (Zeus's wife) sends

---

[61] Saller 1994: 52, 58. [62] For more on remarriage, see Hübner (this volume).
[63] By the mid-second century CE, Roman fathers judged unfit would lose the right to have their children live with them, but would maintain legal control: *Dig.* 43.30.1.3, 3.5 (Ulpian).
[64] Children raised in the home of their dead father's brother: Isae. 1.15. Children raised in their stepfather's household: Isae. 9.29. For Demosthenes, Apollodorus, and their stepfathers, see below. For further discussion of stepfathers in Greco-Roman antiquity, see also Hübner (this volume).
[65] Golden 1981: 329. [66] Krause 1994–5: I, 73.
[67] Dem. 28.15; 29.43; 36.8; 45.28. [68] Watson 1995: 39–42.

snakes to kill them both. Phaedra lusts for her stepson Hippolytus and her lies lead to his death. Despite the predilection of Greek men for young wives, their myths are silent on their sexual attention to their stepdaughters. Oedipus is his own stepfather, but as far as I know, none of our sources holds it against him. This flies in the face of everything we know about stepfathers today, when (in Canada, England, and Wales) they kill children under five 60 times as frequently as biological fathers (or those who are thought to be) and are 120 times as likely to beat them to death (as opposed to other, less brutal forms of murder).[69] Daly and Wilson cite similar evidence from New South Wales, Finland, Korea, Hong Kong, Nigeria, Japan, Trinidad, the Ache hunter-gatherers of Paraguay, and pre-modern Friesland and conclude, "having a step-parent has turned out to be the most powerful epidemiological risk factor for severe child maltreatment yet discovered."[70] It is unsettling that this abuse is worse against younger children – these are not commonly cases of more or less equal tussles with unruly adolescents – and that they must therefore tend to occur relatively soon after the children have lost their own fathers.

   Now, this is not to deny that stepmothers may be guilty of violence, if only very rarely of sexual predation; this phenomenon is not called "the Cinderella effect" for nothing.[71] But of course they have plenty of bad press. The virtual silence about stepfathers is all the more interesting because life presented both Greeks and Romans with instances of hostility toward them (justified or not) which is not reflected in imaginative literature.[72] Conflicts concerning stepfathers and stepsons spawned lawsuits in two well-placed Athenian families.[73] Aphobus never did marry Demosthenes' mother, Cleobule, but he was as close to a stepfather as you can be while he was stealing the boy's property. Demosthenes was just seven when his father died in 376/5 BCE and had to wait a decade to start legal proceedings against Aphobus and his associates. He then pursued them unstintingly through the courts until he achieved some satisfaction. When the banker Pasion died

---

[69] Daly and Wilson 1994; Daly 1996. As a gynecologist and mother tells her daughter in Carol Shields's novel *The Republic of Love*: "You've no idea how different it is with kids of your own, you love them ten times more than you love other people's" (Shields 1992: 13). Daly's and Wilson's data suggest that ten times more may be an understatement.

[70] Daly and Wilson 1999: 7, cf. 32–6. Responding to critics of these conclusions, Daly reaffirms them: "There are no known exceptions to the ubiquitous phenomenon of parents discriminating, on average, against stepchildren" (2001: 287).

[71] For an attempt to identify Greek analogues to the Cinderella story, see Anderson 2000: 24–42. However, stepmothers are absent or of little prominence in those he cites, even in the story of Aspasia of Phocaea, who is raised by her father after her mother's death (Ael. *VH* 12.1).

[72] See Hübner (this volume) for a discussion of ancient views of stepfathers.

[73] Pomeroy 1997: 162–91.

in 370, he betrothed his wife, Archippe, to his ex-slave employee Phormio in his will; their sons, Apollodorus and Pasicles, were then twenty-four and eleven years old. In his essay *On Brotherly Love*, Plutarch recommends that brothers stick together after their father's death.[74] But when Apollodorus later brought suit against Phormio (after their mother's death), Pasicles chose to stand by their stepfather. Apollodorus' enmity was so intense that he insinuated that Pasicles was the result of an adulterous affair between Archippe and Phormio, then still a slave.[75] Financial interests may have led to this split: Apollodorus took a shield factory and a boarding-house as his inheritance from his father, leaving Pasicles the family bank, managed by Phormio.[76] And Pasicles could hardly let Apollodorus' aspersions against Archippe go unchallenged without imperiling his own citizenship. Perhaps too Pasicles, still a child when Pasion died, did not know (or like) him as a father as well as his older brother or was less troubled by Phormio's replacing him in Archippe's bed. In still another court proceeding, in North Africa in the middle of the second century CE, Apuleius tells a magistrate that an acquaintance nominated him as his mother's new husband because of a fear for her property and his (and his underage brother's) interest in it.[77] In royal courts, some stepfathers played for keeps; when the stakes are higher, people are burned at them. Among Hellenistic kings, Ptolemy Ceraunus (of Macedon) and Ptolemy VIII Physcon (of Egypt) each killed a new bride's children at their wedding.[78] Physcon is said to have killed his victim in his mother's arms amidst the preparations for the marriage banquet and rites and to have entered her bed still dripping with the gore of her son. These murderous monarchs aped the many animal species among which alpha males rid themselves of their predecessors' offspring, especially if they are still nursing. Nevertheless, their misdeeds (and others') do not seem to outweigh those of stepmothers. Cicero, to be sure, upbraids Antonius for choosing to take after his stepfather – executed as one of Catiline's co-conspirators – rather than his mother's brother, but even he, master of the rhetorical flourish as he is, satisfies himself with the example at hand.[79] We may reflect that mother-in-law jokes have finally vanished from most comics' repertoires – but there never were any father-in-law jokes.

---

[74] Plut. *Mor.* 483c.   [75] Dem. 45.83–4; 46.21.
[76] Dem. 36.11, 34.   [77] Apul. *Apol.* 71.
[78] Just. *Epit.* 24.3; 38.8; Ogden (1999: xxi–xxii) notes Justin's tendency to rhetorical embellishment, but accepts that the murders took place.
[79] Cic. *Phil.* 2.6.14–18.

Despite the perils of stepparents, Daly and Wilson allow that many, maybe most children, are better off with them than with single parents.[80] Some elite women chose not to remarry.[81] Cleobule (according to her son) stayed single for the sake of her children after her engagement to Aphobus fell through, and it does seem that Demosthenes, a sickly child, was educated at home.[82] She was presumably under the control of a male family member, her *kyrios*, but it is hard to say just who: she had no brothers and had been raised far away, near the Black Sea. In practice she was probably free to manage her affairs and those of her children much as she wished.[83]

Of course, Cleobule was a wealthy woman, even after Aphobus' depredations. So too Cornelia, mother of the Gracchi, who rejected even royal suitors in order to devote herself to her children, her jewels.[84] Women of the Roman elite controlled their own property, eventually freeing themselves even of the nominal oversight of a *tutor* in many cases, and might use it in their children's interests just as their husbands did: to finance political careers for their sons and advantageous matches for their daughters. But even wealthy women needed the help of an adult male citizen to gain access to the courts.[85] Cleobule figures as an ally and informant in Demosthenes' speeches against his guardians, but these had to wait until he came of age. The widow of Diodotus entrusted her young children to her father, who drove them out when the eldest reached majority.[86] She could and did criticize him at a family council but was powerless to protect her son on her own. How much worse off would be poorer women, the great majority, and their children? Without dowries or influential connections, they might be unable to find new husbands whatever their wishes; and Augustus' laws clearly had little impact outside the circle of heirs and office-holders. Aristophanes puts on stage a market woman whose husband died on Cyprus, leaving her with five little children. "It was hard to feed them by weaving myrtle garlands," she says.[87] The Athenian audience may have met her real-life equivalent: Nicarete, the mother of a client of Demosthenes,

---

[80] 1999: 38. We should also consider that the loss of a mother may have been more harmful than fatherlessness, especially to very young children and above all to boys, biologically more vulnerable; cf. Reher and González-Quiñones 2003.

[81] See Hübner (this volume) for a discussion of remarriage in Greco-Roman antiquity.

[82] Dem. 29.26; Plut. *Dem.* 4.3.   [83] Hunter 1989a.

[84] Val. Max. 4.4 pr. See Hallett (this volume) for a discussion of Cornelia and her relationship to fatherlessness.

[85] Compare the experience of the Jewish widow Babatha, who, despite her evident confidence in her own capabilities, needed the assistance of her *epitropos* to summons one of her orphaned son's guardians for not supplying his share of the boy's maintenance in the early second century CE (see Hanson 2005).

[86] Lys. 32.5, 9–10, 16–17.   [87] Ar. *Thesm.* 446–8.

had two young children when her husband was away on campaign within a few years of Aristophanes' play. She worked as a wet-nurse, a slave's job which led to her being taken for a foreigner. By the time of her husband's death, she too had had five children and went to work in the Agora alongside an adult son.[88] As for Rome, "sub-elite Roman society had a vast number of unmarried, and quite unmarriageable, widows, many of them young and burdened with minor-age children."[89] Andromache's lament echoed down one thousand years of Greek and Roman history.

EFFECTS OF FATHERLESSNESS

So, fatherlessness might lead to financial setbacks even for wealthy children, real deprivation for the many who were poor. Can we go further? There is no shortage of speculation about the consequences of fatherlessness for famous individuals of antiquity. Demosthenes (it is thought) yearned to repair his family's fortunes – and to replace his dead father – by becoming a successful orator and statesman; the eccentric and anti-social behavior reported by (hostile or late) sources stemmed from his lack of a father or father-figure to mold or be a model for him.[90] At seven, Brutus lost his father. His mother remarried and Brutus was later adopted by another man. But the main father-figure in his life was Julius Caesar, his mother's longtime lover and for many years Brutus' patron and protector. According to a pioneering psychohistorical essay by T. W. Africa, "Caesar was both a seducer and a false 'father,' and Brutus hated him on both counts."[91] In the end, Brutus sided with Pompey – the killer of his natural father – and then joined Caesar's assassins. Attractive as they are, these diagnoses will not persuade everyone.

Working on a much larger scale, J. K. Evans argued that fathers' long absences in warfare outside Italy during the middle Republic – absences from which many never returned – caused far-reaching transformations in Roman society.[92] The father's power over his household was ineffective at a distance; sons, wives, and daughters nominally under his control had more scope for independent action, all the more as *tutores* too might be unavailable. *Patriapotestas* as an institution weakened as a result. This was of most consequence for the elite, who had access to the political and legal means by which to circumvent or diminish *patriapotestas* over the ensuing centuries. Most of the mass of soldiers who fought Rome's wars, however, were

---

[88] Dem. 57.30–5, 42, 45. [89] McGinn 1999: 625. [90] Pomeroy 1997: 174.
[91] Africa 1978: 612. [92] J. K. Evans 1991.

farmers of limited means and less influence. Their absence too had significant effects, on the women of their households above all, but these were less
positive. Without husbands and fathers to work their farms, many families
were forced by hunger or the pressure of land-hungry neighbors to move
into urban centers. Here their options were few: essentially work in the
textile trade – organized on a family basis and so hard for displaced peasants to
enter – or prostitution. Evans stresses that the extent of this upheaval and of
its effects cannot be determined with any precision; some widows and
orphans remained on the land through remarriage or with the help of other
male relatives, and (as usual) there was much local and regional variation. But

> in striking contrast … to the social and economic emancipation that the conquest
> of an empire brought to so many aristocratic women, for literally thousands of the
> anonymous wives and daughters of the equally anonymous men serving in the
> ranks, Rome's unending wars of conquest held out only the promise of a bleak
> present and still more hopeless future.[93]

Nathan Rosenstein has recently subjected the impact of Rome's rise to
power in the Mediterranean on its rural economy to a sophisticated and
searching re-examination. Deploying comparative studies of contemporary
peasant populations, he demonstrates that even a husbandless household
could survive (if not prosper) with the inputs of women and children (and of
other men left at home). "Claims of destitution and helplessness among the
women and children left behind on farms are overdrawn."[94] More fundamentally, Roman men married for the first time at about thirty but were
conscripted much younger, from the age of seventeen. As a consequence,
few soldiers serving abroad would be fathers of families in need of them at
home. In fact, the end of the period of military obligation seems designed to
correspond to the time at which Roman farmers expected to marry and
father children. Evidence from Greco-Roman Egypt suggests that men
in the ancient Mediterranean continued to father children well into their
fifties – the median age of paternity was thirty-seven or thirty-eight;[95] the
delay in siring children contributed to the high number of orphans we
imagine for antiquity but also preserved some from the poverty and degra-
dation Evans depicts so movingly.

This alternative (and more upbeat) scenario clearly depends on our
acceptance of thirty as the likely age of first marriage for Roman men.[96]
However, Richard Saller's groundbreaking studies of the commemorative

---

[93] J. K. Evans 1991: 144.   [94] Rosenstein 2004: 21.
[95] Bagnall and Frier 2006: 146.   [96] Cf. Rosenstein 2004: 82–4.

patterns revealed on inscriptions are based on Romanized and urban sectors of the population.[97] The age of first marriage (as is generally agreed) was lower among the elite, by five years or even more. If rural citizens – who made up the bulk of Rome's army in the middle Republic – also married at twenty-five or even earlier, they would be only slightly less likely to die before their children reached fifteen.[98] However, it is much more probable that they would leave children at home when they enlisted and therefore orphans when they died. Evans explicitly rejected the relevance of Saller's methodology to the Roman countryside;[99] other scholars have stressed variation – by region and by residence in cities or outside them as well as by social status – in better-documented parts of the Mediterranean;[100] and the most comprehensive collection of evidence posits a normal age of first marriage for Roman men much lower, at between seventeen and twenty-two.[101] Even if these scholars' skepticism is warranted and if – another step in the argument – the age of first marriage for men in the Italian countryside in the middle Republic was as low as twenty or so, Evans' picture might still be overdrawn. Conscription still began before the notional age of first marriage and was in any case relatively ineffective.[102] Young fathers who did not want to fight might well have dodged the draft in the face of all except the most urgent demands for recruits (as some thirty thousand Canadians did even in a developed modern state during the Second World War).[103] Nevertheless, our uncertainty about the age of first marriage for Roman men outside major urban centers means that we can be no more optimistic about the numbers of orphans left in the wake of Rome's rise to predominance in the Mediterranean.

There is no more certainty when we return to the search for useful generalizations, not of the kind we can build on. Let us take children's ages at their fathers' deaths as an example. Young orphans were neediest and (likely) most at the mercy of stepfathers. On the other hand, older sons (like Apollodorus) might be most resentful of their fathers' replacements. Other issues could affect them, as well: Epaminondas allegedly said that he drew most pleasure from his parents' surviving to see the trophy he won at Leuctra; a son's greatness (Plutarch notes elsewhere) is something most fathers do not live to enjoy – they just witness their lisping, learning to

---

[97] Saller 1987; 1994: 25–42. [98] Cf. Scheidel (this volume).

[99] J. K. Evans 1991: 205, n. 53. [100] McGinn 1999: 629.

[101] Lelis, Percy, and Verstraete 2003: 14, 53–4, 103. But see Scheidel's conclusion (this volume: 33–4) that the model they suggest effects only "modest" change in the demographic scheme as a whole, so it would have limited impact on rates of fatherlessness.

[102] Rosenstein 2004: 59–61, de Ligt 2004: 738–44. [103] Wade 1968: 963.

speak, rivals, love affairs ...[104] And a father's death would be a stronger intimation of mortality for older children. "Now that my father is dead there's no one ahead of me any more," as the fictional Swedish policeman, Kurt Wallander, puts it.[105] Then again, such children were better placed to take advantage of any opportunity death afforded (though this would mostly be true of those newly or already adults). The terrible mortality of the Black Death left new land for survivors to work and fewer mouths to feed with it; its availability allowed young men to move away from the control of their fathers and their lords. The slaughter of the best and the brightest in the First World War opened a path for those with other attributes (Harding, Coolidge, Mackenzie King ...).[106] Miltiades died in disgrace and left his son Cimon (then about twenty) a crushing debt to the state; Cimon made excellent marriages for himself and his sister, paid what was owing, and then benefited from both sympathy and the regret the people felt at their harsh treatment of the hero of Marathon since his father could not. A Roman father's death entailed the end of his *patriapotestas*; his sons who had not yet been emancipated – we cannot tell how common this was – were now free to arrange their financial affairs as it suited them (though they would formally require a *tutor* if they were under fourteen and might have the guidance of a *curator* until they were twenty-five). Those still left *in potestate* might resent it more when they saw others escape its restraints – a reaction to which we will return below.[107] It seems that some Romans even pretended to be fatherless (*spurii filii*) in order to cover up their humble birth.[108]

Finally, the emotional effects of the disruption caused by a father's absence or death: more imponderables, or elements which are hard to weigh, to say the least. Much of the impact of a father's loss must depend on the role he plays when he is around. We would not expect to find many Greeks and Romans involved to the extent of the Aka of the Central African Republic, whose fathers spend about half their time holding their babies or within arm's reach, and even let them suck their nipples for comfort.[109] But in poorer families, boys must often have worked beside their fathers in a home workshop or in the fields. This might lead to mutual respect and

---

[104] Plut. *Cor.* 4.3, *Mor.* 193a, 786d, 1098a; cf. 496f.   [105] Mankell 2005: 165.
[106] Bob Friend, the Pittsburgh Pirates pitcher of the 1950s and 1960s, was a fine pianist as well as an athlete, but he gave up aspirations for a concert career in favor of baseball at sixteen, after the death of his father, a bandleader.
[107] Cf. Cantarella 2003: 298.   [108] Buraselis 1996: 55–9.
[109] Hewlett 1991. For a valuable overview of varieties of paternal involvement and their determinants, see Katz and Konner 1981. See also the Introduction for discussion of fathers and the roles they play (7–10).

regard but also to conflict. (Remember the Egyptian weavers who apprenticed
out their sons.) In richer Roman households the elements of fatherhood were
divided among a range of men – slaves, friends, visitors, clients – and boys'
fathers (to maintain that focus) might draw upon their acquaintances outside
for expertise or experience they lacked.[110] Indeed, this circulation of children
seems to have been surprisingly common among Romans outside the elite as
well. The more time a child spent with such "proparents" (as Esther Goody
calls them), the less, perhaps, the loss of a father was a crippling blow.[111] Or, to
put it another way, the regular movement of father figures, surrogates, and
substitutes into the household, and of children out of it, probably made the
changes occasioned by a father's loss less harrowing.[112]

A last consideration: a father's death stood in the mid-range of life's
tragedies in the ancient world. It was not devastatingly rare, as a child's
death is today, nor as inevitable as we might imagine the death of a parent in
our own middle age. Judging from Walter Scheidel's presentation of the
probabilities in this volume – between 25 and 50 percent of teenagers mourned
a father – it was about as common as divorce in North America.[113] And despite
the ongoing investigations of social scientists of every stripe, there is no
agreement on the emotional cost of divorce for contemporary children in
general. (One recent study argues that divorce itself is less harmful than the
environment, often of longstanding, which leads to it.)[114] What is accepted is
that sensible and sensitive behavior by adults can combine with a child's
temperament and personality to prevent any lasting trauma and that some
children, for whatever reasons, fare poorly nonetheless. When fate strikes only
a few, the victims feel unfairly singled out for sorrow; they gain strength and
support by bonding together, in groups such as The Compassionate Friends
for parents who have lost children. When almost all face loss, they bear it
with greater or less equanimity, as part of the human condition. It is in the
mid-range, where the distribution of affliction and escape is more evenly

---

[110] One thinks of Cicero and the young Caelius: Cic. *Cael.* 4.9.   [111] Goody 1999: 378.
[112] The point was made as long ago as Laslett's pioneering piece on English orphans and stepchildren, "Parental deprivation in the past": "A little boy or a little girl with such a plurality of parental figures would seem to have felt the deprivation and the sudden change rather less keenly …" (1977: 166); cf. Bradley 1991a: 143–5, Dixon 1999: 217–20.
[113] For the rough equivalence of orphans in seventeenth- and eighteenth-century England with modern children who have lost a parent by divorce, death, or separation, see Laslett 1977: 162. Laslett complains that it was "peculiarly difficult to find numerical calculations" for the number of children who had experienced divorce (Laslett 1977: 161, n. 3). This is still true thirty years later. I am grateful to my colleague Michael Wahn for the rough estimate I use here. See also the Introduction (5–9).
[114] Strohschein 2005. It also concludes that while children's level of depression rises in the aftermath of divorce, anti-social behavior decreases.

balanced, where we would expect to find most variation, and where comparisons with the lot of others are likely to lead in more directions. A glance through the *Greek Anthology* reveals both Apollonides' epitaph for Menoetus, who drowned hurrying home to see his sick father, and Strato's envy of Euclides: his father has died and cannot meddle in his love life (unlike Strato's).[115] This is without taking into account ambivalence within individuals.[116] I suspect that more evidence for antiquity would make generalizations even less reliable, not more.

---

[115] *Anth. Pal.* 7.642, 12.231.

[116] See, e.g., Strauss (1993: 3–4, 125–6) on Theseus and sons succeeding fathers at Athens, and Evans (1985) on the mix of joy and grief at a Roman *paterfamilias*'s death. Mind you, if Theseus' forgetting to change his sails on his homecoming and Aegeus' subsequent suicide count as evidence for filial hostility (as argued in Sourvinou-Inwood 1979: 21), what should we make of the death of Odysseus' dog (*Od.* 17.326–7)?

CHAPTER 4

Callirhoe's dilemma: remarriage and stepfathers in the Greco-Roman East

Sabine R. Hübner

INTRODUCTION

The wicked stepmother is a famous social type in Greek and Roman myth and comedy; we hear, however, comparatively little about the stepfather in antiquity. This is indubitably the reason why the stepmother in antiquity has already received a thorough treatment in a full-length study,[1] while the stepfather has been widely neglected thus far in scholarship on the Greco-Roman family. In order to rectify this situation, I propose to survey his portrayal in the literary, legal, and documentary sources from the Roman and late antique East with a view to determining the relevance, influence, and authority he held over children who were not his own. By means of this investigation I hope to discover what the introduction of a stepfather might have meant for an otherwise fatherless child with respect to his living arrangements and emotional and economic welfare. Of course, stepfathers entail remarriage. Accordingly, this study will also attempt to shed some light on attitudes toward remarriage for widows from different ideological, sociological, and economic points of view, as well as on the relative frequency of children growing up under a stepfather in these centuries.

The stereotypical stepmother is notoriously wicked.[2] According to Patricia Watson, this picture is "an encapsulation of the negative traits assigned to females in general by a misogynistic tradition which flourished in Greece and Rome."[3] While stepmothers are almost invariably shown as evil and jealous intruders, stepfathers, who occur much less frequently in our sources,[4] are

---

[1] Watson 1995. Cf. Gray-Fow 1988b; Noy 1991.
[2] Watson 1995, *passim*. See, e.g., *Dig.* 5.2.4 (Gaius) for the bad influence a stepmother could exert on the children's father.
[3] Watson 1995: 2. For the stereotype of the wicked stepmother see also Dixon 1988: 49, 155–9; Gray-Fow 1988b.
[4] Greek terms for "stepfather" are πατρυιός (e.g. *CIG* 3445 from Lydia), or πατρυός (*Catalogus codicum astrologorum* 2.174), πατρῳός (*P.Oxy.* 2.266 [96 CE]); μητρυιός (Theopomp. Com. 12), and κηδεστής (Dem. 36.31; more often, however, used to mean "brother-in-law" [e.g. Eur. *Hec.* 834],

depicted in a much more balanced manner. Instead of constituting a strongly delineated caricature like the "stepmother," the image of the stepfather was a flexible one, apparently dependent on a highly contingent set of circumstances, such as the economic and social background of the family. In many cases the stepfather is portrayed as a surrogate father, a protector of fatherless children, and indeed, we sometimes see him even adopting his stepchildren as legitimate heirs when he had no viable heirs of his own.[5] Yet, at other times we also hear of prejudices and widely held assumptions about a stepfather's purportedly selfish motives in marrying a widow with children. Nevertheless, we never find stepfathers who are "cruel" or "amorous," the defining character traits of stepmothers in Greek and Roman literature.[6]

THE SITUATION OF THE ORPHANED FAMILY: WIDOWS AND THEIR CHILDREN

The father in the ancient family was the undisputed head of household, social representative to the outside world, and often main economic provider. Therefore, the loss of a husband and father was a blow to most families, especially to those which, for one reason or another, could not rely on a network of relatives and friends for support.[7] The main concerns a widowed mother faced after her husband's death were: to feed and clothe her children; to provide dowries and arrange suitable marriages for her daughters; and to secure adequate education or apprenticeships for her sons. Of course, these concerns were even more pressing for mothers of low economic and social status. Normally, the costs for these expenses would be covered by her late husband's patrimony, held in trust and managed by a guardian or the mother herself until the children came of age.[8] However, if the patrimony was not sufficient, the mother had to cover the remaining expenses from her own possessions or any other resources

---

"son-in-law" [Isoc. 10.43; *SEG* 24 (1974): 228], "father-in-law" [Ar. *Thesm.* 74.210] or even "guardian" [*P.Cair.Isid.* 62 (= *SB* 6.9167) (296 CE)]). All of these terms are attested very rarely. Sometimes a stepfather is referred to periphrastically as "the husband of my mother" (*P.Mich.* 3.191/2 [60 CE]).

[5] Corbier 1991: 72–3; Cox 1998: 89; Patterson 1998: 199.   [6] Watson 1995.

[7] That widows needed support and protection was a commonplace all over the ancient Mediterranean: For Archaic times see Wöhrle (this volume): 162–74; for ancient Israel see Sigismund (this volume): 83–102. In Classical Athens the eponymous archon was the legal protector of orphans and widows, *Ath. Pol.* 56.7; Isae. 6; Lys. 32; [Dem.] *Or.* 43.75; cf. Hunter 1989a: 295; Günther 1993: 308–25. Divorce was another quite common reason for dissolution of marriage in antiquity; children, however, usually stayed with their fathers (Treggiari 1991a: 473–82; Treggiari 1991b; Parkin 1992: 123–4; Bagnall and Frier 2006: 123).

[8] Cf. below on the stepfather in antiquity and the frequency of remarriage.

which she could call upon.[9] Moreover, aggravating this situation, some fathers left their children with debts, which creditors tried to recover all the more relentlessly after the father's death.[10] As an example of just how straitened circumstances could become, a poor widow from sixth-century Oxyrhynchus justified her decision to give up her nine-year-old daughter for adoption thus:

My husband died, and I was left, toiling and suffering hardship for my daughter by him in order that I might provide her with necessary sustenance; and now, not having the means to maintain her … she being now nine years old, more or less, I have asked you … to receive her from me as your daughter.[11]

Beaucamp provides us with many more examples from early Byzantine papyri, which show that widows lacked economic support and social status.[12] Presumably, at least some of these widows' complaints should be attributed to rhetorical tropes, employed by women who had every reason to present themselves as vulnerable, poor, and weak, in order to attract sympathy and aid when appealing to officials.[13] In fact, we have in contrast to these petitions many private letters that show women actively running households without any difficulties while their husbands were either away or dead.[14] However, if a widowed mother lacked sufficient economic means and was unable to find support from relatives or adult children, she and her children found themselves in a precarious situation.[15] The options for these widowed mothers were grim, to say the least: manual labor,[16] selling their children into prostitution,[17] slavery,[18] or perhaps more mercifully, giving them up for adoption.[19]

This is not to say that widowhood was easy for wealthy mothers. As we shall see below, widowed mothers in the Greco-Roman East who resided

---

[9] *Cod. Iust.* 2.18.22 (227 CE).

[10] For Roman Egypt see *P.Mich.* 5.232 (36 CE); *SB* 1.5761 (91–6 CE); *P.Soterichos* 22–5 (103–9 CE); *P.Oxy.* 3.493 (early second century); *P.Monac.* 3.80 (102–17 CE); *BGU* 7.1654 (118 CE); *P.Oxy.* 3.494 (156 CE); *SB* 1.5343 (182 CE); *P.Ryl.* 2.121 (second century); *SB* 4.7339 (late first century); *BGU* 2.378 (second century); *P.Giss.* 34 (264/5 CE); *P.Cair.Masp.* 1.67026/7 (551 CE); *P.Cair.Masp.* 2.67156/7 (570 CE); *P.Cair.Masp.* 2.67131 (sixth century). cf. Bowman 1986: 98; Krause 1994–5: III, 138–45.

[11] *P.Oxy.* 16.1895; cf. Rowlandson 1998: no. 234.   [12] Beaucamp 1985.

[13] *Dig.* 16.1.2.2–3 (Ulpian); Evans Grubbs 2002: 51–4; Hanson 2000: 156; Hanson 2005: 100.

[14] Bagnall and Cribiore 2006: 79–81. See, e.g., *P.Mich.* 8.464.

[15] E.g. in *P.Oxy.* 34.2711 (268–71 CE), the late father's uncle had taken in his orphaned grandnephews and grandniece, whom their father "had left quite utterly destitute."

[16] Cf. Bradley 1985: 326–9; Krause 1994–5: II, *passim*; Rowlandson 1998: 218–79; Golden (this volume): 54–5.

[17] E.g. *BGU* 4.1024 from the end of the fourth century CE. Cf. Rowlandson 1998: no. 208; Bagnall 1993: 196–7; Krause 1994–5: III, 190–3.

[18] *Cod. Iust.* 2.4.26 (294 CE), 4.43.1 (294 CE); *Cod. Theod.* 3.3.1 (391 CE); Krause 1994–5: III, 133–5.

[19] E.g. *P.Oxy.* 16.1895 (554 CE). Cf. Krause 1994–5: III, 130–45, esp. 134–6; Rowlandson 1998: no. 234.

with their orphaned children usually lived alone with them, not with their natal families or their late husbands'. So, even if the patrimony was managed by the children's guardians, these widows bore sole responsibility for the everyday affairs of parenting.[20] Of course, fathers in antiquity provided not only financial support for their families: the father was also an authority figure who protected his children from external dangers and kept them on the straight and narrow. Thus it comes as no surprise that there were quite a few single mothers who did not feel equal to the task and complained – much as they do today – about the stresses and burdens of raising children alone. Gregory of Nyssa reported that his widowed mother Emelia, who was left with ten minor children, "was distracted with various anxieties" and suffered under a "heavy load of sorrows."[21] Thus, even if money was not an issue, raising a family on one's own could prove to be a daunting challenge nonetheless.[22] The widow who was able single-handedly to manage her affairs, raise her children, see to their education and marriages – and all without damaging their patrimony – was highly esteemed, to say the least.[23]

THE "STEPFATHER" IN THE GRECO-ROMAN EAST

As the previous section makes clear, there were many advantages and rewards that could lead a widow with children to consider remarriage. However, although stepfathers were not so continuously maligned as step-mothers in antiquity, there does seem to have been a persistent prejudice against their raising children inherited from a previous marriage. Such general notions may be misleading, however; it is therefore appropriate to begin with a chronological examination of a stepfather's depiction in the various literary, legal, and documentary sources pertaining to the Greco-Roman East. In exploring this evidence, we want to learn more about the various factors a widow took into consideration when contemplating remarriage, such as the effects a new marriage would have on her children, their economic situation, and their living circumstances. In particular, I want to focus on the way in which a stepfather either successfully filled the void left by a father's death or posed a threat to the orphan's well-being. In addition, I wish to provide some insight into the ancient "patchwork

---

[20] Cf. below, 67–9; 73.   [21] Gr. Nyss. *Vita Macrinae* 7 (ed. P. Maraval, Paris, 1971).
[22] Jo. Chrys. *De sacerdotio* 1.2 (ed. A. M. Malingrey, Paris, 1980); Lib. *Or.* 14.68.
[23] Compare, e.g., Dem. 27.13–15, 29.26; *P.Cair.Masp.* 2.67156 (570 CE); Lib. *Or.* 1.26, 58; Jo. Chrys. *Sacerd.* 1.2; Gr. Nyss. *Vita Macrinae* 6. Cf. Krause, 1994–5: III, 130–45; Van Dam, 2003: 102–3.

family" and the nature of the stepfather–stepchild relationship from eco-nomic, legal, and emotional points of view.

In fifth- and fourth-century Athens, a paternal relative would normally have been appointed after a father's death to guard the orphan's inheritance. Should the mother subsequently remarry, most often her children would remain with their late father's family rather than follow their mother into her new marriage.[24] Sometimes, however, and especially when there were no close relatives either living or willing to take the orphans in, a widow would take her children with her, an arrangement that often seems to have worked well whenever we find evidence of it. Stepfathers in fourth-century Athenian court speeches are shown as affectionate and supportive of their stepchildren at private and public occasions.[25] For instance, from Isaeus we know of a certain Archedamus who took in his stepson Apollodorus and brought him up after the boy's paternal uncle and guardian had embezzled his patrimony. When the boy reached majority, Archedamus helped his stepson to recover all his fortune by bringing an action against Apollodorus' corrupt uncle.[26] Apollodorus, mindful of his stepfather's kindness, later returned the favor by ransoming his stepfather from captivity, supporting him with his money when he was in need, and even adopting his half-sister's son, the grandson of Archedamus, as heir when his own son died.[27] In another speech of Isaeus we learn of the stepfather of an Astyphilus, Theophrastus, who cherished Astyphilus no less than the biological son he had by Astyphilus' mother. Astyphilus entered Theophrastus' home when he was a little boy, where he was brought up and provided with the same education as his younger half-brother. Theophrastus even tilled the land that Astyphilus had inherited from his father, thereby doubling its value.[28] In yet another speech we hear that a certain Callias brought an action against the lessees of his stepson's paternal estate while serving as the boy's guardian, thereby justifying the trust placed in him.[29] The orator Isocrates, after having married a widowed mother of three sons and with no child of his own, even adopted one of his stepsons, the youngest one, Aphareus. Aphareus was also one of

---

[24] Lys. 32; Isae. 7.5; Hunter 1989a: 295–7.

[25] This finds cultural support in Greek myths where we find Amphitryon rearing his stepson Heracles together with his own son; Telegonus adopting Egaphus, the son of his wife, Io, and Zeus; and finally Asterius marrying Europa and raising her three sons, Minus, Rhadamanthys, and Sarpedon. For the striking contrast between stepfathers and stepmothers in Greek myths, see Watson 1995: 39–42.

[26] Isae. 7.5–7; cf. Hunter 1989a: 296.   [27] Isae. 7.15; cf. Cox 1998: 152.

[28] Isae. 9.3–5, 27–30; Cox 1998: 89.   [29] Andoc. 1.124–7; cf. Cox 1998: 90.

Isocrates' most talented students and later became a famous orator and tragedian himself.[30]

Not all relations between stepfathers and stepsons, however, proceeded so smoothly: a certain Phormio quarreled with one of his two stepsons over the guardianship of their paternal estate and their mother's possessions.[31] Yet, the stepson apparently used this step-relationship merely as a distraction: the true cause of this quarrel arose from the young man's profligate and litigious misbehavior rather than from Phormio's purportedly malicious actions as stepfather. In fact, Phormio had been entrusted with the guardianship by the natural father himself (who had also asked him to marry his widow), and, moreover, Phormio's other stepson supported his stepfather's case. We see another example of a strained stepfather–stepson relationship in that between Cnemon and his stepson Gorgias in Menander's *Dyscolus*.[32] However, in this case the friction was probably meant by Menander to be an expression of Cnemon's misanthropic view of the world in general rather than a portrayal of the stepfather–stepson relationship as stereotypically doomed. In any event, Cnemon eventually decided to adopt Gorgias when the latter saved him from drowning, and Cnemon, having no son of his own, realized that "a man needs someone, someone there and ready to help him out."[33] In sum, even though in these two examples we encounter step-relationships that lead to discord and disharmony, it must be stressed that in the evidence as we have it, the friction is ultimately attributable to other sources. In fact, close relations between a stepfather and his stepson could lead to friction between the young man and his paternal relatives, as whenever a stepson preferred to bequeath his property to a half-sibling (i.e. a child of his mother and stepfather) instead of a distant relative on his paternal side.[34]

Moving from Hellenistic to Roman times, we lack the literary evidence of the sort that we discussed above. Our best evidence for studying the stepfather in the Eastern Mediterranean in Roman times is Roman law, particularly after 212 CE when it became the law of the land. Another vital source is the papyri of Greco-Roman Egypt, which provide us with a unique insight into the daily life of the ancient patchwork family, a view that one cannot acquire from literary sources alone. This evidence is in

---

[30] [Plut.] *Mor.* 838a, 839b; cf. Isae. 8.40–2 (a certain Diocles contended that his stepfather adopted him posthumously, even though the latter had three daughters with Diocles' mother). See Rubinstein 1993: 87, 96, 101; Corbier 1991: 72–3; Cox 1998: 90; Patterson 1998: 199. For Greek myths, see Watson 1995: 39–42.

[31] Dem. 36, 45; Cox 1998: 90.   [32] Men. *Dys.* 5.   [33] Men. *Dys.* 708–47.

[34] Isae. 9.3–5, 27–30; cf. 7.7–15, 8.40–2, 11.8–9; [Dem.] 43.4; Cox 1998: 89.

turn supplemented by some epigraphic evidence from other parts of the Greco-Roman East.

Taking Roman law as our starting point, we encounter here a completely different picture of the stepfather than in our Athenian court speeches. In Roman law stepfathers are generally depicted as legacy hunters aiming at embezzling their stepchildren's inheritance. However, we should be cautious in attributing this discrepancy to changing or different conceptions of the stepfather from Greek to Roman society rather than to the nature of the evidence.

Roman jurists were chiefly concerned with the economic consequences of remarriage and therefore endeavored to protect a fatherless child's estate against a mother's second spouse in diverse and manifold ways.[35] Thus, it was obligatory for every orphaned child to have a guardian appointed, usually the nearest male relative on the father's side, who was responsible for administering the fatherless child's property, to provide the child with daily maintenance from its revenues, and to turn over the estate with a full accounting when the child reached his or her majority.[36] Under this arrangement the widow might have responsibility to raise the children,[37] but no legal authority over their property.[38] Therefore, her remarriage would not have threatened her children's patrimony, which was safeguarded against the stepfather's grasp by the child's guardians.

These laws, however, applied only to Roman citizens. In Roman Egypt and Asia Minor we find evidence of numerous mothers acting as guardians for their fatherless children. For instance, there are several examples in the papyri[39] and inscriptions[40] recording widowed mothers, regardless of whether

---

[35] Dixon 1997: 155. [36] Saller 1994: 183–5; Evans Grubbs 2002: 23.
[37] *Cod. Iust.* 5.49.1 (223 CE). Cf. *Nov. Iust.* 22.38.
[38] *Dig.* 26.1.16.pr. (Gaius); *Dig.* 26.6.2.2 (Modestinus); *Dig.* 38.17.2.23 (Ulpian); *Dig.* 38.17.2.26 (Ulpian); *Dig.* 38.17.2.28 (Ulpian); *Dig.* 38.17.2.45 (Ulpian); *Cod. Iust.* 5.31.3 from 215 CE; *Cod. Iust.* 5.31.1 from 224; *Cod. Iust.* 2.12.18 from 294; *Cod. Iust.* 2.34.2 from 294; *Cod. Iust.* 5.35.1 from 224; *Cod. Iust.* 5.31.8 from 291; *Cod. Iust.* 5.34.6 from 293; *Cod. Iust.* 6.56.3 from 315; *Cod. Theod.* 3.18.1 from 357; *Cod. Iust.* 6.56.6 from 439; *Cod. Iust.* 6.58.10 from 439; *Nov. Theod.* 11 from 439; *Cod. Iust.* 5.31.11 from 479; cf. Chiusi 1994: 163. In fact, a widow was obliged to request a guardian for her underage children if her deceased husband had not named one in his will or no *tutor legitimus* was available. If she failed to do so, she lost all rights of succession to her children's property should they predecease her (*Dig.* 26.6.2.2 [Modestinus], cf. 38.17.2.23 [Ulpian]. See De Filippi 1980: 61–3; Chiusi 1994: 157–8. For women from Roman Egypt who submitted a petition for a guardian, cf. *P.Oxy.* 34.2709 (206 CE); *P.Oxy.* 6.888 (after 287). Cf. Taubenschlag 1955: 157–70; A. Lewis 1970: 116–18.
[39] E.g. *SB* 16.12720 (142 BCE; cf. Rowlandson 1998: no. 125; Bagnall and Derow 2004: no. 123); *SB* 5.7568 (36 CE); *BGU* 8.1813 (62 CE); *P.Oxy.* 2.265 (81–95 CE); *P.Oxy.* 6.898 (123 CE); *P.Oxy.* 3.496 (127 CE); *P.Oxy.* 3.497 (early second century CE).
[40] For early Roman Asia Minor see Balland 1981: no. 81 from late first century BCE – early first century CE; *SEG* 6 (1932): 672 from the late first century CE.

they remarried or not, who were in control of their minor children's property, a custom apparently going back to a time before the arrival of Roman rule.[41] After Roman law became applicable to all free inhabitants of the Empire in 212, we find several attempts to adapt this prevailing custom to the new legal dispensation: Evidence from third-century Egypt shows mothers acting only as "assistants" (ἐπακολουθήτρια or παρακολουθήτρια) of their fatherless children's guardians.[42] However, in the later Roman period (from the late third century onwards) we again find widows in our papyri who act as sole guardians of their minor children.[43]

One result of mothers being in control of their orphaned children's property was that a minor orphan lived with the fear that his mother might spend his father's estate, alone or with her new partner, before he or she was able to assume the inheritance.[44] A petition from Karanis in the Arsinoite nome from 175/6 CE provides us with an exemplary case of just such a family drama: a young man, who had lost his father early in life, sued his mother for recovery of his patrimony.[45] His mother had acted as his guardian after his father's death. However, she had remarried and when her son by her first husband reached maturity, she refused to cede to him rightful ownership of his late father's estate. It is therefore understandable that when Roman law later, at the end of the fourth century, officially granted mothers the right to administer their children's patrimony, it was on the condition that they promise not to enter a new marriage: "Mothers who request the guardianship of administering business affairs for their children after the loss of their husband, are to avow in the public records that they will not enter a second marriage, before the confirmation of such a duty can come to them legally."[46] It was also feared that a widow who was in charge of her children's inheritance would be tempted to use part of it to increase her dowry and thereby her chances of remarriage,[47] or perhaps later

---

[41] See also Montevecchi 1981: 113–15; Chiusi 1994: 175–91; Van Bremen 1996: 228–30; Evans Grubbs 2002: 254–7; Wolff 2002: 78, n. 31.

[42] *P.Oxy.* 58.3921 (219 CE); *P.Oxy.* 6.909 (225 CE); *P.Oxy.* 6.907 (276 CE); Montevecchi 1981: 113–15; Evans Grubbs 2002: 256.

[43] *P.Sakaon* 31, 36, 37 (= *P.Thead.* 15; *P.Ryl.* 3.114; *P.Thead.* 18) from 280, 280/1, and 284 CE, respectively; Beaucamp 1990–2: II: 172–9; Evans Grubbs 2002: 257–8.

[44] Cf. Wöhrle (this volume): 169–70.

[45] *P.Lond.* 2.198. Cf. *P.Oxy.* 6.898 (123 CE) for a mother apparently defrauding her son of his property. See also Evans Grubbs 2002: 255–6.

[46] *Cod. Iust.* 5.35.2 = *Cod. Theod.* 3.17.4 (390 CE), trans. Evans Grubbs 2002: 247. See also *Nov. Iust.* 118.5 (543 CE). Cf. Taubenschlag 1955: 157–70; Lewis 1970: 116–18; Humbert 1972: 410–13; Gardner 1986: 150–1; Beaucamp 1990–2: I, 325–30; Chiusi 1994: 192–3; Krause 1994–5: III, 91, 124–7; Arjava 1996: 91–2.

[47] *Cod. Iust.* 5.12.13 (293 CE), 7.33.3 (293 CE). Cf. Krause 1994–5: III, 39–40; Arjava 1996: 98–105; Evans Grubbs 2002: 115.

embezzle it in favor of her second husband and any children she had by him.[48] If a mother did subsequently renege on her promise not to remarry, she would not lose the guardianship, but she *and* her new husband would have to stand surety for the children's patrimony with their own property, and they could be held liable in a case of clear mismanagement.[49] In any case, it must be stressed that these later Roman laws were meant first and foremost to safeguard the welfare and property rights of a widow's children, not necessarily to prevent remarriage per se: even up to the Justinianic period two or more successive marriages were not forbidden either by Roman law or by the Church canons.[50]

Even if the law was ambivalent about remarriage, it is clear that the *ideal* widowed mother refrained from remarriage for the sake of her children, at least in families in which there was a significant estate to protect.[51] Of course, in families in which there was no patrimony, the stepfather who was willing to marry the widow and take in her children would have been seen not as a threat but as a beneficial surrogate, the last resort for securing the family's survival.[52] For instance, we hear of the mother of the later empress Theodora, who was widowed with three young daughters, the eldest not yet seven years old. Theodora's mother hastily remarried after her husband's death in order to win another man who would take over her first husband's

[48] It might be exactly for this reason that we occasionally find clauses in Roman wills in which a man forbids his widow to remarry before their children reach adulthood (*Dig.* 35.1.62.2 [Clementius]; Humbert 1972: 208–13; Krause 1994–5: I, 93–4; III, 33–48; Saller 1994: 175. So, it was with the aim to prevent such abuses that Theodosius ruled in 382 that a widow with children who remarried was required to transfer everything she ever received from her first husband to her children by him (*Cod. Theod.* 3.8.2 [382 CE]; *Cod. Iust.* 5.10.1 [392 CE]; cf. Dixon 1988: 50). She was entitled only to a usufruct of the property, thus preventing her from alienating the possessions of her former husband during her lifetime or by will to anyone other than his children (*Cod. Theod.* 3.8.2.17 [382 CE], 3.9.1 [398 CE], 3.8.3 [412 CE]. See Yiftach-Firanko 2006.

[49] *Cod. Iust.* 5.35.2.2 (390 CE); *Cod. Iust.* 8.14.6 (439 CE); *Nov. Iust.* 22.40 (536 CE); cf. Kaser 1971: 163, nn. 31 and 168; Chiusi 1994: 161. A novel of Justinian from 539 stresses that it was taken for granted that maternal love would prevent a mother from embezzling her children's inheritance (*Nov. Iust.* 94). Cf. Clark 1993: 60; Krause 1994–5: III, 13–14.

[50] *Cod. Iust.* 6.60.4 (468 CE); 5.9.6.pr. (472 CE), 6.41.4.pr. (472 CE). Majorianus in the West in 458 ordered all widows under the age of forty to remarry within five years (*Nov. Maior.* 6.5). Justinian expressively conceded to widows that they might enter a new marriage whether they already had children or not (*Cod. Iust.* 6.40.2 [531 CE]; cf. *Nov. Iust.* 2.3 [535 CE]). Cf. Kaser 1971: 348; Humbert 1972: 283–5; Gardner 1986: 55; Krause 1994–5: III, 123–9; Arjava 1996: 170, 189–90. Legal sources implying high rates of remarriage for widows at least in the upper social strata are *Cod. Theod.* 13.10.4 (368–70 CE), 13.10.6 (370 CE); *Nov. Maior.* 6.5 (458 CE).

[51] *Cod. Iust.* 5.37.22.5 (326 or 329 CE); *Cod. Theod.* 8.13.1 (349 CE); *Cod. Iust.* 6.56.4 (380 CE); *Cod. Theod.* 3.8.1 (381 CE), 3.8.2 (382 CE); *Cod. Iust.* 5.10.1 (392 CE); cf. Humbert 1972: 375–92; Arjava 1996: 167–77; Evans Grubbs 2002: 223–5. For the diverging views of Church fathers on remarriage see, e.g., Jer. *Ep.* 54.15.4; August. *Ep.* 104; Jo. Chrys. *Adviduam iuniorem* 1–2. Cf. Bremmer 1995: 46; Watson 1995: 10–11; Nathan 2000: 121.

[52] Plin. *Ep.* 6.33.2; 8.18.7–8; Krause 1994–5: I, 63, 129.

job as the bear keeper at the Hippodrome in Constantinople and thereby provide for her and her daughters.[53] Although this story is filtered through the polemical view of Procopius, it nonetheless paints a reasonably realistic picture of the sort of considerations that motivated widows from the lower reaches of society as they sought new marriages in order to secure the survival of their families.

How beneficial a stepfather could be for his new family is illustrated by a marriage contract from sixth-century Antinoopolis in Middle Egypt. This contract was drawn up between a certain Aquilinus and his bride, Euprepeia, who brought with her her minor son Victor from a previous union. Aquilinus, the future stepfather, pledged himself to cherish his stepson and raise him like his own child, obviously not a matter of course.[54] Aquilinus apparently had no children of his own, so if the new relationship produced no offspring, his stepson Victor could have even hoped to become his stepfather's heir.[55] At all events, we may presume that under these conditions a man who considered marrying a widow with children was far from resembling the legacy-hunting stepfather depicted in Roman law codes; instead, he was likely to be put off by the thought of the obligations and financial burden he was going to shoulder for a family that was not his own.

Of course, the prejudice of the Roman jurists against stepfathers was not merely theoretical. It had its basis in the propertied classes, as we see in the case of Apuleius, the second-century CE rhetorician from Madaura.[56] Apuleius' stepson accused him of having married his mother only for money and of trying to persuade her to disinherit him and his brother in his favor, "fearing that … she might, as often happens, transfer her whole fortune to the house of her new husband."[57] Apuleius took pains in court to argue that he received only a very modest dowry from his wife Pudentilla: "You will see that Pudentilla's dowry was small, considering her wealth, and was made over to me as a trust, not as a gift."[58] Far from displacing her children in the

---

[53] Procop. *Historia arcana* 9.2–4; Krause 1994–5: I, 130.

[54] *P. Cair. Masp.* 3.67340 recto. 54–65: ἔτι ὁμολογεῖ [[Ἀκυλλῖνος]] ὁ θαυμασιώτατος ἔχειν Βίκτορα τὸν τεχθέντα παρὰ τῆς προγεγραμμένης [[Εὐπρεπείας]] ἀπὸ το(ῦ) γενομέ(νου) αὐτῆς ἀνδρὸς, οὐ μὴν ἀλλὰ καὶ [?] ἀναλημφθεῖσαν παρ' αὐτῆ[ς ?] καὶ τοὺς ὡς εἰκὸς τεχ[θησομ(ένους) ἀπ' αὐτο(ῦ) θάλπειν] καὶ ἀποτρέφει[ν ?] ὡς εἰκὸς τεχθησομέν[ους].

[55] See n. 54 above.

[56] Apul. *Apol.* 71 (trans. Butler 1909); see also Apul. *Apol.* 91, 93. Cf. the case of Septicia in Augustan times, who disinherited her two sons from her first marriage in favor of her second husband (Val. Max. 7.7.4); cf. also Petron. 110.6–7; *Miracula Theclae* 20 (Dagron 1978: 344); Ambrose, *De viduis* 15.86 (Migne, *PL* 16.274); Amphiloch. *Or.* 2.8 (*CC ser. Gr.* 3.60–1).

[57] Apul. *Apol.* 99–100 (trans. Butler 1909). Cf. Gardner 1986: 55; Dixon 1997; Evans Grubbs 2002: 225–7.

[58] Apul. *Apol.* 91 (trans. Butler 1909).

will, then, Apuleius had even tried to reconcile her with her two sons so as to dissuade her from disinheriting them:

All these concessions I extorted from Pudentilla with difficulty and against her will I wrung them from her by my urgent entreaty, though she was angry and reluctant. I reconciled the mother with her sons, and began my career as a stepfather by enriching my stepsons with a large sum of money.[59]

In fact, Apuleius claimed that their marriage only took place on the following condition:

If my wife should die without leaving me any children, the dowry should go to her sons Pontianus and Pudens, while if at her death she should leave me one son or daughter, half of the dowry was to go to the offspring of the second marriage, the remainder to the sons of the first.[60]

Given the rhetorical positions adopted in this case, it is safe to conclude that the image of the fortune-hunting stepfather depicted in Roman legal sources seems to have been a view widely held by Roman society.

As we see from the above example, remarriage did not only involve paternal property: we must realize that if the mother had property, it was also at stake. Even if the management of guardians protected a father's inheritance, a mother's remarriage inevitably meant some sort of financial disadvantage for the children of a previous union, since at least her dowry would go to the stepfather.[61] Also, there was a definite anxiety that a mother would favor her second husband – and, even more, the children she had by him – in her will. We have a vivid depiction from early eighth-century Jeme in Upper Egypt, opposite modern-day Luxor, for such a family tragedy.[62] Several documents of a family archive revolve around a certain Georgius, son of the craftsman Loula who died while Georgius was still in his early teens. His mother Elizabeth, who had remarried soon after and had two children by her second husband, apparently should have held the boy's patrimony in trust after his father's death. However, when Georgius later reached majority, Elizabeth not only refused to hand his rightful possessions over to him[63] but also gave over her entire estate, which was quite substantial, to her second husband when she drew up her will a few years

---

[59] Apul. *Apol.* 93 (trans. Butler 1909).   [60] Apul. *Apol.* 93 (trans. Butler 1909).
[61] For references see below, n. 68.
[62] Wilfong 2002: xvii; cf. Krause 1994–5: I, 86–9. The law found in these Coptic documents originating from the early period of Muslim rule in Egypt generally appears to have been based in later Roman provincial law. Steinwenter 1955: 53, 57; Wilfong 2002: xi. In any case, we are here interested in the family scenario, not the substantive law.
[63] *P.Kru.* 37.17–48; cf. Wilfong 2002: 64–5.

later.[64] Her explicit aim in this will was, as she states, to exclude Georgius, her son from her first marriage, from all rights to her property.[65] We might wonder whether she acted out of pressure from her second husband. After his mother's death, Georgius instituted proceedings against his stepfather and stepsiblings and obtained a settlement in which he was granted the portion of his mother's inheritance to which he was entitled.[66]

Despite such justifiable fears, we also have evidence that shows mothers having children from several spouses and allowing for all of them equally in their wills.[67] Thus, although some new husbands tried to ensure that their own children would gain the lion's share of the property, our evidence gives us several examples of mothers who protected their children by their first husbands, even after remarrying.[68] Of course, any existing children would have to compete with potential stepsiblings for resources, if any were born in the new marriage: any new stepbrothers and stepsisters from a mother's second union necessarily meant that a smaller proportion of the mother's estate would go to the children of her first marriage. If the mother remarried, it was therefore always better from the point of view of the children from the first marriage if she did not have any children by her second husband.[69]

---

[64] *P.Kru.* 68; cf. Wilfong 2002: 58–61.

[65] Cf. Livy 39.9.6; *P.Lond.* 2.198 (*c.* 175/6 CE); Lib. *Ep.* 319, 426, 837, 1169; *Cod. Iust.* 6.2.3 (215 CE); *Nov. Iust.* 155 (533 CE); see also Krause 1994–5: III, 38–9.

[66] *P.Kru.* 38.18–31; see Wilfong 2002, 65–6. Cf. *Cod. Iust.* 9.32.2 (215 CE). Cf. the case of T. Sempronius Rutilus who served as his stepson's guardian and together with the young man's mother wasted his inheritance (Livy 39.9).

[67] *P.Oxy.* 6.968 (second century CE); *P.Oxy.* 4. 837 (117/18 CE); *P.Ryl.* 2.76 (late second century); *P.Harr.* 1.68 (225 CE); *CPR* 6.78 (265 CE); *P.Oxy.* 9.1208 (291 CE); *P.Prag.* 1.42 (early sixth century). Regarding the provision for children by different fathers, we can see the social ideal advertised in a grave inscription from first-century Rome, which praised a certain Murdia who had made her sons from her two marriages equal heirs and in addition passed to her son from her first marriage the entire estate she had received from his father (*CIL* VI.10230 = *ILS* 8394; cf. Evans Grubbs 2002: 225).

[68] If a mother wanted to disinherit her children, she had to bring proof that her children had behaved undutifully. Although there were similar laws on the books concerning fathers and freedmen, mothers are singled out in several instances: e.g. *Cod. Theod.* 2.19–21 (319 CE); *Cod. Iust.* 3.28.28 (321 CE); *Cod. Theod.* 8.13 (349 CE), 3.8.1–2 (381 CE); *Cod. Iust.* 5.9 (472 CE); cf. Humbert 1972: 410–13; Dixon 1988: 59, 65. All of her children together were entitled to inherit at least a quarter share of her estate. In fact, a mother was not allowed to give her second husband a dowry that was so big that her children could no longer receive at least a quarter (*Cod. Theod.* 2.21.1 [358 CE], 2.21.2 [360 CE]; Krause 1994–5: III, 38), nor was she allowed after 472 CE to give as a dowry or by will a larger share to her second husband than to any of her children (*Cod. Iust.* 5.9.6). A woman who had married again had no right to disinherit her children from her first marriage (*Cod. Theod.* 3.8.1). The right to freely dispose of her possessions was granted only as a privilege to a woman who had married once and remained a widow after her husband's death.

[69] Watson showed, however, that some stepfathers also took pains to raise a stepson even if they already had children of their own (1995: 41–2); cf. Bagnall and Frier 2006: 187-Ar-22.

Apart from the preservation of an orphan's inheritance, a mother's remarriage could also have an effect on the fatherless children's living situation. Independent of questions of inheritance, in Roman society we find a general aversion to stepfathers raising stepchildren. In the case of a mother's remarriage, the clear preference, legally and socially, was the placement of the child with relatives or guardians for their upbringing. We can adduce here a rescript of the emperor Alexander Severus from 223 CE which stated that when it was to be decided with whom fatherless children should live – their mothers or their legal guardians – remarriage was a negative factor to be weighed against the mother.[70] Justinian later referred to this edict when he ruled that no one would be better suited to raising such children than the widow, but only on the condition that she refrained from remarrying.[71] Jerome, presenting a very rigorous Christian attitude against remarriage, warned a widow against remarrying because she would then give her children "not a stepfather but an enemy, not a parent but a tyrant."[72] Her new husband would not stand her affection for her children since his jealousy would lead him to believe that she still loved her first husband. Even though Jerome is known as a staunch critic of remarriage, jealousy is in fact a traditional objection to giving one's children a stepfather, and especially as a reason against the cohabiting of stepfather and stepchildren.

On the other hand, as we have seen above, some stepfathers lived harmoniously with their stepchildren. The census returns from Roman Egypt (to which we will return below) provide us with even more cases of stepfathers who had taken in their stepchildren. And just as we see mothers treating all of their children by all marriages equally, so – despite the fear that a stepfather might commandeer his stepchildren's property – we also see some stepfathers in Roman Egypt (as we did in Classical Athens) entrusted as guardians of their stepchildren's inheritance. A certain Tapeteuris, for instance, married for the second time, bequeathed the better part of her property to her son from her first marriage and appointed her second husband, the boy's stepfather, guardian until her son reached maturity.[73] This seems to imply that although there was suspicion, in at least some cases, mothers felt comfortable with

---

[70] *Cod. Iust.* 5.49.1 (223 CE): "The bringing up of your wards should be entrusted to their mother in preference to all other persons, if she has not given them a stepfather" (S. P. Scott 1932). In fact, many fatherless men of the upper social strata in Republican and early imperial times were raised by relatives when their widowed mothers remarried (cf. Hallett, Müller, Harders, Bernstein, all in this volume).

[71] *Nov. Iust.* 22.28 (536 CE); cf. Krause 1994–5: III, 13–14.

[72] Jer. *Ep.* 54.15.4 (trans. Watson 1995: 10); cf. *Ep.* 123. Cf. Bremmer 1995: 46; Nathan 2000: 121.

[73] *P.Fouad.* 33 from an unknown location in Egypt. As mentioned above, it was suggested for Classical Athens that a woman only brought her children into her new marriage if her new husband was simultaneously entrusted with the guardianship of her children. cf. Krause 1994–5: I, 249–54.

making stepfathers guardians of their children's interests. We have further evidence that stepfathers acted as *kyrioi* for their adult stepdaughters, a function that implies close ties and strong trust between a stepfather and his stepdaughter.[74] For married daughters, their paternal homes usually served as a refuge if they were disregarded or maltreated in their husbands' homes, and occasionally we see the stepfather filling that role as well.[75]

We have heard about some documented cases from the Greek period for stepfathers taking the additional step of legally adopting their stepchildren.[76] For Roman times we have two funerary epitaphs erected by stepsons for their stepfathers from third-century CE Galatia: both men had adopted the children from their wives' previous unions.[77] To adduce another example, from Roman Egypt we have two consecutive census returns from 131 CE and 145 CE from the Prosopite nome for a family consisting of the father, Chentmouphis, his wife, Demetrous, their son, Anikos, and his sister, Thamistis, who was four years older than her brother.[78] In both returns Thamistis is declared as the daughter of Chentmouphis and Demetrous and as the full sister of Anikos. However, in the cover letter dated to 161 CE, which accompanied these two copies of the census returns, Thamistis is said to be only the half-sister of Anikos on the mother's side and her father unknown.[79] It is therefore not going too far to assume that Chentmouphis, perhaps upon marriage, had adopted the daughter of his wife whom she had from an earlier relationship.[80]

To offer a vivid insight into the everyday affairs between a stepfather and his stepchild, I want to draw attention to an exceptional contract on papyrus from sixth-century Aphrodito, drawn up between a stepfather and his stepson.[81] Despite its uniqueness, it tells us a great deal about the hurdles that had to be cleared in blending two families into one. In this contract a certain Senuthes, a clerk in the praetorian office in Antinoë, promises to take in his stepson, Johannes, the son of his second wife, to live together

[74] *P.Mich.* 3.191/2 (60 CE. A certain Achilleus served as *kyrios* for his married stepdaughter); and *P.Oxy.* 2.266 (96 CE. A certain Onnophris was the *kyrios* for his married stepdaughter Thaesis).
[75] The major problem for orphaned girls was to find a dowry. Fatherless women without dowries who nonetheless succeeded in marrying often found themselves subsequently with little or no leverage in the marriage: without a father to fall back on or a dowry to rescind, such a woman had no means of applying pressure on her husband if he threatened her with a divorce. For this reason Ambrose admonished orphan girls who were not in the position to expect a dowry to remain unmarried (Ambr. *Exhort. virg.* 4.2 [Migne, *PL* 16.357]).
[76] Cf. 65–6 above.   [77] Calder 1930: 373–4.
[78] Bagnall and Frier 2006: 131-Pr-1; 145-Pr-1.
[79] Bagnall and Frier 2006: 218, 233. Thamistis was, in other words, an *apatōr*. See Youtie 1975 and Malouta (this volume): 120–38.
[80] For examples see Krause 1994–5: III, 44–5.   [81] *P.Cair.Masp.* 3.67305 (568 CE).

with him in harmony, to clothe him, and generally to provide for him. In addition, he pledges to do his utmost in his modest circumstances to care for the boy, at this time probably a youth in his early teens. Overall, this contract recalls apprenticeship arrangements. Through the several apprenticeship contracts that survive in our papyri we know that apprentices, mostly boys from the lower classes, worked and lived for several months to a couple of years in the households of their masters, received room and board, and were integrated into their masters' families.[82] The contract between Senuthes and Johannes is, however, unusual for two reasons: first, apprenticeship contracts were normally negotiated between a master and the apprentice's parents or relatives, not by the apprentice himself;[83] and second, there are terms in this contract that exceed those drawn up in typical apprenticeship contracts, terms in fact that properly belong to adoption contracts. So, for instance, the promise of Senuthes to raise Johannes in place of natural children is a guarantee usually furnished by adoptive parents in adoption contracts from the same period.[84] However, this does not seem to imply that Johannes was to become his stepfather's legal son or heir, as would have been the case in adoption.[85] In fact, Senuthes even reserves for himself the right to turn out his stepson if Johannes is not obedient or does not work assiduously.[86] A real adoption of a child, however, could not be revoked that easily.[87] Added to this unusual mix of adoption and apprenticeship is the fact that Senuthes had stood surety for Johannes, who owed a moneylender 36 carats, presumably debts he had inherited from his late father. It also could have represented the inheritance tax that came due when Johannes succeeded to his father's patrimony.[88] Senuthes insisted that the boy had to hand over to him from his monthly earnings the sum of 6 carats for the following ten months. This money was thus for the repayment of his stepson's debts and for the expense of maintaining him.

---

[82] For apprenticeship contracts: Bradley 1991a: 107; Krause 1994–5: III, 183–8; Rowlandson 1998: 267–8, no. 204; Van Minnen 1998; Cribiore 2001: 82.

[83] We have only one exception, *P.Oxy.* 38.2875 from the early third century CE; but also here the mother was present and consented to this agreement.

[84] Compare *P.Cair.Masp.* 3.67305.9–10 (καὶ πᾶσαν [ἐπ]ιμέ[λειαν] καὶ φροντίδα θέσθαι τῇ σῇ εὐτεκνίᾳ ἐν τάξει γνη[σί]ων τέκνω[ν]) with, e.g., *P.Oxy.* 9.1206 (335 CE): ἀπογράφομαι αὐτὸν εἰς ἐμαυτοῦ γνήσιο[ν υἱόν]. For adoption in the papyri see Taubenschlag 1959: 327; Kurylowicz 1983: 61–75; Beaucamp 1990–2: II, 48–52; Krause 1994–5: III, 80–1; Hübner 2007.

[85] Cf. *P.Lips.* 1.28 (381 CE); *P.Oxy.* 9.1206 (335 CE); *Dig.* 45.1.132.pr. (Paul); Krause 1994–5: III, 81.

[86] *P.Cair.Masp.* 3.67305.12–13: [μ]ηδ[έποτε ἐ]κβαλεῖ[ν] σε τῆς κο[ιν]ῆς βιώσεως ἄκοντα, χωρὶς ῥᾳδιουργίας καὶ ἀταξίας.

[87] Kurylowicz 1983.   [88] Cf. Krause 1994–5: III, 138–45.

Unfortunately, we do not know whether a provision for subsidy was standard in the case of a stepfather taking in his wife's children from a previous union: this is the only contract we have between a stepfather and a stepson.[89] A stepfather was in no way obliged to support his stepchildren; rather, their sustenance had to be met by their paternal inheritance. If this was not sufficient, the mother would be held liable, not, as one might suppose, the children's guardian or even less the stepfather.[90] If a stepfather financially provided for his stepchildren, it was generally assumed that he acted *paterna adfectu*, "out of paternal affection."[91]

To return to our contract between Senuthes and Johannes, it is striking that it is the stepson who is made to support himself out of his own labor. The sum of 6 carats per month, which Senuthes demanded to be paid for the next ten months, comes to 60 carats for the whole period. If Johannes reimbursed his stepfather regularly for the given period on this schedule, he would have repaid his debt of 36 carats, as well as an additional 24 carats, which perhaps was meant to include interest on his debt and the cost of his maintenance. All in all, these 24 carats probably represented a sum equal to the total expense that Senuthes expected to incur on Johannes' behalf.[92]

In any case, we see that the relationship between Senuthes and his stepson was defined largely by economic considerations rather than the emotional ties of a caring father–son relationship. A father who raised a son expected to be cared for and supported in return by his son when he reached old age. However, since even the expectations of natural parents with respect to reciprocal care and support in old age were sometimes disappointed, a stepfather was therefore in a much worse position in terms of relying on his stepson's future benevolence.[93] Stepsons and stepfathers legally owed each other nothing. As stepchildren, neither were they in the *potestas* of their stepfathers,[94] nor was their relationship governed in any way by legal or moral obligations. Thus a stepfather's authority over his stepson was very limited. From the preceding considerations, it is understandable as to why

---

[89] In late medieval Florence we find some sort of compensation for a stepfather who raised his stepchildren. He was paid for their keep by the children's paternal relatives (Klapisch-Zuber 1985: 125).

[90] *Dig.* 25.3.5.4 (Ulpian); cf. Krause 1994–5: 1, 129.

[91] *Cod. Iust.* 2.18.15 from 239: "If, influenced by paternal affection, you have furnished means of support to your step-daughter (Scott translates *privigna* here with daughter-in-law), or have paid out money as salaries to teachers, you will have no right to recover such expenses" (S. P. Scott 1932).

[92] Note that 24 carats or one *solidus* equaled 10 *artabae* of wheat, i.e. about 300 kilograms (Bagnall 1993: 332), enough to feed a child for a year, but not sufficient for many further expenses.

[93] Parkin compared Greek and Roman notions about what children owed their aging parents (2003: 203–36).

[94] Gai. *Inst.* 1.64.

Senuthes regarded it as necessary to draw up such a contract. Senuthes appears to have used the debt he had assumed on his stepson's behalf as a source of leverage over the latter: should Johannes behave in an undisci-plined or licentious way, Senuthes threatened that he would cast him out "naked, naked, together with your debt" at a moment's notice.[95] For Johannes, however, it was a hard, but necessary bargain: obviously hard-pressed by creditors, he had little choice in the matter and at least ended up with a guarantor and a home, if not a father.

The risks and disadvantages of giving a child who had lost his father a stepfather by remarrying were obvious to any mother in antiquity. We may see some of the emotional and economic distress of single motherhood dramatized in Chariton's novel *Callirhoe*. Recently having lost her husband and having been sold into slavery, the noble heroine Callirhoe discovers that she is pregnant. In a heart-rending internal debate, Callirhoe realizes that she is forced to choose between honoring the memory of her "lost" hus-band, Chaereas, and safeguarding the future of her unborn son. While she considers whether or not to marry Dionysius, the leading man of Miletus, since he is the only person able to provide her son with the appropriate social status, economic support, and education, she has a dream in which her husband tells her to take good care of their child. She thus opts for remarriage out of concern for her son, later pretending that it is Dionysius' child with which she is pregnant. Callirhoe is convinced that if Dionysius knew that he was not the biological father, his jealousy would not let her raise another man's child in his house.[96]

Unlike the romantic world of the Greek novel, the widows who most stood in need of remarrying – poor widows with minor children, even those still of childbearing age – probably faced the most formidable challenges in finding new marriage partners. The wealthy, the childless, or those who were able to leave their children for others to raise would have had a much easier time finding a suitable second husband.[97] Particularly the wealthy, however, faced impediments related to their status when it came to remar-riage. It was precisely their attractiveness as potential brides with property that created the suspicion that in remarrying they might abandon their children by their first husbands and endanger their inheritance prospects – in effect putting their interests before their children's. We thus find an interesting

---

[95] *P. Cair. Masp.* 3.67305.26–7: δηλαδὴ, εἰ δ[ὲ καὶ] σὺ ἀγ[ά]γωγος φανείης [κα]ὶ ἄνετ(ος) ἐν [πᾶσ]ι τ[οῖ]ς ἔργ[ο]ι[ς, ἀ]κρ[ί]τω[ς ἐξ]ελθεῖν ἀπ' ἐμο(ῦ) γυμνὸν … γυμ[νὸ]ν, μετὰ καὶ τοῦ [σ]ο(υ) χρ[έους] τῶν αὐτῶν [δύ]ο νομισ[μ(άτων).
[96] Chariton, *Call.* 2.10–11. [97] Firm. Mat. 5.3.3, 25; Jer. *Ep.* 22.16; Krause 1994–5: I, 128–9.

dilemma confronting nearly all widows with children of all social strata with
respect to remarriage: poor widows, on the one hand, desperately needed to
remarry in order to hold their families together, but found it difficult to find
new husbands willing to take them;[98] wealthy widowed mothers, on the other
hand, were attractive prospects, but faced significant familial and social
disapproval in remarrying. For neither, then, was remarriage an easy option.
But let us now turn to the question of the implications of a mother's
remarriage for her fatherless children and, particularly, the relative frequency
of living with a stepfather.

LIVING WITH A STEPFATHER

We must start by looking at the statistical evidence, which can give us some
clues as to the frequency of the introduction of stepfathers into orphaned
families. The best evidence in antiquity concerning this question is the
census returns from first- to third-century Roman Egypt, recording for the
most part inhabitants of the towns and villages of Middle Egypt. Every
fourteen years the head of a household was obliged to identify the members
of his household – wives, parents, siblings, lodgers, and slaves – to the
Roman authorities.[99] In these returns we find only nine cases of remarriage
of widows or divorced women.[100] None of these women was over the age of
thirty-five when she remarried. On the other hand, we have forty-five cases
recorded in the census returns of widowed or divorced women living
alone with their children and not having remarried. In eleven of these
cases the children were no older than fourteen and therefore legal minors.[101]
Apparently, many women who lost their husbands did not remarry in
Roman Egypt, even if the widowed or divorced woman was still young
and capable of bearing children.[102]

It is hard to estimate how many widowed mothers remarried but left their
children to others to raise (usually the late husband's family), as the returns
do not show us these cases of remarriage: "Since surviving issue of prior
marriages provide the invariable occasion for mentioning remarriage, its
incidence was certainly higher than the returns indicate."[103] In any case, we

[98] E.g. Jer. *Ep.* 54.15.   [99] Bagnall and Frier 2006.
[100] Bagnall and Frier 2006: 117-Ar-7; 131-Me-1; 145-He-2; 173-Ar-2; 173-Ar-11; 187-Ar-22; 187-Ar-29; 187-Ar-32. If not explicitly stated it is not possible to differentiate between divorced or widowed.
[101] Bagnall and Frier 2006: 33-Ar-2; 103-Ar-9; 117-Ar-5; 145-Ar-2; 173-Pr-4; 187-Ar-29; 187-Ox-4 (?); 243-Ar-1 (?); 243-Ar-3; 257-Ar-1; *P. Oxy. Census* (Bagnall, Frier, and Rutherford 1997): 89-Pt-51. Cf. Bagnall and Frier 2006: 126–7.
[102] Bagnall and Frier 2006: 126–7; Hanson 2005: 86–7.   [103] Bagnall and Frier 2006: 126.

have only four unambiguous instances in the census returns that record widows who remarried and took their fatherless children into their new marriages.[104] We can only speculate as to the reasons: perhaps there was no one else to whom the widowed mother could have entrusted her children; or perhaps her new spouse did not object because he had no children of his own. In fact, three of these four stepfathers did not have children of their own at the time of remarriage and were therefore probably willing to take in their brides' children (in all three cases, these children were sons).[105] In one instance the widow was also the owner of the house into which the step-father moved after the marriage.[106] Apparently he did not have much choice but to accept his stepson. Compared with these four cases of a co-residential stepfather, we find sixteen widowed fathers in the census returns who had remarried and had given their children a stepmother.[107] Perhaps, then, the imbalance we find in the literary and mythological representations of step-mothers and stepfathers does not reflect only the general misogyny of the ancient world; perhaps we should also understand this imbalance in light of the relative rarity of cohabiting stepfathers as opposed to cohabiting step-mothers, who were by far the more common phenomenon.[108]

CONCLUSION

The main concern in our literary and legal sources about a widowed mother's remarriage focuses not on the emotional impact that remarriage

[104] Bagnall and Frier 2006: 117-Ar-7 (a woman brought a son from a previous union into her second husband's family; her husband was the head of a household consisting of him, his married two brothers and his widowed elderly mother; the couple had not yet any common children); 131-Me-1 (a woman lived with her second husband and her thirty-three-year-old son from her previous marriage in a house of which she was the owner. The couple did not have any common children); 145-He-2 (a woman had brought her twenty-six-year-old son into her new husband's household. The couple later had their own adult son; both sons were married and still lived with their mother and their (step)father under one roof); 187-Ar-22 (a forty-year-old woman had brought her two children, no older than sixteen and twelve upon her remarriage, into her second husband's household and he already had two children by two previous marriages. When the return was drawn up, the couple had a five-year-old girl together). To these four families we can probably add those two cases in which a woman had children living with her from two or more subsequent marriages but was again divorced or widowed (173-Ar-11; 187-Ar-29). It is possible, however, that these women summoned their children into the homes which they headed only after the dissolution of their second marriage.
[105] Bagnall and Frier 2006: 117-Ar-7; 131-Me-1; 145-He-2.   [106] Bagnall and Frier 2006: 132-Me-1.
[107] Bagnall and Frier 2006: 131-Ox-1; 159-Ar-5; 173-Pr-5; 173-Pr-10 (*bis*); 187-Ar-8; 187-Ar-22; 186-Ar-32; 201-Ar-2; 201-Ar-5; 215-Ar-4. To this number we can add those five cases in which a man had children from two or more subsequent marriages living with him but was again divorced or widowed or had died, but where the half-siblings were still living together (131-Ar-11; 131-He-4; 145-Ar-9; 173-Me-1; 215-He-2).
[108] Cf. Watson 1995: 80–1.

would have on the children, but rather on the financial consequences. There was a particular problem facing propertied families when it came to remarriage, namely the presumed conflict between the children from the former union and the new lines of succession created by the new marriage. Stepfathers marrying into the propertied elite often had to defend themselves against accusations that they married with an eye to embezzling the orphan's patrimony, and this prejudice prevailed regardless of whether or not the stepfather and stepchildren lived under the same roof. In those cases in which the mother acted as guardian for her orphaned children, her new husband and stepfather of her children could have been held liable should his stepchildren's patrimony suffer any loss while he was married to their mother. While in the propertied social strata a stepfather was regarded as a threat to his stepchildren's inheritance prospects and suspected of legacy hunting, in the lower strata a stepfather who was willing to marry a widow and take in her children was seen as a last resort. In any event, the proportion of fatherless children who grew up under one roof with a stepfather seems to have been low, while cohabiting stepmothers outnumbered cohabiting stepfathers by a good margin.

Moving beyond the limitations imposed on us by the ancient preoccupations with property and succession, we may ask ourselves what effect a stepfather would have had on a child's life. Even though we cannot reconstruct a full picture of such a relationship because it was, of course, shaped by individual circumstances, living arrangements, and economic aspects, we may safely assert that living in such a patchwork family was difficult for all involved. The non-residential stepfather presumably had only a minor impact on the child's daily life; moving into a stepfather's home, however, was altogether a different proposition. In these few cases the major issues between co-residential stepfathers and stepchildren appear to have centered on problems of authority and obedience, as we have seen in the case of Senuthes and his stepson Johannes. Such problems as these were exacerbated whenever fathers left their children destitute. While in wealthy families such problems might not arise too often since children were provided for from their paternal property, we can easily imagine that when a stepfather became their only provider, such an arrangement could easily develop into a source of constant friction in the home, with the stepfather regularly complaining about the cost of raising his wife's children. Such friction must be seen in the light of the prevailing duties (or lack thereof) that characterized the stepfather–stepchild relationship. In this connection, it is important to stress that no legal relationship between a stepfather and his wife's children from a previous union was established by a remarriage: a stepfather was not legally obliged to support his stepchildren financially, nor did these stepchildren fall under his *patria potestas*. These responsibilities came only with the adoption of his stepchildren, not remarriage to their mother. Yet this lack of legal and social commitment was symmetrical: while the stepfather was not necessarily expected to help pay for his stepchildren's upbringing, neither were the stepchildren later compelled to care for him in his old age.

Notwithstanding the limits of this legal relationship, we have seen that some stepfathers went beyond the bounds of law and took on a quasi-paternal role, and that this role was indeed defined by parental affection. These stepfathers welcomed their stepchildren into their homes, served as guardians, shielded them against wrongful claims of relatives, and even occasionally adopted them as their heirs. Likewise, we see considerable trust placed in those stepfathers who acted as guardians for their minor stepchildren, and also for their adult stepdaughters. Individual accounts provide us with further evidence that some stepchildren developed close bonds with their stepfathers and half-siblings.

Overall, it becomes clear that the role of the stepfather was much less emotionally charged than that of the stepmother. We do not find an equivalent to the *saeva noverca* (cruel stepmother) or the *noverca venefica* (stepmother as poisoner) aiming at seducing her stepson, or stealing her stepchildren's patrimony or trying to murder them, so common in our sources from antiquity.[109] The only prevailing prejudice against stepfathers in antiquity is the accusation of legacy hunting – at least for those men marrying into the propertied classes. In the lower strata a stepfather was more likely to improve his stepchildren's financial situation than to further endanger it.

Astonishingly, we hear next to nothing in our sources about stepfathers mistreating or sexually abusing their minor stepchildren, which flies in the face of everything we know about stepfathers today, as Golden rightly remarks.[110] The currently widespread stereotype of the bullying or sexually violent stepfather does not appear in our ancient sources, and his relatively benign character (apart from the threat he posed to the inheritance) stands in stark contrast to the stereotype of the wicked stepmother that dominates ancient literature. Apart from ascribing this difference to the inherent misogyny of the ancient tradition, this discrepancy might be at least partly attributed to the fact that a cohabiting stepfather was the

---

[109] Watson 1995: 39–40.   [110] Golden (this volume): 52.

exception rather than the norm in antiquity.[111] All this stands in contrast to the modern Western world, where we find at least four to five times more residential stepfathers than residential stepmothers, a situation primarily attributable to the fact that mothers today usually retain physical custody of their children regardless of marriage status.[112]

---

[111] In fact, this is also the case in the European fairy-tale tradition: one rarely, if ever, reads of the wicked stepfather!

[112] Coleman and Ganong 2004: 134 for the USA. For the UK it is estimated that there are about seven times as many cohabiting stepfathers as stepmothers (Jensen and McKee 2003: 4).

CHAPTER 5

"Without father, without mother, without genealogy": fatherlessness in the Old and New Testaments

Marcus Sigismund

The engagement of scholars of antiquity with the topic of "fatherlessness" is of high importance because the problem of fatherlessness presents a conspicuous gap in the otherwise well-studied field of the ancient family.[1] However, a study on the topic should not be pursued simply on account of some desire to fill a historiographical lacuna. Instead, by entering into a dialogue with practicing social scientists, scholars of antiquity may be able to provide useful comparative data on this phenomenon, a collaboration which could in turn help us to understand better the manifold problems associated with modern fatherlessness. As we shall see, the New Testament and other contemporary, non-canonical texts represent a rich source of ancient data with respect to how the early Christian community understood and engaged with the problem of fatherlessness.

A quick survey of contemporary Christian writings reveals that fatherlessness is an increasingly contentious topic within several Christian denominations, since the modern phenomenon of children growing up without a father runs counter to the traditional Christian family image.[2] Unsurprisingly, this state of affairs has occasioned many – often highly emotional – discussions in the Christian media, particularly in Anglo-American Evangelical circles. The inherent dependence of this discourse on the Bible as the normative authority of religion, which understands God as its "Father,"[3] underscores the Biblical rootedness of the modern Christian, family-oriented model of society. However, this discourse is

---

[1] The issue of fatherlessness is ignored almost completely in current handbooks (see below). The following, however, are helpful as background for this essay: Cohen 1993; Osiek 1996; Perdue 1997; Moxnes 1997; and Osiek and Balch 1997. I am grateful to David Ratzan for his comments and suggestions on the English version of this paper.

[2] The growing number of single parents and children being raised in such homes has increasingly become a pastoral concern. See, e.g., Graham 1998 and Domsgen 2006. See also the Introduction to this volume for the issue in contemporary politics.

[3] On the theological interpretation of God the Father, see Strotmann 1991; Grelot 1994; Böckler 2000. For a general account on this topic, see Schlosser *et al.* 2001.

unable to represent fatherlessness in a fully defined manner. In fact, we find that this "problem" is not infrequently omitted even from didactic literature on Christian family values. Typical in this regard is the *Compendium of the Social Doctrine of the Church*, a text which stresses both the importance of the family and the centrality of fatherhood to the family, but apparently has nothing to say about the endemic problem of children growing up fatherless.[4]

The absence of guidelines on fatherlessness in modern Christian literature is ostensibly due to the putative silence of the Biblical sources on the subject. The New Testament in particular appears at first glance to be unconcerned with the topic. The only passage that addresses fatherlessness explicitly, and has therefore been chosen as the title of this paper (Heb. 7:3), has a Christological, not an ethical or larger social meaning.[5] According to normal Christian interpretive practice, the Christian social ethic, the Christian life, must of course be based in Biblical authority, so the apparent paucity of scriptural references to fatherlessness presents a real problem for any Christian.[6] A careful historical analysis of the Biblical sources is therefore necessary.

How are we to understand this supposed silence of the New Testament? First, we must note that the Greek word for "fatherless" (ἀπάτωρ / *apatōr*) is a word which appears only once in the New Testament, here in Hebrews 7:3.[7] The word for "orphan" (ὀρφανός / *orphanos*) appears only twice. Furthermore, it is clear that the contexts in which *orphanos* is attested are dominated by theological concerns. Thus, in John 14:18 Jesus announces that he is not going to leave his disciples behind as "orphans," but will return to them; while in James 1:27 the care of widows and orphans is held up as an essential element of true piety. But must we therefore assume that for the early Christians there was no difficulty with fatherlessness simply because

---

[4] See the *Päpstlicher Rat für Gerechtigkeit und Frieden (Pontifical Council for Justice and Peace)* 2004: 167–98. In this document, only §246 addresses the issue of supporting orphans (as well as old or disabled persons). Moreover, it is a remarkable fact that the chapter on family is the only one in the entire second part of this compendium that does not contain a sub-section on "Biblical aspects." See also the Apostolic Exhortation *Familiaris consortio* of John Paul II (*Acta Apostolicae Sedis* 74 [1982]). Although seemingly engaged with the family in all respects, it has nothing significant to say about fatherlessness, noting simply: "As experience teaches, the absence of a father causes psychological and moral imbalance and notable difficulties in family relationships" (25.72).

[5] Biblical quotations are taken from the New International Version (NIV) and New American Bible (NAB) for the deuterocanonical books, unless a more literal translation according to the Greek is needed (such adaptions will be noted).

[6] Cf. *Compendium of Social Doctrine* §§62–3 with reference to *Gaudium et Spes* 40, esp. §74: "The Church's social doctrine finds its essential foundation in Biblical revelation … From this source, which comes from above, it draws inspiration and light to understand, judge and guide human experience and history."

[7] See Malouta (this volume) for a discussion of *apatores* in Roman Egypt.

these particular passages have a primarily theological aspect? Anyone who is familiar with modes of Biblical representation knows that the exact opposite must be true. We will certainly not be able to ascertain from these texts the actual incidence of fatherlessness within early Christian communities nor define its precise social nature, but the very fact that fatherlessness is employed so naturally as a metaphor clearly suggests that the early Christians were well aware of the phenomenon and the difficult situation of orphans. The extent to which the New Testament engages with fatherlessness and what approach the text appears to adopt regarding the problem will be discussed below. The focus of this chapter is thus decidedly socio-historical, and its scope restricted to purely historical sources and events. For this reason, the alleged father-lessness of Jesus will have no part in this study.[8]

THE OLD TESTAMENT AND EARLY JEWISH BACKGROUND

The world of the New Testament is not easily recovered by means of traditional hermeneutical practice. One must always take care to remember that the Christians of the New Testament represent a culture in the process of self-conscious transformation. We are dealing here with a group that was at once aware of its roots in, and so its ongoing commitment to, Palestinian Judaism, while also consciously entering into a dynamic engagement with Hellenistic

---

[8] Andries Gideon van Aarde has recently attempted over the course of several studies an analysis of Jesus' alleged fatherlessness in the light of today's sociological debate over the nature of single-parent households (van Aarde 1999; 2001; and 2002). Van Aarde's arguments turn on the assumption that Mary was not married to Joseph, and that this situation had the effect of robbing Jesus of his social identity. This in turn led Jesus to assemble about himself a close circle of friends and to imagine himself as the "Son of God." But Aarde obviously overinterprets the absence of Joseph in the New Testament: it is clear from the Gospels that Jesus was widely recognized as the son of the carpenter (which, of course, calls into question Aarde's basic assertion that Jesus suffered from a lack of social identity), e.g. John 1:45; 6:42; Luke 3:23. Furthermore, we have several texts which insist upon the actual marriage of Joseph and Mary, e.g. Matt. 1:20–4; cf. Luke 4:22; Mark 6:3; cf. 3:31–5. Again, Luke 1:21–5 demonstrates Joseph's parental relationship to Jesus by his naming of his son according to Jewish law (on this, see Gnilka 1986: 19). Also, the conflicts between Jesus and his family so frequently alluded to in older exegetical works point to the fact that Jesus was indeed seen as a problematic member of the family, but not for that any less of an integral member. In any case, it is much more profitable to understand Jesus' conflicts with his family as the result of tension between his preaching and pre-existing social norms, such as we often find with both OT and NT prophets (e.g. Elisha or Jesus' disciples). Of course, Jesus was fatherless at the point when Joseph died. However, we know from Luke (2:41–51) that Joseph lived at least until Jesus' twelfth year, since the family undertook a pilgrimage to Jerusalem when Jesus was that age. By this time he was almost an adult according to Jewish law and his social identity would certainly have already been formed. Finally, there is no awareness of Jesus as a fatherless person in the New Testament or the subsequent Christian tradition. Perhaps the most revealing statement in the Christian literature in this regard comes from the Gospel of Philip 17c (TU 143:22f.): "And the Lord would not have said 'My Father who is in Heaven' (Matt. 16:17), unless he had had another father, but he would have said simply 'My father'."

Jewish and pagan ideas and cultural practices. The result was the incorporation of various cultural influences and social norms. An examination of fatherlessness in the New Testament must therefore begin with the Old Testament roots.

Before turning to the OT texts themselves, a closer examination of the terminology is in order. The English term "orphan" – like the German *Waise* – is not specific: it most commonly refers to a child who has lost both parents but may occasionally be used of a child who is motherless or fatherless. It is never understood in modern parlance to mean "fatherless" without further qualification.[9] The terminology in the OT literature is similar. The Septuagint speaks continuously of *orphanoi*, a term that has several attested meanings (e.g., it can express the childlessness of a couple).[10] The Hebrew equivalent (יתום/ *yātôm*), however, is much more specific, as is common in other Semitic languages.[11] *Yātôm* can stand for both orphan in the wider sense above and in a narrower sense to denote a boy without a father. This is clearly the meaning in Lamentations 5:3: "We have become *yᵉtômîm*, | our mothers like widows."[12] Here the stress of the term lies precisely on the aspect of fatherlessness, regardless of the fact that *yᵉtômîm* can also be orphans who have neither mothers nor fathers.[13] The specification of *yātôm* as "fatherless" is also attested

---

[9] The Oxford English Dictionary defines an orphan as "a person, *esp.* a child, both of whose parents are dead (or, rarely, one of whose parents have died). In extended use: an abandoned or neglected child." It is nevertheless interesting that some quotations in this article (especially those from the sixteenth and seventeenth centuries) emphasize the fatherless aspects of orphans, e.g. "Drayton *Heroic. Ep. iv. 95* Make'st me an orphan ere my Father die" and "Heywood *2nd Pt. Iron Age v. Wks.* 1874 III. 429 Sweet Orphant do; thy fathers dead already." Early German meanings of *Waise* are "the abandoned" and "the robbed" (Grimm and Grimm 1922: 1043). Regarding usage, the Grimm brothers emphasize its primary meaning as a juridical category for children who lack parents and so need guardians, and then secondarily as a child who has lost only his or her father. "Waise ist zunächst ein rechtlicher Begriff. Es bezeichnet in der alten Sprache einen Knaben oder ein Mädchen, die ihre Eltern oder wenigstens den Vater durch den Tod verloren haben und daher bis zur Mündigkeit unter Vormundschaft stehen; … es kann auch von einem Kind gebraucht werden, das nur die Mutter verloren hat; … es steht in der neueren Sprache auch von einem Kind, das von Vater oder Mutter verlassen ist" (1047). Apparently only recently has the meaning come closer to that of orphan in English, such that *Waise* now commonly refers to children who have lost either or both parents.

[10] Cf. Seesemann 1954 and the Introduction to this volume (20). The Vulgate also uses *orphanus* and (far more frequently) *pupillus*, the latter more strongly emphasizing the aspect of minority. *Orbus* and *orba* are not found in the Vulgate at all.

[11] The term is attested forty-two times in the Old Testament. Cf. Ugaritic *ytm* (fem. *ytmt*); Punic *ytm*; Aram. *yatmā'*. On the etymology and usage of equivalent terms in Egypt and Mesopotamia, see Ringgren 1982: esp. 1075–7.

[12] NIV: "We have become orphans and fatherless, our mothers like widows." Cf. Golden (this volume), who points to the fact that in his use of *orphanos* Homer provides a particularly moving testament to the effects of a father's loss. Homer's use of this term thus seems to be quite similar to the meaning of Hebrew *yātôm*.

[13] In my view Renkema goes too far in his criticism of Ringgren when he alleges that the latter interprets *ytwm* exclusively as "fatherless," saying that "*ytwm* … must have the same meaning as orphan, i.e., a

in other OT passages.[14] While no one today would deny that a mother's loss or absence is a matter of serious concern, the Hebrew points to the fact that in OT Judaism greater importance was attached to fatherlessness than mother-lessness. Therefore, being an orphan was in almost all cases tantamount to being fatherless. This held true for the intertestamental and rabbinic eras as well, and thus certainly for the time of Jesus and the early Palestinian Christians.[15]

When one turns to consider fatherlessness in the Old Testament proper, the recurrence of the same basic aspects of the phenomenon through all eras of Biblical history is striking, particularly when one juxtaposes this con-tinuity against the changes in Jewish culture which took place over the same period.[16] The fundamental aspects of fatherlessness in the Old Testament are the loss of rights and protection; the poverty resulting from the loss of one's father; and last, but not least, the role of God as surrogate father and champion of orphans.

Central to the characterization of fatherlessness in the Old Testament is the first theme, the orphan's lack of rights and protection. Regardless of date or circumstances of composition, the OT texts universally portray the father as a protector, a guardian who presides over his family and who is held accountable in his performance of this role by God. A father's absence has

---

child who has lost both father and mother" (1995: 120). It goes without saying that *ytwm* can indicate an orphan who has lost both parents. But as Böckler (2000: 375) argues, Job 24:9 and perhaps Lam. 5:3 demonstrate that at least these orphans still have their mothers, and in essence it means "fatherless."

[14] E.g., Gesenius 1995 cites s.v. *yatum* the following instances: in the narrow sense of fatherless children (with reference to KAI 14.3): Exod. 22:22; Pss. 68:6, 109:9–12; Job 24:9; Lam. 5:3; Sir. 4:10; orphan in the non-specific sense: Jer. 5:28; Hos. 14:4; Pss. 10:18 (BHS), 82:3; Job 6:27, 29:12, 31:21 (problematic on textual grounds); Exod. 22:21; Deut. 10:18, 14:29, 16:11, 14, 24:17 (similarly problematic on textual grounds), 24:19–21, 26:12, 27:19; Isa. 1:17–23, 9:16, 10:2; Jer. 7:6, 22:3 (BHS), 49:11; Ezek. 22:7; Zech. 7:10; Mal. 3:5; Pss. 94:6, 146:9; Job 22:9, 24:3, 31:17; Prov. 23:10; Sir. 32:17.

[15] Although the evidence for these other periods is meager (we have only two references, and these from apocryphal texts), Beyer is obviously right in translating יתם / *yatem* as "orphan, fatherless youth" in his glossary (1984: 601). Baumgartner (1974) considers the Aram. and Tigr. radicals *yatomim* and *yetomaiw* as both terms for orphans, or "boys who have become fatherless," citing KAI 24.13. In Ketub. 6.6 the Mishna comes close to the linguistic usage of the New Testament by speaking of an orphan who still has a mother and brothers but obviously lacks a father. There appears to be no noticeable change in the usage of *ytm* until the Babylonian Talmud. But here also – following the Biblical Hebrew – the primary meaning of *yatom* as an "abandoned boy or young man" prevails (see Levy 1963: 277–8, with reference to bPesah. 118a [to Ps. 136:1]). However, other instances of the word indicate that these orphans clearly lack both parents; at other times the emphasis is laid on the deceased mother (e.g. bSanh. 19b, cf. 2 Sam. 21:8). Female orphans are rarely visible in these texts. When one does catch a glimpse of orphaned girls, they are always destitute. This is significant, since a lack of sustenance is a general characteristic of fatherlessness (not of motherlessness).

[16] In contrast to the NT texts the social-historical content of the OT passages is easier to grasp. Accordingly, the subject of orphans in the Old Testament has a relatively well-developed biblio-graphy. In addition to previously cited works, see also Fensham 1962; Weiler 1980; and Norrback 2001, as well as the summaries of Baab 1962; Hasler 1966; Perdue 1997: 193–4; and Lang 2001.

fatal consequences: children without fathers in the Old Testament are routinely shown to be oppressed (e.g. Exod. 22:21), open to attack (e.g. Job 31:21), or even, on occasion, murdered (e.g. Ps. 94:6). The Wisdom literature of the Old Testament (surely to some extent reflecting historical experience) also refers to the drawing of lots for orphans, most likely for use or sale as slaves (Job 6:27, cf. 24:9).[17] The OT texts also frequently refer to the material consequences of losing one's father and protector, wherein one is left open to opportunistic theft (e.g. that of a donkey in Job 24:3) or even the outright appropriation of one's entire patrimony (e.g. Prov. 23:10). All of these texts refer to orphans who had not succeeded in finding a surrogate protector (עוזר/ 'ozer) to take the place of their absent fathers.[18] We thus see that God is called upon to fulfill this role of עוזר/ 'ozer (e.g. Ps. 10:14; cf. God as guarantor of their rights in Deut. 10:17–18 and Ps. 10:17–18).[19]

Since the majority of the OT texts referring to orphans stress their lack of protection and rights, we may assume that this was the major problem associated with fatherlessness during the whole of this era.[20] For instance, it seems that whenever orphans sought to enforce their rights in court, they were often not only denied justice (Isa. 1:23; Jer. 5:28), but even found the legal system perverted and biased against them (Deut. 24:17). This injustice occasioned constant criticism by OT authors, and yet it apparently persisted over the centuries until at least the post-Exilic period, as we may see by the spread of references to the matter.[21] Thus, we see Isaiah illustrating the moral decline of Jerusalem by decrying the fact that the duties owed to orphans were neglected (1:23). Ezekiel likewise notes that orphans and widows were oppressed in Jerusalem (22:7). Finally, Job's insistence on the help he had given to the poor and the fatherless (29:12; 31:16–23) and his impartiality towards orphans (31:21) speaks for itself.

Compared with the lack of protection, an orphan's penury and welfare seem to be second-order themes. Also, with regard to these themes we must differentiate between orphans who had found a surrogate after their fathers' deaths (in most cases a kinsman, or occasionally a stepfather in case of the

---

[17] See Michel 2006: 138, n. 7, who highlights orphans as victims of debt-slavery.
[18] Cf. the radical עזד, which implies the idea of protection. In this context, Böckler (2000: 375) draws a comparison with the noun 'azara, i.e. enclosure.
[19] We find striking parallels in other cultures of the ancient Near East. Cf. Volk 2006: esp. 58–70.
[20] The stereotypical OT context for widows and orphans is almost always legal in aspect, e.g. Deut. 10:18, 27:19; Isa. 7:5, 22:3; Ezek. 22:7; Zech. 7:9–10).
[21] The Old Testament does not simply point to the fact that defenseless orphans were frequently taken advantage of (Ps. 94:6; Job 22:9; Isa. 10:2; Jer. 5:28), but does so in order to enjoin people not to exploit their weakness (Exod. 22:21; Deut. 24:17; Prov. 23:10).

mother's remarriage)[22] and those who did not. Regarding the latter, the Old Testament frequently points out the duty to aid such orphans (e.g. Exod. 22:22–7; Deut. 16:11, 14). Such exhortations, of course, point to the social decline and poverty that most orphans without surrogates experienced. Compared with the loss of a father, the consequences of a mother's loss seem to have been negligible with regard to social status and economic welfare. However, the loss of social and financial status need not have been the inevitable consequence of fatherlessness. Despite Lang's belief that widows with children who did not remarry were relegated to the margins of society,[23] in my opinion such an outcome could have been prevented if the widow had a large estate to fall back on.[24] Nonetheless, the risk of the loss of status was very real, as we see by the report of a widow in 2 Kings 4:1: "Your servant my husband is dead … But now his creditor is coming to take my two boys as his slaves."[25] Several sacral laws in fact refer explicitly to the financial distress typically suffered by orphans: every third year there was to be a special tithe dedicated to the fatherless and other oppressed persons (Deut. 14:28–9, 26:12–15). Like widows, orphans were to have the right to claim forgotten or left sheaves as well as the gleanings of vineyards and orchards (Deut. 24:19–22), and the Pentateuch additionally calls for general public relief for the fatherless (Exod. 22:22–7; Deut. 16:11, 14). However, the texts emphasize that the care of the fatherless was not to be understood merely as a charitable act, but rather as a duty rooted in the law of Israel, as may be seen in the Deuteronomical reform (e.g. Deut. 27:19) and the social agenda of the prophets (Isa. 1:17, 23; 10:1; Jer. 7:6, 22:3–5; Ezek. 22:7).[26] Again, Job's mentioning of his aid for the fatherless clearly assumes just such a pre-existing social obligation (24:9), although his

---

[22] Even though the rabbinic writings have much to say about guardianship and also occasionally testify to the existence of stepfathers (an indication that both relationships were established in pre-Mishnaic times), we nevertheless lack a scholarly analysis of surrogate fathers in the OT era. However, one must note that Biblical Hebrew had no term for "stepfather," and further that the word for "guardian" (אפיטרופוס) is a Hellenistic loan-word from Greek (ἐπίτροπος / *epitropos*). These facts indicate that the OT categories here only partially map onto Greco-Roman or modern analogues.

[23] Lang 2001.

[24] In view of the following quotation, Baab (1962) seems to arrive at too rosy a conclusion when he assumes that the ancient law of Israel provided for the care of fatherless children. However, some texts do imply a heightened consciousness of the plight of orphans (e.g. Deut. 14:29, 24:19–21, 26:12, 27:19).

[25] Of course, we must consider that such statements were often mere rhetorical tropes. See Hübner (this volume): 63.

[26] But cf. Bennett (2002), who suggests that the provisions governing widows and orphans – like other charitable laws of the Deuteronomic legislation – were introduced to bolster the position of the privileged by staving off potential uprisings by the peasantry.

comments as well as those of the prophets indicate that the obligations out-
lined in the Pentateuch were often neglected.[27]

The ultimate refuge for the fatherless in the Old Testament is God,[28] and
while this is theologically comforting, it remains historically unedifying as
to the reality of OT society: (only) God in his mercy sets a bound to human
arbitrariness, giving both justice and sustenance to the oppressed (Deut.
10:17–19; Ps. 146:9). In Psalm 10 he is a reliever (*'ozer*) of the fatherless (v. 16)
and their fair-minded judge (v. 18; cf. Deut. 10:17). His role as surrogate
father is summed up in Psalm 68:6 (dated to the Second Temple period)
with the title "Father of the fatherless (*yᵉtômîm*)."[29] Associated with this
function is a guarantee of sacred protection for the fatherless: whoever
violates them is cursed (Deut. 27:19) and is left to God's severe judgment
(Mal. 3:5). Renunciation of evil in the eyes of Isaiah is tantamount to the
enforcement of justice for orphans (1:17–23).

The texts from Hellenistic times show only slight changes from the basic
pattern set out above. One of them is apparently the possibility of adoption,
which was unknown to OT law.[30] Even so, the only case of adoption
mentioned in the Old Testament seems to be Esther, who was raised by her
cousin Mordecai (Esth. 2:7, 15).[31] Again, just as prescribed in Deuteronomy
(14:22–9), the tithes – now collected in the Temple – provided public
resources for the welfare of orphans.[32] The Book of Tobit (written in the
second century BCE) is most interesting in this context. At 1:8 the protagonist
stresses that he gave a third tithe to the orphans (as well as to widows and
proselytes) of Israel "in keeping with the decree of the Mosaic law and the
commands of Deborah, the mother of my father Tobiel." Tobit in fact tells us
why he learned these commands from his grandmother and not from his
father: he himself was fatherless: "for when my father died, he left me an
orphan." From this we may infer that the grandmother took over the role of

---

[27] E.g. Isa. 10:2 excoriates the perversion of justice. Cf. Jer. 5:28. In his message at the Temple gate Jeremiah
requests (7:6) that orphans not be oppressed any longer (cf. Jer. 22:3). In the oracle against Edom (Jer.
49:7–23) the prophet affirms that YHWH himself will take care of the orphans. Cf. Zech. 7:10.

[28] See Ps. 27:10: "Though my father and my mother forsake me, the LORD will receive me."

[29] On the place of the Psalms in literary history, see Böckler 2000: 363–76. On the chronology, see 365.

[30] However, some OT texts adumbrate a specific Israelitic affiliation not entirely dissimilar to adoption
(cf. Gen. 48:5, 19–29; 50:23).

[31] See Wahl 1999.

[32] The traditional interpretation (when the question is taken up at all) is that the orphans' property
mentioned in 2 Macc. 3:10 was in fact a portion set aside from the regular tithe collected from the
people of Israel for the poor (e.g. Abel 1949: 319–20 with reference to Deut. 14:25, 29).

   Furthermore, 2 Macc. 8:28 notes that after the victory over Nicanor part of the loot was given over
to the widows and orphans. While this gesture clearly relates to the regular allotment from the tithe,
such extraordinary grants were probably uncommon.

the father (at least with respect to religious education) and was obviously quite successful. However, Tobit's support for the orphans ultimately traces back not merely to empathy stemming from his own experience, but also to the commandments of the Pentateuch.[33] Another hint as to the possible thought-world that supported the care of orphans in the Old Testament is found in the Wisdom of Ben Sirach, who associates his exhortation with the principle that one reaps what one sows: "To the fatherless be as a father ... Thus will you be like a son to the Most High, and he will be more tender to you than a mother" (4:10).[34]

Unfortunately, we lack Jewish sources for fatherlessness during the NT era, but the unbroken continuation of the OT guidelines, rearticulated by rabbinic Judaism, clearly indicates that they retained their force throughout this period.[35]

FATHERLESSNESS IN THE NEW TESTAMENT

As with the Old Testament, when attempting a sociological or historical inquiry into a phenomenon such as fatherlessness in the New Testament, one must always bear in mind that it is a theologically charged text. This is especially important as the theological mindset of the NT Christians was particularly significant for their social behavior. Most of the older scholar-ship on fatherlessness in early Christian society discounts it as a social problem for the early Christians: since they were eagerly anticipating the imminent arrival of the *parousia*, or the Second Coming, they were not

---

[33] Cf. Schüngel-Straumann 2000: 55–8.   [34] Cf. Beentjes 1998; Sauer 2000: 70.

[35] The Babylonian Talmud considers the raising of orphans as particularly praiseworthy: "Whoever brings up an orphan in his home, Scripture ascribes it to him as though he had begotten him" (bSanh. 19b; bMeg. 13a). Moreover, this kind of care was seen as the right way to practice uninterrupted *zedaka* (charity): "Happy are they that keep justice, that do righteousness at all times [Ps. 106:3]. Is it possible to do righteousness at all times? ... This refers to a man who brings up an orphan boy or orphan girl in his house and enables them to marry" (bKetub. 50a). Further evidence from the Babylonian Talmud suggests something of an established welfare system for orphans, one which is deeply rooted in OT ethics, but which seems far more elaborate than anything that existed previously. For instance, the court adopts a prominent role in many cases, asserting: "the court is the father of orphans" (bB.Qam. 37a; cf. Maim., Yad, Nahalot 10:5). Among other things, we find the court assigning guardians for fatherless orphans in such cases when the father had not determined one. This guardian was apparently selected with great care and he had to see to all physical, mental, and religious needs of his ward (see the regulations in bGit. 52; cf. Grunwald 1922: 11). As before, destitute orphans were supported by a relief fund (cf. Grunwald 1922: 12), but it is remarkable that girls not only could receive dowries from the fund but were in fact preferred over boys, who had no claim to alimentation if the fund did not suffice for the girls (cf. bKetub. 76ab). Furthermore, if the community was wealthy enough, orphans were to receive alimentation commensurate to their social class and former standard of living (yKetub. 6:5 and bKetub. 67b). Finally, the charitable attitude of early rabbinic Judaism toward orphaned children is well documented by many anecdotes, see Grunwald 1922: 13–14.

likely to be concerned with the social problems of this world.[36] This thesis is not to be dismissed lightly. In fact, the later NT texts, representing the third and fourth generations of Christians, are more apt to seize on social problems and offer solutions to them than are earlier texts. Of course, this does not change the fact that such problems had to be faced, if not resolved, in the first two generations of Christians as well.

The existence of fatherlessness as a social problem in this era cannot be doubted. At about the same time as the first NT texts were being composed and collected, we find Seneca in Rome explaining that only a few parents could expect to reach an age when they would be able to enjoy the gratitude of their own children (*Ben.* 5.5.2). In the next generation Plutarch pointed out that the majority of the fathers died before seeing the end of their children's education (*Mor.* 496e). Most scholars now agree that husbands were in fact more likely to die before all of their children were of age.[37] This demographic pattern was largely attributable to two factors: the age differential at the time of marriage (with men typically being five to ten years older than their wives on average) and the fact that most women would have experienced multiple pregnancies until menopause. Depending on the particular conditions, it is now assumed that between 28 and 37 percent of all individuals had already lost their fathers by age fifteen.[38] There is no *prima facie* reason why the early Christians should have constituted a demographic exception in the Roman Empire.

The demographic fact of fatherlessness raises many important questions as to how the early Christians coped with this phenomenon. For instance, who took over the duties of the father after his death: the mother, relatives of the father, guardians? How did it affect inheritance and succession? Did the position of the fatherless change when they attained majority, and if so, how?[39] Unsurprisingly, we learn practically nothing about questions such as these from the NT texts themselves. As the early Christians were a natural element of their society and shared the same basic assumptions as their pagan contemporaries, they felt no need to comment on what would have seemed obvious to them and their audience.[40] Furthermore, not all Christian communities were the same. Thus, even though one cannot often discern such differences in the New Testament itself, one must nevertheless remember

---

[36] E.g. Hasler 1966: 2133.

[37] For a rigorous discussion of the relevant demography, see Scheidel (this volume). Cf. Krause 1994–5: III, 4–5.

[38] Cf. Scheidel (this volume): 31–6.

[39] See the older, but nonetheless still useful, cross-cultural overview of Weiler 1980.

[40] See Krause 1994–5, vol. III. A study dedicated to the legal rights of Jewish orphans in the NT era is still lacking. See Cohn 1920.

that the Christian communities of Asia Minor were generally well integrated in their Roman-Hellenistic environment, while those of Palestine stayed close to their Jewish heritage and its traditional way of life. That being said, irrespective of their cultural setting, the NT texts address some basic aspects of fatherlessness. One may in fact see the New Testament as somewhere halfway between the OT law and the more fully formed welfare institutions of the Church in late antiquity.[41]

As we learn from many chapters in this volume, the loss of a father in the ancient Mediterranean brought with it the risk of impoverishment, some- times even if the child was old enough to care for him- or herself: the deceased father might have outstanding debts for which his children were liable; there could be funeral expenses to pay; any inheritance might be dispersed too widely among the surviving heirs; the children might not have sufficient experience yet to pursue their father's vocation; and so on. Of course, for orphans who still were minors the threat of poverty was much greater, especially if for some reason they did not have a guardian – or worse, if the guardian took advantage of them and misappropriated the orphan's property.[42] Furthermore, the problems associated with fatherlessness were not only material, but social as well: orphaned girls had greater difficulty in arranging marriages, particularly within the social stratum they originally inhabited; while some orphaned boys found it more difficult to pursue an education.[43] In the upper strata the structure of the ancient extended *familia* often helped to mitigate the consequences of losing one's father; but orphans from the lower reaches of society were frequently left to the widow to raise (if she was still alive), who could be overwhelmed by the burden.[44] As a result, for most of antiquity orphans were thought of as young people at the mercy of others and constantly threatened by poverty.[45]

---

[41] On the latter, see Nathan (this volume).

[42] The ancient sources show that it was often difficult for underage children who had been taken advantage of in this way by their guardians to find a supporter outside the family (cf. Krause 2002: 379).

[43] On the latter, see Cribiore in this volume, who finds that elite orphans with strong extended families were able to continue in their studies.

[44] See Krause 1994–5: III, 194. Krause here notes that poorer widows and orphans evinced a much stronger reciprocal dependency on each other than do their wealthier counterparts. On this, see also Hübner (this volume). Unfortunately, the Biblical texts give us no information about the possibility or incidence of mothers acting as guardians. However, as far as Jews of this period are concerned, we may assume that the practice was similar to later rabbinic regulations, in which a mother could be designated as the guardian of her child by her spouse's will (e.g. bB.Bat. 131b; bGit. 52a; tB.Bat. 8.17). In this case, she acted like a regular *epitropos*.

[45] See, e.g., Isae. *Or.* 5.9–11; Dem. *Or.* 27.6–8; 27.63–6; Diod. Sic. 19.8.3–5; Epict. 3.24.14–15; Tert. *De Anim.* 1.2 (*CCL* 2.781–2); Gregory of Tours, *Hist.* 9.35; Jo. Chrys. *In Psalm.* 108.1 (Migne, *PG* 55.258–9). See above, n. 21.

The few NT texts that do mention fatherlessness seem at first sight so superficial – if one disregards their contexts – as to be merely literary reflections of the Old Testament. Thus, James says in his epistle: "Religion (θρησκείαι) that God our Father accepts as pure and faultless is this: to look after (ἐπισκέπτεσθαι) orphans (ὀρφανούς) and widows (χήρας) in their distress and to keep oneself from being polluted by the world" (1:27). The support of orphans – financial or in any other capacity – is thus offered as an example of good Christian behavior.[46] The fact that the author chooses as his example of righteousness the care of widows and orphans is quite revealing for the social relevance of the problem in the early Christian community. It is, of course, not unreasonable to see the author here as using the examples of widows and orphans not in a literal sense, but rather as symbols for all those who were hard-pressed and exposed to lawless force. But the subsequent history of Christian charity and care suggests that we are dealing here with more than just a literary motif. For instance, in 1 Clement to the Corinthians 8:4, a text roughly contemporaneous with the Epistle of James, we may see a link between OT precedents and injunctions and the early Christian establishment of a welfare system, which was more tightly focused on orphans.

We may see the contrapositive of James's formula in the Epistle of Barnabas, who places *not* caring for orphans in a litany of other evil deeds (Barn. 20:2).[47] Even if one wishes to understand this passage primarily as a literary *imitatio* of an OT phrase,[48] or even of James himself, such an interpretation can be excluded by seeing the phenomenon in light of other texts. For instance, Ignatius polemicizes against a representative of some unidentified, but clearly less charitable theological school, which did not advocate the care of orphans (*Epistula ad Smyrnaeos* 6:2).[49] This, of course, implies that Ignatius' community saw itself as duty-bound to provide such care. Similarly, Polycarp reminds the presbyter of the Christian community at Philippi not to disregard his duties towards an orphan (*Epistula ad Philippenses* 6:1).[50]

---

[46] Cf. Mussner 1964: 112; Maier 2004: 94–103.

[47] Interestingly, the care for widows and orphans is one of the attributes that Barnabas adds to those addressed by the *Didache*. See Prostmeier 1999: 558–9.

[48] A particularly clear example of literary interplay between NT and OT texts on orphans is 1 Clem. 8:4, where one finds Isa. 1:16–20 of the LXX quoted. But of course, the use of this phrase does not contradict the social engagement of the early Christians. Rather it underscores how strongly the early Christian ethic was affected by OT guidelines. Cf. Lona 1998: 186–9, esp. 188.

[49] On Ignatius' strategy of listing his opponents' several pastoral shortcomings in order to illuminate their basic spiritual inadequacy, see Bauer and Paulsen 1985: 95; see also Schödel 1990: 372–5.

[50] See Bauer and Paulsen 1985: 119; Bauer 1995: 56.

Perhaps the earliest textual evidence we have of an organized system specifically dedicated to the care of orphans comes from a passage of *Hermas* (*Visions* 2.4.3 [= 8.3]), in which their religious education is explicitly stressed. The injunction to care for widows and orphans (καὶ χήρας καὶ ὀρφανοὺς ἐπισκέπτεσθε) at *Hermas*, *Similitudes* 1.8 (= 50.8) probably contains yet another reminiscence of James 1:27,[51] thus referring back to the authority of the NT epistle and to a social-historical relevance in early Christian times. Many Biblical scholars believe that this passage assigns the task of caring for orphans to the deacons of the early Church.[52] However, in light of other passages in *Hermas* it is obvious that caring for orphans was seen by the author as work generally pleasing to God and an ethical duty for all Christians.[53]

Unfortunately, we know nothing about the particular manner in which this welfare system was organized, but it most probably included financial aid of some sort, for the early Christians were well aware of the material support that parents usually supplied to their children. 2 Corinthians 12:14 is most precise in this matter: "After all, children should not have to save up (θησαυρίζειν) for their parents, but parents for their children."[54] The relationship Paul here describes between parents and children (in this case, employed as a metaphor of what he sees as the similar relationship between a missionary and the Christian community) is obviously characterized in terms of material obligations, with the principal emphasis on financial responsibility.[55] Just as children are obliged to support their aged parents, so parents must care for their children who are not yet self-sufficient. If the family's breadwinner (almost always the father in antiquity) suddenly disappeared, there was obviously a dangerous shortfall in the family economy. This shortfall could be made up, however, if the father's extended family consented to take in the newly fatherless children and raise them, and indeed this seems often to have been the default in such a situation.[56] Much less frequently we hear of the unusual step of orphaned children following their mother into her new house after her remarriage.[57] The demand in 1 Timothy

---

[51] See Brox 1991: 46, 284.   [52] Cf. Brox 1991: 109.

[53] *Hermas, Mandates* 8.10 (= 38.10); *Sim.* 1.8 (= 50.8); 5.3.7 (= 56.7). See Brox 1991: 234, 288.

[54] Apparently, this was a common view in antiquity: see, e.g., Plut. *Mor.* 526a; Philo, *De Vita Mosis* 2.245. See also Yarbrough 1995: 134–5; Balla 2003: 186.

[55] See Gerber 2005: 213.   [56] See Hübner and Nathan, in this volume; cf. Krause 1994–5: III, 49–77.

[57] See Hübner in this volume; cf. Krause 1994–5: III, 33–48. Krause takes great pains to note that the nature of our sources does not permit us to determine the precise ratio of children who went to live with their relatives versus those who entered into the homes of their stepfathers (cf. Hübner [this volume]: 78–9, with specific reference to Roman Egypt). However, one should imagine that this ratio was likely to have been affected by local differences. Thus those Church Fathers who attempted to dissuade widows with children from remarrying appear to have assumed that their fatherless children would be accepted into the house of their new stepfather.

that young widows remarry, and not be fed by the community (5:14), makes much more sense in light of such a practice: the author does not bother to mention children since it would be assumed that any orphans would be provided for by their paternal families.[58] Another option known from ancient Palestine was for the widow to return to her parental home together with her children.[59] And yet another common response of some widows to the loss of their husbands was to stay with their children in the house of the deceased and provide for themselves from some patrimony (either the dead father's or the mother's own).[60] Although we lack unequivocal proof from the sources that from time to time Christian widows did indeed head households in the place of adult males, certain episodes in the Gospels imply just such a scenario, such as the raising of a widow's son in Naïn (Luke 7:11–17) or the faithful Canaanite woman (Matt. 15:21–8, cf. Mark 7:24–30).

Notwithstanding such escape routes from the consequences of fatherlessness, the Christian injunction to care for orphans indicates that at least some fatherless children became destitute – almost certainly those who were not integrated into new families. Unlike the more regimented Jewish distribution system in place during the Second Temple period described above, the amount of individual contributions for Christian orphans was apparently left to the discretion of the donor. For instance, in the second century Justin Martyr (*Apol.* 1.67) says that "those who have in abundance … give freely, each as he wills, and what is collected is given over to him who presides, and he aids the orphans and widows (καὶ αὐτὸς ἐπικουρεῖ ὀρφανοῖς τε καὶ χήραις)." We find an even more well-organized orphan-welfare system in the late second century, when Tertullian informs us of a fund "to aid the boys and the girls who have neither fortune nor parents" (*Apol.* 39).[61] Although the New Testament is generally silent about such institutions, the Epistles and

---

[58] Cf. Roloff 1988: 298–300; Neudorfer 2004: 196–7. Christianity here follows the example of its environment: "Younger women are to follow the societal and legal requirements for women of their age so that the Christian reputation will be preserved" (Schüssler-Fiorenza 1983: 312).

[59] See Perdue 1997: 194. However, the situation is not as clear as one would hope. Perdue refers to Lev. 22:13, Gen. 38:11, and Ruth 1:8 as evidence for this custom. True, such verses prove that a woman had the possibility to return to her father's home, but the women mentioned in these passages are all childless! In fact, Lev. 22:13 explicitly states that the woman has to be without a child. Also, Lev. here is referring solely to the daughters of priestly families. However, in the commentary to this passage in mYebam. 7.4a and bYebam. 67b–68a, one finds that a widowed daughter of a priest may have had open to her the possibility of returning home even if she had her child with her. Unfortunately, we have no discussion either in these passages or in Scripture generally of non-priestly widows, so we cannot say what the usual practice was for them.

[60] Cf. Perdue 1997: 194.

[61] It is remarkable that similar pagan welfare institutions were established at almost the same time as Christian ones. Under the reigns of Nerva and Trajan, for example, we have evidence of several alimentary foundations for the relief of destitute children, obviously including poor orphans. Under

Acts often point to the existence of similar relief funds for the poor, including destitute orphans.[62]

Another way of helping orphans endorsed by the early Christians was to take such children into their homes. By the second half of the fourth century at the latest the Church was actively urging its members to take in and educate orphans and similarly to donate dowries for orphaned girls (*Constitutio Apostolica* 4:1–2). This practice ultimately may be traced back to one of Jesus' sayings in the New Testament: at Matthew 18:5 (cf. Mark 9:37) he says: "And whoever will receive one such child in my name receives me."[63] Although the passage does not speak of orphans per se, the context suggests that the children he is speaking about have no provider. Of course, this social-historical interpretation of the text is debatable, since the main point of the entire passage is theological.[64] For instance, one cannot fail to notice that Jesus' overall message is that Christians must become as humble as little children (παιδία) in order to enter into the Kingdom of Heaven. But here, as in so many of Jesus' calls to charitable action, we may see his theological statements bound up with a specific social agenda.[65] Nor was this integration of the social and the theological accidental or coincidental: the Evangelist Matthew frequently takes an interest in the situation of children. As Eltrop demonstrates, Matthew mentions that children could lose their means of support by circumstances other than the death of their father, as, for instance, in following the call of an itinerant preacher.[66] Thus the children mentioned in Matthew 18:5 need not have been orphans in the usual sense, though they appeared to have been nonetheless fatherless. In the parallel passage of Mark it is also uncertain whether the children are orphans or whether they had been left or abandoned by their parents for other reasons.[67] Whatever the specific circumstances they had in mind,

---

Antoninus Pius we find several foundations dedicated particularly to girls. See Weiler 1980: 186 with reference on Mrozek 1973. For further bibliography on the *alimenta*, see Nathan (this volume): 275, and the Introduction: 14, n. 48.

[62] See for instance the (certainly idealizing) testimony in Acts 2:44–7, 4:32–7, 5:1–10. For widows, see 1 Tim.

[63] NIV: "And whoever welcomes a little child like this in my name welcomes me."

[64] See Luck 1993: 201; cf. Nolland 2005: 729–34, esp. 733; and France 2002: 374–5 on the parallel passage in Mark.

[65] Thus Luz assumes that Matt. 18:5 refers to "the taking in of a real child" (1997: 15). He explicitly points out that the meaning of this verse differs from that of Matt. 10:40, where the context suggests that hospitality to itinerant preachers is meant. However, Luz wishes to leave open whether this act is intended as "one of guest-friendship, toward homeless and parentless children, or in some figurative sense as one of adoption of children who have a home" (1997: 16). Regarding Mark 9:37, Schüssler-Fiorenza (1983: 149) notes: "This form of the tradition would seem to reflect a very concrete situation in which the community took care of its baptized children."

[66] Eltrop 1996: 120. [67] See Stegemann 1980: 129.

both Evangelists obviously speak of real, and not merely metaphorical, children who have lost their place in the *oikoi* of their parents, and who were therefore fatherless. With Eltrop I agree that it is impossible to determine whether Matthew 18:5 refers to the outright adoption of orphans or the children of slaves, or instead to some form of temporary accommodation of homeless street urchins, and similarly that "as both a permanent and temporary abode for children, the Christian household represented for them a definite source of protection."[68] While the precise status of these children must remain ambiguous, their common need was certain, so they were counted among those who had a claim to aid according to Christian principles.[69]

After poverty and defenselessness, abandonment is the theme most often linked to fatherless children in early Christianity.[70] In the New Testament this image is evoked by Jesus himself. For instance, in John 14:18 he comforts his disciples in his final instructions before his apprehension by the authorities: "I will not leave you as orphans; I will come to you." Referring to John 13:13, where the disciples are called "children," some scholars here see Jesus also representing himself as a father-figure, though this is a questionable interpretation: to the best of my knowledge this title is reserved for God alone.[71] In any event, this theological point is unimportant for the purposes of this investigation.[72] The force of the metaphor comes from the Evangelist's comparing the disciples without Jesus to children abandoned by their father, although the nature of the abandonment is not made clear. However, the verse does not depict any of the specific consequences of abandonment, such as impoverishment, but rather it is the abandonment itself that is stressed, as the final clause, "I will come to you," shows. The scenery of the passage is redolent with an atmosphere of a loss and suggests all the future consequences attendant on such a catastrophe.

The New Testament thus first addresses the problem of fatherlessness as we should expect, theologically. Just as the Old Testament understands

---

[68] Eltrop 1996: 181–2; cf. 183, n. 530: "The early Christian practice of taking in orphans meant in the first instance that children otherwise unprovided for received a secure place to live, and were not simply provided with alms." The protection character becomes particularly clear in the Syriac recension of Aristides' *Apologia*: "and they rescue the orphan from him who does him violence" (15.7; cf. the Greek recension: "they despise not the widow, nor oppress the orphan.").

[69] Cf. Eltrop 1996: 122.

[70] See, e.g., Pl. *Phd.* 116a; Lucian, *De mort. Peregr.* 6; *Vita Antonii* 88.4; Jo. Chrys. *Epistulae ad Olympiadem* 8.12b; Gregory of Tours, *Hist.* 2.23; Sulpicius Severus, *Ep.* 3.10.

[71] See Keener 2003: 943–6. For another interpretation, see Schnackenburg 2001: 88; cf. Wengst 2001: 123: "Jesus speaks here not as a father to his children, but as a teacher to his students."

[72] On the theological background, see Beasley-Murray 1999: 258.

God as the protector of the orphans, so the New Testament sees Christ as coming for all those who have been abandoned and who through his coming are no longer alone (John 14:18; 2 Cor. 4:9–10). But the verb *episkeptesthai* in James 1:27 suggests that the Christian community was already seeking to alleviate not only the material deprivation suffered by many orphans, but also the psychological loneliness that afflicted the fatherless. Again, to put such texts in their proper context, we must look beyond the texts themselves to the larger arc of the history of Christian charity. So, as Aristides notes (*Apol.* 15.7f–8), Christians were in the habit of visiting the children of imprisoned martyrs (cf. Jesus' instructions concerning ministration at Matt. 15:35). Therefore, within Christian communities the abandonment of the fatherless (as well as of any other oppressed group) was ameliorated not only by financial support from the community, but also by constant social interaction.

The author of the Letter to the Hebrews represents Melchizedek, the king and high priest of Jerusalem,[73] as an image of the Son of God, in order to prove that Jesus' own anomalous high priesthood had a scriptural precedent.[74] In this context Melchizedek is characterized in Hebrews 7:3 as: "Without father or mother, without genealogy, without beginning of days or end of life, like the Son of God he remains a priest forever." Again, I shall leave the deeper theological import of this passage to one side in order to concentrate on what the phrase "without father, without mother, without genealogy" can tell us about the social reality of the fatherless.[75] Here we see the passage addressing the identity of a person, and further that this identity is defined by a certain genealogy, which in turn is defined primarily by the identity of the father. The immediate problem of Hebrews 7:3 is that priests were obliged to establish their genealogies in order to serve as priests; those without the appropriate pedigree (ὁ δὲ μὴ γενεαλογούμενος, Heb. 7:6) were duly excluded from priesthood.[76]

The importance of this genealogical identity for the society in which the early Christians lived is frequently attested by the NT texts.[77] For instance, Jesus' genealogy comes at the beginnings of the Gospels of Matthew (1:1–17) and Luke (3:23–37) as a sort of programmatic statement. In Matthew 13:55,

---

[73] Cf. Gen. 14:17–20 in the LXX.   [74] See Gräßer 1993: 11.

[75] For theological exegesis, see Bensel 2005; cf. Craddock 1998: 86–7 and DeSilva 2000: 266.

[76] On this law, cf. Num. 3:10, 15–16, 17:5; Lev. 21:7, 13, 15; Ezek. 44:22; Neh. 7:63–4; Joseph, *AJ* 11.71. See also Bensel 2005: 23.

[77] For the importance of a genealogical identity in other ancient societies, cf. Pratt (this volume) on Homeric heroes and Golden (this volume) regarding Classical Greek antiquity, esp. 41: "Cecrops, it seems, discovered paternity as a biological fact and then presided over its establishment as a prime marker of social identity." Cf. Nathan (this volume): 105–11.

Jesus' identity is defined primarily by his relationship to his relatives, especially his father, the carpenter. Similarly, the brothers James and John, two of his first disciples, are introduced as the sons of Zebedee (Matt. 4:21). Even a social nonentity such as the beggar Bartimaeus is characterized by the name of his father, Timaeus (Mark 10:46). We see that the identity of a person is therefore fundamentally determined by one's father, as was almost always the case in antiquity. The actual genealogical filiation was thus vital to one's identity, far more so than one's social environment, which is so often thought of today as having a more formative influence on the development of an individual's personality. Paul insists that "even though you have ten thousand guardians (παιδαγωγούς) in Christ, you do not have many fathers, for in Christ Jesus I became your father (ἐγέννησα) through the gospel" (1 Cor. 4:15).[78] This was especially so if the fatherlessness has its origin in an extramarital birth, leaving the bastard child without any legitimate genealogy at all. We do not learn much about the various practical consequences of this lack of identity from the New Testament, but obviously they had great consequences for such a child for the rest of his or her life.[79] Among those who never had known their father we likewise encounter the feeling of abandonment. In addition, it was not only the lack of a father, but also the ignorance of one's descent that could represent a decisive social disadvantage.

Finally, orphans were not always destitute, nor did they have to be infants or adolescents. The NT texts seldom shed light upon the lot of grown-up men and women without fathers, but when they do it is clear that such fatherless people had to shoulder heavy responsibilities. For example, an adult male might have suddenly found himself thrust into the role of head of household. We may see just such an instance in the story of Jesus raising a widow's son in Luke 7:11–17.[80] For our purposes, it is important to note the emphasis placed on the mother's grief. At Luke 7:12 she is explicitly characterized as a widow, one who has now also lost her only son. The

---

[78] Here Paul emphasizes the uniqueness of this relationship by metaphorically establishing himself as the biological father (*gennān*) of the "child," which is the Christian community at Corinth. His role as progenitor qualifies him as exceptional, while he relegates a good deal of Christian education to certain other *paidagōgoi*. Cf. Gerber 2005: 409–10, and esp. 411: "The father remains a father, regardless of whether he is alive or dead; guardians, however, once they have discharged their duties, become irrelevant."

[79] Vice versa, an honorable descent could be used in order to distinguish the quality of a person and the integrity of his (or her) identity. Cf. the remarks of Josephus on his grandparents and father at the beginning of his *Vita* (1–2).

[80] Cf. Schürmann 2001: 405. In its content and narrative technique this story borrows from 1 Kings 17:10, 17–24. On this, see Nolland 1989: 320–5.

large crowd of people who had gathered to commiserate with the widow signals the significance of his death to the widowed mother he left behind. In this respect we may see a connection between this passage and other ancient evidence that represents women after their husbands' deaths as emotionally and financially dependent on their adolescent or adult sons, in whose households they often lived.[81] Apart from the other basic functions of a head of household, these fatherless men, among them the young man from Naïn before his untimely death, took responsibility for supporting their aging mothers. Without her only son the widow from Naïn was left without protection and financial support in her old age.[82] Although the passage does not give us much background information, it reminds us that we must remember that through their fathers' death most young men became fathers themselves – heads of household in their own right.

FATHERLESSNESS IN THE NEW TESTAMENT, FATHERLESSNESS TODAY

The present survey shows that the problems of fatherlessness in the New Testament are not comparable to those of modern fatherlessness in all aspects. While the OT and NT texts direct their attention to minor children whose fathers had died,[83] the modern discussion focuses on a fatherlessness that derives from a fairly recent pluralization of family values and structures.[84] Also, as we have seen, both the Old Testament and the New Testament remain quite general on most questions of social history, and the phenomenon of fatherlessness is no exception to this rule. Furthermore,

---

[81] See Krause 1994–5: III, 223, 273.

[82] Loss of protection: Krause 1994–5: III, 223; financial loss: Schürmann 2001: 398–405; Eckey 2004: 338–44.

[83] This is at least suggested by the frequent contextualization of widows and orphans. We perhaps have to assume, that some fathers left their families in order to become itinerant preachers, but there is no evidence for this in the NT sources.

[84] For example, in 2000 51.5 percent of the children in East Germany and 18.6 percent of the children in West Germany were born out of wedlock. For all German families with children under age eighteen, 15.4 percent were headed by single parents without any partner living in the same household. See the report put out by the Bundesministerium für Familie, Senioren, Frauen und Jugend, entitled *Die Familie im Spiegel amtlicher Statistik. Lebensformen, Familienstrukturen, wirtschaftliche Situation der Familien und familiendemographische Entwicklung in Deutschland.* (2003: 77). Other developed Western nations exhibit the same trends: some useful data about the USA has been collected by the National Center for Fathering (www.fathers.com/research/extent.html), but beware that this is not a US government institution, but a private foundation whose mission is "to improve the well-being of children by inspiring and equipping men to be more effectively involved in the lives of children." It was founded "in response to a dramatic trend towards fatherlessness in America" in 1990. On the issue of fatherlessness in the United States, see the Introduction to this volume.

these texts are avowedly theological: although this fact is often a hindrance to the social historian looking to describe the social conditions of Biblical antiquity, it proves a strong point from the perspective of dealing with modern fatherlessness. The relationship of modern Christian ethics to ancient family values and structures always raises the question of the relevance and applicability of such vastly different cultural conditions to modern life.[85] However, the Biblical statements on fatherlessness are so basic as to transcend the particulars of time or culture.

Deriving from the OT literature, the NT texts emphasize that it was a believer's duty to care for the fatherless, who were not able to care for themselves. This duty encompassed both financial support and social care, such as offering protection in the courts or visitations. The New Testament further encourages the taking in of such children, even though the precise legal nature of this sort of "adoption" remains unclear. Given the background of Jewish parallels, some form of adoption seems likely, although it is not the only possible interpretation and it is never termed as such, *expressis verbis*, in the New Testament. As a further consequence of the nature of our sources, though we may see that charitable response of the early Christians toward fatherlessness in large part grew out of the elaborate Jewish welfare system of the Second Temple period, the differences and divergences between the two as Jewish guidelines and laws were adapted to the new circumstances of the growing Christian communities cannot be precisely determined. In the final analysis, any investigation of fatherlessness in the New Testament does not tell us very much about how such welfare for fatherless children was organized but reveals the important fact that it was highly valued by the early Christians. These texts therefore show not only that in the Christian communities of the NT era caring for the fatherless was an integral part of religious life – part and parcel of what it meant to follow Christ – but also that this religious and moral program found expression in the practice of daily life.

---

[85] This question is discussed in Osiek 1996; Barton 1998; and Purvis 1998.

PART II

Virtual fatherlessness

CHAPTER 6

Bastardy and fatherlessness in ancient Greece

Daniel Ogden

When Diogenes saw the son of a prostitute hurling stones into a crowd he admonished him with the words, "Watch out, young man, lest you wound your father, whom you clearly do not know."[1] To link the terms "bastardy" and "fatherlessness" in the modern West is to conjure up images of such children of unmarried lone mothers, with their biological fathers either unidentifiable or long gone. Children of this sort, who might be termed "mother's bastards," presumably were to be found, albeit scarcely, across the broad span of the ancient Greek world, but we have little information about them. Almost all the bastards – the principal term in ancient Greek is *nothos* – that we do hear about, real or imaginary, are rather "father's bastards."[2] That is to say, it is in connection with their fathers that they are named and identified. We hear typically of "X, the bastard of father Y," as opposed to "X, the bastard of mother Z." This pattern of evidence might initially suggest that there is no place for a chapter on Greek bastardy in a volume devoted to fatherlessness, but place there is indeed, for despite bastards' connections, loose or tight, with their fathers, the concept of bastardy was nonetheless often strikingly imbued with the imagery of fatherlessness. In the first part of this study, we will look at the tendency of Classical Athenian culture to construct a legal, social, religious, and even physical distance between a father and his bastard child. In the second part we will look at a range of myths

---

[1] Eustathius on Hom. *Il.* 24.49; cf. Kindstrand 1990: no. 16.

[2] For bastardy in general in the ancient Greek world see Ogden 1996; a revised version of chapter 3 is to be found in Ogden 1997b. A more systematic account of the *gynaikonomoi*, treated in an appendix in Ogden 1996, is now to be found in Ogden 2002. The subject as a whole is approached from a slightly different angle in Ogden 1995. The link between the imagery of bastardy and deformity is discussed in Ogden 1997a. The special case of bastardy – or allegations thereof – in the context of the Hellenistic dynasties is discussed by Ogden 1999. Published subsequently to 1996, though evidently drafted somewhat before this year, are the useful discussions of the social and legal aspects of illegitimacy and related matters in Cox 1998: 170–89 (Classical Athens) and Patterson 1998 (the wider Greek world). The literary aspects of Ogden 1996 are now supplemented by Ebbott 2003. Despite its promising title, Hartmann 2000 has little to say about bastardy as such. Of pre-1996 material, much of value is still to be found in Wolff 1944; Vatin 1970; Humphreys 1974; Patterson 1990.

which imagined bastardy as a variety of fatherlessness. In the words of the volume's editors, in the ancient Greek world bastardy could often be seen as a variety of "virtual fatherlessness."[3]

But before we begin, let us make it clear that the term *nothos* applied equally to "father's bastards" and "mother's bastards" alike. Detlev Lotze contended that the term *nothos* almost always denoted a relationship with the father rather than the mother. After him Cynthia Patterson, reviewing the uses of the term *nothos* from Homer onwards, observed that, "Typically the *nothos/ē* is the child of a concubine and is known and acknowledged as such by his or her father."[4] These generalizations do indeed account for the bulk of extant references to *nothoi* in the Greek world, but a series of texts, all produced in Classical Athens, demonstrate that the term *nothos* also embraced "mother's bastards." First, Ion, in Euripides' play of that name written shortly before 412 BC, knows nothing of his father's identity and is unaware of any relationship with him (the father in question transpires to be the god Apollo). When he learns that he is the child of Creusa, who was raped when a virgin, he declares himself to be "the *nothos* child of an unmarried woman" (*nothon … partheneuma*).[5] Secondly, Xenophon tells that in 400 BC Lysander successfully argued before the Spartans that Leotychidas was a *nothos* because he was not the son of his putative father, Agis, but rather the adulterine bastard of Agis' wife, Timaia, fathered by the Athenian Alcibiades. There is no suggestion that Alcibiades recognized the child as his *nothos*. In context it is clear that Lysander tied Leotychidas' *nothos* status rather to his relationship with his mother. Thirdly, in 351 BC Demosthenes referred to the mercenary leader Charidemus as a *nothos* in his home town of Oreos, on the basis that he had a citizen mother. Here, again, the status of *notheia* (bastardy) is clearly defined from the mother's point of view.[6] The word is so seldom found applied to mothers' bastards for two reasons. First, our sources are predominantly interested in relationships between males. Secondly, in practice individuals in the category of "mother's bastard" had very little chance of being brought to birth and then reared, at any rate by their own mothers.[7] Prostitutes' sons of the type supposedly addressed by Diogenes were no doubt

[3] It would be fatuous to attempt here a formal comparison of bastardy in Roman society, which was structured according to radically different principles. Suffice it to say that Roman bastardy was dominated by the phenomenon of military *spurii*, the recognized and cherished children of soldiers in stable and quasi-marital relationships. Soldiers were not permitted to make formal marriages before discharge. See Wolff 1945; Syme 1960; Youtie 1975; Rawson 1989; Watson 1989; Olsen 1999.
[4] Lotze 1981: 169–72; Patterson 1990: 41.   [5] Eur. *Ion* 1473, misinterpreted at Patterson 1990: 51, 67–8.
[6] See Ogden 1996: 15–17, with further arguments.
[7] For abortion in the ancient world see now Kapparis 2002, especially 91–132.

rareties. When good Athenian girls are impregnated by rapists or seducers in early Hellenistic New Comedy, the baby is exposed or given away.[8]

THE SEPARATION OF THE BASTARD FROM HIS FATHER IN CLASSICAL ATHENS

For all that most bastards identifiable as such may well have been father's bastards, children acknowledged (as bastard) by their father, produced in concubinal relationships, there was a developing tendency throughout the Archaic and Classical ages for such children to be separated from their fathers, be it literally or metaphorically, physically, legally, or socially.

Indeed, the tendency to separate the bastard from his father is latent in the term *gnēsios* already found in Homer. This term, cognate with *genos*, "family," and *gonos*, "seed," clearly meant at heart "of the blood." In Classical Athens it had two complements, *poiētos*, "adopted," which is a readily intelligible antithesis, and *nothos*, "bastard." When we find the term contrasted with *nothos*, it is of course appropriate for us to render it "legitimate," but we should not lose sight of its core meaning, and we may be sure that the Greeks did not. In short, the *gnēsios–nothos* opposition proclaimed that bastard children were somehow not of the blood of the man recognized to be their biological sire.[9]

Three Athenian laws ascribed to Solon, for what that is worth,[10] but certainly operative in the Classical period, sought to achieve a legal and social separation between a father and his *nothos*. To Solon, first, is attributed a definition of legitimacy often rehearsed in the Attic orators:

Whichever woman her father or brother born of the same father or paternal grandfather should betroth on a just basis to be a wife (*damar*), from this woman the children are to be legitimate (*gnēsioi*).[11]

The use of the Archaic term for "wife" (*damar*) and the oddly positive phraseology of the law speak of its antiquity. Nothing in this law as its text stands directly requires a separation between the *nothos* and his father, but a formal definition of the categories to be considered *nothos* is of course

---

[8] Thus, Menander *Heros, Hiereia, Perikeiromene, Samia*, Terence *Heautontimoroumenos*, Plautus *Truculentus*; see Powell 1988: 354–61 (= 2001: 364–72) and Ogden 1996: 106–10. We have little information bearing upon the fate of mother's bastards for the wider Greek world; non-royal bastards may have had a better chance of survival – insofar as they could be identified as such – in Sparta: see Ogden 1996: 217–51.

[9] See Ogden 1996: 17–18.   [10] See Ruschenbusch 1966.

[11] Dem. 44.49, 46.18; Hyp. 5.16. The law is F48b in Ruschenbusch's catalogue.

a prerequisite of and concomitant with the attempt to redefine the status of the *nothos*.[12]

In Aristophanes' *Birds* of 414, Heracles is excluded from the new foundation of Cloud-Cuckoo-Land on the basis that he is a *nothos* and therefore not entitled to succeed his father, Zeus. Pisthetaerus quotes a "law of Solon" at him:

A *nothos* may not have the participation-right-of-close-relatives (*anchisteia*) if there are legitimate (*gnēsioi*) children. But if there are no legitimate children, then the estate is to be shared by the nearest kin.[13]

Despite the absurdist comic context, the law quoted gives all appearances of being composed of genuine material: it is noteworthy that it stands outside the meter of the play. But the law's drift as quoted is illogical, and herein lies its comic effect. The first clause invites Heracles to believe that as a *nothos* he might aspire to succeed to his father if he has no legitimate siblings. But the second clause then dashes this expectation as the right of succession is made to leapfrog *nothoi* children and pass in the next instance to their fathers' wider collateral family (his brothers, nephews, etc.). The simplest interpretation is that two laws from different legal eras have been run together here, the first from an earlier period in which *nothoi* enjoyed some possibility of succession, and the second from a later point when they did not.[14] The exclusion of *nothoi* from formal succession of any kind is likely to have been the occasion of the introduction of the *notheia* or "bastard's portion," of which we learn from lexicographical sources. This was a limited sum of either 1,000 or 500 drachmas that a father was permitted to bequeath to his bastard children, either to each or in total, at his own discretion.[15] There is no indication – to address the issue of "social responsibility" – that a father was subjected to any social pressure to make such a bequest. It is difficult to get a sense of the significance of these amounts, but let us recall that in the Erectheum accounts of 407 BC a skilled workman is paid a drachma a day, and an unskilled laborer half that.[16] This would imply that for those of modest income the *notheia* limit would have been equivalent to something between two and five years' worth of wages: for such men, no mean sum.

This law, then, sought to dissolve a father's obligations of finance and maintenance toward his bastard children. Another law preserved by Plutarch

[12] See Ogden 1996: 37–8.
[13] Ar. *Av.* 1649–70. This text (in its totality) is F50a in Ruschenbusch's catalogue.
[14] See Ogden 1996: 34–7.
[15] Harp. s.v. *notheia* (1,000), *Suda* s.v. *epiklēros* (500), schol. Ar. *Av.* 1655–6 (500).
[16] *IG* 1.2 373–4.

(he takes it from Heraclides Ponticus) and again ascribed to Solon sought from the other end, as it were, to dissolve the *nothos* child's reciprocal obligations of finance and maintenance toward his father. It prescribed that:

children born of *hetairai* [presumably in effect "concubines," in such a context] should no longer have the duty of looking after their fathers.[17]

This pair of laws, taken together, speaks clearly of a desire to dissolve bonds of succession, finance, and maintenance comprehensively between fathers and their *nothoi*.

The separation sought between *nothos* and father was not merely financial. It was also religious and social. A law cited by both Demosthenes and Isaeus in the mid-fourth century as operative from the archonship of Euclid in 403 was doubtless a restatement or reformulation of a rather earlier law:

Neither male bastard (*nothos*) nor a female bastard (*nothē*) may have participation-right-of-close relatives (*anchisteia*) in the sacred and holy rites (*hiera kai hosia*) from the archonship of Euclid.[18]

The similarity in language between this and the "Solonian" law of Aristophanes' *Birds* invites us to suppose that a law of this sort originally derived from the same era. However, this law does not (directly at any rate) address economic succession, but rather the religious rites – and, more to the point, rights – that bound an Athenian family together, protected it, and, above all defined it. It seeks, then, to achieve a social and religious separation between a *nothos* and his father, and indeed his father's wider family.[19]

Separation from his father's family also ultimately entailed a bastard's separation from wider kinship groups and indeed the state itself, a "political" separation. In the Classical period the critical point of acceptance within or exclusion from the family and its rites seemingly fell on the tenth day after birth, the culmination of the *amphidromia* ceremony. On this day, the *dekatē*, the child's father publicly acknowledged the child and hosted a feast for relatives at which he presented the child to them. Demosthenes, speaking for Mantitheus, presents the supposed fact that Mantitheus' father had not performed a *dekatē* for his half-brother Boiotos, born of his mother's rival Plangon, as an indication of Boiotos' illegitimacy. So far as we can tell there was no formalized ceremony through which a father was

---

[17] Plut. *Sol.* 22.4 = Heraclides Ponticus F146 Wehrli. The law is F57 in Ruschenbusch's catalogue. Cf. Wolff 1944: 87; Patterson 1990: 51; Ogden 1996: 37, 39.
[18] Dem. 43.51 and Isae. 6.47.   [19] See Ogden 1996: 36.

able to recognize his *nothoi* children qua *nothoi*.[20] Nor was the father of a *nothos* normally able to include his illegitimate children in the rites of his phratry and his deme, participation in which eventually led to a child's recognition as a full citizen. At the first annual Apaturia after a legitimate son's birth, he was presented to a wider group, and one that exercised responsibilities on behalf of the central state, the pseudo-kinship group of the phratry. His father introduced him to the accompaniment of a *meion* sacrifice and an oath to the effect that he was introducing "his own legitimate (*gnēsios*) son, born of a married woman" or "born of a citizen woman who has been given in betrothal."[21] This introduction was almost certainly accompanied by an act of registration that was, in the long term, to be a critical factor in the eventual recognition of the child as a citizen of the Athenian state by his deme.[22]

The attempt to achieve a political separation between a father and his bastard is found also in the description of the "Constitution of Draco" in the famous *Constitution of Athens* (*Ath. Pol.*). This document is believed to be an archaizing confection pieced together from a range of genuinely historical laws. Within this, the *Constitution* describes the following measure:

They elected … as generals and cavalry commanders (hipparchs) those who proved that they had an unencumbered estate worth at least a hundred minas and their own legitimate (*gnēsioi*) children from a married woman who were over ten years old.[23]

Those who hold no land in a state cannot be trusted to guard the security and therefore stability of that state, upon which their continued enjoyment of their property must depend. Those whose land is mortgaged cannot be trusted to guard the stability of the state, for they may be tempted to seek revolution and the cancellation of debts. Children under ten remain susceptible to the diseases of childhood. A father cannot be confident that they will survive into adulthood and in due course be in a position to receive his land from him under the state's protection. Therefore, they cannot constitute a serious investment in the future stability of the state on his part. The law makes it clear that bastard children, similarly, young or grown, can constitute no investment in the future stability of the state on their father's part.[24] The rationale here may just be specific to succession: if a man has

---

[20] Dem. 39.24 (cf. also 39.20, 22); see Ogden 1996: 88–91.
[21] *IG* II.2 1237.109–11; Isae. 8.19; Dem. 57.54.
[22] Registration at *meion* is entailed by *IG* II.2 1237.118–22; for its importance, see Ogden 1996: 110–15.
[23] *Ath. pol.* 4.2.
[24] For a similar notion that (only) legitimate children constitute an investment in the future security and stability of the state, see the "Decree of Themistocles," Meiggs and Lewis 1969: no. 23, lines 20–2 (a third-century composition doubtless reflecting earlier material); cf., more broadly, Thuc. 2.44.3 (Pericles' Funeral Oration) and Din. 71.

only bastard children, he has less of an interest in the future stability of the state, since he cannot pass his land on to them under its protection. But the rationale is probably a broader one. Almost certainly *nothoi* are viewed as incapable of political succession to their father, in other words, they were debarred from citizenship itself. At the very least, they could not hope to follow their father easily into the offices of general or hipparch: the restrictions of the bastard's portion meant that their father was unable to bequeath to them the hundred minas they would need to acquire a qualifying estate for themselves.

Almost certainly, too, the exclusion of a *nothos* from his father's *hiera kai hosia*, sacred and holy rites, in itself also entailed exclusion from the state. When the Athenians came to grant the Plataeans citizenship, they were granted, as a prerogative of this citizenship, participation in the *hiera kai hosia*.[25]

It is possible that bastards were also separated from their fathers by name. It is possible that they were not normally permitted, or at any rate accorded, their father's name in patronymic. That is to say, they would not have been addressed or referred to with a phrase of the sort "X of Y." There is no simple example of an Athenian bastard's being accorded a patronymic, but the question is complicated not least by the uncertainties as to what sorts of expressions should be taken to constitute patronymics in the formal sense (e.g., did it count as a formal patronymic if one attached the father's name in the genitive not directly to the son's name, but to the word "son" in apposition to it, as in "X, *son* of Y"?).[26] Plutarch tells us that the Athenian people made an exceptional decree to legitimate Pericles' *nothos* son by the courtesan Aspasia after the death of his legitimate ones, and in so doing "allowed him to enrol him in the phratry lists and give him his own name, so that his name and stock should remain." Plutarch probably means by this that Pericles was permitted to confer his own name on his son as a patronymic, something that would not otherwise have been permitted for a bastard. However, it is a complication that the given name of the son concerned was, after the act of legitimation at any rate, also Pericles.[27]

And father's bastards were, it seems, often reared in a house physically separate from that of their father. In the Homeric poems the expectation seems to be that father's bastards will not normally be reared in their father's house. When Agamemnon addresses the bastard Teucer, he tells him that his father, Telamon, reared him and looked after him in his own house,

---

[25] Dem. 59.104; cf. Ogden 1996: 42, 98–100, where the argument, somewhat more complex than may be suggested here, is laid out in full.
[26] Discussion at Ogden 1996: 93–4.   [27] Plut. *Per.* 37.2 and 5; cf. Ogden 1996: 91–3.

"even though a *nothos*."[28] In more vague terms in the *Odyssey* Odysseus, in spinning a yarn about being the bastard son of a rich Cretan, claims that he was honored by his father on a par with his legitimate half-brothers, who then proceeded to mistreat him after his father's death. The context, for all that it is a lying one, again implies that such treatment was not the norm, or at any rate could not automatically be expected.[29]

There are numerous indirect indications that a man of Classical Athens was not expected to rear a *nothos* child in the house in which he lived with his legitimate wife. The implication of this is seemingly that concubinal *nothoi* born to a married man could not normally have expected to spend a great deal of time in their father's company. Apollodorus' famous adage, for all that it is confusingly vague about the role of concubines, *pallakai*, serves to make a fundamental point:

Courtesans (*hetairai*) we keep for pleasure, concubines (*pallakai*) for the daily care of our body, and wives to procreate children legitimately (*paidopoieisthai gnēsiōs*) and to have a trusty guardian of the things inside.[30]

The tie between the wife's legitimate procreation and the interior of the house is here made explicit, and the normal exclusion of courtesans and concubines is implicit. Even when unmarried men lived with courtesans or concubines, it is possible that it was thought improper that the *nothos* children they had by these women should be reared within the house in which they themselves were normally resident. The point is made by a lacunary passage of Menander's *Samia*. Here Demeas mistakenly believes that his courtesan Chrysis has had his child and begun to rear it behind his back, and he expresses his anger at this turn of events to his son Moschion with a sarcastic paradox:

MOSCHION: Why are you pulling a face?
DEMEAS: Why? Because I've been keeping a married courtesan (*gametēn hetairan*), as it seems, without realizing it.
MOSCHION: "Married?" How can that be? I don't understand what you're saying.
DEMEAS: A son has been born to me, as it seems, without my knowing anything about it … Well she can take it and get the hell out of the house.
MOSCHION: Don't do that!
DEMEAS: Why not? Do you expect me to rear a *nothos* inside my house for somebody else? … what you speak of is not at all in my character.[31]

---

[28] Hom. *Il.* 8.284. Sophocles on Teucer's bastardy: *Aj.* 1304. See Ogden 1996: 21–6.
[29] Hom. *Od.* 14.199–214.   [30] [Dem.] (i.e. Apollodorus) 59.122.   [31] Men. *Sam.* 129-36.

This exchange makes clear the radical separation in the roles of courtesan and concubines on the one hand, and wives on the other. It is the wife's part to bear children, not the courtesan's. It is the wife's part to rear her children in the house, not the courtesan's. Most striking is Demeas' strong implication that if he were to rear the *nothos* he would be rearing it for someone else as opposed to himself – presumably, in immediate context, his courtesan Chrysis. But there is also dramatic irony here, for the audience knows that the child is in fact Moschion's by another woman, and that it would in effect have been for Moschion that Demeas would have been rearing the child.[32]

There was no normal legal method by which a father could legitimate his *nothoi* children, except by marrying the child's mother, if he was permitted to do so. After Pericles' citizenship law and the reestablishment of its provisions in 403, this meant that the mother had to be a citizen woman. It is upon the premise of this possibility that many New Comic plots were resolved in the early Hellenistic period.[33] As we have seen, it took a special decree of the assembly to legitimate Pericles' *nothos* by his Milesian courtesan Aspasia, also called Pericles. Adoption offered no hope, for when one introduced an adopted son to one's phratry, one again had to swear an oath to the effect that he had been "born legitimately" (*gegonota orthōs*).[34] But it may have been possible for older families and richer families to smuggle their illegitimate offspring into a life of ostensible legitimacy and citizenship by various means. One such backdoor route to such a life may have been via the *genē*. Certain kinds of *genē*, whether they consisted principally of aristocratic families or of families that monopolized a range of priestly offices by right,[35] seem to have had a privileged, albeit shadowy, relationship with the phratries to which they were linked, and they may have been able to offer an easy route to legitimacy and citizenship for their members' bastard children. Either in the age of Pericles, as some believe, or rather earlier, perhaps in the Pisistratid period, as I prefer, it had been decreed that phratries should mandatorily accept members of *genē* into themselves.[36] This of itself suggests *genē* could exercise laxer admission criteria than phratries and that they could, henceforth, force their members, admitted according to laxer criteria, into the phratries. We have to wait until 399 to

[32] See Ogden 1996: 100–6.
[33] So end Menander's *Epitrepontes, Fabula Incerta, Georgos, Samia*, Plautus' *Aulularia* and *Truculentus*, and Terence's *Adelphoe* and *Andria*, amongst others. See Harrison 1968: II, 68–70 and, more generally, Brown 1990; Omitowoju 2002: 137–239; Lape 2004.
[34] E.g. Isae. 7.16; cf., more generally on adoption, Rubinstein 1993.
[35] Bourriot 1976 and R. C. T. Parker 1996, especially 56–66 and 282–342.
[36] Philoch. *FGrH* 328 F35ab; cf. Ogden 1996: 47–53; *pace*, e.g., Andrews 1961.

observe a *genos*'s admission procedures in action, and they do indeed appear to be laxer. In this year Callias was able to have his supposedly *nothos* son enrolled into his *genos* of the Ceryces by swearing to no more than that the boy was his own son *tout court*.[37] As for the mechanisms available to richer families, Apollodorus tells us of the rich Stephanus' supposedly illegitimate daughter Phano, born, as he alleges, of the courtesan Neaera. Both as illegitimate and indeed as the daughter of a non-citizen woman, she could not legally be given in marriage to an Athenian citizen. But Stephanus succeeded in persuading two poor Athenian men, Phrastor and Theogenes, to marry her in turn, doubtless with the enticement of a healthy dowry, and so to confer a spurious aura of legitimacy upon her. We bear in mind too Isaeus' observation that poverty often constrained men to make fraudulent adoptions of rich foreigners.[38]

GREEK MYTHICAL PROJECTIONS OF BASTARDY AND FATHERLESSNESS

The Athenians developed or adapted for themselves a number of myths that explained the development of the concept and institutions of legitimacy as arising out of an earlier condition in which all children had been fatherless. These myths, then, tended to give out the message that the illegitimate remained in some sense fatherless. Let us consider two.

First, the mythical founder of the Athenian state, Cecrops, was also held to have been the one who led the Athenians from a condition of promiscuous sex into a culture of marriage and thereby established a link of legitimacy between fathers and their children.[39] His dual form (he was a man above the waist and a snake below) came to be held as symbolic of the stable yoking of those heterogeneous creatures, man and woman, in marriage:

Some say that Cecrops was also of double nature, since he had the upper parts of a man, and the lower parts of a beast. Or that he found many laws for men and led them from wildness to civilization. Or that it had been the case that men had been having sex with women randomly, and that as a result of this sons were not known by their fathers, nor fathers by their sons, but he made laws that men should mix with women in a more public fashion, and be contented with one, and he

---

[37] Andoc. 1.126–7; cf. Ogden 1996: 115–17.
[38] [Dem.] 59.50, 72; Isae. 12.1. See Ogden 1996: 124 and 206; cf. also Trevett 1992: 100–2 and Patterson 1994: 207–9. More generally on Neaera, see Carey 1992; Kapparis 1999; Hamel 2003.
[39] Cf. Golden (this volume): 41.

discovered the two natures of the father and the mother, and was called "of double nature" on account of this.[40]

But Cecrops' twisted lower-body might also be considered emblematic still of the age before legitimacy, as will become clear. Compatible with Cecrops' establishment of marriage, we learn that it was under his rule too that women were comprehensively subjected to their husbands. Augustine, recycling Varro, notes that this was the point from which children were no longer permitted to take their mothers' name: in other words, this was the point at which (legitimate) children were first given their father's name, their patronymic.[41]

Secondly, the phratries' festival, at which legitimate children were introduced to their fellow phratrymen and recognized as such was, as we have seen, the Apaturia. Numerous foundation myths grew up for this festival.[42] One of particular interest, preserved by the twelfth-century AD *Etymologicum Magnum*, based itself upon a predictable folk-etymology of the festival's name:

Apaturia … In this festival the fathers registered their children who had been produced in that year, swearing that they were Athenians born of Athenians. Before this the children had appeared to be fatherless (*apatores*), but then they appeared to have fathers …[43]

The myth reads the initial alpha of *Apatouria* as privative, although it was in fact copulative, and the festival had all along been a festival of "those of the same fathers," as other ancient scholars realized.[44] However that may be, our Apaturia myth, like that of Cecrops, envisages the emergence of a regime of social order and legitimacy being born out of some sort of chaotic prehistoric condition in which no ties could be discerned between a father and his children.[45]

Wider Greek thinking about legitimacy tended to conceive of and represent it in terms of a metaphorical straightness and physical perfection, and bastardy concomitantly in terms of a metaphorical crookedness or

---

[40] Schol. Ar. *Plut.* 773.
[41] August. *De civ. D.* 18.9bc; cf. Ogden 1996: 181–2 and more generally R. C. T. Parker 1987 and Tyrrell and Brown 1991: 133–57. For Cecrops, see now the exhaustive study of Gourmelen 2005, especially 175–208 and 329–49 for the matters referred to here.
[42] Discussed at Vidal-Naquet 1981a and Lambert 1993: 144–52.
[43] *Etym. Magn.*, s.v. *Apatouria*.   [44] Thus schol. Ar. *Ach.* 146.
[45] The term *apatores*, "fatherless," in due course seems to have been used as the Greek equivalent of the Latin term *spurii* in Roman Egypt, the designation for the distinctive class of Roman military bastards. See Youtie 1975 and Malouta (this volume) and (forthcoming).

deformity, in particular lameness, linked to fatherlessness.[46] In a banal example of the former, Attic orators could talk of legitimacy in terms of being "born straight," as we have seen. The same idea may already be apparent in Homer, when the lying Odysseus, in making up the story in which he is the bastard son of a rich Cretan, refers to his legitimate half-brothers as *ithaigeneessin*. The etymology of this term remains obscure, but it seems that the later Greeks at any rate derived the first element from *ithy-*, "straight," and so read the term to mean "straight born."[47] In the *Laws* Plato speaks of the scrutiny to which candidates for his priesthoods will be subjected: it will be necessary to ensure that they are all "sound in all parts" (*holoklēros*) and legitimate (*gnēsios*).[48] Here the term *holoklēros* is interestingly ambivalent between denoting physical perfection and full possession of one's lot or inheritance (*klēros*). In the *Republic* Plato explains that legitimate (*gnēsios*) souls are born for philosophy unlike bastard (*nothos*) ones, which are crippled (*anapēros*) and lame (*chōlos*).[49]

A strikingly practical example of this association is found again in the case of the would-be Spartan king Leotychidas. Xenophon explains how the Eurypontid throne was disputed between the lame Agesilaus and the (supposedly) bastard Leotychidas. The oracle-monger Diopeithes intervened to support Leotychidas by producing an oracle that bade the Spartans beware of "lame kingship," which looked bad for Agesilaus. But then Lysander, intervening on Agesilaus' behalf, succeeded in persuading the Spartans that the oracle was deploying the concept of lameness as a metaphor for illegitimacy, "for the kingship would be lame when it was not the descendants of Heracles that were at the head of the state."[50]

We might be tempted to think that the metaphor of lameness attached to illegitimacy initially in the context of father's bastards, born not by the straight and direct line of descent represented by a wife, but a crooked, indirect one represented by a concubine. But in all probability this imagery was initially associated with mother's bastards before being generalized to father's bastards. Again it is worth noting that it was as a mother's bastard that Lysander attempted to characterize Leotychidas.

The point becomes clearer when we consider the *Homeric Hymn to Apollo*, which narrates a primeval competition in autonomous generation between the male Zeus and the female Hera. To Hera's dismay, Zeus is able

[46] See Ogden 1997a: 33–4 and *passim*.
[47] Hom. *Od.* 199–214; cf. Ogden 1996: 22–3, 1997a: 183, n. 54, with further references.
[48] Pl. *Leg.* 759c.   [49] Pl. *Resp.* 535cd.
[50] Xen. *Hell.* 3.3.1–4. The text of the oracle is supplied, with variations, at Plut. *Mor.* 399bc; *Ages.* 3; *Lys.* 22 and Paus. 3.8.9. See Fontenrose 1978: 322 (Q163).

to produce of his own accord the beautiful and perfect Athena. But Hera's attempts to reply in kind are doomed to failure: she can only produce the lame and ungainly Hephaestus, twisted of feet and so disgusting that she herself casts him out of heaven; and then the even more monstrous Typhon, serpentine below the waist (cf. Cecrops, above). Hera speaks:

Hear me, all gods and goddesses, how the cloud-gatherer Zeus begins to dishonor me, unprovoked, after making me his chaste wife. Without any contribution from me, he brought to birth gray-eyed Athene, who stands out among all the blessed immortals. But my child Hephaestus, whom I bore myself, was born halting among the gods, shrivelled of feet … I took him in my hands and threw him and cast him into the broad sea. (*Homeric Hymn* [3] *to Apollo* 311–18)[51]

In short, mothers can only produce misshapen monsters on their own. Only fathers (with or without mothers) can produce perfect offspring. Similar ideas resurface in Plutarch:

It is said that no woman ever produced a child without association with a man, but they call the shapeless and flesh-like embryos that form of their own accord as a result of infection "moles." One must take care that this does not happen in the souls of women. If they do not receive the seed of good arguments and share with their husbands in education, they conceive of their own accord many strange things and base designs and passions. (*Moralia* 145d–e)

The crookedness and deformity associated with bastardy, then, seems to attach primarily to womens' bastards, these effectively fatherless children. The point emerges, too, from the well-known legend of the birth of Cypselus, tyrant of Corinth. Herodotus tells how Corinth was run by the strictly endogamous Bacchiad aristocracy. The Bacchiad Amphion ("Going on two legs") had a lame (*chōlē*) daughter Labda (i.e. lambda, the letter-form illustrative of the crookedness of her leg), whom, accordingly, none of the Bacchiads would deign to take in marriage. So instead she was given to a man outside the Bacchiad group, Echecrates of the deme of Petra, to whom she bore a son. Learning from oracles that the boy was destined to overthrow them and make himself tyrant of Corinth, the Bacchiads attempted to destroy him, but were thwarted when Labda hid him from them in a ceramic beehive, a *kypselē*, from which he supposedly derived his name, *Kypselos*. In consequence, Cypselus survived to complete his destiny and secure the tyranny of

---

[51] For Hephaestus, cf. Hom. *Il.* 18.371, 394–7, 410, 20.270; *Od.* 8.310; Hes. *Theog.* 927–30; Apollod. *Bibl.* 1.3.5; Paus. 5.19.8. For illustrations of his twisted feet, see *LIMC* s.v. "Hephaestus," nos. 21, 43, 103a, 117, 129, 142, 157d and "Hephaestus/Sethlans," 18a. See Delcourt 1957: 110–36; Detienne and Vernant 1978: 259–76; T. Carpenter 1986: 13–29; Ogden 1997a: 35–7. For Typhon, see *Hom. Hymn. Apollo* 343–55 and Apollod. *Bibl.* 1.6.3.

Corinth.[52] But Cypselus' name sustains other readings too: a *kypselos* was in
fact a sandpiper, and it was doubtless the sandpiper's distinctively shaped nest
that had caused ceramic beehives to be called *kypselai*. Now we know from
Aristotle that sandpipers, *kypseloi* were also known as *apodes*, "footless birds."[53]
This will have been, no doubt, either because the sandpiper's feet are invisible
as it characteristically wades in shallow water, or because its feet are in any case
so delicate and often angled as direct extensions of the leg. It is, of course,
from the perspective of the endogamous Bacchiads that Cypselus, sired by a
non-Bacchiad father, is a bastard. He is, then, a mother's bastard. And the
point is well made through the imagery of lameness, which in this case tightly
binds him with his mother.[54]

CONCLUSION

Such, then, was the wider context of thought about bastardy and fatherlessness against which Athenian legislation and morality enforcing separations of various kinds between bastards and their fathers unfolded and
operated.

What ideas and legislation of this sort might have meant on the ground,
in Athens or the wider Greek world, it is unfortunately impossible to tell.
We have no data of the sort to permit us to track the life-experiences of any
historical Greek *nothos*, beyond, possibly, those of the royal bastards of the
Hellenistic dynasties, and they, for reasons both obvious and unobvious,
constitute a very special case.[55] Certainly, we have no possibility of inves-
tigating any emotional or psychological response on the part of an ancient
nothos to his situation. Nor, indeed, is it possible even to begin to quantify
the proportion of citizens' children in Athens or in any other Greek city that
were born or considered to be *nothoi*, be they mother's bastards or father's
bastards.[56] Even if, by some miracle, we could arrive at the overall number
of bastards in Classical Athens (let alone any distribution of bastards across
classes), it would not get us very far, because we still would not know how
many citizens there were.[57] Comparative studies for those historical societies
where reliable demographic data are available, however, would seem to

[52] Hdt. 5.92.   [53] Arist. *Hist. an.* 618a31.
[54] The imagery of lameness and bastardy in the Cypselus legend is investigated at length at Ogden
1997a: 87–94. See also Roux 1963; Lambrinoudakis 1971; Vernant 1982; and Jameson 1986.
[55] Ogden 1999: *passim*.
[56] It was once erroneously believed that the *nothos*-inscriptions of the Milesian Delphinium (Kawerau
and Rehm 1914: nos. 34–93) might offer such a possibility, but see Ogden 1996, 304–10.
[57] See, e.g., Hansen 1986.

suggest that reproductive culture tends to be more conservative and stable than marital and legitimacy legislation and the policing and enforcement of these. Change in the numbers and proportions of bastard children, or those deemed to be such, therefore, is primarily a function of changes in a state's legislation and recording activities rather than of changes in the reproductive culture of its people.[58] So far as bastardy legislation across the wider Greek world and across the centuries is concerned, our evidence for it is very patchy indeed, but it does permit us to detect a general trend through the Classical and Hellenistic periods. This trend is the movement from regimes applying more restrictive definitions of legitimacy toward those applying more lax ones.[59] Thus, in Athens' own case, for example, having a citizen mother was no longer a necessary qualification for legitimacy after 229 BC.[60] The significance of the fact that Athenian bastardy law moved, to some degree at any rate, in line with panhellenic trends, has still to penetrate the minds of those scholars who continue to explain the causes of Pericles' citizenship law for us without looking beyond the borders of Attica.

Against such a background of ineluctable ignorance, optimistic hypotheses remain available, should we choose them. Despite his legal, social, religious, and economic separation from his father's family, nothing ultimately prevented a bastard child from clinging closely to his father in Classical Athens, if that was what suited them both. And no doubt it normally did suit fathers who had no legitimate children to compete with their bastards. Nor, despite these separations from his biological father, was a bastard left wholly without social context. In Classical Athens, as a resident, free non-citizen, he would have belonged to the "metic" class, which, for all that it had to pay an additional variety of tax, constituted a large, for the most part thriving and in part even rich, parallel community (which, incidentally, must have had its own laws on marriage and succession, though they remain largely obscure to us).[61]

---

[58] Laslett, Oosterveen, and Smith 1980. This work is warmly recommended to those with an interest in the comparative study of bastardy across diverse (or not so diverse) societies.
[59] Ogden 1996: 277–317.   [60] Ogden 1996: 81–2.
[61] For the metic community in general, see Whitehead 1977; for their marital system, Ogden 1996: 131–5.

CHAPTER 7

Fatherlessness and formal identification in Roman Egypt

Myrto Malouta

INTRODUCTION

My contribution to this volume is concerned with the phenomenon of fatherlessness as it is attested in the papyri and ostraca of Roman Egypt. The kind of fatherlessness considered in this paper is not to be understood as the physical, or possibly even actual, absence of a father, such as would make one a child of a single-parent family or an orphan. Rather, it is a legal formality that figures in the documents from Egypt in the Roman period, a compulsory self-designation for any free individual who could not establish legitimate paternity and was thus forbidden from using the name of his or her father (a patronymic) for the purposes of legal self-identification. Such individuals are attested fairly frequently and the terms used to describe them are *apatōr* (literally, "without a father" or "fatherless") and *chrēmatizōn mētros* ("officially described [by the name] of the mother"). Both are legal terms to mark a fatherless person, who must give his or her mother's name instead of the normal patronymic when officially declaring his or her identity. They are synonymous and have roughly the same chronological span, as we shall see, but they are not interchangeable: the former is the more common of the two, since it is used in all parts of Egypt, other than Oxyrhynchus, where the latter is used instead.[1]

The main issue I wish to examine in this chapter is the position of these fatherless individuals within the social fabric of Roman Egypt, exploring their roles within city or village life, their family situations, and their personal functions. In order to do so with more precision, I analyze the entire body of available evidence and thereby attempt to establish a proper

---

[1] *Apatōr* has a literary life before becoming a legal term: see Calderini 1953: 358–9; cf. Ogden (this volume): 115. *Chrēmatizein* is commonly employed in a host of situations dealing with legal naming, but the particular phrase here is clearly an alternative expression for *apatōr* (see Gradenwitz 1903: 97–100; cf. Youtie 1975: 726, n. 3). For a discussion of the terminology and the geographical divide between the terms, see Malouta 2007.

understanding of the phenomenon with respect to certain matters of demography and the geographic and chronological distribution of the evidence. The reasons behind this kind of fatherlessness, as well as its significance for the status of those individuals affected by it, for the most part still remain obscure. The articles written on this topic by Calderini and Youtie converge on the opinion that some or most of the fatherless individuals who appear in the papyri and ostraca must have been children of soldiers, who under imperial law were not legally allowed to marry and therefore could not be legal fathers to their children.[2] Yet, as we shall see, the time span of this phenomenon largely occurred within the second and third centuries and thus overstepped the lift on the marriage ban of soldiers by more than a century. Also, as Phang has observed, if all such fatherless individuals were children of soldiers, the predominance of Greco-Egyptian names among them would suggest a higher rate of relationships with Egyptian than Roman women, a situation which contradicts the general picture for soldiers.[3] So, while it is quite clear that we should be looking for a Roman legal institution behind the sudden emergence of this new legal status – though not necessarily one that remained unassimilated to its new context – the extent to which its explanation relates to soldiers should perhaps be reconsidered. The purpose of the present study, however, is not to engage with the question of the underlying reasons for this type of fatherlessness, but instead to explore the documentary evidence and develop something of a demographic and social profile of those who were legally "without a father."[4]

DATA AND METHODOLOGY

The data used in this study have been collected and arranged to form an exhaustive database comprising those individuals from Roman Egypt who describe themselves or are designated as *apatores* or *chrēmatizontes mētros*.[5]

---

[2] Calderini 1953: 361; Youtie 1975: 737.   [3] Phang 2001: 391, n. 18.
[4] See Rowlandson 1998: 232–3; Malouta forthcoming 2008.
[5] As opposed to Calderini and Youtie, I have decided not to include other terms, such as *spourios*, or cases where the patronymic is simply absent in this study, since it is not certain that they reflect the phenomenon in question. For the uses of the word in Latin see Kubitschek 1929 and Rawson 1989: 15, 29–38. *P.Select.* 14 is the best example of the meaning of *spourios* in Greek, where a father uses it in connection with a daughter he obtained with a freedwoman. This, of course, could not have been used interchangeably with *apatōr*, see Youtie 1975: 726, n. 1. In the light of this document, Youtie's rejection of Calderini's conjecture should possibly be reconsidered. The reader is asked to bear in mind that the numbers mentioned by these two authors appear larger than they would if they focused only on *apatores* and *chrēmatizontes mētros*.

They include men and women, children and adults. Based on the documents published at the time of writing, there are some 590 such "fatherless" individuals. Overlaps have been eliminated wherever they could be determined with certainty, but some cases may have slipped through, since there was not always enough information preserved to warrant confidence.[6]

The database has been set up in electronic "cards." Each individual has his or her own card (or cards), on which as much information as could be gleaned from the document (or documents) containing his or her name has been set out. There is a reference to the document itself, as well as information concerning its nature, date, and provenance. Then, the name of the fatherless individual in question is recorded, along with the following information: the terminology used to characterize him or her as such (i.e. *apatōr* or *chrēmatizōn mētros*), the name of the mother, gender, age (where not recorded, at least whether they were adults or children), any other known relatives or guardians, profession, level of literacy, type of household in which they lived, type of house, ownership of immovables, tax quotas, any designations of higher status, identifying scars, area of residence, role in the particular document, and, on a case-by-case level, anything else that would contribute to a better understanding of the phenomenon of fatherlessness. These categories of information clearly represent what we would ideally like to know. That is to say, they represent *desiderata* rather than anything approximating the reality of the kind or amount of information actually available. That reality is in turn directly related to the kind of document which preserves the reference to a particular individual. Documents associated with certain private or public business, such as census returns, birth and death declarations, are the most productive of personal data, usually preserving a wealth of information concerning his or her person, family and/or household setup, and often even touching upon matters of property and land ownership. Lists, on the other hand, usually preserve only the name of the individual, the term of fatherlessness, and the name of the mother (though even that is sometimes omitted). Clearly, lists cannot be of much help with personal data, but they nonetheless constitute a valuable source of information in the process of examining the geographical and chronological distribution of the phenomenon.

Identifying and collecting fatherless individuals from among all published papyri and ostraca was made possible through the extensive use of the search

---

[6] Indeed, the total number of references exceeds eight hundred, but there are many instances where the same person is mentioned twice or more, such as in long tax-registers where the taxes are paid in instalments, as well as, in a few cases, in different documents.

function of the *Duke Data Bank of Documentary Papyri*, with additions through the *Wörterliste*. The final number of individuals included in this database is the outcome of examination of the results of the electronic searches, with any references that have resulted from editorial errors, such as erroneous resolutions of abbreviations of the word *apatōr*, being carefully excluded.[7] It must be made clear early on that in collecting data of this kind there is always the likelihood that a small number of relevant cases have been inadvertently omitted. For example, if a key word in a text is misread by its editor (always a possibility in papyrological editing), that document will necessarily not be included in the results of an electronic search. But the chances are that such cases, if indeed there are any at all, are negligible in number and so not likely to skew the conclusions drawn from the available data.

There are, however, two potentially serious shortcomings in this data set. First, as is often the case with data drawn from ancient sources, there has been a major loss of unique information due to the partial preservation of many of the texts, and there is no way to recover or reconstruct this information. Furthermore, we must bear in mind that not all of the relevant texts have yet been published, and this constitutes another potential source of valuable information that is not easily available for study at this time. In this chapter every effort is made to present the available data in a way that does not take the information at face value but incorporates it into the general pattern of demography, geography, and chronology. Second, it is worth noting that the pattern of specific kinds of individuals we see in the total of preserved instances of *apatores* is not therefore necessarily representative of the existence and function of *all* fatherless individuals in Roman Egypt. Rather, it is representative of the phenomenon as it was *recorded*. Therefore, although some important aspects of the phenomenon, namely those not captured by the usual types of documents, are now lost to us, the information that has been preserved is likely to be qualitatively, though probably not quantitatively, representative of the ways that the phenomenon was recorded in general.

GENDER, AGE, AND STATUS

Among the attested fatherless individuals there is a clear preponderance of men, but there are enough women to show that the phenomenon could and did concern both sexes. There are approximately five hundred men as

---

[7] These are errors which have either been recorded in the *Berichtigungsliste* or more recent articles, or which I identified during this work.

opposed to sixty-two women, and this difference may be in large part explained by the fact that the documents, which record mainly the financial dealings of village populations, would naturally overrepresent the male population, which was more active in this arena.[8] In other words, women typically are not found in official documents concerning labor, capitation tax, officialdom, liturgies, and such like. Instead, the sixty-two fatherless women attested are found in letters, documents about land and property (mainly the sale and lease thereof), census-related documents, loans and tax lists (from Karanis). The identifiable children among the present set are very few; probably for the same reason as the women discussed above, though here the effect is even more pronounced since they usually had even less opportunity or need to participate in the civil and fiscal spheres in such a way as to be recorded.[9] To be exact, there are just twelve cases where the fatherless individual is certainly a child, the fact being reflected either by an exact age or circumstantial evidence which suggests that the person is a minor. There are, however, just over a hundred cases of individuals of unconfirmed age where it cannot be gauged even whether the subjects are minors or adults. This is a large enough group to prevent us from attempting to draw any firm conclusions based on the numbers we have, but at least it is clear that fatherlessness of this sort is recorded as a description among children, that is, it appears to be a status one is born into, not a designation acquired later in life.

The number of confirmed slaves among the set of fatherless individuals is nearly nonexistent. In fact, it is surprising that they appear at all, since legitimate paternity is by definition precluded in the case of slaves.[10] A list of names from Soknopaiou Nesos from 200 CE preserves an entry in which a certain Sotas, a brother of an *apatōr*, is referred to as a *doulos*.[11] The name of the mother is not recorded, and the function of the list is unknown. It is only among the dike workers preserved in a list of 193 CE from Tebtunis that

---

[8] There are approximately thirty cases where the name of the person concerned is damaged or lost, and there are no other clues as to gender. All in all, women had an active economic role as property owners, but they were recorded less often than men since they did not pay poll tax and were not required to discharge liturgical duties (see Hobson 1983). For discussion of the bias toward village settings in the documents, see the section entitled "Geographical distribution" below.

[9] I consider anyone under the age of fourteen a child. This is obvious for boys, since this is the age when they would have started to pay poll tax. For the sake of uniformity I apply the same limit to girls, although some of them would have been married before then.

[10] See Bagnall 1991: 7–8.

[11] Brother of Soterichos [87], *BGU* 2.630 iv.2. Where there is no particular need to refer to a fatherless individual by name and to avoid confusion potentially caused by names that are similar to other names, too long-winded, incomplete, or missing altogether, I use the unique identification number assigned to each individual in the database. These are the bold, bracketed numbers. Their order follows the order of the documents in which the names were found, according to the *Checklist* (or the first of the documents in cases in which there is more than one attestation).

we find an *apatōr* who is unambiguously stated to be a slave.[12] The word *apatōr* is written out in full, so there is no chance of a false resolution of an abbreviation. However, the mention of a slave's father is suspicious, and in fact it may be a scribal error, possibly caused by inadvertent repetition of the word from the line above. Some indirect light on slavery and the *apatores* is cast by the presence of freedmen and freedwomen in our documents. In a census document from the Memphite nome of 188 CE, a female *apatōr* lists her forty-five-year-old mother as a freedwoman.[13] Also a freedwoman is the mother of another *apatōr* in a third-century document from the Arsinoite nome.[14] In a third-century list of lodgers of unknown provenance we find an *apatōr* whose son is a freedman,[15] and a similar situation arises in a list from Theadelphia, of 138–61.[16] It must be borne in mind, of course, that in the "gray area" of unskilled labor recorded in the papyri, there may lurk several more slaves who were never named as such.[17]

The pattern emerging from this basic demographic survey of the *apatores* does not exhibit any major idiosyncrasies as compared with the overall situation of the recorded population: the activity of men is recorded more frequently than that of women, and children appear in documents only rarely, and as marginal characters. While there is no easy way of determining statistical "totals" or even representative samples of the overall population to juxtapose with the present figures, a rough comparison and perhaps a rather optimistic use of empirical common sense would suggest that the only group that might appear underrepresented here is that of slaves. Slaves, of course, appear only in certain types of documents and fulfill a restricted repertoire of functions, but that almost none of the *apatores* are slaves would appear to be below the expected ratio. This is, however, not an indication that the *apatores* never inhabited the lowest rungs of the social ladder; rather, the reason clearly is that when one is a slave and happens to be an *apatōr*, the latter is beside the point: it is, as mentioned above, a legal redundancy, since slaves by definition do not legally have fathers, but owners, and this is how they determine their identity and are designated in official documents. The very existence of "fatherless" slaves is suggested only by the exceptional (and probably erroneous) reference to one slave's parents and those more interesting (and certain) cases where family connections between slaves and *apatores* can be attested or inferred.

---

[12] [**659**], *SB* 1.5124 ii.55.   [13] [**201**], *BGU* 9.2019 i.19.
[14] [**726**], *SB* 6.9069.16.   [15] [**45**], *P.Ryl.* 2.285.3.   [16] [**639**], *P.Stras.* 9.829 iv.99 recto.
[17] See for example *SB* 12.10948 ii, a name list from first- or second-century Tebtunis, in which [**738**] and [**739**] appear. In that list at least nine people out of the thirty-four preserved seem to have been slaves.

PROFESSIONS AND LITURGIES

As would be expected, several documents attest to the connections of *apatores* with land. Whether they are explicitly called *geōrgoi* (farmers) or are involved in transactions involving land or are seen paying land taxes or other taxes in grain, many of the *apatores* appear in the contexts associated with land and its use. But this is unexceptional: land dominates official papyri as a whole, as it constituted the most important productive asset in the agricultural economy of the ancient world. I shall therefore leave this to one side. Instead, I focus on explicitly named professions and offices that the *apatores* of Roman Egypt are documented to have held, as well as attestations of seasonal work.

There are few kinds of documents in the ancient world that required one to state his or her profession, so explicit descriptions of this sort are few and far between. Luckily, some information can be gleaned from lists of workers and liturgists. Thus, for just over 20 percent of adult males in our set of *apatores* we may draw some conclusions about the offices they held or work they did apart from cultivation. Of course, some professions and kinds of work are bound to appear disproportionately in the papyri, owing to the type of document in which they are preserved. Our interest here, however, is not in the comparative numbers of individuals who practiced certain professions, but in the raw number and types of professions that *apatores* appear to have practiced.

In documents related to agriculture, such as name-lists of farmers, we find a few individuals who are described as "specializing" in a certain area of agriculture. Apart from the nominated *geōrgoi* of the village, or of a certain clerouchy or public and *ousiac* land, we also find trade specialists, such as millers (*mylōnikoi*)[18] and cattle-keepers (*ktēnotrophoi*).[19] Some *apatores* are recorded as having carried out specific functions within the context of agricultural work: there are a few shepherds[20] and weavers.[21] We also find two individuals who may be craftsmen (*tektones*), as well as an apprentice

---

[18] [178]–[191] and [193]–[206] are included in *BGU* 9.1900, a list of farmers from Theadelphia from 196–8 CE. Of them, [190] and [195] are further described as *mylōnikoi*, and [206] as a substitute farmer.

[19] [155] in *P.Col.* 2.1 recto 4.

[20] [192] is a *poimēn* found in *BGU* 9.1900 vi.113, a list of farmers of 196–8 CE from Theadelphia. [689] is a *boukolos*, found in *SB* 1.5124 vi.178 of 193 CE from Tebtunis.

[21] [694] is a weaver mentioned in *SB* 1.5124 vii.225, and [698] is described as a *gnapheus*, or fuller, viii.239. [650] is included in a list of persons of 153 CE from Tebtunis (*P.Tebt.* 2.584.1 verso), under a heading concerning weavers.

builder.[22] Another is described as a door-keeper (*prosthyraios*), a custodian of the *logistērion*.[23] In the tax lists from Karanis, we find an undertaker (*entaphiastēs*).[24] We find only one fatherless individual personally involved in shipping, a *nauklēros*, in a third-century grain receipt of unknown origin.[25]

Apart from unskilled labor used in agriculture, seasonal work, and low-level trades, there are numerous *apatores* who are attested to have held liturgies and village-level offices. A great number of *apatores* are found to be working on dikes and canals, but conclusions based on this must be drawn with caution, since most of the references come from a single document.[26] Other than that, the most common liturgy among the preserved sources for the *apatores* seems to have been the *phylakeia*. Six individuals are referred to simply as guards (*phylakes*),[27] while there are others more specifically described as guards of the threshing floor (*alōnophylakes*),[28] estate guards (*pediophylakes*),[29] a policeman (*androphylax*),[30] and a night guard (*nyktophylax*).[31] Furthermore, we find four councilors (*presbyteroi*),[32] two police chiefs (*archephodoi*),[33] a tax collector (*apaitētēs sitikōn*),[34] two bailiffs (a *praktōr sitikōn*[35] and a *praktōr argyrikōn*[36]), one *gyarchēs* (land

---

[22] [561], a rather uncertain reading from a grain tax document of 184–5 CE from Ptolemais Hormou (*P.Petaus* 53 i.24), and [770], also uncertain, from a third-century document from Soknopaiou Nesos (*Stud.Pal.* 22.52.9). The apprentice builder, [25], comes from a third-century apprenticeship contract from Oxyrhynchus (*P.Oxy.* 38.2875.2).

[23] [59], *C.Pap.Gr.* 2.1, App. 3 (*P.Oxy.* 43.3104.3), Oxyrhynchus, 228 CE.

[24] *P.Mich.* 4.1.223 lxxviii.2380 recto.   [25] [727] in *SB* 6.9088.2.

[26] Over sixty *apatores* ([657]–[723]) are listed in *SB* 1.5124, a list of dike workers from Tebtunis of 193 CE, some with further specializations, such as shepherds, donkey drivers, etc., discussed below. A further four unspecialized dike workers ([207], [626], [736], and [774]) are found in four different documents, in order: *BGU* 13.2236.17, a list of canal workers of the mid-second century from Soknopaiou Nesos; three penthemeros-receipts, *P.Stras.* 4.249B.6, from Bacchias (122 CE); *SB* 10.10543.6, from Tebtunis (159 CE); and *Stud.Pal.* 22.160.6, of the same date from Soknopaiou Nesos.

[27] [2], a *phylax* of the Sarapaeum in Oxyrhynchus, named in *P.Harr.* 1.64.2, from the third century; [23], also mentioned above as a donkey driver, charged with the *phylakeia*, in *P.Oxy.* 18.2131.3/6 of 207 CE; [359], listed among village officials as a *phylax* in 200/1 CE in *P.Lond.* 2.199.13; *P.Oxy.* 17.2121 ii.53, a list of Arsinoite village officials, includes [551] and [552]; and [569] features in *P.Petaus* 67.24, a list from Ptolemais Hormou of 185 CE.

[28] [57] and [58], *SB* 16.12494, Oxyrhynchus, 222–35 CE.

[29] [221] and [222], *P.Berl.Leihg.* 1.6, Theadelphia, 165–7 CE.

[30] [308], *P.Col.* 2.1 recto 4 ii.19. This is the only occurrence of this term.

[31] [553], *P.Oxy.* 17.2121 ii.64, Oxyrhynchus, but refers to Arsinoite village officials, 209/10 CE.

[32] [535], *P.Mil.Vogl.* 2.98 ii.38, Tebtunis, 138–9? CE; [550], *P.Oxy.* 17.2121 i.13, Oxyrhynchus, 209/10 CE; [573], *P.Petaus* 88.3, Ptolemais Hormou, 184–7 CE; [618], *PSI Corr.* 1.1244 i.4, ii.40, Oxyrhynchus, but refers to liturgies in Arsinoite villages, 208 CE.

[33] [11], *P.Oxy.* 1.80.9, Oxyrhynchus, 238–44 CE, and [56], *SB* 16.12494.4, Oxyrhynchus, 222–35 CE.

[34] [17], *P.Oxy.* 3.514.1, Oxyrhynchus, 190/1 CE.   [35] [32], *P.Oxy.* 43.3097.5(r), Oxyrhynchus, 224/5 CE.

[36] [769], *Stud.Pal.* 22.6.3, Soknopaiou Nesos, 205 CE.

supervisor?),[37] two granary officials (*sitologoi*),[38] one superintendent of *ousiac* land (*epitērētēs ousiakōn ktēmatōn*),[39] and another tax farmer (*epitērētēs telōnikōn*).[40] Donkey driving is attested as a liturgy after 136 or 166 CE,[41] and we find a few *apatores* among them.[42] We also find two who have been nominated to transport grain and oxen, respectively, both of whom are on their way to Syria.[43] A further eleven individuals are listed in documents containing suggestions for liturgies.[44] Finally, in a letter of 171 from Bacchias, to which a list of priests is appended, two individuals are described as *apatores* who are priests and are said to have been examined and assessed at twelve drachmas, and to have paid the relevant *eiskritikon*.[45] This is unexpected, since priesthood required purity of lineage among its members.[46]

The above picture might be statistically useful, since it is based on the entire preserved set of fatherless individuals from Roman Egypt. However, in trying to form an impression of an overall pattern of distribution of professions among those individuals, there are some obvious and some less obvious pitfalls one must try to avoid. First of all, the set is complete, but only in the sense that it comprises everything that has survived and been published; this can in no way be assumed to be a representative portion of all documentary evidence written. Secondly, even in the hypothetical situation in which everything ever written had survived, it cannot be assumed that a piece of information such as one's profession would have been adequately recorded for the entire population. Thirdly, even though a certain number

[37] [230], *B.Berl.Leihg.* 2.41 A.7, Theadelphia, second century. The term only appears here and in *P.Hib.* 2.260. The exact nature of this liturgy is not known.

[38] [562], *P.Petaus* 59 ii.29, Ptolemais Hormou, 185 CE; [563], *P.Petaus* 59 iii.68, Ptolemais Hormou, 185 CE.

[39] [570], *P.Petaus* 76.5, Ptolemais Hormou, 184 CE.

[40] [75], *BGU* 1.277 ii.1, Arsinoite nome, second century.   [41] N. Lewis 1982: 40.

[42] [706] and [718] are found in a list of dike workers, *SB* 1.5124 (see above), and [23], for whom being a donkey driver appears to be one of several functions (he was also a farmer and a *phylax*), in *P.Oxy.* 17.2131.3, 6, a copy of a petition of 207 from Oxyrhynchus. See Youtie 1973: 86–7.

[43] Both are found in Oxyrhynchite documents recording undertakings on oath, namely [30] in *P.Oxy.* 43.3091.2 of 216/7? CE, and [33] in *P.Oxy.* 43.3109.10 of 253–6. The former undertakes to carry barley down to Alexandria on the way to Syria (and offers to act as a guarantor for another *chrēmatizōn metros*, [31]), and the latter is one of the fourteen villagers nominated to convey plowing oxen to Syria.

[44] [574], unknown liturgy, *P.Petaus* 90.6, Ptolemais Hormou, 183–4 CE; [575], unknown liturgy, *P.Petaus* 90.23, Ptolemais Hormou, 183–4 CE; [63], unknown liturgy, *BGU* 1.91 ii.17, Arsinoite nome, 170–1 CE; [64], unknown liturgy, *BGU* 1.91 ii.18, Arsinoite nome, 170–1 CE; [566], for *praktores dēmosias*, *P.Petaus* 63 i.7, Ptolemais Hormou, 185 CE; [567], for *praktores katoikias*, *P.Petaus* 63 i.12, Ptolemais Hormou, 185 CE; [568], unknown liturgy, *P.Petaus* 65 i.28, Ptolemais Hormou, 185 CE; [607], in list of officials, *P.Ryl.* 2.91.6, Arsinoe, early third century; [624], unknown liturgy, *P.Stras.* 1.55.12, Arsinoite nome, 173 CE; [748], unknown liturgy, *SB* 16.12498.5, Arsinoe, third century; [749], unknown liturgy, *SB* 16.12498.17, Arsinoe, third century.

[45] [216] and [217], *P.Bacch.* 2 i.19, ii.41. See Youtie 1975: 733–4.   [46] Youtie 1975: 733.

of individuals among the surviving documents are described as *apatores* or *chrēmatizontes mētros*, it cannot be assumed that this is an absolutely consistent practice at all times and in all parts of Roman Egypt. For instance, as will be discussed later, there may have been some individuals who tried to conceal their status from the authorities.[47] Fourthly, the picture formed with regard to the segment of the population in question, whether complete or incomplete, cannot take us very far statistically, since there are no reliable complete data concerning the distribution of professions in the population as a whole, either synchronically or diachronically, against which to compare the current findings. That is not to say that the data presented here are not useful; while they cannot make for a complete picture, they do allow us certain interesting glimpses into the social role of an *apatōr*, as can be deduced from his professional status. For example, the evidence of *SB* 1.5124 should not be dismissed as merely a fortuitous over-representation of dike workers within the set. If examined separately, the fact that of a total of about three hundred and fifty workers more than sixty are described as fatherless is certainly significant, if only for the specific region and chronological instance.[48] Similarly, the data we have on fatherless individuals charged with liturgies cannot suggest how often they were called upon to perform such services as compared with the rest of the population, but the fact that the most commonly attested liturgy for *apatores* is the *phylakeia* may indeed be seen as significant.[49]

FAMILIES AND HOUSEHOLD STRUCTURE

A fatherless individual, when being described as such, will have his status declared by the terms we have seen so far, namely *apatōr* or *chrēmatizōn mētros*

[47] See the discussion on *P.Lond.* 2.324 below and Rawson 1989: 16. For the present study individuals who were really fatherless but went through life concealing their identity are not statistically significant: since their real status would have been a reality known only to themselves and those in their immediate environment, it would not have had any legal implications visible in the documentary evidence. Their necessary absence from this data set does not therefore skew the results in any way other than in terms of absolute numbers.

[48] Three hundred and fifty is the approximate number of those names that are legible. The text actually provides numbers of the people listed, and only those that are preserved add up to 396. From what remains in the very fragmentary parts of the text, one can calculate that the text would have comprised more than one thousand workers, perhaps a good deal more depending on how much has been lost at the end. There is, however, no reason to assume that the ratio of fatherless individuals over the whole would have been much different than the average we find in the legible part.

[49] Admittedly, the *phylakeia* was a common liturgy, and one which was served by more than one person at a time. Also, it had many variations, and it was held for one year or less. All of these factors would have contributed to there being more attestations of *phylakes*, but this would apply to other liturgies as well. See N. Lewis 1982: 51–2; Homoth-Kuhs 2005.

and, more often than not, the name of his or her mother. This means that in
any given document the minimum information that we can expect to have
about a fatherless person's family (other than nothing at all) is usually just the
name of the mother. However, because of the varied nature of the documents
in which fatherless individuals are attested and the roles they fulfill, for about
a hundred of these individuals we know of more members of their family than
just the mother. The family member we most often know about is the
brother, mostly because in several documents brothers are listed together.
In fact, we have references to almost forty brothers.[50] References to sisters,
however, are scarcer and only come in census-related documents and wills; in
all, we know of only ten, from eleven references.[51] Sons occur very often, over
thirty instances,[52] while daughters less often, only eight times,[53] mostly
because when children figure in the documents their fatherless fathers provide
their patronymics, and so must identify themselves as *apatores* in the process.
Wives and husbands appear in all sorts of documents for different reasons, in
three and eleven instances, respectively;[54] also, there is some overlap between
spouses and siblings. Finally, grandparents are named less often, with eight

[50] *P.Köln* 2.100.6 ([5]–[6]); *P.Oxy.* 4.728.2 ([18]–[19]); *P.Oxy.* 47.3365 ii.60 ([39]–[40]); *P.Ryl.* 2.285.3
([45]–[46]); *PSI* 15.1532.14 ([53]); *BGU* 1.91 ii.17 ([63]); *BGU* 1.91 ii.18 ([64]); *BGU* 2.630 iv.2 ([87]);
BGU 9.1891 iii.73 ([105]); *BGU* 9.1891 iii.74 ([106]); *BGU* 9.1891 iii.75 ([107]); *BGU* 9.1891 iii.83
([108]); *BGU* 9.1891 iii.84 ([109]); *BGU* 9.1891 iv.116 ([115]); *BGU* 9.1891 iv.117 ([116]); *BGU* 9.1891
iv.121 ([117]); *BGU* 9.1891 iv.122 ([118]); *BGU* 9.1891 iv.123 ([119]); *BGU* 9.1891 vi.186 ([125]); *BGU*
9.1891 vi.187 ([126]); *P.Col.* 2.1 recto 3 ii.30 ([298]); *P.Mich.* 15.715.8 ([532]); *P.Mich.* 15.715.9 ([533]);
P.Petaus 1.5 ([555]); *P.Stras.* 8.710 i.13 ([634]); *SB* 1.5124 iv.121 ([670]); *SB* 1.5124 iv.122 ([671]); *SB*
1.5124 v.134 ([675]); *SB* 1.5124 v.135 ([676]); *SB* 1.5124 vi.165 ([682]); *SB* 1.5124 vi.166 ([683]); *SB*
6.9100.2 frA.4 ([728]); *SB* 6.9100.2 frA.5 ([729]); *Chr.Wilck.* 1.208.29 ([752]).

[51] *P.Köln* 2.100.6 ([4]–[6]); *P.Oxy.* 58.3929.3 ([41]); *BGU* 9.2018.10 ([198]–[200]); *BGU* 9.2019 i.19
([201]–[202]); *BGU* 9.2019 i.20 ([202]–[203]).

[52] *P.Köln* 2.100.6 ([5]); *P.Oxy.* 1.100.7 ([12]); *P.Ryl.* 2.285.3 ([45]); *BGU* 2.497.5 ([82]); *BGU* 3.971.13
([94]); *BGU* 9.1891 v.127, *P.Col.* 2.1 recto 1 and 2 ([120]); *BGU* 9.1891 vi.175 ([124]); *BGU* 9.1891
viii.229 ([132]); *BGU* 9.1891 viii.254 ([133]); *BGU* 9.1891 ix.261 ([135]); *BGU* 9.1891 xi.351 ([145]); *BGU*
9.1891 xii.380 ([149]); *BGU* 9.1891 xiii.393 ([150]); *BGU* 9.1891 xviii.540 ([162]: This is probably the
same *apatōr* as [132], but here we hear of one more son); *BGU* 9.1900 ii.30 ([181]); *BGU* 9.1900 iii.47
([183]); *P.Bas.* 22(c) ii.14 ([219]); *P.Berl.Leihg.* 2.29 i.26 ([227]); *P.Col.* 2.1 recto 1a v.27 ([260]?); *P.Col.*
2.1 recto 1a vii.17 ([268]); *P.Col.* 2.1 recto 2 vi.19 ([291]); *P.Col.* 5.1 verso 3 iii.58 ([319]); *P.Col.* 5.1 verso
3 iii.69 ([320]); *P.Col.* 5.1 verso 3 iv.94 ([323]); *P.Mich.* 4.1.224 lviii.2374, 3626 recto ([451]); *P.Mich.*
4.1.225 cxxix.2173 ([517]); *P.Mich.* 6.360.9 ([530]); *P.Stras.* 7.651.11 verso ([632]); *P.Stras.* 9.829 iv.99
recto ([639]); *SB* 14.11355.15 ([745]); *P.Bas.* 22 ii.14 ([782]).

[53] *P.Oxy.* 1.104.10 ([13]); *P.Oxy.* 19.2231.7 ([24]); *PSI* 5.450 v.1.50 ([48]); *P.Mich.* 6.360.9 ([530]);
P.Petaus 1.3 ([554]); *P.Petaus* 1.5 ([555]); *P.Petaus* 15.4 ([558]); *P.Stras.* 8.768.4, 18 ([637]).

[54] Not all cases clearly refer to a wife as such; most of these are references to those documents that record
a mother for the child of a fatherless father. I list here only the ones that are referred to as such, or
those who clearly cohabit with their presumed spouse: *P.Oxy.* 1.100.7 ([12]); *BGU* 2.497.5 ([82]);
P.Petaus 1.3 ([554]). Husbands: *PIFAO* 1.15.2 ([3]); *P.Köln* 2.100.6 ([5]); *P.Matr.* 2.2/10/15 ([8]); *P.Oxy.*
19.2231.7 ([24]); *BGU* 1.90.12, *BGU* 1.224.13, BGU 1.224.14, BGU 2.410.13, BGU 2.537.13 ([62]);
P.Mich. 4.1.224c.3988 recto ([469]); *P.Mil.Vogl.* 3.194a.12 ([537]: divorced); *P.Soter.* 7.7 ([622]); *SB*
10.10294.10 ([735]); *SB* 14.11355.15 ([745]); *SB* 18.13850.1 ([751]).

grandfathers and two grandmothers appearing in the documents, either in their own right or as part of extended identifications.[55] For the latter purpose, one great-grandfather is also mentioned three times, in the same document.[56]

Thanks to census-related documents, we are also allowed the occasional glimpse into household structure: we find a couple of very small households, where only a single person is registered.[57] Then, there are nuclear families (where the fatherless individual is one of the parents) or families with single mothers (where the fatherless individual is the mother or one of the children).[58] In some cases an extended family lives together under the same roof.[59] More extended households might include family members and some non-kin,[60] while no exclusively non-kin households are attested. We have no further indications concerning the setup and size of houses, except two cases in which we know that the property in question is one-quarter of a house.[61] But still, this does not shed much light on the actual living situation within each household, since evidence for houses from Roman Egypt would suggest that the sizes varied to a very great extent.[62] There is evidence of slave ownership in about one-third of cases, which may be low, since in many documents the part where slaves would have been registered is lost or damaged. Most households that have slaves declare one slave, but there are cases of three, six, and nine slaves.[63]

In general, not much is explicitly revealed in the documents about the personal status of *apatores*, other than reference to their fatherlessness. For example, only two of the *apatores* seem to have belonged to the privileged class of *katoikoi* themselves, as well as the sons and heirs of two more,[64] and a further two appear in the Oxyrhynchite corn-dole register.[65] More

[55] Grandfathers: *P.Köln* 2.100.6 ([4]–[6]); *P.Oxy.* 38.2875.2 ([25]); *P.Oxy.* 40.2913 ii.4 ([26]); *P.Mich.* 4.1.223 lxxviii.2380 recto ([406]); *P.Ross.Georg.* 5.54.11 ([605]); *P.Stras.* 8.768.4, 18 ([637]); *SB* 6.9206.6, 8 ([730]); *SB* 10.10294.10 ([735]); grandmothers: *P.Köln* 2.100.6 ([4]–[6]); *PSI* 5.450 1.50, 2.83 ([47]).
[56] *P.Köln* 2.100.6 ([4]–[6]). [57] *P.Oxy.* 3.475.14–15 ([14]); *SB* 18.13289.3 ([750]).
[58] *BGU* 9.2019 i.19 ([201]); *P.Mich.* 6.360.9 ([530]); *P.Mil.Vogl.* 3.193a.13 ([536]); *SB* 14.11355.15 ([745]).
[59] *P.Ryl.* 2.285.3 ([45]–[46]); *BGU* 1.90.12 ([62]); *BGU* 1.117.19 ([66]–[67]); *BGU* 2.447.11 ([79]); *BGU* 9.2018.10–11 ([198]–[200]); *P.Mil.Vogl.* 3.194a.12 ([537]); *P.Stras.* 8.768.4, 18 ([637]).
[60] *BGU* 2.496.6 ([81]); *BGU* 2.497.5 ([82]).
[61] *BGU* 2.496.6 ([81]); *BGU* 2.497.5 ([82]). [62] See Alston 2002: 52–8.
[63] One slave: *P.Oxy.* 3.475.15(r) ([14]); *BGU* 9.2019 i.19 ([201]–[202]); *P.Mil.Vogl.* 3.194a.12 ([537]); *P.Stras.* 4.257.14 ([627]). Three slaves: *P.Stras.* 8.768.4, 18 ([637]). Six slaves: *BGU* 2.447.11 ([79]). Nine slaves: *SB* 14.11355.15 ([745]).
[64] *SB* 6.9370 iv ([731], [732]), 170 CE, Tebtunis. The first is damaged and assumed abbreviated, and therefore, uncertain; *P.Stras.* 7.651.11 verso ([632]), second century, Bacchias; *P.Vind.Bosw.* 16.13 recto ([653]), second to third century, unknown provenance. On the *katoikoi*, see Bowman and Rathbone 1992: 121.
[65] *P.Oxy.* 40.2936 ii.8 ([27]) and 23 ([28]).

information however can be derived from family connections. The most interesting kinship relation to observe is that of siblings: in most cases a brother or sister of a fatherless individual will be explicitly identified as fatherless him- or herself, or else by inference, since there is no patronymic following the name. In two cases, however, we find a clear reference to a fatherless and a non-fatherless child of the same mother: in a tax list from Theadelphia of 135–45(?) we find a man called Heracles, designated *apatōr*, who has a brother of the same name(!), whose name is followed by a patronymic.[66] Most interestingly, in a census-related document of 161 from the Prosopite nome, we find a woman called Tamystha, designated *apatōr*, who has a brother of the same mother and who has a father.[67] What is remarkable in this case, is that Tamystha and her brother, Anikos, can be identified in census declarations of the previous two cycles, where they are declared as children of the same mother and father, that is, Tamystha does not have the status of *apatōr*.[68] The exact circumstances here are not clear, but Youtie suggests that this is a case in which the true identity of a concealed *apatōr* was revealed later in life, perhaps on purpose in an interfamilial fight over inheritance where legal paternity would have a definite effect on succession, and he argues that cases such as this one were not likely to have been altogether uncommon.[69]

CHRONOLOGICAL DISTRIBUTION

The distribution of the documents used in this study clearly marks the *apatores* as a second- and third-century phenomenon. More than half of all the documents preserving mentions of fatherless individuals are dated to the second century CE. Almost all the rest come from the third century, with only a handful coming in the first,[70] and one sole document from the fourth.[71] The fourth-century document, an account of tax collections from

---

[66] *P.Col.* 2.1 recto 3 ii.30 ([298]).

[67] *Chr.Wilck.* 1.208.29 ([752]). To these clear references should be added the aforementioned case of Sotas, a slave, referred to as brother of an *apatōr* ([87]) in *BGU* 2.630 iv.2. Whether or not he was an *apatōr* as well is not stated, and in any case may have been beside the point, as discussed above.

[68] Youtie 1975: 723–5; the previous census returns are *P.Lond.* 2.324.1–24 and *P.Lond.* 2.324.25–29; for details see Bagnall and Frier 2006: 217, 233.

[69] Youtie 1975: 725.

[70] *P.Oxy.* 1.104.10 ([13]); *P.Leid.Inst.* 28 ii recto ([352]–[355]); *P.Lond.* 2.256D.18 recto ([357]). First to second century: *P.Lond.* 3.901 ([360]–[363]); *P.Stras.* 9.843 ([640]–[641]); *SB* 12.10948 ii ([738], [739]).

[71] *P.NYU* 1.12 i.19 ([544]), re-dated to 336–7 CE. The search also yields one occurrence in the sixth century, *P.Ryl.* 4.714.3 ([611]). There is considerable uncertainty concerning the contents of this document and strong reason to believe that the reading is erroneous. In any case, if one supposed that the practice of designating oneself as fatherless (be it during its latest stages legal necessity or habit) ceased toward the end

Karanis, constitutes the latest mention of a fatherless individual in the published papyri and ostraca, a fatherless woman called Atous.[72] The earliest seems to be from an Arsinoite account of *sitologoi*, dated to around 11 CE, where we hear of a man called Aphrodisios, designated *apatōr*.[73] The rest of the first-century documents, however, do not further substantiate the existence of this phenomenon for most of the century: two out of the three that bear a secure date in the first century occur in the last decade of that century,[74] and the undated ones which are assigned to this century are always assigned to the "first or second," except one case where the papyrus is assigned to the "late first."[75] The Oxyrhynchite documents, that is, those using the term *chrēmatizōn mētros*, also span this time more or less, with the earliest attestation being in a will of 96 CE,[76] and the latest two names in the corn-dole register of 271/2,[77] while several documents are dated in the third century.

Although the time span of this phenomenon is not long enough to allow us to examine long-term trends of distribution, it is interesting to investigate whether its distribution pattern is comparable with the overall chronological distribution of (published) documents, at least within its narrow time confines.[78] The necessary hypothesis which would allow this comparison is that a papyrus that mentions a fatherless individual has the same chances of survival, discovery, and publication as any papyrus. If this is true, then we should expect the number of fatherlessness-related documents in the second century to be a percentage of the overall number of documents in that century which would not be too different from the relevant percentage in the third century.

In the graphs of Figure 7 I have set side by side the percentage of documents per century in each of the two best-documented nomes and in the rest of Egypt with that of the overall numbers of documents. It is evident that the percentage of the total number of papyri and of the papyri mentioning fatherlessness follows roughly the same pattern. This implies that the phenomenon, for the amount of time that it can be attested at all, had a fairly regular

---

of the third century, then the renegade *apatōr* of the sixth century must actually be a literal use of the word, with no reference whatsoever to its use as a technical term in the second and third centuries. Youtie attributes the word to the document's Christian background (1975: 732, n. 2).

[72] Youtie (1975: 732, n. 2) is justified in expressing some doubt as to the certainty of the reading of the word *apatōr* in this document, since the last two letters are lost, and what could be meant is the name of the father in the genitive, e.g. *Apat[os]*. I chose to include this document, since in fact it is not certain that the editor's reading is wrong. In any case, the second latest document recording a fatherless individual is the Oxyrhynchite document mentioned just below, of 271/2 CE.

[73] *P.Lond.* 2.256D.18 recto ([**357**]).

[74] *P.Oxy.* 1.104 of 96 CE; *P.Soter.* 7 of 91 CE; but *P.Lond.* 2.256D of 11–15 CE.

[75] *P.Leid.Inst.* 28, assigned to the late first century; *P.Lond.* 2.901, first or second century; *P.Strass.* 9.843, first or second century; *SB* 12.10948, end of first or second century.

[76] *P.Oxy.* 1.104.10 ([**13**]); see Youtie 1973: 380–2.   [77] *P.Oxy.* 40.2936 ii.8 ([**27**]) and 23 ([**28**]).

[78] For specific numbers see Habermann 1998: 147.

Chronological distribution by nome

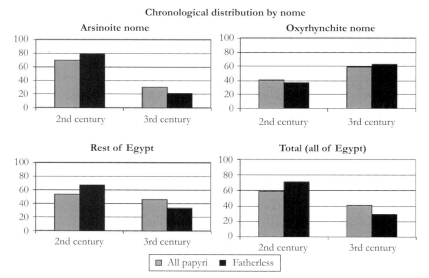

All papyri: *Arsinoite: second century, 4437; third century, 1937. Oxyrhynchite: second century, 875; third century, 1281. Rest of Egypt: second century, 3124; third century, 2687. Total: second century, 8436; third century, 5905.*

Fatherlessness-related papyri: *Arsinoite: second century, 161; third century, 42. Oxyrhynchite: second century, 17; third century, 29. Rest of Egypt: second century, 18; third century, 9. Total: second century, 196; third century, 80.*

Figure 7 Percentage of papyri over second and third centuries.

chronological distribution. Consequently, an overall preponderance in second-century documents, followed by some in the third, is pretty much what we would expect. Furthermore, it is notable that in the specific case of the Oxyrhynchite documents with references to fatherless persons, those coming from the third century actually outnumber those from the second. This also conforms to the expected pattern of distribution, since the Oxyrhynchite nome, as opposed to the general trend, has yielded more documents from the third century than it has from the second (or any other).[79]

An exacting statistical approach would suggest that the percentage difference between fatherlessness-related documents and the sum of all papyri is in fact not insignificant. Especially in the case of the Arsinoite documents, an abundance calculation (ratio of fatherlessness-related documents to all documents) would indicate that, although the percentage remains very

[79] Habermann 1998: 148. The figures of course refer to published documents.

small, in the second century it is in fact almost double what it is in the third. However, in a situation such as the present one, where so many variables are impossible to assess, and many of the data are only a plausible approximation of what may have been the case, this difference is not significant enough to undermine the overall impression that the documents mentioning fatherless individuals do not notably diverge from the overall pattern formed by the sum of published documents.

All in all, the chronological spread reveals the *apatores* – or, more probably, the legal requirement of their designation as such – as a uniquely Roman phenomenon of the second (or very late first) to third centuries. Within that time, the amount and quality of information that we derive from the documents absolutely depends on the type of document in which it appears. Anything that is disclosed is nothing more than is absolutely necessary depending on the requirements of each document. One exception to this would be private correspondence, where on occasion we can learn much about the people writing to each other. Unfortunately this is of no help in the case of the fatherless individuals in question, since the designations *apatōr* and *chrēmatizōn mētros* would only be required in documents that have some sort of legal status or fulfill a legal function.

GEOGRAPHICAL DISTRIBUTION

The provenance of all but twenty-six documents is known or conjectured, and in the case of Oxyrhynchite documents we have the added element of terminology as extra confirmation. To establish the geographical distribution of fatherless individuals we must again turn to the documents: simply counting the individuals themselves would be pointless and would provide us with a completely false impression – suffice it to say that over eighty of the known *apatores* are attested in Theadelphia in 134/5 in only two documents.[80] This, of course, shows that these documents are exactly the type in which we would expect such identifications to appear, and that it is easy to find the section of the population that we are looking for in a document that lists most of that population, rather than that there was an exceptionally high number of *apatores* in Theadelphia (though there may or may not have been). The same point can be made in connection with the chronology, where a simple count would reveal exceptionally high numbers of *apatores* in *circa* 193 CE, because of the high number of *apatores* in the *Charta Borgiana*.[81] Instead,

---

[80] *BGU* 9.1891–2 and *P.Col.* 2.1 recto 1a–b.
[81] *SB* 1.5124. More than sixty of the workers whose names are legible are described as *apatores*.

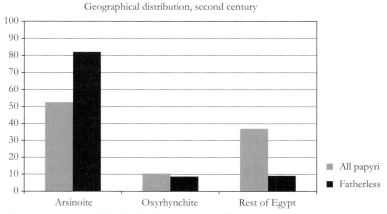

All papyri: Arsinoite, 4437; Oxyrhynchite, 875; Rest of Egypt, 3124.
Fatherlessness-related papyri: Arsinoite, 161; Oxyrhynchite, 17; Rest of Egypt, 18.

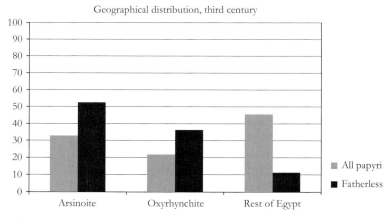

All papyri: Arsinoite, 1937; Oxyrhynchite, 1281; Rest of Egypt, 2687.
Fatherlessness-related papyri: Arsinoite, 42; Oxyrhynchite, 29; Rest of Egypt, 9.

Figure 8 Percentages of papyri by area in the second and third centuries.

we should again examine whether there is a pattern in the distribution of the documents in question compared with the overall geographical distribution of documents. In Figure 8 I compare the percentage of fatherlessness-related papyri to that of all papyri, separately for the second and third centuries, in both of the better attested nomes and the rest of Egypt.

The picture which emerges is not as straightforward as the one regarding chronology. The vast majority of documents mentioning one or more *apatores* come from the Arsinoite nome. Very few are from the metropolis, and of those with specific provenance within the rest of the nome most come from Theadelphia, while quite a few come from Ptolemais Hormou, Soknopaiou Nesos, Tebtunis, Karanis, a few from Philadelphia and only a couple from Lagis, Hiera Nesos, and Polydeukeia. The Oxyrhynchite is the next best represented in the documents, with less than a third of those from the Arsinoite. The Heracleopolite, Memphite, Hibite, Prosopite, Kynopolite, and Mendesian nomes all feature in the documents, but with only a couple of documents each, as do Hermopolis and Elephantine. It is clear from the chart that in the fatherlessness-related documents the rest of Egypt is pointedly underrepresented. In both the second and the third centuries the percentage of Arsinoite fatherlessness-related documents is considerably higher than that of the total number of documents, as is the case with the third-century Oxyrhynchite documents. As is obvious in the bars representing the documents from the rest of Egypt, the percentage of fatherlessness-related documents among the total number is significantly smaller than would be expected if the two had a similar distribution to each other. The factors creating this discrepancy are impossible to establish with certainty, but they could represent one (or more) of three possibilities: perhaps there were more fatherless individuals in these two nomes, for whatever reason; or the requirement to record them was more strictly applied; or this discrepancy may be due to the arbitrary discovery and/or publication of documents mentioning fatherless people. In any case, the present picture could be seen to suggest a variation between Upper and Lower Egypt, but this is not something that can be substantiated based on the evidence to hand.

The documents offer very few opportunities for a closer look into the distribution of fatherless individuals within a village, and the Karanis tax rolls are our best chance to compare the number of those individuals with the overall population. The rolls preserve lists of tax dues, mainly the *laographia* and other taxes, for the years 171–5. The rolls are not complete, since parts of them, mainly the ends of rolls, have been damaged or lost. However, the names of taxpayers occur several times as the taxes were paid in installments, which means that the overall loss of names is much smaller than the damage to the document would suggest. Over the preserved years only a small number of taxpayers has been lost.[82] Boak calculates a maximum of 644 and a minimum of 575 male Greco-Egyptians over the age of fourteen.[83] Based on this, Youtie calculates that the fourteen fatherless men who are attested paying the poll tax in the rolls accounts for 2.1–2.6 percent

---

[82] The rolls are *P.Mich.* 4.223–5. See Boak 1955: 157–62; Geremek 1969: 36–40.   [83] Boak 1955: 159.

of the total of poll-tax payers.[84] To the upper estimate of the latter figure Rathbone adds approximately one hundred Roman citizens, based on which he calculates the total population of Theadelphia in the 170s CE to be about 2,300.[85] If we accept that fatherlessness of this sort is a phenomenon which permeates people of both genders and any social status without much distinction, then Youtie's figure could be applied to the total estimated population of Karanis, suggesting that between forty-eight and fifty-nine people may have been fatherless.[86]

CONCLUSION

The purpose of this survey was to explore the question of the social status of one class of fatherless individuals in Roman Egypt, particularly with respect to their financial situations, their household structures, and other important aspects of their civic lives and legal positions. The ultimate goal was to gain an impression of their function and standing within the social fabric of Roman Egypt, and to identify any distinguishing features that would set them apart, favorably or unfavorably, from the general population. The overall picture that emerges from the above discussion indicates that this sort of fatherlessness permeated the society of Roman Egypt demographically and chronologically, while it appears to have been more restricted geographically. Men and women, adults and children could be designated as *apatores*. Furthermore, though fatherlessness technically is only seen to affect free persons, this is because slaves do not have legally recognized parents, not because as a phenomenon it occurs only in higher social echelons. The professions, trades, and liturgies that we know about would position the *apatores* in a middling social position, extending from dike workers to village officials. Two *apatores* surprisingly even appear as priests. The evidence discussed in this paper suggests that fatherless individuals were not restricted to certain statuses or professions, but that the phenomenon of legal fatherlessness was inextricably linked with the overall structure of society. And although there was a legal obligation on the part of fatherless individuals to designate themselves clearly as such, this did not seem to taint those individuals in a way that was especially damaging.

---

[84] Youtie 1975: 731–2.
[85] Rathbone 1990: 132, 134. The calculation is based on an index of 3.1 percent.
[86] Theadelphia also offers tax documents in which there are ample references to fatherless individuals, but the total population cannot be reconstructed with the same confidence as in the case of the more complete Karanis rolls. See Sharp 1999: 164.

PART III

Roles without models

CHAPTER 8

Diomedes, the fatherless hero of the Iliad

Louise Pratt

INTRODUCTION

In this study I will explore a literary representation of a single fatherless son, Diomedes in the *Iliad*. Though the *Iliad* cannot be used as a reliable source for the depiction of social norms and practices in any single period of Greek history, its broad influence and high status in antiquity make it an integral part of Classical culture. As children in Classical Athens studied the *Iliad* in school from an early age and were sometimes even required to memorize it in full, as it was regularly performed at major festivals and contests all over Greece in the Classical period, and as it is clearly alluded to in multiple ways in multiple texts and works of art, both Greek and Roman, from various periods, so we may assume that it shaped the consciousness of a broad range of different kinds of ancient audiences in powerful ways.[1] Thus, though Diomedes represents only one view of a fatherless son and a fictional one at that,[2] his example must have been extremely well known. In a world in which many children never knew their fathers and in many cases suffered the isolation that might go along with fatherlessness but still frequently found great social success, as is detailed in many of the chapters in this volume, the complex characterization of Diomedes in the *Iliad* surely had a particular resonance. The *Iliad*'s Diomedes would discourage any ancient audience from imagining that fatherlessness was an impediment to social success: Diomedes is a more than competent participant in many aspects of Homeric culture. At the same time, the poem's portrait of the fatherless

---

[1] On the use of Homer in childhood education in Athens, see, e.g., Pl. *Resp.* 377a–e and *Prt.* 325d–26a (Homer is not explicitly named, but surely must be included among the good poets listed). For memorization, see Xen. *Symp.* 3.569. For Homer's more general role as the "educator of Greece," see Pl. *Resp.* 606e and *Ion*, the latter of which is also useful as a source for the performance of Homer at festivals in the Classical period. Lamberton 1997 offers a helpful overview of the reception of Homer in antiquity and cites many additional primary sources.

[2] Some may prefer the term "mythical" to "fictional," but in any case I mean not grounded in historical reality.

hero suggests a subtle psychological toll that marks the fatherless hero and keeps him from certain forms of insight and integration valued in the poem.

Thomas Greene once labeled the *Iliad* "a great poem of fatherhood,"[3] and numerous scholars and critics have commented on how fatherhood figures as a major theme of the poem. From the first action in its plot, when Chryses, an aged father, enters the Achaean camp to ransom his daughter, to its surprising close, when the poem's hero, Achilles, finds reconciliation and fellowship with the father of his slain enemy through pity of his own mortal father, Peleus, fathers figure prominently in the *Iliad*'s action and imagery.[4] In a poem so grounded in the father–child relationship, it is not surprising to find some reflection of the demographic reality that a large percentage of children in antiquity were in fact growing up fatherless.[5] Indeed, the *Iliad* comments directly on the consequences of fatherlessness to a small child through Andromache's vivid and detailed imaginings of Astyanax in the wake of Hector's death.[6] The poem also shows awareness of the economic consequences of fatherlessness in the simile of the upright widow, toiling over her careful balance to win a pittance for her fatherless children (*Il.* 12.433–5).

But the *Iliad* gives its most sustained treatment of fatherlessness through its depiction of an adult male, Diomedes, who asserts at *Iliad* 6.222–3 that he has no recollection of his father, who left him when he was small (Τυδέα δ'οὐ μέμνημαι, ἐπεί μ' ἔτι τυτθὸν ἐόντα | κάλλιφ'). The contention of this chapter is that Diomedes' fatherlessness is a significant component of his characterization, maintained throughout the *Iliad*, which enhances his role as a foil for Achilles, whose complex relationships with various fathers – his own father (Peleus), his surrogate father (Phoenix), his second surrogate (Agamemnon),[7] his enemy's father (Priam), and his dearest friend with the significant paternal name (Patroclus)[8] – are an important motif in the poem. Strikingly, the *Iliad* suggests that the absence of a father has left Diomedes without empathy, a quality that the poem presents as the hallmark of a civilized humanity through the reconciliation of Achilles and Priam in

[3] Greene 1963: 47.
[4] Important work on fathers in the *Iliad* includes Redfield 1975: esp. 110–12; Finlay 1980; Macleod 1982; Crotty 1994: esp. ch. 2, also 81–2, 97; Wöhrle 1999; Mills 2000; Felson 2002.
[5] See Scheidel (this volume).
[6] See esp. *Il.* 22.487–507. See quotation and discussion in Wöhrle (this volume) with additional passages from both the *Iliad* and *Odyssey*.
[7] See Avery 1998 for Agamemnon as a surrogate father.
[8] See Finlay 1980 for Patroclus as a substitute father for Achilles.

Book 24. Unlike Achilles, Diomedes never learns to pity the father,[9] nor does he develop the emotional capacity for care on which the *Iliad* puts a premium, a kind of care explicitly associated in the poem with parental concern for children, as I have argued elsewhere.[10] Thus, the fatherless Diomedes remains cut off both generationally and emotionally: lacking a father, Diomedes also does not become a father, either literally or metaphorically.[11]

Diomedes is not a failure as a warrior; his utter pitilessness, together with the support of Athene, makes him a ruthless and highly successful killer. Moreover, despite his brutality on the battlefield, Diomedes finds it easier to maintain peaceful relations with those in authority than does Achilles, so that at several points in the poem we may be tempted to take Diomedes as far superior to the selfish and sullen hero whose struggles with his surrogate father, Agamemnon, lead to such disaster for the Achaeans, in a conflict that many readers have seen as at least vaguely Oedipal. Nonetheless, overall the *Iliad* suggests something different. When the two heroes are compared – and the poem suggests many similarities that encourage such a comparison – Diomedes emerges as second to Achilles. Unlike Achilles, who is fated to surpass his father, Diomedes in the *Iliad* remains in the shadow of his famous father. More important still, Diomedes' inability to comprehend paternal care and loss keep him from sharing the tragic vision of Achilles and of the poem itself.

THE UNIQUENESS OF DIOMEDES IN THE *ILIAD*

Diomedes is highly unusual in the *Iliad* in being explicitly presented as a fatherless hero. In general, the *Iliad* highlights parents' care for children and hence the terrible grief and loss of parental investment at their children's deaths. Thus, even in cases in which we may be tempted to deduce that a hero must have grown up essentially fatherless, as in the many cases of sons

---

[9] In this he is like Virgil's Neoptolemus, whom Priam accuses of falsely claiming to be born of Achilles, because he defiled a father's eyes by forcing him to witness his son's death (*patrios foedasti funere vultus*, *Aen.* 2.540), instead of following Achilles' example in respecting his enemy's father's supplication. See Golden (this volume) for the suggestion that Neoptolemus' fatherlessness might be adduced as contributing to his brutality.

[10] Pratt 2007.

[11] In this he can be both compared and contrasted with Phoenix. Like Phoenix, who comes from a dysfunctional patriline that makes it impossible for him to reproduce (cf. 9.453–6, 493), Diomedes will never have his own children. Unlike Phoenix, who tells us that Peleus treated him like his own son and who acts in turn as father to Achilles (9.481–95), Diomedes never develops the emotional capacity for paternal care in the *Iliad*. See Felson 2002: 41–2 on the dysfunctional patriline of Phoenix, and Felson 1999 and 2002: 40–2 on the importance of a healthy patriline in the development of successful masculinity in Homeric epic.

of gods, the *Iliad* undermines our assumptions in its representation of divine parents. For example, though we may find it hard to imagine that Zeus was readily available to Sarpedon in his youth, we witness the divine father profoundly moved by his mortal son's death, weeping tears of blood (16.459) and tenderly overseeing his burial (16.665–83). Zeus's grief and care make it impossible to see Sarpedon as fatherless.[12] Divine fathers overturn several norms.[13] They will always outlive their sons and therefore *must* mourn them. Moreover, despite surpassing mortal fathers in virtually every capacity, they cannot rescue their mortal sons from death, and this gives special pathos to their loss. As with Sarpedon, so in the case of Ascalaphus, son of Ares, the *Iliad* is clearly interested in exploring the pathos of divine fatherhood in the face of the mortal child's death. In Book 13 Ares' ignorance of his son's death and his detention on Olympus are pathetic (13.516–25); two books later, the poet comes back to this minor character to focus on Ares' paternal rage and sorrow (15.110–18). Indeed, as Thetis is frequently shown interacting with Achilles to underscore that same theme of the immortal parent who, for all her love and concern, cannot save her child from death, the poem does not allow us easily to infer that immortal parents are necessarily absent or uninvolved, despite their inevitable grief.[14]

In a perhaps more typical case of a divinely sired son, that of Eudorus, a Trojan son of Hermes, we are told that an old man, Phylas, took him in "and brought him up kindly | and cared for him, in affection as if he had been his own son" (16.191–2).[15] It seems reasonable to infer in this case that Eudorus is not imagined to have any contact with his real father, Hermes. But this example, too, raises questions about whether divine sons of this sort should really be considered fatherless, since it suggests that sons of gods brought up by mortals might have relationships with their adoptive fathers that could scarcely be distinguished from those with their biological ones.[16]

---

[12] Late sources (schol. *Il.* 12.292; Apollod. *Bibl.* 3.1.2; Diod. Sic. 4.60.3) tell us of a stepfather to Sarpedon, Asterius, but the *Iliad* makes no mention of him. On Asterius and other mythological stepfathers, see Watson 1995: 38–42; Hübner (this volume).

[13] In addition to the differences discussed here, divine fathers do not want their sons to be better than them nor are they the repositories of cultural values and memories, as are human fathers.

[14] On Thetis as a mother, see Murnaghan 1992: 251–7.

[15] Cf. Menesthius, son of the river god Spercheius, but brought up by Borus, who married his mother (16.170–8), a virtual doublet of Eudorus. All quotations of the *Iliad* in English are adapted from the translation by Lattimore (1951) unless otherwise noted.

[16] Watson (1995: 40) notes that "in most myths where a stepfather adopts a stepson, he has no son of his own." See also Hübner (this volume). See also Watson's discussion of Amphitryon as Heracles' adoptive stepfather, as well as other examples (Watson 1995: 39–42). There are, however, exceptions to this general rule in Homeric epic, e.g. the children of Tyro (cf. *Od.* 11.256–9) and of Leda.

Perhaps most relevant here is that the poet cares to provide an affectionate father even for a relatively minor figure.

Indeed, when one considers the obituaries of minor warriors, it is striking how many actually mention living fathers who will not be able to be repaid for the tender upbringing they provided or whose special talents as a seer or priest have nonetheless not enabled them to preserve their sons' lives.[17] Another motif that recurs is the father who has sent his son off to war with some piece of advice, advice that death will soon render meaningless.[18] Thus, the general tendency of the *Iliad* is to depict war as disrupting the ideal that the child should outlive the father, in order to emphasize the pathos of parental care and loss.

In contrast, we hear almost nothing about fatherless heroes. There is a brief obituary of a Thracian Iphidamas (11.221–5), intriguing because like Diomedes he marries his own aunt (5.412); the pathos in his case is generated by the fact that, again like Diomedes, he never procreates. Achilles' son, Neoptolemus, is being raised on Scyros apart from both his father and paternal grandfather, Peleus, something Achilles hoped that Patroclus would remedy at the end of the war, vainly, as he laments over his friend's corpse (19.326–3).[19] But these two fatherless sons are balanced by countless numbers of sons whose deaths ensure that they will never repay their still-living father's loving investment. Of course, frequently the poem tells us nothing whatsoever about the hero's father beyond his name. Verisimilitude would require that many of these fathers left their sons fatherless at an early age, but the poet generally does not call our attention to this, presumably because it does not fit the themes of fatherhood that he wishes to emphasize. Diomedes exists as a striking exception to the normal pattern.

Moreover, though later sources report that heroes, including Achilles, were frequently turned over to Chiron and other surrogate fathers for their upbringing, and so presumably spent a considerable amount of time apart from their fathers, part of what Shapiro has called the "absent father syndrome,"[20] the *Iliad* itself shows almost no awareness of this pattern. The few brief mentions of Chiron emphasize only his gifts to a very few heroes and do not necessarily imply any extended separation between father

---

[17] E.g. see Griffin 1980: 123–7 for discussion and many examples.
[18] Examples are Pandarus' father (5.196–202); Glaucus' father (6.206–10); Peleus (11.781–3; 9.252–9); and Menoetius (11.764–89).
[19] The contrast with the reestablishment of the healthy patriline of Odysseus after his return is striking. See Felsen 1999 on the importance of the union of all three generations in this family.
[20] Shapiro 2003: esp. 85–92.

and son.[21] Phoenix's memorable description of his care for Achilles as a baby
at 9.485–95 makes it clear that Phoenix was a surrogate father to Achilles and
may even suggest that the child was more attached to Phoenix than to his
real father. Phoenix says:

> … godlike Achilles, I made you all that you are now,
> and loved you out of my heart, for you would not go with another
> out to any feast, nor taste any food in your own halls
> until I had set you on my knees, and cut little pieces
> from the meat, and given you all you wished, and held the wine for you.

Nonetheless, Peleus is hardly absent from the picture of Achilles' childhood.
Phoenix says earlier in that same speech that Peleus acted as a surrogate father
to Phoenix himself, loving him "as a father loves his own son | who is a single
child brought up among many possessions" (9.481–2). Phoenix's characterization of the father–single-son relationship here has implications for Peleus'
relationship with his only son, as well as making it clear that Peleus was not a
distant or removed member of the household. In Book 23 Patroclus' ghost
testifies that Peleus took him into his house and brought him up carefully
(ἐνδυκέως) alongside Achilles. Nestor and Phoenix both describe interactions between Peleus and Achilles that cast Peleus in a typical paternal role,
and, as I will argue below, Achilles' memory of his father plays an essential role
in the poem.[22] Thus, the Achilles of the *Iliad*, far from suffering "absent father
syndrome," is oversupplied with fathers, having not only Peleus, but Phoenix,
perhaps briefly Chiron, and, less obviously, Patroclus and Agamemnon, all
serving as father figures at points in the poem.[23] Whatever later sources may
suggest, nowhere else in the *Iliad* itself does the poet or any hero other than
Diomedes comment on the absence of a father from an adult hero's life or
memory; Diomedes thus emerges as a special case.

DIOMEDES AND HIS FATHER

The *Iliad* ensures that we remember that Diomedes is fatherless by the way
in which Tydeus' name and reputation are used rhetorically by speakers in

---

[21] Medicine to Asclepius (4.219); knowledge of medicine to Achilles (11.832); and the Pelion ash spear to
Peleus (16.143–4).

[22] E.g. *Il.* 11.781–3, where Peleus gives standard paternal advice in saying farewell to Achilles (cf. Glaucus'
father at 6.206–10). Cf. 9.252–9, 9.438–43 for Peleus in the role of advisor and guide to his son
(discussed below). At *Il.* 23.89–90 Peleus is said to have brought up Patroclus alongside Achilles. The
presence of Menoetius at the departure of Achilles and Patroclus (11.764–89) likewise suggests that
Menoetius did not abandon Patroclus after bringing him to the household of Peleus.

[23] See Finlay 1980; Avery 1998; and Mills 2000 on these father figures to Achilles.

the poem and by the frequent reiteration of his name whenever Diomedes appears.[24] Tydeus is repeatedly held up as a precedent and model for Diomedes in a way that is not characteristic of the living fathers of heroes in the poem. A particularly developed example occurs in our first extended encounter with Diomedes in *Iliad* 4, during Agamemnon's rallying of the troops (the so-called "Epipolesis"). The last and the longest in a series of five exhortations to major leaders, Agamemnon's address contrasts Diomedes' current behavior to the glorious deeds of his father, Tydeus, clearly exploiting the young man's desire to match up to his dead father:

> Ah me, son of Tydeus, that daring breaker of horses,
> why are you skulking and spying out the outworks of battle?
> Such was never Tydeus' way, to lurk in the background,
> but to fight the enemy far ahead of his own companions.   (4.370–3)

Agamemnon then proceeds to relate at length (374–98) one of Tydeus' great exploits, in which he first bested in contests the many Cadmians he faced and then defeated and killed all but one of fifty Cadmians who waited in ambush for him on his way home, apparently enraged by their humiliation. Agamemnon concludes his speech by saying, "This was Tydeus, the Aetolian; yet he was father | to a son worse than himself in fighting, better in conclave" (399–400). The considerable attention Agamemnon gives to Diomedes' father here is clearly distinct from his approach to other heroes in his previous four exhortations and is certainly part of the poem's overall characterization of Diomedes as particularly engaged with the reputation and fame of his dead father.

The responses that Agamemnon's rebuke generates are also essential to our understanding of Diomedes' character as particularly beholden to his dead father's example. Diomedes responds to Agamemnon's rebuke with silent awe (4.401–2), an unusually passive response to such a rebuke for a Homeric hero. In contrast, Diomedes' companion Sthenelus responds with considerable heat, defending himself as well as Diomedes, though in fact Agamemnon has said absolutely nothing about Sthenelus or his father:

---

[24] Many scholars have noted the unusually close association between Diomedes and his father in the *Iliad*. See particularly Andersen 1978: 15–16, 34, 41, 51 and *passim*. See also Schnapp-Gourbeillon 1982: 46; Kirk 1983: 26 on Tydeus in Books 4–6; Kirk 1990: 67 *ad* 116; Rabel 1997: 90–1. Tsirpanlis 1966: 244–5 shows that the patronymic Τυδείδης is used about fifty times in the poem, thus almost as many times as Achilles' patronymic, Πηλιάδης (fifty-eight times), despite Diomedes being much less of a presence in the poem than Achilles. This is considerably more than any other patronymic (with the likely exception of Ἀτρείδης, used of both Agamemnon and Menelaus, which Tsirpanlis does not quantify).

> Son of Atreus, do not lie when you know the plain truth.
> We two claim we are better men by far than our fathers.
> We did storm the seven-gated foundation of Thebes
> though we led fewer people beneath a wall that was stronger.
> We obeyed the signs of the gods and the help Zeus gave us,
> while those others died of their own headlong stupidity.
> Therefore, never liken our fathers to us in honor.   (4.404–10)

Sthenelus' touchy self-defense both offers a more complex view of Tydeus' achievements and is more characteristic of the Homeric hero's response to suggestions that others are better, as we have seen in previous scenes with Achilles.[25] Odysseus' very angry retort at 4.350–5 to the only other rebuke in the Epipolesis immediately preceding likewise presents a particularly strong contrast to Diomedes' silence.[26]

Not only is Diomedes at first silent in response to Agamemnon's rebuke, but he directly responds to Sthenelus' defense by defending Agamemnon:

> Friend, stay quiet rather and do as I tell you; I will
> find no fault with Agamemnon, shepherd of the people,
> for stirring thus into battle the strong-greaved Achaeans;
> this will be his glory to come, if ever the Achaeans
> cut down the men of Troy and capture sacred Ilion.
> If the Achaeans are slain, then this will be his great sorrow.
> Come, let you and me remember our fighting courage.   (4.412–18)

His response is strikingly sympathetic to Agamemnon's point of view as leader of the army; his words contrast particularly sharply with the barbs thrown at Agamemnon earlier in the poem by Achilles and Thersites. The exchange is clearly the climax of the extended Epipolesis and draws our attention to Diomedes immediately before he begins his *aristeia* (a period of greatest glory for a Homeric warrior). Containing his first words and deeds of the poem, the scene thus highlights Diomedes' abiding interest in his absent father and his desire to live up to his reputation, a desire that makes him particularly susceptible to Agamemnon's manipulation.

When we compare the way in which living fathers are used to motivate heroic sons, we see something different. Commonly, a speaker will remind the son of what his father said, as, for example, when Nestor reminds

[25] Sthenelus is presumably another fatherless son, but the *Iliad* does not develop his character nor make a point of his fatherlessness.
[26] For Idomeneus and the two Aiantes, he offers brief and mild exhortations with no rebuke (4.257–64, 4.285–91); for Nestor he comments briefly and approvingly on the spirit the old man shows and wishes only that Nestor were younger (4.313–16).

Patroclus of his father's parting words (11.764–89). Nestor spends a considerable amount of time here recreating the entire scene, using abundant
detail to trigger Patroclus' memory of the moment of separation for its
emotional effect. Similarly, Odysseus and Phoenix try to move Achilles to
follow their advice by invoking his father's advice on parting (9.252–59;
9.438–43). Like Nestor, these speakers use the emotional effect of the
memory of separation as well as the father's authority to help persuade,
but they do not hold up the father himself as an example to imitate.

This in turn reflects the rhetorical strategies fathers themselves employ
when they are shown directly offering advice to their sons on how to excel:
they do not invoke themselves as examples. To do so would perhaps create
competition between father and son that is inappropriate to the cooperative
father–son model generally embraced by Homeric epic.[27] Nestor's advice
to his son, Antilochus, on how to win the chariot race is a particularly
illuminating example of paternal tact. He prefaces his advice with the
remark, "Zeus and Poseidon | have loved you and taught you horsemanship
in all of its aspects. | Therefore there is no great need to instruct you; you
yourself | know well how to double the turning-post" (23.306–9). He then
proceeds to deliver almost forty lines of detailed advice (309–48), covering,
as the poet comments, "each stage of the contest." Unusually for Nestor,
who frequently recounts in detail his own notable example to inspire the
rest of the Achaeans, he does not mention his own successes when speaking
to Antilochus. Peleus and Hippolochus offer a much terser piece of advice
to their sons, Achilles and Glaucus respectively, "to be always best in battle,
and pre-eminent beyond all others" (11.783 = 6.208). Both heroes are urged
to compete with other people rather than to live up to their father's
example. It is true that Achilles in particular differs from Diomedes in
being destined since birth to surpass his father, but it also may simply be
safer to invoke the Oedipal urge when the father is already dead.

During Diomedes' *aristeia*, his next appearance closely following
the Epipolesis, Athene twice speaks to Diomedes of Tydeus, once telling
him that she has put the might of his father (μένος πατρώϊον) into his
chest (5.125–6) and once comparing him unfavorably with Tydeus, who
performed impressive feats among the Cadmians, which, like Agamemnon,
she relates at some length (5.800–13). Again, the absent Tydeus plays a
considerable role in motivating Diomedes to action. Indeed, Diomedes
often seems to exist in the shadow of his father's name. From his first brief

---

[27] See Felson 2002: 38–40 and work cited there (esp. 40, n. 6) on epic's embrace of a cooperative rather
than competitive model of the father–son relationship.

mention in the poem (2.406), where he is called simply "son of Tydeus" (Τυδέος υἱόν), to his final appearance in the funeral games for Patroclus (23.824), where the patronymic Τυδείδη is used by itself, Diomedes is actually called the son of Tydeus more often than he is by his given name.[28]

Although the *Iliad* strongly associates Diomedes with his father's name and reputation, it consistently presents Diomedes as a man with no personal knowledge of the long-dead Tydeus. Diomedes repeatedly invokes Tydeus to win the support of others, but in ways that are compatible with his claim in Book 6 that he does not actually remember him.[29] At the outset of his *aristeia* in Book 5 and again in Book 10 when he is embarking on his other major exploit in the *Iliad*, the Doloneia, Diomedes mentions his father in asking Athene for help: "If ever before in kindliness, you stood by my father | through the terror of fighting, be my friend now also" (5.116) and "Come with me now as you went with my father, brilliant Tydeus" (10.285). Diomedes clearly accepts Tydeus' function as precedent and example for him. Later, in his final speech of the poem, he invokes Tydeus to give credence to his counsel before the Achaeans. He acknowledges that his youth may stir up some resentment of his advice, but suggests that this is mitigated because he is born "of an excellent father, | Tydeus, whom now the heaped earth covers over in Thebes" (14.110–14). The burial of Tydeus at Thebes, far from Argos, seems to underscore the dissolution of the patri-line.[30] A few lines later (119–25) he gives a summary account of Tydeus' life, which emphasizes his wealthy estate in Argos, presumably Diomedes' childhood home, and briefly mentions his outstanding spearsmanship, but notably omits anything personal as well as all the negative elements in Tydeus' life story (14.121–5).[31] The poet thus creates in Diomedes a psycho-logically plausible example of a fatherless son: a man constantly aware of his father's name and reputation, which he uses to win the support and respect of others and which others use to spur him to greater success, but whose knowledge of his father, uninformed by personal experience, remains not only colorless and devoid of emotional content but idealized.

---

[28]   It is telling that his first mention comes in a catalogue of Achaean heroes, the rest of whom are identified by their given names. Again, over the course of his final appearance (23.811–25), he is referred to by his patronymic three times (812, 820, 824), but only once by his name (following his patronymic at 812).

[29]   Though see Andersen 1978: 105–7 for the importance of the fathering theme to this scene.

[30]   I am grateful to Margaret Foster for this suggestion.

[31]   As Higbie (2002: 188) comments, "Diomedes' performance of his genealogy is as notable for the stories it omits as for those it tells, as the scholiasts themselves observed. Diomedes overlooks his father's crimes and exile and simply states that Tydeus wandered to Argos, married a daughter of Adrastus, and was part of the Seven against Thebes." See Janko 1992: 163–4 *ad* 114 and 115–20 for details of the omissions.

DIOMEDES AND FATHER SURROGATES?

Later sources give fatherless sons like Diomedes powerful father surro-gates;[32] indeed, later sources put Diomedes himself in Chiron's care. But the *Iliad* does very little with this theme of a surrogate father for Diomedes, as though it would undermine the characterization of the fatherless hero it is carefully creating. Thus, we hear virtually nothing of Diomedes' childhood in the *Iliad* apart from the reiterated theme of the absent father-hero. We do learn at 14.119 that Tydeus' own father, Oeneus, stayed behind when Tydeus settled in Argos, strongly suggesting the absence of the paternal grandfather from Diomedes' upbringing and thus further underscoring the dissolution of this entire patriline. But we hear nothing of the male relatives on Diomedes' mother's side whom we would expect to assist with the upbringing of a male child in these circumstances.

Diomedes' positive relationship with the aged Nestor is the closest thing we see to a substitute father relationship for Diomedes. The scene in *Iliad* 8, in which Diomedes rescues Nestor, whose horse has just been struck by Paris' arrow, as Odysseus flees, unresponsive to Diomedes' appeal (8.80–112), has been thought to have been inspired by a scene in the *Aethiopis*, in which Antilochos dies rescuing his father from his wrecked chariot.[33] In the *Iliad*, however, Diomedes plays the son's role. Moreover, at 9.53–9 Nestor both praises Diomedes in strong terms and comes close to suggesting that he is virtually a son to him ("you are a young man still and could even be my own son | and my youngest born of all"). In this limited way Nestor does act as something of a father figure to Diomedes; indeed, the association of Diomedes with particular skill as a speaker and his ability to mediate between Agamemnon and more outspoken members of the army make Nestor his natural ally and an appropriate mentor for him. As we have seen repeatedly in this volume, such male mentors and surrogate fathers were essential parts of the social structure that kept fatherless sons as successfully functioning members of the group. Athene's support likewise makes Diomedes an early example of a "fatherless favorite of the gods," who achieves considerable success without his father's direct guidance and advice and with only minimal support from any other mortal.[34]

---

[32] See Bernstein (this volume) on the importance of surrogate fathers for many fatherless sons.
[33] See Whitman 1958: 166 and bibliography cited there.
[34] See Müller (this volume) on two such favorites, Cyrus and Sulla.

THE PITILESSNESS OF DIOMEDES

Nonetheless, even if successful within the competitive warrior culture depicted in the poem, Diomedes falls short on a competing scale of values that the *Iliad* presents as more important: he lacks a fundamental human capacity for pity and care, a capacity rooted in the poem's conception of fatherhood, as I have argued elsewhere.[35] In his *aristeia*, the very high point of his success, he is an automaton, heeding Athene's bidding rather than making his own decisions.[36] Moreover, the poem puts particular emphasis on the harm Diomedes does to children and fathers to emphasize his pitilessness and possibly also his generational isolation. The wounding of Aphrodite, who is clearly not fit for war, and whose response in running tearfully to the lap of her mother is that of an injured and vulnerable child, diminishes Diomedes' stature, making him at once brutal and inconsequential. Though Ares, god of war, would, in contrast, seem to be a worthy opponent for a human warrior, he too comes across as strangely childish in this book, particularly when confronted with the far more cunning and thoughtful Athene, who directs all of Diomedes' actions, even driving home the thrust of the spear to Ares' belly (5.856–9). Ares' subsequent whining to Zeus about his oldest sister, Zeus's favorite (5.872–87), and Zeus's comically paternal response at 5.889–98, where he labels Ares' problems as "all your mother's fault" while acknowledging that, as a father, he cannot bear to see even his most troublesome child in pain (5.895–6), reinforce the impression of Diomedes' actions as brutal and unfeeling, but also insignificant and even comical in their effects.

When Diomedes encounters mortal victims, these comic elements are lost but Diomedes remains particularly brutal and pitilessness. Thus, he boasts:

> … if one is struck by me only a little, that is far different,
> the stroke is a sharp thing and suddenly lays him lifeless
> and that man's wife goes with cheeks torn in lamentation,
> and his children are fatherless (*orphanikoi*).   (11.391–4)

This is no formulaic vaunt; it is, in fact, the only time the word *orphanikoi* (fatherless) is used in the *Iliad* apart from its use in Andromache's speeches,

---

[35] On the importance of pity and care as essential Iliadic values, see esp. Crotty 1994; Lynn-George 1996; Kim 2000. See Mills 2000 and Pratt 2007 for the association with parents.

[36] On this quality of Diomedes, see Erbse 1961: 184. He calls Diomedes a "Werkzeug." Schnapp-Gourbeillon (1982: 69) refers to him as "mécanique meurtrière."

when she describes her fears for Astyanax.[37] Thus, though Diomedes' own fatherless state enables him to envision clearly the broader consequences of his actions, it does not generate any pity for the children he himself leaves fatherless.[38] Himself deprived, he has no mercy for those he deprives in turn.

Even more notable, in contrast to the moving meeting of Achilles with the father of his slain enemy at the poem's brilliant close, Diomedes shows a striking lack of sympathy toward the fathers of those he is slaying. Thus, in the opening part of his *aristeia*, the poet puts particular emphasis on the harm Diomedes does to *fathers*. His first kill is one of the sons of Dares. We hear that he was on the verge of killing the other, "but Hephaestus caught him away and rescued him, shrouded in darkness, | that the aged man might not be left altogether desolate" (5.23–4). But though this father, a priest of Hephaestus, is helped by the god, others are not so lucky, as Diomedes goes on to kill several pairs of brothers:

> He … went on after Polyidos and Abas,
> son of the aged dream-interpreter, Eurydamas;
> yet for these two as they went forth the old man did not answer
> their dreams, but Diomedes the powerful slew them. Now he
> went after the two sons of Phaenops, Xanthos and Thoön,
> full grown both, but Phaenops was stricken in sorrowful old age
> nor could breed another son to leave among his possessions.
> There he killed these two and took away the dear life from them
> both, leaving to their father lamentation and sorrowful
> affliction, since he was not to welcome them home from the fighting
> alive still; and remoter kinsmen shared his possessions.   (5.148–57)

The first father, the priest or prophet whose divine connections and skills offer inadequate protection to his sons, is a standard Iliadic type but is particularly associated with Diomedes through three separate examples;[39] the second is a uniquely detailed and consequently particularly vivid elaboration of the standard motif of a father bereft of sons.[40] Immediately following the sons of Phaenops, Diomedes goes on to kill a pair of Priam's sons, one of many pairs of sons lost by the long-suffering Priam in the poem; Kirk suggests that the connection to Priam makes them "more real than their shadowy predecessors," hence a fitting climax to the series.[41] This

---

[37] See Wöhrle (this volume) for discussion of Andromache and fatherlessness.
[38] See also Schnapp-Gourbeillon 1982 on Diomedes' brutality and lack of human feeling, particularly the connotations of *krateros* and the similes he is associated with.
[39] On this type, see Kirk 1990: 54 *ad* 9–26 and 73 *ad* 148–9. In addition to the example here, Diomedes kills a priest's son at 5.23 (mentioned previously) and a seer's sons at 11.328–34 (see below).
[40] Kirk 1990: 74 *ad* 155–8.   [41] Kirk 1990: 75 *ad* 159–65.

series is then followed by a lion simile (161–4) that underscores Diomedes' brutality.

Diomedes' harm to fathers is again prominent in his other major exploit in the *Iliad* in Book 10, where he cold-bloodedly slays Dolon, whom the poet pointedly says is an only son with five sisters (317), despite his pleas in the name of his father and promises of ransom (380). At 11.328–33 Diomedes kills the two sons of Merope of Percote, a skilled prophet, who "tried to prevent his two sons | from going into battle where men die." Diomedes even comments directly on his grievous effect on fathers at the opening of Book 6, when he boasts to Glaucus "unhappy are those whose sons match warcraft against me" (127).

DIOMEDES AND ACHILLES COMPARED

Now, warriors kill, and the *Iliad* often comments on the effects of death on those left behind, so that the association of bereft fathers with Diomedes does not put him in the wrong or make him atypical. Moreover his father, Tydeus, was clearly something of a brutal figure in the epic tradition, as can be seen in the act that so repulsed Athene, his drinking of the brains of his slain enemy. Though the *Iliad* glosses over this event so far as to ignore Athene's subsequent refusal to act as Tydeus' patron, it was almost certainly known to the audience. It is therefore entirely possible that, as with Telemachus in the *Odyssey*, Diomedes' character in many respects reflects that of his absent father rather than his father's absence.[42] Nonetheless, just as Telemachus seems frozen at the threshold of manhood until Athene pushes him into action and toward greater knowledge of his father, so Diomedes is a static figure, frozen in time, who in lacking the memory of his father or the potential for reunion with him, will never take the crucial step toward a more human understanding. It is precisely in this respect that he most differs from his obvious foil in the *Iliad*, Achilles.

For, as many scholars have noted, the poem clearly asks that Diomedes and Achilles be compared by creating many direct parallels between them. For example, while the *aristeiai* of the two heroes, the first and last in the poem and the two longest, are unusual in the degree of divine involvement each shows, Achilles' encounters with the gods take on a cosmic

---

[42] It is important to acknowledge that, though the Greeks clearly did see a strongly inherited quality to human character, they could simultaneously recognize external influence contributed to shaping character. Thus, Phoenix can say to Achilles, "I made you all that you are now" (9.485). Although perhaps a boastful overstatement, this kind of language clearly acknowledges that character was not exclusively inherited.

significance as his battle with the river god evolves into a battle of the elements (21.214–376); Diomedes' encounters with Ares and Aphrodite, however, are more comic than cosmic. Similarly, both heroes are alone in the poem in taking serious but abortive action against Hector (11.338–67; 20.419–54), and both deliver the same insult when he escapes (11.362–67 = 20.449–54), but Achilles goes on later to kill Hector, while Diomedes, for all the killing he does and all the praise he receives, never kills a major Trojan hero or ally. Moreover, immediately after Diomedes insults Hector, Paris wounds him with an arrow to the foot (11.372–95), an event that seems to allude to the death of Achilles, which though not narrated in the *Iliad* could have been known to the poet.[43] But the wound that destroys Achilles is, in Diomedes' case, a surface wound that provokes only his taunts (385–95). Thus, where the poet creates deliberate parallels between the two, these underscore Diomedes' relative lack of consequence and his essentially untragic nature.

Similarly, though Achilles' arguments with Agamemnon alienate him from the rest of the Achaeans and often have a profoundly selfish cast, particularly early in the poem, his willingness to adhere to principle in the face of conflict is strikingly different from Diomedes' rather mindless obedience. Even when Diomedes voices disagreements with other members of the army in Books 7–14, his message remains a very simple and consistent one: "we must stay the course." The simplicity of his position contrasts dramatically with Achilles' gropings in Book 9 to understand the justifications for dying in warfare (316–43). Diomedes is certainly, as Taplin characterizes him, an "Achilles without the complications."[44] But without these complications, Diomedes is not very interesting or sympathetic, not fully human.

To be perfectly fair, at moments in the poem, Achilles is as brutal and utterly pitiless as Diomedes, and he certainly wreaks as much havoc on fathers as anyone in the poem, as Priam's words at 24.493–503 show.[45] And yet the striking difference is that Achilles becomes over the course of the poem profoundly aware of the meaning of paternal loss, as he mourns his dead friend Patroclus in the manner of a father bereft of his son. The similes of the poem make this relation explicit, as they compare Achilles in his

[43] So Erbse 1961: 173. See also Kullman 1984: esp. 313–15 and works cited 313, n. 14 for this claim. Gantz (1993: ii, 625–6) points out that Achilles' foot is not actually mentioned in Proclus' summary, but selected seventh- and sixth-century vase paintings make it plausible that Apollodorus' account, the earliest surviving mention of the foot, is taken directly from the *Aethiopis* or some other early source (Gantz 1993: ii, 626–8).
[44] Taplin 1992: 135.
[45] Indeed, Achilles is the only other character in the poem who uses the identical line, "unhappy are those whose sons match warcraft against me" (at 21.151).

mourning first to a father lion mourning his dead cubs (18.318–22) and, second, to a human father laying to rest the bones of his newly married son:

> And as
> a father mourns as he burns the bones of a son, who was married
> only now, and died to grieve his unhappy parents,
> so Achilles was mourning as he burned his companion's
> bones, and dragged himself by the fire in close lamentation.   (23.222–5)

The similes suggest that Achilles in losing Patroclus has come to understand what it means to lose a son. Indeed, these two similes are part of a larger pattern in the *Iliad*. As we move toward the end of the poem, Achilles is increasingly associated more with fathers and less with mothers, seen more as a parent and less as a child.[46] Thus, Achilles mentions his son Neoptolemus for the first time in Book 19, where he explicitly compares his loss of Patroclus to the loss of his father or his son; at the same time, Achilles suggests that the loss of Patroclus also represents loss of his hopes for his son's upbringing by Patroclus in Phthia, as he assumes the death of his own father Peleus by this time (330–7). Thus, with the loss of Patroclus, who plays the roles of both father and son to Achilles in these books, Achilles anticipates the dissolution of his entire patriline, and he therefore becomes through the poem's imagery a bereft father.

In contrast, Diomedes never attains this tragic insight, this peculiarly parental perspective, in the poem. This is perhaps to his credit, as he never makes the foolish decisions that lead Achilles to the loss of his friend.[47] And yet, the *Iliad* seems to insist that the ability to understand loss in the manner of a father is an important component of human sympathy. In contrast to Achilles, Diomedes, the fatherless son, the sonless hero, is entirely without significant attachments that allow him the *Iliad*'s fundamental tragic insight. He has a wife who is mentioned once by Dione (5.412), but never by Diomedes himself. He mentions his mother briefly and unemotionally in recounting Tydeus' story: "he married one of the daughters of Adrestos" (14.121). Even Sthenelus, who so passionately defends Diomedes following Agamemnon's rebuke in the Epipolesis, is distanced when Diomedes takes Agamemnon's side. It is impossible to imagine Achilles treating Patroclus in the same way. The poem further suggests the relative weakness of that friendship by giving Sthenelus a closer friend than Diomedes: at 5.325–6 Deipylos is described as Sthenelus' "close friend, whom beyond all | others

---

[46] See Pratt 2007.
[47] So some scholars would see this as a mark of Diomedes' greater prudence. See, for example, Rutherford 1982: 146, n. 9.

of his own age he prized, for their hearts were intimate." Diomedes'
cold-hearted interest in his father's reputation (πατρὸς κλέος) precludes
his developing an emotional tie to a real Patroclus.

But the effects of Diomedes' fatherlessness are made most clear in Book
24, where we are shown that Diomedes can never reach the degree of human
sympathy that we witness in the encounter between Achilles and Priam. For
the fact that Diomedes cannot actually remember Tydeus, for all that he
constantly mentions him, leaves his recollections of Tydeus entirely without
emotional content. And this makes it impossible for Diomedes to make the
extraordinary leap that Achilles does at the end of the *Iliad* in forging an
emotional bond with his enemy through thoughts of his father. As the
language of the passage clearly shows, Priam's appeal to Achilles is based in
his *memory* of his father.

It begins: "Remember your father" (μνῆσαι πατρὸς σοῖο, 24.486). And
it ends:

> Honor then the gods, Achilles, and take pity upon me,
> remembering (μνησάμενος) your father, yet I am still more pitiful;
> I have gone through what no other mortal on earth has gone through;
> I put my lips to the hands of the man who has killed my children.   (503–6)

It is precisely that ability to remember his father that Diomedes lacks
(cf. above, Τυδέα δ'οὐ μέμνημαι, 6.223). But it is that *remembering* that
creates the emotional effects essential to this scene:

> So he spoke, and stirred in the other a passion of grieving
> for his own father. He took the old man's hand and pushed him
> gently away, and the two remembered (τὼ δὲ μνησαμένω), as Priam sat
>   huddled
> at the feet of Achilles and wept close for manslaughtering Hector
> and Achilles wept now for his own father, now again
> for Patroclus.   (24.507–12)

Lacking memories of his father, Diomedes can invoke his father's name and
reputation only. Without grounding in experience, these invocations lack
emotional content and so remain on a superficial level. Thus, where Achilles
achieves a kind of tragic insight into paternal care and loss through the loss
of Patroclus, Diomedes remains verbally but never emotionally engaged
with his father's *kleos* (reputation).

Fineberg has argued that the encounter between Diomedes and Glaucus
in Book 6, in which the two men meet on the battlefield and exchange
genealogies, only to discover their grandfathers were guest-friends, thereby
putting an immediate end to their fighting, anticipates the reconciliation of

Achilles and Priam in Book 24.[48] As he rightly notes, there are clear
structural and thematic parallels. Both meetings result in the reconciliation
of two enemies, one of whom is the pre-eminent Achaean warrior of the
moment, having recently completed an extended *aristeia*; and both encounters temporarily suspend the competitive quest for personal honor through
killing in favor of more cooperative values and human connections. But
while Fineberg emphasizes the similarities between these two episodes,
I suggest that the differences are just as telling.[49] Though this scene has
been subjected to many different interpretations, it is typically felt to have a
very different tone from that of the tearful reconciliation of Book 24, one
almost comic or at least ironic.[50] Moreover, one of the most striking and
memorable features of the Priam–Achilles reconciliation is the way that it
makes a tired and defeated old man momentarily an equal to the poem's
greatest hero as they gaze wordlessly at one another in mutual wonder
(24.629–34);[51] the Diomedes–Glaucus incident has an imbalance so great –
the exchange of Glaucus' gold armor for Diomedes' bronze – that it
becomes a byword for inequity.[52] Thus, their meeting is consistently
interpreted as one in which one or the other of the two men emerges
as dominant – socially, intellectually, or morally – instead of, or in addition
to, Diomedes' obvious material advantage.[53] Moreover, though the link
between the two is grounded in paternal ties, as is the Priam–Achilles link, it
emerges not through emotional insight, through actual memories of the
father, but through social ties and conventions, through memorized lineages.
These elements – its greater affinity to comedy than tragedy, the absence of
real feeling, ties that are social and verbal rather than personal, and the

---

[48] Fineberg 1999.

[49] Subsequent scenes do not strongly or clearly support Fineberg's contention that Diomedes has been
transformed by the encounter with Glaucus "from a warrior who eagerly assaults the helpless children
of his enemies to a man whose thoughts turn to his own orphaned condition and to a renewal of
ξενία" (1999: 31). The emphasis on Diomedes' leaving fathers bereft is nowhere again as pronounced
as in the opening of Book 5, particularly if one omits Book 10 as non-Homeric (though this is far from
certainly the right decision. See, for example, Andersen [1978: 125–33] on the consistency of the
portrait of Diomedes in *Iliad* 10, which he adduces as partial evidence for Book 10 as an integral part
of the epic). But given that nowhere else does Diomedes attain the same prominence as in Book 5
except in Book 10, the continuing harshness of his words at 11.391–3 and the slaughter of another pair
of priest's sons just before this at 11.322–3, coupled with his unrelenting insistence on continuing the
war when others propose peace or withdrawal (e.g. 7.400–2, 9.32–49, 14.110–42), I do not think that
the change Fineberg adduces is evident.

[50] On comic/ironic tone, see, for example, Kirk 1990: 191; Scodel 1992. On the many interpretations of
this scene, see note 53 below. I follow particularly Gaisser 1969; Scodel 1992; Alden 1996.

[51] On this equality, see Pratt 2007 and bibliography cited there.

[52] See, for example, Pl. *Symp.* 219a.

[53] See Alden 1996: 257, n. 2 for a concise summary of the multiple interpretations of the significance of
this unequal exchange. To her bibliography, add Maftei 1976; Traill 1989; Scodel 1992; Harries 1993.

emphasis on the resultant inequity – create a very different kind of encounter between the two that neatly reflects the differing characters of Diomedes and Achilles.

The poem underscores at this parallel moment in the reconciliation the element that most distinguishes Diomedes from Achilles: his inability to remember his father. As Diomedes recites the genealogy that ties Glaucus' family to his own, he says, "I do not remember my father, Tydeus, who left me behind when I was small," the line I have cited previously in this paper.[54] This absence of memory keeps Diomedes from attaining a true sympathy with his opponent, comparable to that Achilles attains with Priam. Moreover, because Diomedes does not remember his own father but has only an idealized view of him that omits all the negative elements, he seems to miss entirely the relevance of the story of Bellerophon that Glaucus tells him, a story that, as Scodel points out, "implicitly recalls Tydeus," who like Bellerophon ultimately fell out of favor with the gods.[55] Echoing as it does the larger themes of the *Iliad* itself about the fragile nature of human success, the story should serve as a warning to Diomedes.[56] But the superficial and untragic Diomedes, though he emerges "the victor in material terms," fails to perceive "any but the surface meaning of what Glaucus says to him,"[57] instead taking comfort in the story of Lycurgus, which offers the more optimistic message that those who do not oppose the gods can avoid their wrath.[58] In fact, in dutifully following the commands of Athene and in avoiding serious conflicts with authority, the prudent Diomedes does avoid real tragedy in the *Iliad*. But as he avoids tragedy, he misses out on greatness, and the *Iliad* clearly represents him as Achilles' inferior.

A perennial question of Homeric scholarship, already raised in antiquity, has been, "why does Homer choose Diomedes rather than Ajax to be Achilles' substitute [by giving him an *aristeia* following Achilles' withdrawal from battle], when he has previously called Ajax 'the best of the Achaeans by

---

[54] My translation. Because it is not immediately relevant to the genealogy in which it is embedded, the comment seems to be a response to what Glaucus has just said about his father at the end of his recitation of his genealogy at 6.206–8; this contains Glaucus' recollection of his father's advice to him on parting. This passage is echoed later in the *Iliad*, as Peleus is said to have given Achilles the identical piece of advice on parting. The echo strongly suggests that the poet deliberately opposes Diomedes' absence of memory of his father to figures who remember their fathers in a highly emotional context.

[55] Scodel 1992: 81.   [56] Gaisser 1969.   [57] Alden 1996: 260.

[58] So Gaisser 1969: 175. She elaborates, "Diomedes is fundamentally an optimist, a non-tragic hero. In the story of Lycurgus he makes the point that the gods punish mortals who dare to oppose them; by implication, the man who does not oppose the gods will be safe from their wrath. Glaucus, on the other hand, is pessimistic; the story of Bellerophon, as he tells it, shows mortals as the victims of the gods. Diomedes' outlook is closely bound up with his own character and fate; that of Glaucus informs the poem as a whole."

far after Achilles' (*Il.* 2.768)?"[59] Though the ancient answer, that Ajax is more of a defensive than an aggressive warrior, has obvious merit, I suggest that, given the poem's interest in the fatherhood theme, Diomedes' father-lessness makes him a particularly interesting foil to Achilles, whose inter-actions with fathers, surrogate fathers, and fatherhood the poem clearly explores through its plot and imagery. Moreover, a desire to give a full characterization to the fatherless hero and to emphasize through parallels significant contrasts with Achilles encourages the poet in his surprising decision to recount an elaborate *aristeia* of Diomedes in Book 5 and its related incidents in Books 4 and 6, even though it reverses the plot direction suggested by Zeus's previous decision to support Achilles by giving victory to the Trojans in his absence.[60]

As a fatherless son, Diomedes experiences none of the tensions that bring Achilles into conflict with the rest of the army; he does not have the same Oedipal impulse, the desire to surpass the father, that Achilles manifests in his conflict with Agamemnon.[61] At the same time, however, Diomedes lacks the empathy and depth of human understanding that allows Achilles his moment of transcendence at the end of the *Iliad*, the moment that allows him to achieve, through his memories of his own father and his consequent sympathy for Priam, an appreciation of the shared humanity of his enemy. Diomedes remains an automaton, who knows obedience but not love; he remains forever cut off from others, not reproducing either literally or metaphorically. Unlike Telemachus, whose reunion with his father and grand-father brings his story of fatherlessness to a satisfying conclusion, Diomedes remains forever fatherless, a child of fortune alone.

The *Iliad* is forged in the imagination of Greek poets; it does not seek to convey social or historical reality, and no doubt in many respects it fails to conform to that external reality. But the *Iliad* must have been as influential as it was in antiquity at least partially because of the quality of its emotional insights. Homer must have seemed divine in part because he appeared to understand better than others the human heart. For this reason, the *Iliad* offers at least a glimpse into what is otherwise entirely lost to us: what the ancients felt might be lost to the son who never knew his father. The *Iliad* certainly does not offer a picture of the broad range of different emotional responses experienced by different fatherless children under many different

---

[59] See Kirk 1990: 52–3 *ad* 5.1 and bibliography cited there.
[60] This offers better motivation to the episode than Kirk (1990: 53) grants it: "The poet has decided to devote a long episode to Diomedes' triumphs and seems to offer the warrior's desire for glory as a rather cursory excuse." But see also Erbse 1961: 184–5 for additional arguments.
[61] See Austin 1999; Avery 1998.

conditions, but, as it does with so many other character types, it offers a paradigmatic view of the fatherless son: a man capable of achieving great social success through the support of mentors and the gods and through his desire to live up to his dead father's name but personally isolated and missing an important memory that might both encourage his own paternity and increase his understanding of and empathy toward other human beings.

CHAPTER 9

Sons (and daughters) without fathers: fatherlessness in the Homeric epics

Georg Wöhrle[1]

Ioanni Kramer
collegae optimo
viro doctissimo
vere philologo sexagenario

As always in Homer we have before us an imaginary setting, one projected onto a time long before the written composition of the epic, based on oral tradition and reflecting the conditions of his own time, perhaps those of the last half of the eighth century BCE. One must therefore exercise extreme caution in drawing conclusions about any underlying social realities: first and foremost the narrative must be understood in the context of its poetic world. At the most general level one can say that the figure and role of the father in both Homeric epics assumes a special importance: he is a symbol of a thoroughly patriarchal society and through him are projected the positive and negative aspects of this society. Some years ago I dealt at length with the image of the father and the relationship between fathers and sons in the *Iliad* and *Odyssey*, and I thereby attempted to describe how the idealization of the father, the social default, is undermined by bad fathers, and further how the very process of sons' becoming fathers calls into question this idealization.[2] Now, as then, I am of the opinion that the concepts "father" and "son" cannot be mapped neatly onto kinship relations, since they also carry figurative meanings. Thus, for instance, Andromache describes her husband Hector as her "father" (*Il.* 6.429).[3] Similarly, as we shall soon see, Telemachus has several surrogate or virtual "fathers."[4]

In the past I have argued that the *Odyssey*, the father–son story par excellence, is designed as a positive counter-image to the *Iliad*, an image

---

[1] Translated by David M. Ratzan and Sabine R. Hübner.   [2] Wöhrle 1999.   [3] Cf. also below p. 164.
[4] See pp. 169–70; cf. also Pratt (this volume): 142; 145–6, for Achilles and "his complex relationships with various fathers."

of the harmonious resolution of intergenerational conflict.[5] Following on from my previous study, I want to return to father–son relationships, but with a view this time to those passages in which the loss of the father constitutes the main theme. Of course, this is a central aspect of the Telemachus story, and indeed one could interpret the greater part of the *Odyssey* from the perspective of the aforementioned figurative meanings of "father" and "son." What did the loss of a "father" like Odysseus, who was "as kind as a father" to the Ithacans over whom he ruled (*Od.* 2.233–4), signify in the society described in the Homeric epics? While interesting, that is not a question I will address here; in the following I will only explore the discourse of "fatherlessness" in its literal sense.

We will begin with a couple of passages in the *Iliad*. The loss of a father had social, material, and so psychological, effects.[6] Andromache made this clear in her insistent words to her husband Hector as she attempted to keep him from voluntary self-sacrifice. In the famous scene on the Skaian Gates in Book 6 of the *Iliad*, Andromache, carrying the little Astyanax in her arms, exhorted her husband not to forget that the death he believes he owes to his sense of valor would inevitably bring misery to his family:

> Dearest, your own strength will be your death, and you have no pity
> on your little son, nor on me, ill-starred, who soon must be your widow;
> for presently the Achaeans, gathering together
> will set upon you and kill you; and for me it would be far better
> to sink into the earth when I have lost you, for there is no other
> consolation for me after you have gone to your destiny –
> only grief; since I have no father, no honored mother.   (407–13)[7]

To better understand Andromache's speech, we must make recourse to Homer's introduction to this scene just a few lines before (401–3), in which he digresses on the naming of Astyanax, "Hector's son, the admired, beautiful as a star shining, | whom Hector called Scamandrius, but all of the others | Astyanax – lord of the city; since Hector alone saved Ilion." In relating the etymology of his name, derived as it is from his father's role, "Ruler of the City" (Ἀστυάναξ), these verses foretell that just as the fate of the beloved son is bound up with that of his father, so also is the fate of the entire city. Andromache, however, makes it clear in her words that should

---

[5] See Wöhrle 1999: esp. 145–9.
[6] See the Introduction to this volume for a systematic account of the effects of father-absence or fatherlessness.
[7] Trans. Lattimore 1951. All further translations of the *Iliad* will be from this edition, though spellings have been brought into line with the conventions of the volume. Translations of the *Odyssey* will be from Lattimore 1965.

Hector fall, she would absolutely prefer death to life as a widow since she has
no other family to support her. As we hear in the subsequent lines (414–28),
Achilles had killed her father and her seven brothers when he took Cilician
Thebe, and although her mother was ultimately ransomed, nonetheless she
later died a natural death. Thus, it is consistent with her situation when
Andromache then goes on to say:

> Hector, thus you are father to me, and my honored mother,
> you are my brother, and you it is who are my young husband.
> Please take pity upon me then, stay here on the rampart,
> that you may not leave your child an orphan (παῖδ᾽ ὀρφανικόν),
> your wife a widow …   (429–32)

In his reply (440–65) Hector refers to his sense of shame before the Trojan
men and women that compels him to fight despite his knowledge that Troy
is doomed. He also knows – and this grieves him the most, as he says at lines
450–63 – the hard fate that awaits Andromache if she should fall into
slavery: with her husband missing, who could hold off the day of slavery
(463)? The future of their child is not addressed here. In fact, in this scene
which foreshadows his own imminent death, Hector casts the ominous
premonitions of disaster aside and instead takes his son into his arms and
utters a short prayer, hoping that one day Astyanax might become a
renowned ruler of Troy, and a warrior even better than his father (476–81).

   Homer returns to Astyanax's fate in Book 22, when Andromache hears of
Hector's death, thus recalling the foreshadowing of Book 6. Yet, in her
lament for her lost husband Andromache performs a sort of inversion of the
scene in Book 6: she allows the widow's lot to recede into the background
and instead brings the fate of her child to the fore, depicting it in great
detail. I quote here the entire passage as it is the most elaborate portrayal of
an orphan's fate in the Homeric poems:

> Now you go down to the house of Death in the secret places
> of the earth, and left me here behind in the sorrow of mourning,
> a widow in your house, and the boy is only a baby
> who was born to you and me, the unfortunate. You cannot help him,
> Hector, any more, since you are dead. Nor can he help you.
> Though he escape the attack of the Achaeans with all its sorrows,
> yet all his days for your sake there will be hard work for him
> and sorrows, for others will take his lands away from him. The day
> of bereavement leaves a child with no agemates to befriend him.
> He bows his head before every man, his cheeks are bewept, he
> goes, needy, a boy among his father's companions,
> and tugs at this man by the mantle, that man by the tunic,

and they pity them, and one gives him a tiny drink from a goblet,
enough to moisten his lips, not enough to moisten his palate.
But one whose parents are living beats him out of the banquet
hitting him with his fists and in words also abuses him:
"Get out, you! Your father is not dining among us."
And the boy goes away in tears to his widowed mother,
Astyanax, who in days before on the knees of his father
would eat only the marrow or the flesh of sheep that was fattest.
And when sleep would come upon him and he was done with his playing,
he would go to sleep in a bed, in the arms of his nurse, in a soft
bed, with his heart given all its fill of luxury.
Now, with his dear father gone, he has much to suffer:
he, whom the Trojans have called Astyanax, lord of the city,
since it was you alone who defended the gates and the long walls.　　(482–507)

This depiction derives its particular force from the contrast it establishes between the life of a child growing up in the household of an illustrious aristocrat and the sort of life this same child could expect to lead should his father then die. Andromache here speaks not so much of the slavery that awaits a defeated enemy, but rather of the social status of an orphaned child in general. That his lands will be seized arbitrarily is assumed, but above all she knows that the community – the adults as well as his "agemates" – would only tolerate her son as a begging suppliant. His name, Astyanax, once more explicitly connecting father and son, now takes on a bitter and ironic note.

But does this depiction conform to reality? Aristarchus, the famous Hellenistic Homeric scholar, apparently was of a different opinion. As Ameis and Hentze say, he "took offence at the exaggerated depiction of the royal prince's hardships and bodily privation, as well as the too generalized nature of the representation in lines 490–99 … and so athetized lines 487–99."[8] Of course, Aristarchus could not have known the realities of the eighth century BCE, but regardless we find the universality of this depiction interesting precisely because it does not specifically address the later fate of Astyanax but rather presents the universally bleak future of any orphaned son.[9] Homer was naturally bound by existing myth (i.e. the older oral epic), so the fall of Troy and the enslavement or massacre of its population was in a sense predetermined. For this reason, one could argue that this depiction of the life of a fatherless aristocratic child – even allowing a certain degree of

[8] Ameis and Hentze 1965: 36. Cf. Richardson 1993: 158.
[9] Similarily, see Ulf 1990: 115, who says that Andromache's lament proceeds from the assumption that Hector's murder does not entail the destruction of Troy.

exaggeration to a mother worried to death about the future of her newly orphaned son – is not completely unrealistic. This is especially so regarding the first point mentioned above: there was certainly a danger that he could be dispossessed of his inheritance. Hesiod's *Works and Days* affords us an almost contemporary insight into this problem, as the poet warns his audience of the divine *nemesis* that attends ill-gotten riches. In addition, he must also fear the anger of the gods who mistreats suppliants, commits adultery with his brother's wife, and "foolishly wrongs fatherless children (ὀρφανὰ τέκνα)" (330). In fact, this also could be read as referring to the wrongful appropriation of fatherless children's property.[10] Hermann Strasburger is probably correct in assuming that Andromache in her prophetic words on her son's fate did not count on the respect normally due a royal family.[11] Her words thus mirror something of the aristocratic reality of the age, including the conflicts among its members.

Also of interest here for a later period is a passage in Book 11 of Plato's *Laws* which deals with the legal care of orphans.[12] Among other things, Plato writes that "if a man refuses to comply and harms a child deprived of its father or mother (τινα πατρὸς ἢ μητρὸς ἔρημον), he must pay double the damages that he would have to pay for a crime committed against a child with both parents living (τὸν ἀμφιθαλῆ)" (927d1–3).[13] Apart from the fact that this passage underlines the problems of orphanhood, it is also notable that Plato uses the term ἀμφιθαλής, which occurs in Homer only at *Iliad* 22.496.[14] For this reason we cannot rule out that Plato here alludes to this passage.

The fate of Andromache and Astyanax is mentioned yet a third and final time in the *Iliad*. In her lament of Book 24 Andromache addresses her late spouse for the last time with the certainty of what will follow on her husband's death (725–38). Though young, Hector lost his life and left her now a widow in his house. Their son is just a baby and yet will never come of age, since before this Troy will be sacked now that Hector, the bulwark of the city and defender of its wives and children, lies dead. Before long the women and children will be led away on enemy ships, and among them will be Andromache herself and possibly even Astyanax, perhaps destined to toil in slavery for a harsh master. Or perhaps her son will be thrown from a tower by one of the Achaeans, angry at Hector because in battle he once killed a brother, father, or son.

[10] Cf. also Hes. *Op.* 464: "fallow land is a defender from harm and a soother of children."
[11] Strasburger 1990: 24 with n. 43.   [12] See Weiler 1980: 175.   [13] Trans. Saunders 1970.
[14] This is the only attestation of this word in archaic poetry; see Richardson 1993: 161 *ad loc.* 496.

Andromache thus glimpses both her own fate as well as that of her son in the realization of Hector's death and the anticipation of the fall of Troy. Against this background, slavery for her and her child, or even her child's death, seem inescapable. It is an old question whether this scene alludes to Andromache's and Astyanax's fate as we know it from later sources. According to subsequent tradition, Neoptolemus, Achilles' son, casts Astyanax from the walls and abducts Andromache as his slave. Andromache, however, here speaks of this as an act of revenge, which could not possibly apply to Neoptolemus. It remains open whether Andromache in Book 24 refers to events already handed down in the epic of Troy's fall, or whether her thoughts "spring entirely from her psychological condition."[15] This problem, however, does not address the core question of this essay, since slavery and death after the capture and destruction of an ancient city would have been the routine fate of its population.[16] To Andromache's mind, Hector's death seals this destiny once and for all.

Apart from the passages given above we find only short, incidental allusions to the consequences of a father's death for his children, as, for instance, in the swaggering speech of Diomedes in Book 11.384–95. Wounded by Paris with an arrow through his foot, Diomedes contemptuously exclaims that the sole of his foot was merely scratched as if a girl or some silly boy had hit him. His own arrows, however, would kill a man:

> But if one is struck by me only a little, that is far different,
> the stroke is a sharp thing and suddenly lays him lifeless,
> and that man's wife goes with cheeks torn in lamentation,
> and his children are fatherless (παῖδες δ' ὀρφανικοί), while he staining the
>   soil with his red blood
> rots away, and there are more birds than women swarming around him. (391–5)

Nothing more is said about the orphans' fate;[17] they are named here only as those whom a warrior's death would afflict most immediately and profoundly. The rest, presumably, could be left to the audience's imagination. The same applies to statements in which the consequences of a father's death are only implied or foreshadowed. Thus, for instance, Acamas,

---

[15] Kullmann 1992: 235–6 with n. 39. See also Kullmann 2002b: 172–3.   [16] See, e.g., *Il.* 9.590–4.
[17] Technically (i.e. in our terminology) such a child would be a "half-orphan," since it is presumed that his mother would still be alive (see the Introduction, 20, for discussion and bibliography on the terminology of orphans and fatherlessness). Diomedes himself had lost his own father while still a young child (*Il.* 6.223), and he and others refer to this fact at various points in the *Iliad*. For a psychological analysis of Diomedes as a "fatherless hero," see Pratt (this volume).

fighting for the body of his fallen brother, declares, "Therefore a man prays he will leave behind him | one close to him in his halls to avenge his downfall in battle" (*Il.* 14.484–5). Or, in Book 5 of the *Iliad* the wounded Sarpedon begs Hector not to let his body fall into the hands of the Danaans, "since I could return no longer | back to my own house and the land of my fathers, bringing | joy to my own beloved wife and my son, still a baby" (685–8). Previously in Book 5 Sarpedon had pointed out to Hector that he had left his wife and his infant son back in Lycia in order to come and fight at Troy (479–80). Again, at *Iliad* 6.310 Athena is called upon to take pity on "the town of Troy, and the Trojan wives, and their innocent children." And, of course, it was not only boys but also little girls who suffered. Therefore, Helen regrets having left her daughter Hermione behind in Sparta (*Il.* 3.171–5): although she is no orphan, she is yet likely to meet the same fate since both her parents are at (or in) Troy.[18]

The realistic awareness in this poem of the fact that wives and children were utterly without protection should the husband and father die is arresting, and it is to this condition that Andromache gives such forceful point and expression. And yet it is equally remarkable that characters in the poem turn around and use the safety of women and children as an argument to die on the battlefield. We find this very tension bound up in Hector's own motivations. While in Book 6 in the passage above (p. 164) he claimed that his sense of honor prevented him from withdrawing from battle, now in Book 15 he encourages the Trojans and Lycians to fight on behalf of their wives and children. He who must die, should die:

> He who among you
> finds by spear thrown of spear thrust his death and destiny,
> let him die. He has no dishonor when he dies defending
> his country, for then his wife shall be saved and his children afterwards,
> and his house and property shall not be damaged, if the Achaeans
> must go away with their ships to the beloved land of their fathers.   (494–9)

Hector's ideology, however, is ultimately undercut by Andromache's words in Book 22.

Let us now turn to the *Odyssey*. As indicated above, fatherlessness is one of the central topics or themes of this poem. This is connected to the fact, to quote Hermann Strasburger once more, that "the figure of Odysseus ought to reveal an ideal in which the political and the social, the king and the father, are not only indivisible for us, but in which the two ought not even

[18] At *Od.* 4.5–7 we discover that Menelaos before the walls of Troy had promised Hermione to Achilles' son, Neoptolemus. The wedding took place after the return.

to be able to be kept apart."[19] In this sense one could see the people of Ithaca as "orphaned" until Odysseus finally returns, and this is made clear when in Book 2 the people of Ithaca assemble for a congregation and declare at the outset that this is the first such meeting to be held since Odysseus had left for Troy. This raises questions as to the social order on Ithaca, such as why Laërtes did not reign over Ithaca while Odysseus was away.[20] However, as stated above, I do not intend to address in this chapter the issue of the figurative meanings of fatherhood and fatherlessness in Homer, except insofar as they condition Telemachus' belief that on the basis of Odysseus' paternal leadership the Ithacans are morally obligated to support him in his domestic conflict with the suitors (*Od.* 2.40–79).

Telemachus is the paradigm of a child growing up literally without his father, and here I wish to address, though only in passing, the social and psychological consequences of his fatherlessness.[21] Of course, we have to acknowledge that he was not considered a true orphan since Odysseus' return was still thought possible. However, this was more pertinent to the social, and not the psychological, consequences of his father's absence. In point of fact, Telemachus grew up without his father. When Odysseus sailed away to Troy, Telemachus must have been a toddler, since upon his return twenty years later, the hero finds his son on the verge of mature adulthood, able to attend assemblies and to marry. In view of his uncertain fate, Odysseus had asked Penelope upon his departure (as we hear from her mouth) to "take care of everything" (πάντα μελόντων, *Od.* 18.266), by which he seems to have had in mind particularly the personal care of his aged parents. In the event that he did not return and their son attained the age of maturity, so Penelope tells Eurymachus, he encouraged her to remarry (αὐτὰρ ἐπὴν δὴ παῖδα γενειήσαντα ἴδηαι, | γήμασθ' ᾧ κ' ἐθέλησθα, τεὸν κατὰ δῶμα λιποῦσα. 18.269–70).[22] With respect to Telemachus, however, we hear nothing about the responsibilities of either of his living grandfathers, Icarius or Laërtes. Odysseus instead conferred the care of his whole *oikos* on his old companion, Mentor (ἐπέτρεπεν οἶκον ἅπαντα, 2.226), with no mention of the official status of Laërtes beyond the vague mandate to "obey the old man" (πείθεσθαί τε γέροντι, 2.227).[23]

[19] Strasburger 1990: 25.   [20] See Finley 1979: 83–6.

[21] Cf. for a more detailed analysis Wöhrle 1999: esp. 117–44.

[22] For example, cf. Wöhrle 1999: 118 and Kullmann 2002a: 183–6, who addresses the question whether Penelope really contemplated a second marriage (cf. *Od.* 18.272–3, 281–3).

[23] Cf. however, the commentary of Heubeck, West, and Hainsworth 1988 for this passage (i.e. *Od.* 2.226–7): "A puzzling detail … there is no suggestion elsewhere that Mentor has some sort of responsibility, however vaguely defined, towards Odysseus' dependants, nor does Telemachus think of turning to him for advice or moral support." As we cannot simply erase these lines, we should

The practical care of Telemachus was assigned to the nurse Eurycleia and the swineherd Eumaeus, whom Telemachus affectionately calls "Daddy" (ἄττα, 16.31; cf. 16.11–22). In addition, Telemachus himself mentions the herald, Medon, as a sort of surrogate father (*Od.* 22.356–60). During the fight with the suitors Telemachus pleads with Odysseus to spare Medon since he cared for him (κηδέσκετο) as a little boy. It thus becomes clear that upon his departure for Troy, Odysseus, like any caring and provident father, erected a kind of protective barrier around his minor son in order to shield him from both social and emotional harm. This is certainly understandable in light of the dangers threatening a fatherless child, which we have seen so poignantly depicted above in the *Iliad*.[24]

Telemachus gives an account of his current situation in the assembly at the opening of Book 2. Two great misfortunes have befallen his house:

> I have lost a noble father, one who
> was king once over you here, and was kind to you like a father;
> and now here is a greater evil, one which presently
> will break up the whole house and destroy all my livelihood.
> For my mother, against her will, is beset by suitors,
> own sons to the men who are greatest hereabouts. These
> shrink from making the journey to the house of her father
> Icarios, so that he might take bride gifts for his daughter
> and bestow her on the one he wished, who came as his favorite;
> rather, all their days, they come and loiter in our house
> and sacrifice our oxen and our sheep and our fat goats
> and make a holiday feast of it and drink the bright wine
> recklessly. Most of our substance is wasted. We have no man here
> such as Odysseus was, to drive this curse from the household.
> We ourselves are not the men to do it; we must be
> weaklings in such a case, not men well seasoned in battle.
> I would defend myself if the power were in me.   (46–62)

perhaps read them as details for the audience, confirming the fact that Odysseus had indeed provided for his minor son before leaving for Troy, and the manner in which he did so. A further question is who precisely was meant by γέροντι in line 227. The argument of Heubeck *et al.* that Laërtes cannot specifically be meant here, since he "is not elsewhere regarded as taking an active interest in Odysseus' household," is unconvincing. We are dealing here with a formal appointment made at Odysseus' departure two decades earlier. Furthermore, the suggestion that Mentor is the one described by γέροντι is unpersuasive given the syntax of the passage.

[24] Telemachus does not avoid Astyanax's fate "because he was able to grow up under his mother's care, who for his sake delayed remarriage even at the price of the plundering of the *oikos*" (Ulf 1990: 115). In fact, the suitors plundered the household only in the seventeenth year of Odysseus' absence. In Astyanax's case, however, we are dealing particularly with the fate of a child who was still an infant.

It is difficult to unravel conclusively this complicated social and "legal" situation, which is further obscured by inconsistencies in the story with its interweaving of fiction and contemporary moral values. It is clear, however, that even while the aristocratic suitors woo Penelope, and so strive for sovereignty over Ithaca, they still respect Telemachus' right to his father's throne (*Od.* 1.386–7, cf. 11.184–7). It is also clear that Telemachus does not possess the δύναμις ("power" or "influence") to enforce his claim. Thus the nature of Telemachus' authority in his paternal home remains altogether murky, particularly with respect to his mother's potential remarriage, now that he has come of age.[25] These inconsistencies and obscurities reflect the instability produced by the uncertainty surrounding Odysseus' return.[26] In any case, since with Telemachus we are not dealing explicitly with an orphaned son, we should speak of "father-absence" rather than of "father-lessness," in line with the modern psychological literature on this phenomenon.[27] Therefore, we should consider in more detail the masterly depiction of a fatherless boy's psychological condition as he stands at the threshold of adulthood. First, we must consider the problem of the quest for self-identity, described by Homer in the first four books of the poem, the so-called "Telemachy," and second the problem of maturation, which is represented from Book 15 until the end of the poem as a developmental process that results in a partnership between father and son.

The difficulty of his search for identity is addressed from the very beginning of the "Telemachy." When in response to Athena's question, posed in the guise of Mentes, as to whether he was the son of Odysseus, since he resembled him in so many ways, Telemachus answers:

> My mother says indeed I am his. I for my part
> do not know. Nobody really knows his own father.
> But how I wish I could have been rather son to some fortunate
> man, whom old age overtook among his possessions.
> But of mortal men, that man has proved the most ill-fated
> whose son they say I am …   (1.215–20)

Telemachus later adds that it would be better if he at least knew for sure that his father was dead and a glorious tomb had been raised up for him:

---

[25] Cf. *Od.* 2.130–45; 15.16–23; 20.338–44.

[26] See Finley 1979: 83–6. Reichardt recently has discussed the normative regulations for the assemblies which take place in the second book of the *Odyssey* (Reichardt 2003: 25–9). According to his view, everything we learn from this *agora* speaks to "the marginal development of political institutions and against the acceptance of the rule of law in epic" (29).

[27] See Erhard and Janig 2003: 7.

> I should not have sorrowed so over his dying
> if he had gone down among his companions in the land of the Trojans,
> or in the arms of his friends, after he had wound up the fighting.
> So all the Achaeans would have heaped a grave mound over him,
> and he would have won great fame for himself and his son hereafter.
> But now ingloriously the stormwinds have caught and carried him
> away, out of sight, out of knowledge, and he left pain and lamentation
> to me ...
>   (1.236–43)

Quite apart from the significant questions touching on inheritance and succession, we also see a less obvious, but vital, social function of fatherhood manifest in this passage. The Homeric father served as a medium to the outside world for his son – much more so in antiquity than in later times – a sponsor who is responsible both for shaping and then representing his son's identity, his manhood, to the community outside the family. Telemachus, of course, lacks this sponsor.[28] And so, along with the poet we accompany this young man, who in the beginning is still in need of a "Mentor," on his mission to reconstruct the identity of his father and to construct one for himself. His visits to Nestor in Pylos and Menelaus and Helen in Sparta represent important way-stations on his journey towards self-realization, since in each place he receives several confirmations of his paternity. The scene in Book 21 in which Telemachus proves to be able to draw his father's bow represents the symbolic conclusion of this process (21.101–17). The end of the poem also thus metaphorically reenacts the cutting of the umbilical cord, severing the once dependent son from his mother, who, given Odysseus' absence, had naturally assumed a dominant role in her son's upbringing and education.[29]

As was the case in the *Iliad*, so in the *Odyssey* the poet tells us very little about the fate of children whose fathers were dead or absent. An important exception to this rule is found in the story of Orestes who, like Telemachus, was still a young boy when Agamemnon sailed for Troy.[30] The *Odyssey* at

---

[28] Like Telemachus, Diomedes had no personal experience of his father, and yet his father nevertheless remained a permanent point of reference for him and his world (see Pratt [this volume]).

[29] See the fourth chapter ("Mother") in Felson-Rubin's excellent study (1994: 67–91).

[30] Cf. *Il.* 9.142–3 and 284–5. On the term τηλύγετος as an epithet for Orestes, see Heubeck, West, and Hainsworth 1988 *ad loc. Od.* 4.11: "the precise meaning of this epithet was disputed in antiquity, and its etymology is uncertain. In Homer it is always used of a dearly loved, special, or favorite child, once (*Il.* 13.470) with an evidently pejorative sense, 'spoilt darling.' The ancient explanation 'late born, born to aged parents' does not suit very well either this passage or *Il.* 3.175, where Helen so describes Hermione." At the passage cited above in Book 9 of the *Iliad* the three daughters of Agamemnon – Chrysothemis, Laodike, and Iphianassa – are also mentioned, however only by name (i.e. no epithet).

some points offers us important allusions to the story of the house of Atreus, a story that is well known to have provided something of a model and counterpoint for the Telemachy.[31] The chief point of difference between the two stories resides in the fact that while Telemachus gets his father back, who with his son's help will take revenge on the suitors, Orestes must exact his own revenge for the murder of his father at the hands of his mother. However, we receive from the poet only oblique indications of Orestes' life before the murder of Aegisthus and Clytemnestra. Thus, for instance, in Book 11 the shade of Agamemnon inquires about his son's whereabouts, whether he might be in Orchomenus, Pylos, or even Sparta with his uncle Menelaus (457–61). Possibly this question alludes to a certain legend, according to which after the murder of his father Orestes was saved by his wet nurse and brought to the house of Agamemnon's brother-in-law and guest-friend, Strophius, King of Crisa in Phocis.[32] According to *Odyssey* 3.306–8, Orestes returned from Athens eight years after his father's murder in order to take his revenge.[33] It is self-evident that Orestes passed his teenage years after his father's death in grave danger and uncertainty, menaced as he was by the usurper Aegisthus.[34] Agamemnon apparently also understood the basic danger posed by the absence of a husband and father from his own house, when upon his departure for Troy, like Odysseus above, he left someone as a sort of watchdog over his wife, in this case his ἀοιδός, or bard (*Od.* 3.267–8).[35]

Apart from the story of Orestes, the *Odyssey* only occasionally addresses the fate of children kidnapped and sold into slavery, as in the case of the swineherd Eumaeus, who narrates his story to Odysseus in Book 15.403–84. Abducted by some Phoenicians, he was sold to Laërtes on Ithaca. On hearing his life story, Odysseus can only comment that at least after so much suffering Zeus granted him the good fortune to come to the house of a generous man who provided him with enough food and drink to be able to lead a decent life (485–91). So also were the younger daughters of Pandareus this fortunate – the only case of which I am aware in which fatherless girls are mentioned in the Homeric poems. Penelope informs us about their fate in Book 20.61–78. After the gods had murdered their parents, Aphrodite, Hera, Artemis, and Athena for unstated reasons gathered them up and

---

[31] See U. Hölscher 1967: 1–16.   [32] Cf. Pind. *Pyth.* 11.17–37.
[33] See the commentary of Heubeck, West, and Hainsworth 1988 *ad loc. Od.* 3.306.
[34] Pindar in *Pyth.* 11.35 describes him as a "young man" (νέα κεφαλά).
[35] Perhaps a eunuch? Cf. the remarks on this passage by Heubeck, West, and Hainsworth 1998: 176–7.

together raised them.[36] Yet, in the brief moment when Aphrodite went up to Mount Olympus in order to inquire about possible marriage arrangements for the girls, the Harpies abducted them and gave them to the Erinyes as handmaidens.

As I emphasized at the outset, just how much and what sort of reality we find in the above passages of the *Iliad* and *Odyssey* is hard to say. Regardless of the particular resolution to that difficult issue, it is clear that with respect to the question of fatherlessness we get only a glimpse of the underlying, broader social reality, a series of suggestive clues as to what a father's loss or absence might have meant to the very small, elite – perhaps "aristocratic" – segment of the society that Homer portrays.[37] Insofar as we may say anything, then, we may be fairly confident of the fact that in Homer's world a fatherless child's fortunes were precarious – socially, economically, emotionally – sometimes fatally so. In this there is nothing surprising, for in aristocratic societies claims to power are always bound up with claims of heredity. Of the fate of common orphans, we may safely assume that it was hardly a pleasant one, yet on this the epics are silent.

---

[36] Weiler takes this as evidence of a "karitatives Denken": "Even the Greek gods were capable of compassion" (1980: 174).

[37] This limited epic perspective also applies to fatherlessness in a more general sense, namely those children who had no legitimate father (cf. the Introduction to this volume, 20–1, and Ogden [this volume]). The *Iliad* mentions (elite) *nothoi* (father's bastards) in a few places. Of course, it goes without saying that they took second place to legitimate children (e.g. 11.101–4, two sons of Priam, one a *nothos*, the other *gnēsios*; the *nothos* serves as the charioteer to his brother). The raising, moreover, of a *nothos* in the house of his natural father appears to have been thought worthy of special mention by the poet (e.g. Teucer, *Il.* 8.281–3; cf. Ogden [this volume]: 112). Especially interesting in this regard is the description of Pedaeus at *Il.* 5.69–71, a *nothos* who grew up in the household of his father Antenor, but was raised by Antenor's wife, Theano, "with close care, as for her own children, to pleasure her husband" (71).

CHAPTER 10

Absent Roman fathers in the writings of their daughters: Cornelia and Sulpicia

Judith P. Hallett

As a point of comparison with the topic of this essay – two Roman daughters of the Classical era, and how they write about their own absent fathers – I would like to begin by looking at the presence of a Roman father in an autobiographical work written by his son, the Augustan poet Ovid. In *Tristia* 4.10, while recounting some significant and emotionally charged moments from his own life, Ovid makes several references to his father. These references testify to the considerable control that Ovid's father managed to exert over Ovid's life, and to Ovid's deferential stance toward him. Their prominence in Ovid's literary autobiography also testifies to the importance that Ovid accorded, and wished his audience to accord, to his father's influence.

As long as Ovid's father lived, of course, Ovid was legally a *filiusfamilias* under *patria potestas*, his father's power of life or death over his children.[1] As such, he was in no position to contest his father's authority. Throughout *Tristia* 4.10 – written from exile on the Black Sea, several years after his father's death – Ovid acknowledges his father's role in his life, both directly and obliquely. Yet even there Ovid does not challenge, or criticize, his father's decisions, presumably out of deep reverence for his memory.

At *Tristia* 4.10.15–16 Ovid informs us that because of his father's attentiveness (*curaque parentis*), he and his brother – exactly one year Ovid's senior – left their hometown of Sulmo as small boys to be educated by the most distinguished teachers in Rome. In lines 21–2 Ovid matter-of-factly relates that his father frequently disparaged his poetic gifts: *saepe pater dixit,*

Earlier versions of this paper were presented at St. Mary's College of Maryland in March 2006 and the Albert Ludwigs University of Freiburg in January 2007; I would like to thank my hosts on these occasions – Iris Carter Ford and Linda Jones Hall at St. Mary's, and Therese Fuehrer and Ann-Cathrin Harders at Freiburg – as well as Marilyn Skinner for their helpful comments and criticisms.

[1] On *patria potestas*, see Nicholas and Treggiari 1996. It merits emphasis that Ovid does speak critically of others in *Tristia* 4.10: the friends and slaves who behaved disloyally at the time of his exile at lines 101–2 as well as his first wife in line 69.

"studium quid inutile temptas? | Maeonides nullas ipse reliquit opes," "often my father said, 'why do you attempt a useless pursuit? Homer himself, son of Maion, left no riches.'" In 27–36 Ovid describes how – evidently to please his ambitious father – he then gave up poetry and pursued a political career, intensifying his efforts to climb the political ladder after his politically talented brother died at the age of twenty.

Ovid tells us that he eventually abandoned this career path in favor of poetry. Yet he makes it clear that his father's wishes continued to play a key role in other areas of his life. In 69–70, when discussing the first of his three marriages, Ovid characterizes his first wife as "neither worthy nor useful," and as wed to him only briefly when he was "little more than a boy." He also claims that she was "given to him" (*est data*) in a marriage presumably arranged by his father.[2] In 71–2 Ovid describes his second, and similarly short-lived, union to a woman he terms "blameless" (*sine crimine*) in such a way as to allow us to infer that his father arranged it too. And Ovid's remarks about his exile at 81–90 express relief that both of his parents were already dead when he was compelled to leave Rome. In line 87 he even addresses their shades (*parentales umbrae*) in the world of the dead, assuring them in lines 89–90 that he took "forced flight owing to an error, not any wrongdoing" *(causam … errorem iussae, non scelus, esse fugae)*.

Various details in *Tristia* 4.10 also suggest that Ovid's father was able to exert control over Ovid's life for a long time. In lines 77–84 Ovid indicates that his parents, first his father and then his mother, had both died shortly before he was banished from Rome to Tomi on the Black Sea:

And already my father had completed his allotted fate and had added another nine spans of five years [i.e. 45 years] to nine spans of five years [i.e. 45 years]. I did not weep for him in a way that was different from that in which he was about to weep if I had been taken from him. I endured funeral rites next for my mother. Both were fortunate and buried at the proper time, because they died before the day of my punishment. And I am also fortunate, because they did not grieve at all about me.[3]

---

[2] In trying to determine the date of Ovid's second marriage, Green (1982: 31) speculates that "Ovid was in fact pressured into his second marriage by his father after finally (and as late as possible) rejecting a public career."

[3]

Et iam compleat genitor sua fata novemque
  addiderat lustris altera lustra novem.
non aliter flevi, quam me fleturus adempto
  ille fuit; matri proxima busta tuli.   80

felices ambo tempestiveque sepulti
  ante diem poenae quod periere meae.
me quoque felicem, quod non viventibus illis
  sum miser, et de me quod doluere nihil.

From statements that Ovid makes elsewhere in this poem, scholars have concluded that his banishment occurred in 8 CE, when he was fifty. At line 6 he relates that he was born in the year when both consuls died, 43 BCE (*cum cecidit fato consul uterque pari*). At lines 95–8 he states that ten five-year intervals had passed since the time of his birth when "the anger of the injured first-citizen" ordered him to seek the shores of Tomi. We may infer, therefore, that Ovid was likely to have been in his late forties at the time of his father's death. So too Ovid claims at 77–8 that his father died after reaching the age of ninety. Hence Ovid's father must have been in his early forties when Ovid was born, relatively old in the Roman scheme of things.[4]

Ovid's father may have imposed so many, and such heavy, demands on Ovid, particularly after the early death of Ovid's brother, because of his relatively advanced age. And whether or not Ovid's father viewed Ovid's political activities as a way of ensuring that the talents of Ovid's elder brother outlasted his physical lifetime, Ovid himself expected to live on through his own poetry. He thanks his Muse in lines 121–2 for granting a "lofty name to him still living," and at 130 he informs the earth that even when he dies "I will not belong to you" (*protinus ut moriar, non ero, terra, tuus*).

THE WRITINGS AND FATHERS OF CORNELIA AND SULPICIA

Keeping Ovid's portrayal of his father in mind, let us now turn to these writings by Roman daughters. They are similar to Ovid's autobiographical poem in that they too are by elite and cultivated individuals and portray significant and emotionally charged moments in the lives of their authors. One is a letter dated to 124 BCE from the noble matron Cornelia, then a widow in her sixties, to her younger son, Gaius Sempronius Gracchus.[5] The others are love poems dated to approximately 19 BCE in the same elegiac meter that Ovid employs in *Tristia* 4.10: poems by another noblewoman, in her mid-twenties, named Sulpicia.[6]

---

[4] Green (1982: 18) also remarks: "Ovid never mentions his mother … except as the anonymous half of a parental duo, and, finally, to record her death. Since his father was at least forty, and probably older, at the time of Ovid's birth (*Tr.* 4.77–82, 83–8), she is unlikely to have been his first wife."

[5] For basic biographical information about Cornelia, see Badian 1996a; his entry, like Astin's in the second edition of the *OCD*, relies heavily on Münzer's article in *RE*, s.v. "Cornelia 407." See also Hemelrijk 1999: 193–7 and Hallett 2002a; 2006b.

[6] For basic biographical information about Sulpicia, see Watson 1996, as well as Hemelrijk 1999: 151–3; Hallett 2002b; and J. Stevenson 2005: 36–8.

These writings, however, differ from *Tristia* 4.10 in that they are by aristocratic women, not a man of less exalted albeit equestrian status, and by women who had been fatherless for a long time when they wrote. Cornelia's father, the illustrious general and statesman Publius Cornelius Scipio Africanus, who defeated the Carthaginian leader Hannibal at Zama in 202 BCE, died in 184 when Cornelia was still a small child.[7] The death in 43 BCE of the man whom most scholars would identify as Sulpicia's father – the distinguished jurist Servius Sulpicius Rufus, consul in 51 – appears to have taken place when she was very young as well.[8]

The writings of Cornelia and Sulpicia further resemble Ovid's autobiographical *Tristia* 4.10 in that their fathers also loom as significant presences in their literary imaginations. Indeed, their very words evidently recall those of their fathers. Yet these two fatherless women differ from Ovid by their fathers' absences from their actual lives, absences that the writings of both women acknowledge, albeit subtly. These women's writings signal as well that their fathers, like Ovid's father, made major demands on them, despite and yet because of their fathers' absences from their lives. I will argue that the fatherless state of these two women seems particularly to have influenced the ways in which they represent themselves publicly; in their interactions with males inside and outside their family circle; and in their adoption of stances that in certain respects may be regarded as "masculine" behavior according to the expectations of the Classical Roman elite.

I subscribe to the somewhat controversial assumption that Cornelia herself wrote the letter to her son Gaius, from which the late Republican author Cornelius Nepos quotes two long excerpts. This assumption is controversial because many scholars, such as Ernst Badian, who wrote the *Oxford Classical Dictionary* entry on Cornelia, refuse to believe that she is its author.[9] I also subscribe to the even more controversial assumption that Sulpicia wrote all eleven of the elegies associated with her in Tibullus, Book 3, poems 8 through 18. This assumption is even more controversial because

---

[7] For the date of Scipio Africanus' death, see Hallett 1996: 419–20, discussing Cic. *Sen.* 19 and Livy 39.52.

[8] For Servius Sulpicius Rufus, see Badian, Pelling, and Heath 1996; for the view that Sulpicia is this man's granddaughter, see Syme 1981.

[9] Badian 1996a cites Horsfall 1987 when stating, "the authenticity of two fragments addressed to Gaius, and preserved in [Cornelius] Nepos MSS must be regarded as uncertain." For the debate over the authenticity of this letter, see, e.g., Horsfall 1989; Courtney 1999: 136 (also relying on Horsfall 1987 and 1989); and Hemelrijk 1999, 193–4. For recent arguments in favor of its authenticity, see Hallett 2002a; 2004; 2006a.

most scholars, such as Patricia Watson, author of the *OCD* entry, believe that Sulpicia wrote only the final, shorter six poems – if she wrote any of them at all.[10]

I will maintain too that Cornelia may also have written a passage, quoted without attribution, in an anonymously written treatise from the early first century BCE, the *Rhetorica ad Herennium*. It directly addresses her father in language resembling that of Cornelia's letter, as well as that of a speech by a similarly situated woman in a later literary work evoking her letter. It also faults the political conduct of Cornelia's sons. By the same token, I will contend that Sulpicia may also have written a funerary inscription of a Greek female slave who served as a *lectrix* (an attendant who read aloud), named Petale, and that by writing this inscription in the same poetic meter as her elegies, Sulpicia publicly represents her father's household. Consequently, both texts may further illuminate how their fathers' absences inform these women's writings, conduct, and lives.

Given the nature of the sources, my analysis of these women's writings necessarily involves some speculative "reading between the lines." For instance, Cornelia's letter itself does not directly mention her father. The elegies of Sulpicia mention her father only once. Even so, I would argue that both men still command a presence in both women's writings, and that the physical absences of their fathers from their lives affect how both women try to persuade other men to act in ways that they themselves deem satisfying and pleasing.

PUBLIUS CORNELIUS SCIPIO AFRICANUS AND THE LETTER OF CORNELIA TO GAIUS GRACCHUS

The manuscripts of Nepos present the excerpts from Cornelia's letter as follows:

These words are excerpted from a letter of Cornelia, mother of the Gracchi, from the book of Cornelius Nepos *About Latin Historians*:
   "You will say that it is a beautiful thing to take vengeance on enemies. To no one does this seem either greater or more beautiful than it does to me, but only if it is possible to pursue these aims without harming our country. But seeing as that

---

[10]   On the authorship of the eleven Sulpicia-elegies, see in addition to Watson 1996 the discussions of Hinds 1987; H. Parker 1994 and 2006; Holzberg 1999; Hallett 2002b; Hubbard 2004–5; J. Stevenson 2005: 38–43; Keith 2006, but especially Skoie 2002: 126–31, 162–212, and 265–6. Skoie examines the efforts by the nineteenth-century German scholars Rossbach and Gruppe to exclude [Tib. 3.] 8–12 (and in Gruppe's case, 13 as well) from Sulpicia's œuvre. She also notes the efforts by Holzberg and Hubbard to contend that all eleven elegies are not by Sulpicia, but rather a male impersonator.

cannot be done, our enemies will not perish for a long time and for many reasons, and they will be as they are now rather than have our country be destroyed and perish."

The same letter in a different passage:

"I would dare to take an oath solemnly, swearing that, except for those who have murdered Tiberius Gracchus, no enemy has foisted so much difficulty and so much distress upon me as you have because of all these matters. You, who should have shouldered the responsibilities of all of those children whom I had in the past and to make sure that I might have the least anxiety possible in my old age. And that, whatever you did, you would wish to please me most greatly. And that you would consider it sacrilegious to do anything of great significance contrary to my feelings, especially as I am someone with only a short portion of my life left. Cannot even that time span, as brief as it is, be of help in keeping you from opposing me and destroying our country?

"What end will there finally be? When will our family stop behaving insanely? When will we cease insisting on troubles, both suffering and causing them? When will we begin to feel shame about disrupting and disturbing our country? But if this is altogether unable to take place, seek the office of tribune when I will be dead; as far as I am concerned, do what will please you, when I shall not perceive what you are doing. When I have died, you will sacrifice to me as a parent and call upon the god of your parent. At that time will it not shame you to seek prayers of those gods whom you had abandoned and deserted when they were alive and on hand? May Jupiter not for a single instant allow you to continue in these actions or permit such madness to come into your mind! And if you persist, I fear that, by your own fault, you may incur such trouble for your entire life that at no time will you be able to make yourself happy."[11]

In both excerpts Cornelia attempts, in unhappy and outraged words, to convince Gaius not to run for tribune of the people. Gaius' elder brother,

---

[11] I follow the text and translation of Hallett 2002a:

Verba ex epistula Corneliae Gracchorum matris ex libro Corneli Nepotis de latinis historicis excerpta: dices pulchrum esse inimicos ulcisci. id neque maius neque pulchrius cuiquam atque mihi esse videtur, sed si liceat re publica salva ea persequi. sed quatenus id fieri non potest, multo tempore multisque partibus inimici nostri non peribunt, atque uti nunc sunt erunt potius quam res publica profligetur atque pereat. eadem alio loco: verbis conceptis deierare ausim, praeterquam qui Tiberium Gracchum necarunt, neminem inimicum tantum molestiae tantumque laboris, quantum te ob has res, mihi tradidisse; quem oportebat omnium eorum quos antehac habui liberos partes tolerare atque curare ut quam minimum sollicitudinis in senecta haberem, utique quaecumque ageres, ea velles maxime mihi placere atque uti nefas haberes rerum maiorum adversum meam sententiam quicquam facere, praesertim mihi cui parva pars vitae superest. ne id quidem tam breve spatium potest opitulari, quin et mihi aversere et rem publicam profliges? denique quae pausa erit? ecquando desinet familia nostra insanire? ecquando modus ei rei haberi poterit? ecquando desinemus et habentes et praebentes molestiis insistere? ecquando perpudescet miscenda atque perturbanda re publica? sed si omnino id fieri non potest, ubi ego mortua ero, petito tribunatum; per me facito quod lubebit, cum ego non sentiam. ubi mortua ero, parentabis mihi et invocabis deum parentem. in eo tempore non pudet te eorum deum preces expetere, quos vivos atque praesentes relictos atque desertos habueris? ne ille sirit Iuppiter te ea perseverare, nec tibi tantam dementiam venire in animum. ei si perseveras, vereor ne in omnem vitam tantum laboris culpa tua recipias uti in nullo tempore tute tibi placere possis.

Tiberius Sempronius Gracchus, had held this same office when assassinated by personal enemies in 133 BCE: the second excerpt of Cornelia's letter begins by alluding to the pain of this loss. So too had nine of the twelve children whom Cornelia bore died when they were still very young; the letter alludes to all of these dead children as well. Tiberius' death thus meant that only two of Cornelia's offspring – Gaius and his sister Sempronia – still survived. Gaius, of course, did not heed his mother's words: he ran for tribune of the people despite her entreaties, won, and was then assassinated by personal enemies in 121 BCE.[12]

In the first excerpt Cornelia voices an argument against Gaius' political plans on the grounds of moral principle: that revenge on personal enemies (*inimici*) may be great and beautiful, but if such revenge proves harmful to one's country it is unacceptable. In the second excerpt she makes a guilt- and shame-inducing emotional plea, associating Gaius with her *inimici* if he runs for tribune and damages their country. In addition to predicting her son's own unhappiness if he seeks this office, Cornelia stresses her own emotional difficulties and losses, begging Gaius to wait until she is dead and cannot feel if he must run.[13] Cornelia represents her losses of Tiberius and all the other children she had in the past as creating additional family responsibilities for Gaius, among them making sure that she herself suffers minimal anxiety in her old age (*senecta*). But Cornelia also inquires of Gaius, rhetorically, when their entire family will stop behaving insanely. Reminding her son that he will sacrifice to her as a parent when she is dead, she asks if it will not shame him to seek prayers of those gods whom he abandoned and deserted when they were alive: that is, family members such as herself who were worshiped as divine spirits within their households after their deaths. Finally, she invokes the god Jupiter to stop her son's madness.

One is tempted to contend that in this letter Cornelia, whose husband Tiberius Sempronius Gracchus had died in 154 soon after she gave birth to Gaius, the youngest of their offspring, is adopting what would have been her late husband's role in advising her son how to conduct himself in pursuing a political career. But to characterize her demanding, egotistic words to Gaius as mere advice ignores what is striking and to some scholars problematic about them: the high emotional voltage of her rhetoric and the combination of anger and sorrow her choice of language conveys. As I have argued elsewhere, Cornelia's gender does much to account for this emotionally charged

---

[12] For the political careers of her sons, and Cornelia's dead children, see Badian 1996a and 1996b, as well as Hallett 2002a and 2004.

[13] For Cornelia's argument and its emotional dimensions, see Hallett 2002a; 2004; 2006b.

motivational strategy. A woman lacking *patria potestas* and formal political authority, even one of Cornelia's social stature and clout, could not rely on the same punitive powers that a Roman father could wield in trying to bend her son to her will.[14] Furthermore, even if Cornelia is attempting to function in a fatherly capacity to Gaius in this letter, her distinctive, importuning, emotionally charged mode of communication with her son closely resembles that ascribed to women in their dealings with recalcitrant male kin by later Roman authors. Livy's Veturia, whose speech to her son Coriolanus (to be discussed shortly) seems to echo Cornelia's letter, is but one of several examples. It is also significant that Cornelia does not mention her husband among her losses in this letter, only her children. But, as we shall see, she does appear to allude to her father, particularly when invoking their family and Gaius' relationship to it, in order to induce feelings of guilt and shame in her son.

   Her family and its continuity are of paramount importance to Cornelia in this letter. She portrays herself as her family's authoritative representative, connected with and about to join the dead, and consequently able to speak for those already long deceased as well as for living family members. As we have observed, Ovid also characterizes himself as an extra-mortal communicator, addressing his dead parents in the underworld. Both Ovid and Cornelia also claim that they themselves will in some way survive beyond the grave. But Ovid expects to live on after his physical demise through his poetry. Cornelia expects to live on through her family's ancestor worship and her family business, the Roman state.

   Cornelia, to be sure, does not state specifically that her father, Publius Cornelius Scipio Africanus, is among the family members whom she accuses of having behaved insanely (*insanire*). But she may well allude to her father with another phrase, one that I and others have translated as the "god of your parent," *deum parentem*. The phrase is customarily thought to refer to Cornelia herself once she is dead, even though *deum* is a masculine noun.[15] But *deum* might refer to her father instead. Or, if we read *deum* as a masculine genitive plural form (which it is in the next sentence) rather than a masculine accusative singular, the phrase can also mean the "parent of the gods." In this case it would refer to the father-god Jupiter, with whom in his role as Jupiter Optimus Maximus, Jupiter "the best and the greatest," Cornelia's father Scipio Africanus claimed a privileged relationship.[16]

---

[14] For the role played by Cornelia's gender in her motivational strategy, see in particular Hallett 2004.

[15] See, for example, Horsfall 1989: 126; Courtney 1999: 138; Farrell 2001: 58–65. Another, perhaps more accurate, translation of *deum parentem* would be "[you will call upon] that parent as a god."

[16] On this relationship, attested to by, e.g., Livy (22.53.11 and 28.28.11) and Aulus Gellius (*NA* 4.18, 6.1.6, and 12.8), see Hallett 1996.

What renders a connection between the phrase *deum parentem* and either Jupiter or her father Scipio Africanus, or both, more plausible is that Cornelia invokes Jupiter himself in the sentence after that. In so doing, she employs words that resemble those later ascribed to her father by the later historian Livy: *ne ille sirit Iuppiter te ea perseverare* ("May Jupiter not for a single instant allow you to continue in these actions!"). At 28.28.11 Livy states that Scipio, addressing his mutinous soldiers in 206 BCE, proclaimed: *ne istuc Iuppiter optimus maximus sirit, urbem auspicato dis auctoribus in aeternum conditam huic fragili et mortali corpori aequalem esse* ("May Jupiter Optimus Maximus not allow henceforth that the city of Rome – founded with due auspices and the favor of the gods to endure forever – live no longer than my own weak, mortal body"). In so doing, Livy portrays Cornelia's father as resembling Cornelia herself: voicing his commitment to the welfare of the Roman state by emphasizing that it must physically long survive him and the politicians of his own time.

The words of another speech by Scipio Africanus, dated to 185 BCE and provided by the second-century CE writer Aulus Gellius in his *Attic Nights* (4.18.3), also show some affinities with those of Cornelia in this letter. In addition to invoking Jupiter Optimus Maximus, Scipio here refers to Hannibal, enemy of the entire Roman state, with the superlative of the adjective for personal enemy used by Cornelia, *inimicissimum*. Curiously, he refers to his own conquest of Hannibal metaphorically with the phrase "I gave birth to a victory for all of you" (*victoriam vobis peperi*), likening himself to a mother rather than a father. To be sure, Livy's account may only have a loose relationship with what Scipio actually said nearly two centuries before Livy wrote. While Gellius claims to be quoting Scipio's exact words, he does not quote that many words. Even so, the similarities between what Cornelia says and what both authors claim that her father said are striking.

Similarities between what Cornelia says in this letter and the language and tone of a passage from the *Rhetorica ad Herennium*, a treatise dated to several decades after Cornelia's letter, are also striking.[17] The treatise quotes this passage, whose author is never identified, to illustrate the figure of speech known as apostrophe or *exclamatio*. After defining this figure as "expressing sorrow or outrage by an address to some person or city or place or thing," it illustrates this figure with the following example: *Te nunc*

---

[17] For the authorship and date of the *Rhetorica ad Herennium*, see Caplan 1954, xxvi–xxvii; for the earlier authors quoted, including the "poets and historians" (one of whom may have quoted from Cornelia's letter much as Nepos did in *About Latin Historians*), see xvi–xvii.

adloquor, Africane, cuius mortui quoque nomen splendori et decori est civitati.
Tui clarissimi nepotes suo sanguine aluerunt inimicorum crudelitatem ("Now I
address you, Africanus, the name of whom – though you are dead – is also a
source of luster and glory to the state. With their own blood your most
famous grandsons have nourished (*aluerunt*) the cruelty of their personal
enemies (*crudelitatem inimicorum*)"). Here, then, we have a sorrowful and
angry effort to communicate with a dead person who happens to be
Cornelia's father, and who is praised for his achievements that immortalize
the Roman state. What is more, like Cornelia's letter, this instance of
apostrophe criticizes his most famous grandsons, Tiberius and Gaius
Gracchus, and characterizes them as provoking their personal enemies,
called *inimici*, by their destructive – and self-destructive – conduct.

This is why I think it possible that this passage constitutes another
excerpt from Cornelia's sorrowful and angry letter to Gaius. Cornelia,
after all, harshly faults the political behavior of her sons and invokes her
family and "we" as well as the god Jupiter in faulting them. Furthermore,
the verb *alere*, "to nourish," appears in another passage, also from Livy's
history, that contains many verbal and thematic affinities with Cornelia's
letter and thus may echo another passage from the letter which Nepos did
not manage to excerpt. This is a speech that Livy places in the mouth of
Veturia, the mother of the traitor Coriolanus, at 2.40. Here Veturia, like
Cornelia, emphasizes her old age with the word *senecta* when sorrowfully
and angrily begging her son to cease from his disastrous political course.
With a series of rhetorical questions resembling those of Cornelia, she asks
him, *potuisti populari hanc terram quae te genuit atque aluit* ("Have you been
able to devastate this land, which bore and nurtured you?"), metaphorically
ascribing her physical maternal functions to those of his native soil.[18] It
merits notice, too, that in Livy's rendition at 28.29.1 of the speech given by
Scipio Africanus in 206, Scipio speaks of Coriolanus, asserting that personal
devotion to his family (*pietas*) brought Coriolanus back from destroying the
Roman state as if it were his own father (*publico parricidio*).

Whatever the relationship among these different texts with their memorable deployment of parental metaphors for political conduct, and whatever
these texts may or may not disclose about how the words and views of

---

[18] For the similarities between Cornelia's words to Gaius and those of Livy's Veturia to her son
Coriolanus, see Hallett 2002a; 2004; 2006b. The parallels also include the characterization of
Coriolanus as "as if insane" (*ut amens*) and the phrase *nec tibi turpius nec mihi miserius*, "nothing
either more shameful for you or more miserable for myself," recalling the negated and paired
neuter comparative adjectives with dative personal pronouns in *id neque maius neque pulchrius
cuiquam atque mihi.*

Cornelia's father influenced those of Cornelia and a later depiction of an angry aging mother of a recalcitrant son, such evidence warrants careful notice. For it strengthens the supposition that Cornelia identifies with, and thereby appropriates the authority of, her father in the excerpts from the letter quoted by Nepos. She achieves this identification and appropriates this authority in various ways: by invoking her father's patron deity (and perhaps her father in his posthumous status as a deity), by employing language and figures of speech that other authors attribute to him, and by minimizing the distinctions between Gaius' living and dead family members. This final strategy, facilitated by her advanced age, is, as we have observed, later employed by the aging, exiled Ovid. Most important, Cornelia, as her father is said to have done, represents her devotion to the Roman state as an abiding family commitment to a larger-than-life – and longer-than-life – enterprise.

THE ELEVEN SULPICIA ELEGIES AND SERVIUS SULPICIUS RUFUS

The writings of the later and much younger love elegist Sulpicia – poems 8 through 18 in Book 3 of the Augustan elegist Tibullus – differ drastically from Cornelia's letter to her son in both their goals and their values. Whereas Cornelia uses the word *insanire* to criticize her son and her entire family, Sulpicia announces at 12.18 that she would not wish to have been of sound mind (*nec ... sana fuisse velit*), even if it were possible. Her passion for a young lover whom she calls by the pseudonym Cerinthus, celebrated in most of the eleven Sulpicia elegies, requires an emotionally inflamed, unbalanced mental state. In these poems she portrays herself as attempting to control the day-to-day proceedings of a torrid romance with what we might call a "boy toy," not the public image and actions of a politically powerful and prominent family.[19]

Similarly, Sulpicia's invocation and evocation of her father Servius Sulpicius Rufus in her elegies differs from Cornelia's allusions to Scipio Africanus and in fact adopts a somewhat surprising form. Sulpicia does not ordinarily speak deferentially to, or about, living parents and parental surrogates. For instance, in Elegy 14 she directly addresses by name her maternal uncle and presumed guardian, the distinguished general and statesman Publius Valerius Messalla Corvinus;[20] protesting that he is

---

[19] For the literary connotations of the pseudonym Cerinthus, see Roessel 1990 and Hallett 2002b: 46–7.
[20] For Messalla and his relationship to Sulpicia, see Pelling 1996 and Hallett 2002b: 45–6, as well as Hemelrijk 1999: 322–3, n. 28.

planning to separate her from Cerinthus on her birthday, she insists that he lessen his efforts to control her movements, calling him in line 5 *mei studiosus*, "excessively attentive to me." She employs the feminine of the same adjective, *studiosa*, for her mother at 12.5, when resisting her mother's well-intentioned efforts to interfere with her erotic desires. After criticizing Cerinthus' plans to go boar-hunting, and the pursuit of hunting itself, in Elegy 9, she tells her lover at line 23, *et tu venandi studium concede parenti*, "leave the passion for hunting to his father," disparaging his father in the process.

Yet in Elegy 3.16 Sulpicia proudly identifies herself as her father's daughter when she reproaches her lover for preferring a woman of low social station. "I am thankful," she writes,

that you, free from any care about me, are now so indulgent to yourself in order that I, clumsy as I am, may protect myself from suddenly taking a bad fall. May your caring for a woman shamefully clad in a whore's toga and a partner-for-hire loaded with a wool basket be stronger than Sulpicia, daughter of Servius (*Servi filia Sulpicia*). Still, men are anxious about me, to whom it is the greatest cause of sorrow that I may yield my position in your bed to a total nobody.

By mentioning her father's name – indeed his *praenomen*, first name, Servius – she affirms her privileged social status and the exclusive claim on her lover's affections that this status should secure. So too she alludes to the other men concerned on her behalf, presumably her male kin and father-surrogates, such as Messalla, again in order to wield her lofty social status as a love weapon.

In asserting her rights and emotional needs with men, Sulpicia not only poignantly invokes her father's aristocratic social pedigree, but also through her use of legal language evokes his professional expertise as an authority on Roman jurisprudence. In Elegy 3.14, for example, she employs the technical legal terms *vis*, use of force, and *arbitrium*, exercise of judgment, when challenging Messalla's attempts to control her movements by forcing her to spend her birthday in the country rather than in Rome with Cerinthus.[21] In the subsequent elegy (15) Sulpicia depicts herself as having prevailed over Messalla and emphasizes her successful advocacy by exhorting, *omnibus ille dies nobis natalis agatur*, "let this birthday be celebrated by all of us" (3). The Latin verb *agere* can mean "to plead [a case in court]"; the passive voice and jussive subjunctive mood further invest *agatur* with legal overtones.[22]

---

[21] 3.14.8: *arbitrio quam vis non sinit esse meo*. For *vis* in the legal sense of "unlawful force or violence," see *OLD*; also for the various legal connotations of *arbitrium*.
[22] See *OLD* under *ago*, especially subheadings 42 and 44.

It merits note, too, that several Roman authors represent poetry, and indeed erotic poetry, as interests and practices of both Sulpicia's father, Servius, and surrogate father, Messalla. At *Satires* 1.10.86–7, when discussing the type of individuals whose approval he seeks for his verses, Horace lists both Messalla and Servius. Since the first book of the *Satires*, written in the early thirties BCE, postdates the death of Servius Sulpicius Rufus by a few years, Horace may be referring to this man's son. However, the Latin construction – a relative clause of characteristic denoting types of people rather than specific individuals – enables Horace to include the deceased in this list as well. Furthermore, Ovid names Servius as a writer of naughty verses (*improba carmina*) at *Tristia* 2.441–2; and the younger Pliny cites Messalla and Servius Sulpicius as composers of playful poetry (*versiculos severos parum*) at *Epistles* 5.3.2–3.

Jane Stevenson has recently "recovered" a text of some relevance to Sulpicia's role as her father's daughter: a funerary inscription unearthed in the mid-1920s by Paolino Mingazzini and identified as the work of Sulpicia in 1929 by Jerome Carcopino. For the past seventy-five years it has received no attention from Sulpicia scholars, perhaps because of the controversy surrounding Carcopino's later career as Education and Youth minister in the Vichy government of Nazi-occupied France. But it deserves to be recognized as by Sulpicia herself and accorded far more careful study than Carcopino's cursory treatment.[23] The text of the inscription in my translation follows:

Passer-by, look at the ashes of the female reader named (or belonging to or commemorated by) Sulpicia, to whom the slave name Petale had been given. She had lived for three times ten years plus four in number and had produced a son, Aglaon (Greek for "glorious"), while on earth. She had seen all good things of nature, she was flourishing in art, she was glittering in beauty, she had grown in talent. Envious Fortune was unwilling for her to spend a long time in life. Their own distaff failed the Fates.[24]

---

[23] For the inscription, *AE* 1928: 73.4; see J. Stevenson 2005: 43–4; Mingazzini 1926; and Carcopino 1929. For Carcopino's career, see Corcy-Debray 2001.

[24]   Sulpiciae cineres lectricis cerne viator,
                        quoi servile datum nomen erat Petale.
                    ter denos numero quattuor plus vixerat annos
                        natumque in terris Aglaon ediderat.
                    omnia naturae bona viderat, arte vigebat,   5
                        splendebat forma, creverat ingenio.
                    invida fors vita longinquom degere tempus
                        noluit hanc: fatis defuit ipse colus.

Written in elegiac couplets, Sulpicia's signature meter, and datable to the early Augustan period when Sulpicia wrote, this inscription full of learned literary touches commemorates a Greek female slave named Petale who served in the capacity of *lectrix*, a woman who reads aloud.[25] Like Elegies 14 and 15, with their puns on technical legal language, this text provides evidence for Sulpicia's literary skill at playing with words. It also furnishes testimony as to her identification with her late father and her assumption of an important task her father would have performed had he been alive. Sulpicia's penchant for wordplay is, we should note, vividly evinced when she identifies herself as her father's daughter, *Servi filia Sulpicia*, in Elegy 16. Her father's *praenomen*, Servius, derives from *servus*, "slave." The female rival, partner-for-hire in a whore's toga, to whom she favorably contrasts herself, is presumably a slave sex-worker. Thus, as Stevenson, quoting Stephen Hinds, puts it, Sulpicia engages in play with the ironies of women's identity: a prostitute is worlds apart from Sulpicia, but curiously both are *servi filia*, "a slave's daughter" and "Servius' daughter."[26]

In the epitaph the phrase used for Petale's charred remains, *Sulpiciae cineres lectricis*, can mean "the ashes of the female slave-reader named Sulpicia," as any female slave of Servius Sulpicius' household would officially be called in Latin after manumission. But, as Stevenson observes, it can also signify "the ashes of the female slave-reader belonging to the mistress Sulpicia," and Sulpicia may well have inherited slaves of her late father's household, especially female slaves with literary duties.[27] It could even refer to "the ashes commemorated by the mistress Sulpicia, herself a

---

[25] On the linguistic evidence used to date the poem (e.g. the adverb *longinquom* and the form *quoi* for *cui*), see Carcopino 1929: 85–6 and J. Stevenson 2005: 43–4. Another indication of an early Augustan date, not noted by either, is the ending of the pentameter lines with words of three and four syllables: concluding with a disyllabic iamb is standard practice in Augustan elegy after *c.* 20 BCE. One learned literary touch, observed by both Carcopino and Stevenson, is the masculine form *ipse colus*, used only by Catullus and Propertius. Another is an allusion to an epigram in the Greek Anthology (*Anth. Pal.* 7.12.4), which represents the Hellenistic female poet Erinna as sent to Hades by the Moira (fate), the "mistress of the distaff," and draws on metaphoric connections between weaving by Fates and mortal women and poetry. These connections provide a thread, as it were, between the portrayals of Sulpicia as "reader" and "writer" in the first and last lines of the epigram, respectively. As Marilyn Skinner has observed (pers. comm.), the mention of the distaff in line 8 is an honorific tribute to Erinna, and therefore evidence that the author considers herself to be writing within a female poetic tradition; so, too, in this poem does Sulpicia cast herself as Erinna, and the dead Petale as Erinna's beloved companion, Baucis, an amazing tribute to a freedwoman. Propertius also uses the name Petale for a female slave of the dead Cynthia at 4.7.43, written *c.* 16 BCE.

[26] Hinds 1987: 44–5; J. Stevenson 2005: 44, who further points out that the ambiguity of the phrase *servi filia* "is increased by the absence of capitalization in Roman scripts."

[27] It seems likely that we "passers-by" are expected to construe the first line initially as "behold the ashes of Sulpicia the *lectrix*," and only after reading the second line to realize that this Sulpicia is a freed slave originally named Petale – and that *Sulpiciae* is also the *sphragis*, or personal imprint, of the elegist.

reader," which the literarily learned Sulpicia most certainly was.[28] The inscription then describes Petale with a warm and witty collocation of words.[29]

Whether the name Sulpicia refers to the slave Petale, or her freeborn and well-born mistress, or both, its prominent placement as the first word of the inscription represents this dead female slave as belonging to Servius Sulpicius' *familia*. This Latin term, lest we forget, refers to a male-headed household: all persons subject to the control of one man, the *paterfamilias*, whether relations, freedmen, or slaves.[30] By commemorating this member of her dead father's *familia*, Sulpicia, if she is the author of this inscription, has undertaken one of her father's public functions. We might argue that she is merely adopting a role comparable to that occupied by young men, with and without living fathers, who were expecting to become *patresfamiliae* themselves, albeit for a different, less socially elevated, constituency, and albeit by writing rather than speaking. For young Roman males traditionally made their speaking debuts in public by delivering funeral speeches for dead relatives, male and female.[31] Writing verse inscriptions for dead slaves and freed people may have been a parallel, if less politically prestigious, duty for literarily educated young women, such as Sulpicia. But since we do not know of other young women who performed this task, we must assume that Sulpicia is fulfilling duties that would ordinarily have been her father's as head of their household. Ironically, Petale, the dead woman whom Sulpicia commemorates, contributed to Sulpicia's own literary education and served Sulpicia's *familia*, with her voice. However, unless we are to imagine that Sulpicia read this text aloud at a public event, Petale's funerary tribute was communicated in silence.

It is worth noting, too, that Sulpicia seems to have had a younger brother, who also evidently contributed elegies to the third book of Tibullus' poems, under the pseudonymous slave name of Lygdamus. While it is not impossible that he, rather than his sister, wrote Petale's epitaph, his poems lack the

---

[28] J. Stevenson (2005: 43–4) claims that "insofar as it is possible to read any kind of poetic signature off such a tiny œuvre, the epitaph is Sulpician. The ambiguities about naming in the two first lines suggest the same love of paradox as the use of *fama* in 3.13 … the emphasis on [Petale] as a servile name implies she had a non-servile name … and her free name would of course be Sulpicia."

[29] One noteworthy feature is the chiastic order of verb tenses in lines 5 and 6, a series of four asyndetically linked phrases: pluperfect (*viderat*), imperfect (*vigebat*), imperfect (*splendebat*), pluperfect (*creverat*).

[30] *OLD*, s.v. "*familia* (1)."

[31] For funeral orations honoring elite Roman males and females, and the elite young Roman men who often delivered them, see Kierdorf 1980. Ovid's autobiography in *Tr.* 4.10, with its homage to his father, appears to employ some conventions of this literary genre.

verve and subtle artistry of this inscription and of the eleven Sulpicia elegies
generally. If nothing else, it is unlikely that he would have employed the
feminine name Sulpicia to such powerful, punning effect.[32]

Sulpicia's fatherless existence, then, seems to account for her assumption of
this commemorative responsibility for members of the *familia*, properly the
responsibility of her father or whoever was head-of-household. Cornelia
appears also to have been confronted with demands imposed on her time,
talents, and energies, demands which a living father might have assumed.
Indeed, Cornelia was husbandless as well as fatherless during the years in
which she was grooming her sons for political leadership. From what we can
ascertain about both women, Cornelia had to deal with far more emotionally stressful demands than Sulpicia: supervising the education of her sons
when they were children; overseeing their entry into the family business of
Roman governmental service when they reached adulthood; and ensuring
all the while that they adhered to sound moral and political principles,
including responsiveness to her own emotional needs.

   Like Cornelia in her letter, Sulpicia also identifies with her father in her
poems, in her case through the use of legal language and the writing of erotic
poetry as well as the invocation of his name. And whatever demands made
on these two different women as a result of their fathers' early deaths, we can
understand why they would have identified, proudly, with their fathers.
After all, these demands, and their fathers' absences, created opportunities
for these women: Mark Golden's observation elsewhere in this volume, that
the absence of a father could offer opportunity as well as hardship and grief,
is particularly apt in the case of both Sulpicia and Cornelia. Unlike Ovid,
Sulpicia did not have a living father who disparaged her interest in writing
poetry. In fact, her father's death evidently afforded her a forum in which to
write poetry and – if she in fact wrote the epitaph to Petale – in a way that
brought credit to their family. Unlike Ovid, Cornelia did not have a living
father dictating how she was and was not to conduct herself in political and
personal matters (or a husband: she never remarried, even rejecting a
proposal from a Ptolemy of Egypt, after her children's father died).[33]

---

[32] For Sulpicia's brother, Servius Sulpicius Postumius, putative Lygdamus of Tib. 3.1–6, see Butrica 1993.
[33] For the marriage proposal, see Badian 1996a.

Finally, paternal absences meant empowerment as well as opportunities for Cornelia and Sulpicia, emboldening them both. Yes, Cornelia needed to negotiate with her son in her letter, evoking and perhaps invoking her late father while attempting to make her own political and personal demands in a way that a male parent would not have needed to do. Yes, Sulpicia needed to negotiate with both Messalla and Cerinthus, invoking and evoking her late father while attempting to make her own erotic demands. Still, both women exercise agency and a degree of autonomy in their writings, self-assertively expressed. One wonders if Cornelia's fierce opposition to her son's political agenda, or Sulpicia's extra-marital affair with a younger man, would have been possible, much less publicly acknowledged, if their fathers had been alive at the time.

In any event, the independent stances of these fatherless women contrast vividly with the paternally deferential pose struck by the "father-ful" Ovid. To be sure, both Cornelia and Sulpicia differ from Ovid in a number of ways. Not only are they women, and women whose aristocratic lineage afforded them advantages unavailable to a man of his equestrian background. Both also became fatherless at a very early age, and they were never subjected to the controls and pressures of *patria potestas*.[34] Consequently, gender, social class, and the experience of growing up without a father all presumably played a role in how these daughters characterize themselves as interacting with others, and mostly other men, in their writings. And while the writings of Cornelia and Sulpicia offer only a limited glimpse into how fatherlessness affected female children in Greco-Roman antiquity, without that glimpse we would not have a daughter's perspective at all.

---

[34] In contrast to Ovid, who spent nearly fifty years under *patria potestas*, Cornelia and Sulpicia were under the legal control of a guardian, but not the life-or-death power of a father, for most of their lives, including the times at which they wrote; this, too, may have helped to embolden them.

PART IV

Rhetoric of loss

CHAPTER 11

The disadvantages and advantages of being fatherless: the case of Sulla

Sabine Müller

This chapter explores fatherlessness in the political self-fashioning of the late Roman Republic. Specifically, it will examine the political and ideological disadvantages and advantages of being fatherless through a discussion of Lucius Cornelius Sulla's strategic use of fatherlessness as a part of his rhetoric of power. As this chapter will show, Sulla successfully forged a public image of himself as a divinely chosen statesman who surpassed all other men on the basis of his personal virtue and special relationship to the gods. In this he borrowed from Hellenistic and Eastern models of kingship that projected an image of the ruler as a self-made man, and as such did not owe his position of power to family connections or ancestral deities. These models led Sulla to all but disown his family and advertise himself as a "fatherless" politician in a culture that revered both personal and political "fathers." Sulla's *persona* thus provides us with a special view into the role of the father and of growing up fatherless in the political culture of antiquity.

SULLA: BEING FATHERLESS IN THE *COMMENTARII*

At the end of his life Sulla wrote his memoirs.[1] According to Plutarch, he abandoned his work on the last book in 78 BCE, just two days before he died.[2] After he laid down the dictatorship, Sulla was nominally a *privatus* and it was during this time that he wrote his memoirs in his country home near Puteoli.[3] This was, of course, a mere illusion. In fact, Sulla still was the most influential man in Rome, guarded by nearly 100,000 veterans and a troop of 10,000 freedmen called the *Cornelii*.[4] The bucolic idyll described by Appian is therefore misleading, as Sulla was still active in politics.[5] When

---

[1] Presumably written in Latin, not bilingually in Greek and Latin. See Behr 1993: 9.
[2] Plut. *Sull.* 37.1.
[3] For his dictatorship, see Lintott 1999: 113, 210–12; Baltrusch 2002.
[4] Hölkeskamp 2000: 217.
[5] App. *B Civ.* 1.104; cf. Plut. *Sull.* 37.4–5; Behr 1993: 103.

Sulla began his literary work, which eventually filled twenty-two books, the tradition of Roman aristocratic biography and autobiography was already well established.[6] The last book was certainly left incomplete.[7] Sadly, our knowledge of his memoirs is now limited to just twenty-three fragments, most of which are found in the works of Plutarch.[8] Traces of his work can also be found in Appian and Livy.[9] There has been much debate as to the structure, title, and motivation of the *commentarii*, but it is now the *communis opinio* that Sulla's literary propaganda effectively brightened his image in the subsequent historical tradition while blackening the reputations of his political enemies Marius and Cinna, whom he condemned.[10] Cinna was labeled a cruel tyrant,[11] and Marius a slow-witted, uncouth, and politically inept *vir militaris*.[12]

Concerning the structure of the memoirs, most scholars believe that the first book contained a general introduction and established the *leitmotif* of the work, Sulla's *felicitas*,[13] while the bulk of the autobiography was devoted to his account of the Mithridatic and Civil Wars.[14] Holger Behr therefore characterizes the memoirs as an apologetic manifesto justifying his political activities, which had been widely regarded as acts of injustice.[15] It has also been generally suggested that Sulla devoted the whole of the second book to the history of his family and ancestors.[16] According to Badian, this subject was treated at even greater length.[17] While Badian's suggestion is unlikely, it

[6] R. G. Lewis 1991: 512; Brennan 1992: 106–7; Behr 1993: 105; Scholz 2003: 173–5.
[7] R. G. Lewis 1991: 518; Behr 1993: 9.
[8] Peter, *HRR el* 1.195–204. See also Ramage 1991: 95; Behr 1993: 9, 17–18; Christ 2002: 160; Scholz 2003: 180. Despite his obvious reliance on Sulla's own work, Plutarch still patterned him on the model of the Greek tyrant.
[9] Badian 1970: 4. For Livy, see Barden Dowling 2000: 326.
[10] R. G. Lewis (1991: 511, n. 10) doubts that the term *commentarii* was part of the title and suggests that the work was called *L. Sulla de rebus suis, De rebus L. Cornelii Sullae*, or *Res Gestae L. Cornelii Sullae*. Scholz (2003: 176, n. 17) argues that both Sulla and other ancient authors called his memoirs *commentarii*. Cf. Ramage 1991: 95–6: "*Commentarii rerum gestarum*." Letzner (2000: 5) points out that Cicero (*Div.* 1.33.72) speaks of the *Sullae historia*. For Cinna, see Lovano 2002: 137. For Marius, see Behr 1993: 16; Werner 1995: 220–366.
[11] Lovano 2002: 139.   [12] Plut. *Mar.* 2; cf. Ramage 1991: 99.
[13] Candau Morón 2000: 462–4. For a definition of *felicitas*, see Keaveney 2005: "It was ... regarded as his personal quality which would endure unto death ... *Felicitas*, too, carried with it a ... notion of abundance or plentifulness of good things. As a result, it was believed that the personal *felicitas* of the man of *virtus* radiated from him and was transmitted to all who came into contact with him" (34).
[14] Behr 1993: 11–12. Cf. Alföldy 1976: 158. Scholz (2003: 181) points out that Plutarch seems to follow Sulla's chronology very closely (cf. R. G. Lewis 1991: 510, n. 4).
[15] Behr 1993: 11–13. It is important to recall, however, that the work was left unfinished, so Sulla may have never treated the last years of his political life in great detail. Scholz (2003: 181) assumes a short treatment.
[16] The third book is thought to have related his early political career and achievements. Cf. Scholz 2003: 181.
[17] Badian 1970: 4.

is true that Sulla could not leave out his ancestry altogether.[18] Lineage was a central symbol of status in late Republican Rome, carrying prestige and affecting the standing of a young aristocrat.[19] Thus the *homo novus* Marius, who had no glorious and widely known ancestors to rely on, went to extraordinary lengths in order to raise his political profile. According to Sallust, in order to make up for the ancestry he lacked, Marius publicly recalled his military achievements and bared his scars in his famous speech in Rome during his Numidian command.[20] Unlike his contemporaries, however, Sulla clearly played down his ancestry, reducing this section of his work to a minimum, instead choosing to focus on himself.[21] He did not dismiss his ancestors entirely, particularly not the early *maiores*, but rather seems to have emphasized the divine sphere as more important. In Rome ancestors usually were even more impressive than the divine members of the mythical genealogies that entered into aristocratic lineages.[22] And yet, here again Sulla does not seem to have followed the herd of late Republican nobility by inventing legendary genealogies claiming descent from gods or demi-gods, like the Iulii, who traced their origins back to Venus, or the Antonii, who saw themselves as related to Heracles.[23] The lack of a divine ancestor of the Cornelii in the *commentarii* is probably also due to the same process of image construction as that which led to the displacement of ancestors generally in the work. Sulla preferred to inscribe his divine protection as a sign of a heavenly mission and this led him to focus on himself as an individual.

In this context it is also noteworthy that Sulla clearly stressed and exaggerated the decay of his branch of the family tree.[24] Checking the fragmentary evidence in Plutarch, Gellius, Velleius Paterculus, and Livy, we find that Sulla did indeed mention at least one ancestor, P. Cornelius

---

[18] Cf. Lewis 1991: 512, n. 13.   [19] Saller 1984: 342, 349–52.

[20] Sall. *Iug.* 85.4, 10–30; Plut. *Mar.* 9.2.

[21] A fragment in Gellius (*NA* 1.12.16) proves that Sulla mentioned at least one of his ancestors. Behr (1993: 14) points out that this could also be a comment in the context of the description of Sulla's own *cursus honorum* made *en passant*. He further argues that the chapters on Sulla's childhood and familial background were short and by no means an important element. Contra (without argument): Letzner 2000: 22.

[22] Saller 1984: 351; Hölkeskamp 2004: 169–95. Thus Julius Caesar revived the memory of his uncle Marius (Plut. *Caes.* 5.1–2; 6.1–4; Suet. *Iul.* 11). Cf. Mackay 2000: 165–7. Caesar also honored his aunt Julia, the widow of Marius (Suet. *Iul.* 6.1; Plut. *Caes.* 5.3). It was no coincidence that he was running for the quaestorship at this time: in this particular context, recalling the patron deity of his family, Venus, was not politically useful enough.

[23] Wiseman 1974; Huttner 1995. For the Iulii, see Suet. *Iul.* 6.1; for the Antonii, see Plut. *Ant.* 4.2; 60.5; *IG* 11.2 1043.23.

[24] Sall. *Iug.* 95.3.

Rufinus, who was consul in 290 BCE during the Samnite Wars, dictator around 285, and consul again in 277 during the Pyrrhic Wars.[25] He came to a dishonorable end in 275, when he was expelled from the senate for possessing more than ten pounds of silver plate contrary to the law.[26] In succeeding generations his career was transformed into an example of the intolerant attitude toward luxury that was regarded as typical of the early Republic. Rufinus thereby won some dubious fame.[27] Many in both antiquity and more modern times have in fact seen this taste for luxury passed on through the family tree from Rufinus to Sulla,[28] yet this is to misjudge the ideology of abundance that Sulla later adopted when, for example, he acted as a bene-factor of Rome by consecrating a tenth of his wealth to Heracles and funding several days of feasts for the Roman people.[29]

Sulla also probably mentioned Rufinus' son P. Cornelius. He was *flamen dialis* in the mid-third century BCE and perhaps the first to bear the cog-nomen, "Sulla."[30] His son, P. Cornelius Sulla, praetor in 212, founded the *ludi Apollinares*.[31] His son in turn was Sulla's grandfather, who was praetor in 186.[32] Plutarch has little to say about Sulla's grandfather and his son, L. Cornelius Sulla, Sulla's father. To quote Badian: "Of L. Sulla's father we know nothing."[33] Hinard attempted to show that the elder Sulla was a personal friend of King Mithridates VI Eupator and had held a promagist-racy in Asia.[34] This theory, however, is without evidence and has subse-quently been refuted by Madden and Keaveney. They have concluded that while "we must thrust Sulla's father back into the obscurity," "we may … console ourselves with the thought that the father's continuing obscurity serves only to underline, once more, the remarkable nature of his son's rise

---

[25] Vell. Pat. 2.17.2. See Badian 1970: 4; Behr 1993: 25–6; Christ 2002: 54; Keaveney 2005: 5.
[26] Plut. *Sull.* 1.1. See Katz 1982: 148; Keaveney 2005: 5.
[27] Keaveney 2005: 5. Cf. Val. Max. 2.9.4; Tert. *Apol.* 6; Plut. *Sull.* 1.1.   [28] Plut. *Sull.* sync. 3.2–3.
[29] Plut. *Sull.* 35.1–2. Cf. Keaveney 2005: 34: Abundance was regarded as a part of *felicitas*.
[30] Macrob. *Sat.* 1.17.27. Behr (1993: 26) argues that Sulla himself applied the *cognomen* to the *flamen dialis* in order to stress the antiquity and religiosity of the name. Cf. Katz 1982: 148; Keaveney 2005: 6. Keaveney gives several possible explanations for the cognomen "Sulla": it might have derived from a physical characteristic, perhaps as a corruption of the word *sura* (the calf) or connected with the reddish or golden hair for which the family was famous (Plut. *Sull.* 6.2); Plutarch mentions that Sulla was mocked because of his mottled complexion and received this name thus (*Sull.* 2.1; *Mor.* 505b). Cf. Behr 1993: 26–7. It is obvious, however, that Plutarch's description of Sulla's looks followed the doctrines of Peripatetic physiognomy: white skin sprinkled with blotches of red symbolized daring and fierce anger; keen and piercing eyes were a sign of courage; their gray-blue color betrayed a leonine nature. Cf. E. C. Evans 1941: 104–5; R. Carpenter 1945: 357.
[31] R. G. Lewis 1991: 512–13.   [32] Keaveney 2005: 6.   [33] Badian 1970: 5; Christ 2002: 54.
[34] Hinard 1985: 21–2. He argues that Appian (*Mith.* 54.216) refers to a personal friendship between Sulla's father and Mithridates.

and achievements."[35] This is an important argument. Sulla was in no need of a father. A successful father would have cast a shadow on his rise.

The only information we receive about Sulla's father is that he married twice and that his second wife was wealthy. Sulla obviously did not mention the offices or other achievements of his father. Badian suggests that a descendant of praetors who married a wealthy heiress must have held some public office to be considered an attractive bridegroom.[36] But Plutarch, who cites Sulla, states only that he died when his son was still young and left him no inheritance at all. Born in 138 BCE, Sulla probably had just assumed the *toga virilis* and was in his teens when he lost his father.[37] An anecdote illustrates the state of poverty Sulla supposedly endured after the death of his father. It was said that he was forced to rent a room in a lodging house where his neighbor was a freedman who paid not much less than he did for his accommodation.[38] In speaking of "poverty," we must, of course, bear in mind that we have to handle the term carefully. Plutarch adopts the perspective of the Roman nobility that used the term "poverty" as a political slur in order to cast doubt on the *dignitas* of an opponent. Cicero's polemical comments on Marcus Antonius' childhood in the *Philippics* illustrate this strategy.[39] Therefore, "poor" does not mean poverty in the sense of living at the subsistence level or being close to starvation.[40] The definition of poor as used by Sulla in his memoirs is that based on this aristocratic standard of the late Republic; in reality, he likely had an income and a fortune that from our perspective would not classify him as among the "poor" of Rome. In the eyes of the Roman nobility, however, living in a lodging house also inhabited by freedmen was a sign of great poverty that affected one's political status, making it very difficult to embark on a political career.[41] But how trustworthy are Sulla's memoirs concerning his poverty? It is assumed that this story is part of his image.[42] Again, there are signs here that he deliberately manipulated the truth in order to emphasize his rise from nothing. A reassessment of the legend of Sulla's youth is therefore in order.[43]

---

[35] Madden and Keaveney 1993: 141. They argue against Hinard's interpretation of Appian's *philia*, contending that it referred not to a private friendship but to formal relations between states. The elder Sulla may therefore have been part of the staff of a Roman magistrate in the East (1993: 139–40).

[36] Badian 1970: 5. See also Reams 1984: 162; Keaveney 2005: 6.

[37] About fifteen years old according to Letzner 2000: 30. Cf. Keaveney 2005: 6.

[38] Plut. *Sull.* 1.4; see Hölkeskamp 2000: 201.   [39] E.g. Cic. *Phil.* 2.44–5, 48.

[40] Keaveney 2005: 7: "His tiny income might appear impressive when compared with that of a manual worker, but no Roman noble … would ever dream of making such a comparison … By the standards of the class to which he rightfully belonged … Sulla was a very poor man."

[41] Letzner 2000: 32; Keaveney 2005: 7.

[42] Reams 1984: 158–69, who regards Sulla's early poverty as completely fictional.

[43] Eder 1997: 189, who admits that it is nearly impossible to judge Sulla's person and deeds because the ancient sources are strongly influenced by his autobiography.

Sulla received an excellent education in Latin and Greek, as befitted an aristocratic youth, and this stands as a clear contradiction of his alleged poverty.[44] Plutarch stresses Sulla's education as a main difference between him and Marius, who received no Greek *paideia* and purportedly did not want it.[45] Plutarch, as a philosopher, believed that lessons in Greek culture could have helped the general learn to control his vices so that he might not have ended up as a cruel tyrant. He portrays Marius' rejection of Greek wisdom as punished by Nemesis.[46] If one considers Sulla's education, his father could not really have been as unimportant as Sulla wanted to make the reader of his memoirs believe. This was yet another element of his image as the divinely protected, self-made man. Thus, he stressed the decline of his family and depicted his father as degenerate. His intention was to highlight and exploit his poverty in order to shape his image.[47]

Plutarch contributed to this storyline by stressing that Sulla's loss of his father was quickly followed by his loss of status and morals: "when he was still young and obscure he spent much time with actors and buffoons and shared their dissolute life."[48] This theme recurs in later chapters of work and serves to illustrate his principal character traits. Candau Morón is probably right in finding in these passages a literary trope that emphasizes the convergence of great political achievements and an unstable personal disposition, the same sort of *ritratto paradossale* as Theopompus employed in his depiction of Philip II.[49] However, the theme of poverty leading to debts and thus dangers for the Roman state also shows up in the portrait of Catiline painted by Cicero and Sallust.[50] They emphasize that the debts of Catiline, who

---

[44] Sall. *Iug.* 95.3. See Christ 2002: 54.   [45] Plut. *Mar.* 2.4. Cf. Sall. *Iug.* 85.12; Val. Max. 2.2.3.

[46] Plut. *Mar.* 2.4. For Marius as an unpleasant character: Plut. *Mar.* 2.1; 14.2. Cf. Russell 1966: 145; Swain 1990: 133, 137–40; Werner 1995: 239–40, 266: "In this dilemma, however, Plutarch 'invented' a new model of general: militarily efficient and manly, yet tainted by undeniable character flaws."

[47] Here Sulla also had M. Aemilius Scaurus as a model to imitate, since he wrote an autobiography, probably in the 90s, which stressed that his father left him next to nothing: Val. Max. 4.4.11; Plut. *Mor.* 318c. Cf. Badian 1970: 5; Reams 1984: 163; Brennan 1992: 110; Behr 1993: 24.

[48] Plut. *Sull.* 2.2. It is often suggested that he was taught to create a public image by these artists. Cf. Hölkeskamp 2000: 200; Christ 2002: 65. Of course, Sulla could have exploited the idea that he associated with actors and buffoons in order to stress that his rise from misery was such as only a god's favorite could achieve. His continued presence at drinking parties in the company of such theatrical types even after he had reached the peak of his career might have been seen as a demonstration that the gods did not disapprove of this lifestyle.

[49] Candau Morón 2000: 474–5. While fathers obviously have an impact on the moral education of their sons (cf. Cic. *Off.* 1.121; cf. 1.4; 3.121; cf. *Att.* 15.13.6), most explanations of Sulla's moral decline have been too indebted to Freudian psychology. On the connection between fatherlessness and moral education, see the contribution of Neil Bernstein in this volume.

[50] Cic. *Cat.* 2.10–11. Cf. Sall. *Cat.* 5.1–7; 16.4.

figures as the morally corrupt arch-villain, caused him to aim at the total destruction of the state.[51]

In reality, Sulla's family was not as poor and marginalized as he wanted his audience to believe.[52] Neither was Sulla without any political protection, although the early death of his father was undoubtedly a disadvantage for him. Usually it was the duty of the father of a young Roman aristocrat to introduce his son into political life and to take care of his political education.[53] But Sulla turned political disadvantage into ideological advantage. The early death of his father was the setting of the story in which a young man, driven into poverty, made his career out of nothing, fostered by a divine power.[54] Consequently any information about his supporters, mentors, teachers, or friends during the first three decades of his life (regularly seen as one's "youth" in Roman thought) was put to one side.[55] One has to keep in mind that this is fiction built up around his *persona*.

Finally, it is worth noting that Sulla was equally silent about many, but not all, of the important women in his life. He wrote a few sentences about his stepmother but seems to have passed over his biological mother in silence.[56] In fact, it seems that the names of both women were perhaps omitted by Sulla, since it is Plutarch's practice in his biographies to give the name of the protagonist's mother when he knows it.[57] As Plutarch states that Sulla's stepmother left a sizable legacy to her stepson with the result that he became moderately well-off, it is clear that the woman could not have been a disreputable nonentity.[58] The omission is certainly due to Sulla's literary strategy and personal iconography: just as he needed no earthly father, so he had no need for a mortal mother of any sort. After his successes in his Greek campaign he had called himself *Epaphroditos*, or "Aphrodite's favorite," and advertised himself as the foster child of the goddess.[59] The title signified that he claimed to be chosen by Aphrodite in the sense of being divinely chosen.[60] He thus wanted to ascribe his successes to the

---

[51] Philipps 1976: 442.
[52] Madden and Keaveney 1993: 138, n. 1. They call it "shabby gentility rather than outright penury."
[53] Thomas 1996: 325. Cf. Bernstein, this volume.   [54] Plut. *Sull.* 1. sync. 3.2.
[55] Christ 2002: 197. Contra: Reams 1984: 160–1, who thinks that the omission is due to a source hostile to Sulla, on which Plutarch based his account of his youth.
[56] Certainly his motive was not that he lacked an emotional tie to his mother, as Letzner (2000: 27–8) suggests. Sulla also omitted his brother, half-brother and sister (cf. 25–6). See also Reams 1987: 301–5. This omission fits into the pattern of the mythical exposed hero. Rank (1909: 61) points out that the hero needs no brother, who usually turns out to be the rival he has to remove.
[57] Badian 1970: 6, n. 10. He suggests that Plutarch's omission is attributable to Sulla, who stressed his poor beginnings. This is most certainly the reason. Cf. Behr 1993: 14, n. 54; Hölkeskamp 2000: 20.
[58] Plut. *Sull.* 2.4.   [59] Wosnik 1963: 25–6; Ramage 1991: 101; Christ 2002: 207.
[60] Wosnik 1963: 28–30; Fears 1981: 794; Sumi 2002: 416.

goddess and not to the influence of his mother's family, which would have had the effect of diminishing the marvelous character of his career after he had taken such great pains to shape his life on a heroic model.[61]

It is also striking that he seems to say next to nothing about his first three wives. His first wife, Ilia or Julia, was probably a member of the Iulii Caesares, a family that certainly could have supported him as he was starting his political career.[62] His second wife, Aelia, is – apart from her name – a complete unknown.[63] In 88 BCE he divorced his third wife, Cloelia, and married Caecilia Metella, the widow of M. Aemilius Scaurus and niece of Q. Caecilius Metellus Numidicus, the enemy of Marius.[64] He most likely owed his consulship of the same year to this prestigious and illustrious marriage.[65] His last wife, Valeria, was a daughter of M. Valerius Messala and a sister of the orator Hortensius.[66] While his first three wives are mere phantoms in his memoirs, the last two were given greater prominence.[67] The reason seems to be clear: as he was already a successful general when these marriages took place, the respectable tie to the Metelli was presented as a consequence, not a cause, of his success, whereas the marriage to Valeria illustrated the charismatic effect of his *felicitas*. Plutarch tells us that the dictator met Valeria during a gladiatorial spectacle when she plucked a bit of fluff off his mantle, explaining that she merely wanted to have a little part of his felicity.[68]

On the other hand, it is interesting to note that Sulla obviously mentioned his mistress Nicopolis, whom he had loved in his youth.[69] Her name may indicate that she was a former slave and may have gained her fortune by prostitution.[70] As in the Hellenistic monarchies, the royal mistress was associated with Aphrodite in her function as the goddess of beauty, love,

[61] See Fears 1981: 793: "Throughout his 'Memoirs,' Sulla portrayed his rise to power as the work of the gods and himself as the divinely foreordained agent of the deities." See also Syme (1964: 150–1) on Sulla's autobiography: "This curious document, cynical at times in its bold mendacity … "
[62] Plut. *Sull.* 6.1. He married her perhaps in 107 BCE, as suggested by Letzner (2000: 36, n. 62). Cf. Keaveney 2005: 8.
[63] Christ 2002: 199.
[64] Plut. *Sull.* 6.10–12; 33.3; 34.3; 37.2. See Keaveney 1984: 114–15; Eder 1997: 187; Hölkeskamp 2000: 206; Bringmann 2002: 231; Christ 2002: 199.
[65] Plut. *Sull.* 6.5-6. See Syme 1962: 12, 20, 31; Eder 1997: 187.   [66] Plut. *Sull.* 35.4.
[67] They also had higher public profiles, cf. Plut. *Sull.* 6.12.   [68] Plut. *Sull.* 35.4–5.
[69] Keaveney 2005: 9. Plutarch (*Sull.* 2.4) comments that she was a common but wealthy woman who left him her fortune when she died.
[70] See Athen. 13.574e, 587b. Her humble descent seems to have been the reason why she was mentioned at all. She might have known some members of the aristocracy but, if so, on an informal level without being linked to influential political circles. Therefore she could not be regarded as having forwarded Sulla's career. Contra: Keaveney (2005: 10), who calls her a woman of means without any explanation.

and sexuality.[71] This tradition could be a plausible reason for Sulla to mention her. She was said to have been charmed by him and to have fallen in love with him because of his *charis*.[72] This attribute is usually connected to females and often to Aphrodite, but in this passage it is ascribed to Sulla. It seems his complex treatment of Nicopolis in his memoirs points to Aphrodite and his being specially favored by her. Apart from her, however, Sulla extinguished from his memoirs all persons who could have been regarded as nurturers, protectors, father-figures, and supporters of his career. The model he patterned his image upon permitted no other authorities than the gods.

So, from the picture he paints in his memoirs, Sulla appears to emerge on the scene as a completely self-made man, protected by divine power. Of course, the very genre of autobiography tends to invite an emphasis on youthful poverty in order to set off the great efforts necessary for ultimate success.[73] A difficult start to one's political career merely serves to illustrate the virtue of the successful man. Like the phoenix that rises from the ashes, so Sulla entered onto the political stage of Rome. He probably opened his memoirs with a programmatic comment illustrating his "illustrious ancestry and decline in family fortunes, from which his own Blessedness had brought recovery, for his own and the state's benefit."[74] Suggestions that Sulla wrote a great deal on his boyhood and adult life must therefore be corrected.[75] It is plausible that the chapters on his youth consisted of mysterious tales, like the only anecdote we know about his childhood. Keaveney judges it to be "as false as it is charming."[76] When Sulla was a baby, his nurse carried him through the streets of Rome. A strange woman approached and greeted him with the words, *Salve … puer tibi et rei publicae tuae felix* ("Hail … a boy fortunate for you and your Republic"), and then disappeared like a ghost.[77] Stories like this one foreshadow his career and emphasize the benefits he was to bestow on Rome. It is also clear that throughout his memoirs Sulla used dreams, omens, portents, and prophecies as narrative devices to strengthen the illusion that he was a favorite of the gods.[78] We may therefore be

---

[71] Athen. 11.497d; 13.571c, 572e–f; 6.254a; *OGIS* 228, 229; Theocr. 17.17–19, 45–50; 15.106–8. Cf. Carney 2000: 218–19, 223. The first Macedonian noble to associate his mistress with Aphrodite was Alexander's treasurer, Harpalus. He set up a sanctuary and a *temenos* for his Corinthian mistress, Pythionice, in Babylon after her death, dedicating the altar to Pythionice Aphrodite as Theopompus testifies (*apud* Athen. 13.595c, 595f–596a).
[72] Plut. *Sull.* 2.4.   [73] Hölkeskamp 2000: 202.
[74] R. G. Lewis 1991: 516. Cf. Scholz 2003: 182.   [75] R. G. Lewis 1991: 513.
[76] Keaveney 2005: 6. R. G. Lewis 1991: 513, n. 19.
[77] [Aur. Vict.] *De vir. ill.* 75.1. See Behr 1993: 14, n. 53.
[78] Fears 1981: 793; Ramage 1991: 98; Behr 1993: 19; Candau Morón 2000: 456; Christ 2002: 161.

tolerably certain that he did not write much more than Plutarch quotes about his grandfather and father. The reason is clear: Sulla wanted to create the impression that he owed nothing to his family, claiming his legitimacy solely from the divine sphere. His father would have been a disturbing element in the otherwise miraculous story of his career. As a consequence, his father had to be transformed into a no-name loser who left him in the most miserable circumstances. Nothing could be allowed to overshadow his direct relationship to the gods and his star-like rise out of nothing. The depiction of his family as having fallen on evil days served his purpose of presenting himself as having "succeeded single-handedly in bringing his family out of political obscurity."[79]

MARIUS AS FATHER-FIGURE: A REASSESSMENT

Sulla's self-promotion as the fatherless favorite of the gods negatively influenced the picture of Marius in his memoirs. This is significant because Marius could have served as father-figure for the young Sulla: he was approximately twenty years older and had the appropriate age and prestige to be regarded as a suitable protector. But this was not Sulla's intention at all. Rather, he had to eliminate any element in his biography that hinted at any source of protection – whether it was a political foster-father, family member, or even a client – other than the divine. Again, such an admission would have spoilt the impression that he owed everything to his virtue and divine election. As we have seen, Sulla's carefully crafted self-image often necessitated the elision of important figures in his life, and the case of Marius is no exception.

For instance, it was no coincidence that although he had never before held public office, Sulla was nevertheless elected quaestor in 108 BCE, presumably on Marius' consular coat-tails.[80] Both Sallust and Velleius Paterculus confirm the suggestion that they were on friendly terms.[81] Thus Sulla appears to have covered up the nature of his early political dependence on Marius.[82] This political connection must still have been active when Sulla was appointed

---

[79] Gruen 1966: 386.
[80] Plut. *Sull.* 3.1. See Badian 1970: 6–7. Badian believes that the family of Sulla's mother was in some way tied to Marius. There may have been yet another family tie between Sulla and Marius in the Iulii Caesares. As Sulla seems to have married a sister of Caesar Strabo and L. Julius Caesar, while Marius married a Julia, it would not seem impossible for both to have been on friendly terms with the Caesares. Cf. Letzner 2000: 37; Keaveney 2005: 12.
[81] Sall. *Iug.* 96.4; Vell. Pat. 2.12.1. Cf. Val. Max. 9.2.1.   [82] Keaveney 1984: 114; Christ 2002: 62.

legate to Marius in 104 in the German Wars.[83] Clearly, Marius was responsible for proposing Sulla: the senate nominated legates but usually followed the recommendation of the general under whom they were to serve.[84] The idea, then, that Marius' hostility toward Sulla arose out of his junior officer's diplomatic success in the Jugurthine War strains credibility. Sulla may well have boasted excessively about his achievement of having persuaded Bocchus to surrender Jugurtha, even going so far as to commission an infamous signet ring representing the exploit in order to commemorate his role in ending the war;[85] but the campaign was led by Marius and the victory was attributed to him, whereas Sulla had acted as Marius' subordinate.[86] Sulla, of course, told a different version. He depicted himself as the lucky one from the very start, in contrast to the brutal, uncouth, and low-spirited Marius, who was portrayed as his opposite, lacking *felicitas* and divine favor. Sulla thus antedated their hostility and exaggerated the significance of the signet ring, turning it into a symbolic moment that triggered Marius' envy.[87] Plutarch reinforced this picture, focusing on the conflict between the two men, turning them into protagonists of a drama on the political stage.[88] It is uncertain whether Plutarch himself was the first to suggest that Sulla took revenge for Metellus Numidicus, whom Marius replaced as commander,[89] by stealing some of

---

[83] Plut. *Sull.* 4.1. Cf. Cagniart 1989: 139. Hölkeskamp (2000: 204) assumes (without argument) that for some reason Marius had no choice in the matter.

[84] Plut. *Sull.* 4.1. See Behr 1993: 120–1.

[85] Plut. *Sull.* 3.4; *Mar.* 10.5–6; *Mor.* 806d; Plin. *HN* 37.8–9; Val. Max. 8.14.4. See Mackay 2000: 209–10, who suggests that Sulla changed rings after his triumphant return to Rome in the last years of his life. The new signet ring depicted three trophies symbolizing his victories over the Cilician opponents, Mithridates and his personal enemies. Sulla's son, Faustus, represented the image on a *denarius* in about 56 BCE (cf. below, n. 89). According to Plutarch, however, Marius considered Sulla to be beneath his envy (*Sull.* 4.1).

[86] Cagniart 1989: 144; Behr 1993: 116.

[87] Thommen (2000: 190) adopts the version of Plutarch and thus simplifies the history of their enmity. Contra Behr 1993, 28–9; cf. Keaveney (2005: 24–5), who points out that Sulla was at this time politically insignificant and therefore no threat to Marius. In spite of this, he sees the signet ring as a signal for the beginning of the quarrel between them.

[88] The play continued: in 91 Bocchus dedicated a gilded statue group on the Capitol representing Jugurtha being surrendered by Bocchus (Plut. *Sull.* 6.1; *Mar.* 32.4. See T. Hölscher 1984: 17–8; Bringmann 2002: 251; Christ 2002, 65). Mackay (2000: 162–4) suggests that Bocchus supported Sulla, who was looking forward to running for the consulship. Cf. Brennan 1992: 156; Hölkeskamp 2000: 204. According to Behr (1993: 121) this was the first provocation by Sulla, and the ring was only commissioned after the erection of the statues.

[89] Plut. *Mar.* 10.1; Sall. *Iug.* 73.2–7; 82.2–3; 84.1; Vell. Pat. 2.11.1–2. Sulla's son, Faustus, added to this legend by minting coins that depicted his father seated on the *sella curulis*; Jugurtha was being delivered to Sulla by Bocchus, who kneels in front of him with the inscription *FELIX* written above the scene, starting just at the line of Sulla's neck. The *denarii* were minted in about 56 BCE. Cf. Crawford 1983: 426.1, 426.3; Behr 1993: 115; Christ 2002: 57. Probably, they reflected the concept of the gilded group. Cf. Hölscher 1984: 17. For Marius' numismatic propaganda, see Heinrichs 2003: 32–5.

Marius' glory in his victory in the Numidian War, or whether this *topos* in fact derives from Sulla's own hand, as he attempted to play down his close connection to Marius.[90]

In the end, Sulla's literary efforts to conceal the truth have succeeded in making it difficult to date the exact beginning of their enmity. According to Badian, Q. Lutatius Catulus was Marius' "special protégé," being closely related to the family of Marius' wife, Julia.[91] As Catulus would have accepted Sulla in his staff only with Marius' permission, it must have been the hostility that arose between Marius and Catulus over their rival claims to victory over the Germans that forced Sulla to change sides.[92] Cagniart offers a different theory, regarding Sulla's "reduction to the inferior rank of military tribune" under Catulus in 103 BCE as a clear sign that the winds had changed and that now Marius wanted to get rid of Sulla. The reason for the demotion was Sulla's capture of the chieftain of the Tectosages, Copillus, earlier in 104 while Marius was busy training his troops.[93] Sulla in the meantime had capitalized on his success and compared it to his capture of Jugurtha, openly promoting his own glory and criticizing Marius. Annoyed by these constant pretensions, Marius demoted his legate to the rank of tribune and transferred him to the staff of Catulus.[94] Cagniart thus doubts that Catulus stood in a close relationship to Marius and sees no reason to dismiss Plutarch's comment that Sulla attached himself to Catulus because of his hostility to Marius, as he was the candidate of the nobles.[95] Both arguments show how Plutarch's testimony has to be treated with great caution.

For his part, Sulla obviously manipulated the facts in order to support the overarching storyline of his memoirs, his personal *felicitas*, which led him from severe poverty to supreme power. According to his version, Marius jealously opposed his advancement so that Sulla was forced to attach himself to Catulus, who then promptly profited from his lieutenant's *felicitas* in the battle of Vercellae. This battle of the Cimbric War is a significant and illuminating episode in Sulla's propaganda, favorable to him and critical of

---

[90] Werner (1995: 258–60), who suggests that it is a fabrication by Plutarch since Sallust has a different version that criticizes Metellus. Plutarch also creates the impression that the war had already been won when Metellus left Africa. Cf. Vell. Pat. 2.11.2. See also Behr (1993: 19–20), who stresses that Plutarch generally ignores the apologetic and self-justifying character of Sulla's memoirs. Cf. Swain 1990: 139–40; Buszard 2005: 489.

[91] Badian 1970: 9. He regards the fact that Marius was entitled to two triumphs after the German war but shared one with Catulus as a sign of their connection. See also Behr 1993: 42–4.

[92] Badian 1970: 9–10.   [93] Plut. *Sull.* 4.1.   [94] Cagniart 1989: 139–45.

[95] Plut. *Mar.* 14.14. Cagniart (1989: 146) also suggests that Catulus' election was a severe political setback for Marius, a *homo novus*. Cf. Behr 1993: 44–50.

Marius. In fact, in relating this battle Plutarch clearly follows the fairy tale Sulla told in his memoirs. In this version Marius is depicted as an experienced general, but one unable to meet the enemy in decisive battle. According to Sulla, a gigantic dust cloud swallowed Marius and all of his troops when the fighting started. They then wandered aimlessly for hours around the plain, trapped in this fog, searching in vain for the Cimbri. It was therefore up to Sulla, Catulus, and their troops to fight the battle and gain the victory. Predictably, the ominous cloud faded just at the moment when the fighting had come to an end and it was time to divide the booty.[96] Marius and his soldiers therefore wrongly claimed victory and its reward. This story is an incredible piece of propaganda that aims to snatch glory away from Marius, comparable to Sulla's version of the Jugurthine War.[97] This account also appears to have a literary precedent in that it seems Sulla modeled his version of events on Herodotus' story of the dust cloud appearing before the battle of Salamis.[98] This cloud accompanied the Greek fleet and was seen as a heavenly sign from Eleusis that foreshadowed the defeat of the Persians. In Sulla's account, on the other hand, the cloud was a sign that the gods did *not* favor Marius. All of this, however, must be juxtaposed with the fact that it was Marius who received the credit for defeating the Germans.[99] According to the contemporary Cicero (and seconded by Plutarch), Marius was celebrated for his achievements with great enthusiasm, likened to a new founder of Rome, given the title *pater patriae*, and even honored with private libations.[100] He had thus reached the pinnacle of his career while Sulla was the mere subordinate of his co-consul.

Finally, this same hostile contrast between Marius and Sulla is also manifest in the passages on the subsequent Social and Mithridatic Wars. By the time of the Social War, Marius is depicted as an exhausted old man, no longer able to render any great service to the state, while Sulla is represented as having earned the reputation of a great general.[101] In his version Plutarch in fact contradicts this characterization of Marius by admitting that he fought well and gained a remarkable victory, killing six

---

[96] Plut. *Mar.* 26.5; see Hölkeskamp 2000: 206.
[97] Werner 1995: 288–93. Rutilius Rufus and Catulus also tried to stress their military achievements by denouncing Marius. See also Brennan 1992: 108–9, n. 14; Behr 1993: 32, 41; Müller 2002: 208.
[98] Hdt. 8.65.
[99] Vell. Pat. 2.12.4. See R. J. Evans 1994: 88–9; Müller 2002: 208. Christ (2002: 68) does not believe a word of it: "Sulla's part in the decisive victory was nothing short of brilliant, and his efforts to profit at Marius' expense once again nothing short of disgusting."
[100] Plut. *Mar.* 27; Cic. *Rab. perd.* 27; *Sest.* 37–8; *Red. pop.* 9. See Behr 1993: 165.
[101] Plut. *Mar.* 33.1; *Sull.* 6.2–3, 7.1.

thousand of the enemy.[102] Later, on the eve of the Mithridatic War, Marius is once again described as a doddering old man, vainly attempting to deny his age by making a fool of himself, exercising in public with the Roman youth.[103] But again, the events that follow this allegedly pitiful demonstration vividly contradict this characterization.

Peter Scholz has suggested an alternative interpretation of Sulla's propaganda, that he in fact tried to hide his personal excellence by insisting that he was just the tool of a divine plan.[104] He believes that the Roman aristocracy would not have tolerated Sulla's praising his *virtutes* in this way, but would have dismissed the autobiography as the boastful words of a tyrant. This is not convincing. Here Scholz relies on Plutarch, who tells us in his *Moralia* that Sulla adopted the epithet *Epaphroditos* in order to avoid envy, since good luck is more easily tolerated than true virtue.[105] Nevertheless, it is a strange idea that a commander and statesman should play down his skills and create the impression of total reliance on personal luck. In fact, in a different essay, "On the Fortune or Virtue of Alexander the Great," Plutarch treats this very topic, the relationship between *aretē* (virtue) and *tychē* (fortune). In this essay he defends Alexander against the charge that he owed his success mainly or exclusively to *tychē*.[106] Instead, he says, a good general and statesman must be both naturally skilled *and* lucky.[107] This same idea is expressed by Sallust.[108] The Socratic ideal of the general as related by Xenophon also demands cleverness and skills, and not just passive reliance on fortune.[109] In the same vein, Sulla reminded his readers that a successful Roman commander needs not only good fortune, but also the ability to plan (*consilium*) and to act quickly (*celeritas*).[110] Here again Marius served as a foil, when at Vercellae he appeared as an old general lacking these necessary virtues.[111] But fortune is still an important component. Thus Sulla undercut Marius' own propaganda of *felicitas* and divine blessing by

---

[102] Plut. *Mar.* 33.3. He obviously cites a different source, one favorable to Marius. See Gilbert 1973: 106–7; Werner 1995: 315–18.

[103] Plut. *Mar.* 34.3; Diod. frag. 37.29.1. Probably deriving from Sulla. Cf. Werner 1995: 319, n. 458.

[104] Scholz 2003: 192. Cf. R. G. Lewis 1991: 516, who describes Sulla's attitude as one of "false modesty."

[105] Plut. *Mor.* 542e–f. Scholz does not quote this passage but relies on Plut. *Sull.* 6.5. Contra: Behr 1993: 19–21, 88, 119–20, 145, 159–60. Behr cautions against accepting Plutarch's simplified portrait of Sulla as a child of fortune (*fortunae filius*), pointing out that the Greek moralist did not understand the difference between the Roman concept of *felicitas* and the Greek concept of *tychē*. He therefore distorted the meaning of Sulla's *felicitas*. Balsdon (1951: 3, n. 59) had already pointed out that Plutarch's views on this subject are not very consistent.

[106] Plut. *Mor.* 326d–45b. Plutarch stresses his personal qualities as philosopher-king and warrior who always fought in the front line. Cf. Swain 1989: 507–8.

[107] Cf. Plut. *Sull.* 6.2–3; 7.   [108] Sall. *Iug.* 1.3. See Gilbert 1973: 106.

[109] Xen. *Mem.* 3.1.6–7. See Xen. *Cyr.* 1.6.25; Plut. *Mar.* 7.3. Cf. Erdmann 1972: 15–17.

[110] Cf. Ramage 1991: 99.   [111] The depiction of Q. Sertorius serves a similar purpose: cf. Behr 1993: 23.

claiming that the gods Marius appealed to before the battle ignored his entreaties.[112] Plutarch tells us that in his speech to the people after his triumph Sulla enumerated the instances of his good fortune with no less emphasis than his deeds of virtue (*andragathia*).[113] To hide his excellence, then, would have contradicted other elements of his persona as an *imperator* worthy of divine patronage. Traditionally, the god's favorite was recognized by his unusual skills, which were themselves a symbol of one's divine favor and election. Therefore, only the best men were the beneficiaries of divine favor, not, as Scholz put it, the "obediently successful."[114] So, there would have been no sense in Sulla's hiding his qualities unless he wanted to show that the gods had made a mistake.

Thus we see that Sulla either played down or simply denied the fact that he had profited from any kind of political patronage. Instead, the protection and support Marius provided at the beginning of Sulla's military career was transformed into a predated antagonism between the two. Moreover, we find Sulla casting his own virtue and *felicitas* in a favorable light while drawing a contrast with Marius' lack of virtue and *infelicitas*, thus keeping the older general from appearing to be any sort of political father-figure. No human father or protector should stand above Sulla and contribute anything to his successes. Rather, Sulla wanted to make clear that all of his triumphs derived from his own personal qualities, and that these qualities were moreover a sign of the divine favor he enjoyed. Therefore, on the altar of his political self-image he sacrificed not only the memory of his family, but even that of his erstwhile mentors, Marius and Catulus, the latter of whom was portrayed as sluggish and incompetent.[115]

SULLA AND THE BIRTH OF A HERO

To ward off criticism of his extraordinary political position and subsequent reforms, Sulla cultivated a personality cult based on a sort of heroic charisma.[116] His strategic use of fatherlessness was, as we have seen above, part of the construction of this charismatic heroism. It is interesting to see the similarities between Sulla's story and the typical structural elements of heroic biographies. Otto Rank, a pupil of Sigmund Freud, defined this paradigm in 1909. He pointed out that in many folkloric traditions, the hero, often of royal birth, is exposed as a young child only to be saved or

---

[112] Plut. *Mar.* 26.3–4. See Werner 1995: 270–1.
[113] Plut. *Sull.* 34.2.   [114] Scholz 2003: 192.
[115] Plut. *Sull.* 4.2.   [116] Christ 2002: 210.

adopted by wild animals or humble people. When the hero comes to manhood, however, his true nature is recognized because of his personal excellence, evidence of the divine favor he enjoys. A critical component of this mythology is the fact that the hero must be seen to emerge from nothing, in effect proving his true worth. "The difficult circumstances attending the birth and childhood serve, of course, to enhance the miraculous elements of the fact that the future hero manages to attain maturity: the more severe the circumstances described, the more impressive the results are."[117] Thus he must either be abandoned by his family in his early formative years, or sometimes even reject his family: "the hero cannot need a family."[118] Furthermore, according to the categories of rule established by Max Weber the hero is a type of charismatic leader, one whose political legitimacy and authority rests on his being chosen by a higher power and whose success stands as proof of the divine approval of his rule.[119]

The archetype and "model of the world conqueror par excellence" is the third millennium Mesopotamian ruler Sargon of Akkad.[120] The earliest preserved text of his birth legend comes from the eighth century BCE: a pseudo-royal inscription allegedly written by Sargon himself tells us that his mother was a high priestess while his father was unknown. After his birth Sargon was exposed in a basket on the Euphrates, but he was saved and brought up by a humble gardener. He rose to power when the goddess Ishtar favored him and made him king.[121] The closest comparable stories are those concerning the childhood of Cyrus the Great, founder of the Persian Empire. His birth legend was obviously modeled on the ancient regal myth of Sargon.[122] Cyrus' story was also famous in the Greek world because it was told by Herodotus. According to his account, Astyages, a descendant of Deioces and the king of Media, was alarmed by a prophecy that the future son of his daughter, Mandane, would replace him. When she gave birth to Cyrus, Astyages therefore gave the order that the child be murdered by one of his high-ranking relatives, Harpagus. But Harpagus tricked him and handed the child over to a shepherd who was to expose him. As the

[117] Brenner 1986: 257. Cf. Russell 1966: 142; Huys 1995: 13–5, 27–35.
[118] Rank 1909: 61: "der Held keine Familie brauchen kann." Cf. Huys 1995: 16.
[119] Weber 1972: 140–8.   [120] Kuhrt 2003: 347–58. Cf. Rank 1909: 12; Brenner 1986: 257.
[121] Kuhrt 1995: 48: "Sargon, mighty king, king of Agade, am I; my mother was an *entum*, my father I knew not … My mother … conceived me, in secret she bore me; she placed me in a basket of rushes … She cast me into the river which did not rise over me; the river … carried me to Aqqi, the water-drawer. Aqqi … adopted me, brought me up … set me up as his gardener. As a gardener, Ishtar loved me; for [56] years I exercised kingship." Cf. Kuhrt 2003: 350–1.
[122] Binder 1964: 21–2, 25, 27: "The mythical Ur-kings … are nearly always foundlings … " See also Merkelbach 1984: 31.

shepherd's wife had just suffered the misfortune of a still-birth, the couple decided to bring Cyrus up as their own child.[123] Of course, neither the isolation in the mountains among wild animals nor a shepherd's rustic education could conceal Cyrus' divine designation, evident in the qualities he displayed as a child, marking him as a natural-born ruler. At the age of ten his destiny became obvious: while playing "king and subjects" with the other children of the village, he showed his innate aptitude for kingship.[124] According to Herodotus, he had knowledge of all the important institutions of the Deiocid kingship and proved to be both strict and just.[125] Cyrus was the true heir, appointed by the highest of gods, and his right to rule was proven by his skills, which were in turn signs of divine favor. The fact that the name of the shepherd was supposedly Mithridates may also be a hint that the god Mithras was in fact the real foster-father of Cyrus.[126] Metaphorically, the good statesman takes care of his people just as the shepherd takes care of his sheep.

The importance of the divine designation was subsequently emphasized in the propaganda of Darius I, who had to establish an alternative basis for his legitimacy because of certain problems with his lineage, being a usurper of the Persian throne.[127] More interesting, though, is Herodotus' comment – relying on Persian sources – that Cyrus' parents, the Persian Cambyses and Mandane, were responsible for spreading the rumor that the child was brought up by a dog in the desert to make the legend about Cyrus' childhood more marvelous.[128] This again is a common folkloric hero motif: wild creatures saving the hero after he has been exposed as a child.[129] Thus, the Persian Achaimenes, from whose royal line Darius claimed descent, was said to have been nourished by an eagle.[130] In Greek mythology the she-goat Amaltheia fostered little Zeus.[131] In the Hellenistic world Ptolemy I was

---

[123] Hdt. 1.107–13. Cf. Just. *Epit*. 1.4. Ctesias knew a version different from that of Herodotus: Cyrus was the son of a brigand and a female shepherd (*apud* Nic. Dam. *FGrH* 90 F 66.3).

[124] Binder 1964: 20–8. According to him, the play was a symbolic coronation. Cf. Plut. *Artax*. 3.1–2. See also Huys 1995: 20–1.

[125] Hdt. 1.114. Cf. Just. *Epit*.1.5. Herodotus' discussion of Deioces and his establishment of the Median Empire is generally regarded as a Greek account of the creation of absolute power. Wiesehöfer (2004: 22) doubts that there was any Median Empire in this form at all.

[126] Binder 1964: 22, 69. Cf. Merkelbach 1984: 31.

[127] Balcer 1987: 50; Heinrichs 1987: 504–5; Briant 1996: 180–1; Wiesehöfer 2005: 33–43. In the famous inscription at Behistun (Iran), Darius mentions his divine mission at the behest of the highest god, Ahuramazdah, more than sixty times.

[128] Hdt. 1.122.3. Cf. Ael. *VH* 12.42. According to Herodotus, who knew four different versions, the shepherd's wife was named Cyno (1.95.1). This is Greek for "bitch," a literal translation of her Median name, Spaco (1.110.1).

[129] Ael. *NA* 12.21; Suda, s.v. *Lagos*; Hdt 1.107–13. Cf. Rank 1909: 23–37.

[130] Ael. *NA* 12.21.   [131] Callim. *Hymn* 1.47–9.

rumored to be an illegitimate son of Philip II, exposed by his stepfather Lagus but saved by an eagle who took him under his wings.[132] In Roman mythology, the twins Romulus and Remus were nourished by a she-wolf.[133] Such heroic elements even appear in the biographies of Sulla's contemporaries, such as Rome's archenemy, the energetic Mithridates VI, king of Pontus. He claimed descent from Perseus and Dionysus and was said to have escaped from his guardians as a child only to wander in the wilderness for seven years, living with wild animals.[134] Obviously, there were several possible models of heroic leaders available for Sulla to emulate.

If we compare this paradigm to the story of Sulla's childhood, we find that it is missing only one element: the exposure. However, we may understand the early death of his parents as its functional equivalent. Sulla thus rationalized the myth after a fashion. The choice to adopt a heroic persona meant that he could not, unlike his aristocratic contemporaries, advertise an illustrious or divine ancestry. Of course, he emphasized his noble birth and the deeds of his early *maiores*; but these are standard elements of the heroic narrative. Sulla, however, was not the progenitor of a successful family, like Sargon or Cyrus, who were both founders of empire: his family had a glorious past but had suffered a recent decline. This potential political liability may be what led him to adopt this alternative model, relying on and focusing on his individual person. Johan Flemberg, in his studies on Venus Armata in Greek and Roman art, has observed that the honors that late Republican generals such as Sulla and Caesar bestowed on Venus are reminiscent of the relationship that rulers in the ancient Near East had to the goddess Ishtar.[135] This is certainly the case with Sulla, whereas Julius Caesar relied on a family tradition of proclaiming Venus as their ancestral deity, a tradition he helped to articulate and promote.

SULLA AND EASTERN AND HELLENISTIC ROLE MODELS

While the basic heroic paradigm is a cultural narrative of wide currency, the emphasis on divine favor, particularly that shown by Aphrodite, seems to

---

[132] Suda, s.v. *Lagos*; Paus. 1.6.2; Curt. 9.8.22. Clearly this was Ptolemaic propaganda, perhaps invented by Soter himself in order to legitimatize his reign after having assumed the title of king (*basileus*). The eagle of Zeus standing on a thunderbolt appears on Ptolemaic coins as a symbol for their kingship. Cf. Ellis 1994: 3. On some rare issues the eagle has its wings spread.

[133] Livy 1.4–7.3; Plut. *Rom.* 3; Diod. 8.3–5; Ael. *VH* 7.16; Strabo 5.3.2.

[134] Just. 37.2. See Volkmann 1958: 30–6; Bohm 1989: 157–8, 183–5.   [135] Flemberg 1991: 27–8.

suggest that Sulla relied on Eastern and Hellenistic models.[136] As Gerhard
Dobesch has pointed out, the reception of Hellenistic culture reached its
peak in Sulla's last years.[137] Divine patronage was the key element in Sulla's
claim to political legitimacy. This is shown by his wish to be called officially
Felix and *Epaphroditos*.[138] Traditionally the Roman concept of *felicitas*
revolved around the idea that a man of virtue and skills received the blessing
of the gods and that his enterprises were crowned with success. Sulla's good
fortune, however, was a personal charismatic quality that surrounded him
like an aura. In representing *felicitas* as a special aspect of his personality,
Sulla thereby transformed its general meaning.[139] This personal quality
emanated through his family. For instance, the twins he had by Caecilia
Metella received the *praenomina* Faustus and Fausta, both of which are
etymologically connected to the word *felix*.[140] In fact, names bearing ideological significance were common in the Hellenistic monarchies and
marked special connections to divine ancestors or to emphasize the
dynastic tradition. For instance, the eldest son of Ptolemy I Soter was
called Ptolemy Ceraunus, the Thunderbolt. This name certainly implied
that he descended from Heracles, the Argead ancestor, and therefore
ultimately Zeus.[141] Sulla thus borrowed from this Hellenistic-ruler imagery
after his military and political successes, in effect reminding the public that
Rome needed him as the guarantor of victory, safety, and abundance.[142] *Felix*

[136] Balsdon 1951: 1; Fears 1975: 594; Sumi 2002: 419–21. Throughout antiquity Cyrus was celebrated as
the model of the just ruler. In Rome he served as a Stoic *exemplum*, and we know from Cicero that his
story was well known, e.g. *Brut.* 112, where he is most likely referring to Xenophon's *Cyropedia*
(cf. *Off.* 2.5.16). Xenophon, however, does not mention Cyrus' abandonment. Livy also speaks about
the fame of Cyrus (9.17.6). Cf. Fears 1974: 265–6.
[137] Dobesch 2004: 132, 144.
[138] Plut. *Sull.* 34.2; App. *B Civ.* 1.104; Vell. Pat. 2.27.5; Val. Max. 9.2.1. See Volkmann 1958: 36–43; Fears
1981: 794; Ramage 1991: 100; Hölkeskamp 2000: 216–17. It is uncertain whether Sulla himself really
believed in his divine agency or promoted his *felicitas* merely for propagandistic reasons. Keaveney
(2005: 33) attributes to Sulla an "obsessional belief" in his own *felicitas*. Cf. Eder 1997: 189–90;
Heftner 2006: 142. But one might wonder whether there was not a calculated element to this belief.
Alföldy (1976: 143) suggests that Sulla cynically exploited Roman religiosity in order to establish his
power. Hölkeskamp (2000: 200–1) depicts Sulla as a master of propaganda possessed of a "nearly
egomaniacal self-love" and a "delight of posing." Fears (1981: 795) admits that it is not clear whether
the imagery of divine legitimacy actually reflected Sulla's own conviction because it was primarily
used to justify his political authority. Christ (2002: 195) prefers a rationalized interpretation because it
was first of all the ancient authors who styled Sulla as truly believing in his divine mission.
[139] Alföldy 1976: 145; Keaveney 2005: 33.   [140] Plut. *Sull.* 34.3. See Alföldy 1976: 148.
[141] On Heracles and the Argead dynasty, see n. 145 below. See also Harders' discussion (this volume) of
Cleopatra's children, who had equally significant dynastic names.
[142] For abundance, see Plut. *Sull.* 4.3. See also Candau Morón 2000: 464. Sulla wanted to show that his
felicitas served the Roman Republic and its citizens and not only himself.

in this context is parallel to the Hellenistic use of *sōtēr* ("savior") and *euergetēs* ("benefactor").[143]

Taking a brief look at the Hellenistic world, the prototype of the Hellenistic heroic ruler was Alexander the Great.[144] He presented himself in Homeric colors as a youthful, vigorous hero, emulating his ancestors Achilles and Heracles.[145] His ultimate ancestors thus had divine fathers, and since the Argeads claimed to be descendants from Heracles, they were related to Zeus himself. Therefore, Alexander the Great emphasized the divine descent of his family.[146] It is a striking parallel to Sulla's image that the Macedonian ruler also stressed having come from nearly nothing.[147] Alexander was obliged to play down the great achievements of his father, Philip, in order to create the illusion that he alone was responsible for his success. He too would have liked to concentrate on his divine ancestry and patronage, as Sulla did in his memoirs, but political pressure from the Macedonian opposition left him no choice but to deal with the memory of his father. It would have no doubt suited him better not to be limited by the constant comparison with Philip's policies and political attitude toward the Macedonian nobles and soldiers. But Alexander failed in pretending to be fatherless.[148]

It is not the purpose of this paper to prove that Sulla consciously imitated either Cyrus or Alexander. The model of the fatherless hero was an almost universal archetype in the various cultures of the Mediterranean, and certainly familiar to both Greeks and Romans. Yet, while there were certain Roman models available to him, it is clear that Sulla either consciously opted for, or was at least influenced by, Eastern and Hellenistic versions of this archetype. Of course, the Roman political arena at this time was awash with Hellenistic imagery, so in this sense Sulla was a product of his times. But where he innovated was in choosing a particular strain of Hellenistic political ideology which had not yet been deployed by others in the Roman

---

[143] Sumi 2002, 414. Sulla thus used the Ptolemaic symbol of the *cornucopia* on his coins, stressing the connection between his *felicitas* and general prosperity and fecundity.

[144] Exaggerated by Fadinger 2002.

[145] Achilles as Alexander's ancestor: Plut. *Alex.* 2.1; *Pyrrh.* 1; Arr. *Anab.* 4.11.6; Paus. 1.11.1; Curt. 8.4.26. Heracles as ancestor of the Argead dynasty: Arr. *Anab.* 4.7.4; Plut. *Alex.* 2.1; Isoc. *Philippus* 127; Speusippus 3.18. See Wirth 1993: 4–5; Funke 2000: 166–8.

[146] Isoc. *Philippus* 111–15; Arr. *Anab.* 4.7.4. See Koulakiotis 2006: 223–6; Flower 2000: 105.

[147] Plut. *Alex.* 15.1.2; Arr. *Anab.* 7.9.6. Arrian mentions Alexander's complaints in his speech at Opis, where he claimed to have inherited from his father a few gold and silver cups and a mountain of debt.

[148] His propaganda was seen as an insult to the memory of Philip who was transformed after his death into the ideal Macedonian ruler in contrast to Alexander, who was seen as a new Achilles rapidly degenerating into a new Xerxes for his adoption of elements of Achaemenid kingship after Issus (and perhaps already before this). See Wiesehöfer 1994: 27, n. 25; Müller 2006: 280–1.

political class. Instead, they naturally inclined toward Hellenistic ideas that dovetailed with the traditional Roman concerns, such as the cultural and religious emphasis on ancestors. Thus, the Julii, the Antonii, and others adopted the Hellenistic fashion of claiming descent from divine or heroic ancestors, padding their traditional lineages with gods and heroes, as did the Seleucids (Apollo), the Ptolemies (Dionysus), the Attalids (Telephus), and the Antigonids (Heracles). Sulla, however, did not.[149] Instead, he represented himself as being protected and supported by divine power. Yet Venus and Fortuna did *not* favor him because they were genetically related to him or because they were the traditional protectors of his *gens*. In his case, divine patronage was the expression of an exclusive relationship between the deity and Sulla himself. His alleged poverty and the downfall of his family together helped to prove that *fortuna* did not run in the family, but rather that it had been earned by Sulla on account of his *virtus*. Finally, this personal relationship in some sense guaranteed his public or political persona.[150] It is interesting to note that Sulla's propaganda was adopted as a model by Quintus Sertorius as he was waging war in Spain against Sulla and his followers. Evidently, Sertorius styled himself as a charismatic person protected by Diana who represented the legitimate *res publica*.[151]

CONCLUSION

This study of Sulla's fatherlessness has attempted to show how Sulla relied on a basic cultural model, the hero, which was common to many ancient cultures. The chief components of this model are exposure as a child, divine fosterage, and the proving of one's worthiness as a favorite of the gods through personal merit. In his memoirs Sulla stressed that he owed nothing to his father and in fact tried to erase all other possible father-figures from his public image. This strategy stressed his invincibility and helped to legitimatize his deeds by building up a myth around his person to shape the *memoria* of his career. This, of course, was Sulla's motivation in writing his *commentarii* at the end of his life: to commemorate his deeds and to shape an image with lasting historical effect. Sulla, characterized by his enemy Carbo as half fox, half lion,[152] wanted to influence his own historical reception and this necessitated a good deal of idealization. One must bear in mind just how much ill will Sulla had created in his own time. His marches

---

[149] Schmitt 2005: 452.　　[150] Frier 1969: 187–9; Flemberg 1991: 27.
[151] Plut. *Sert.* 11. See Rowland Jr. 1966: 414; Behr 1993: 20–1, 23, 151.
[152] Plut. *Sull.* 28.3. Cf. Cic. *Off.* 1.41. See Frier 1971: 601.

on Rome and proscriptions had provoked widespread disgust.[153] Many were put off not just by his methods, but also by his person and his politics. Even his laws were not generally approved of. It is telling that Sallust, writing a little more than a generation later, had M. Aemilius Lepidus, who was elected consul for 78 with Sulla's tacit approval,[154] vilify Sulla in his *Histories* as a treacherous tyrant, a criminal who depopulated Rome by exile and murder and enslaved the survivors, a caricature of Romulus, feared and hated by the Romans.[155] So Sulla needed to polish his memory, and his efforts in his memoirs were not uniformly successful.

But he was partially successful, and the subsequent blackening of his memory in the history of the fall of the Republic has helped to obscure his partial success in shaping the memory of his career for later generations. Certainly, Sulla had always depicted himself as the favorite of the gods throughout his career, but in his *commentarii* his *felicitas* and image as guarantor of *salus* were combined with both slander and the denial of any kind of political protection, even though his aristocratic peers at the time must have known that he owed a good deal of his success to Marius as a kind of father-figure. According to Plutarch, Sulla was once asked by a nobleman how he could be an honest man when his father had left him nothing and yet he was so rich.[156] Plutarch, unfortunately, does not tell us how Sulla responded, but even at this stage in his career he might have answered that his *felicitas* and his skills had provided for him where his father did not. The nobleman's question effectively encapsulates the crucial elements in Sulla's public image: emerging from an obscure and lowly condition, but ending up with supreme power.[157] Styled *Felix* and *Epaphroditos*, Sulla had no need for his father or any other kind of father-figure. Being fatherless was an integral part of his image and political strategy. It was a strategic father-lessness, a new variation on the ancient myth of the exposed hero.

---

[153] Val. Max. 9.2.1; Vell. Pat. 2.28.2–4.   [154] Plut. *Pomp.* 15. See Behr 1993: 313.
[155] Sall. *Hist.* 1.48.   [156] Plut. *Sull.* 1.1.   [157] Cf. Plut. *Sull.* 3.4.

CHAPTER 12

An imperial family man: Augustus as surrogate father to Marcus Antonius' children

Ann-Cathrin Harders

INTRODUCTION

The final days of Rome's once glorious general Marcus Antonius and Egypt's last queen, Cleopatra VII, are legendary: after his defeat at Actium, Antonius rushed back to Alexandria. Since he thought Cleopatra dead, he plunged his sword into his bowels. Sometime afterwards Cleopatra followed him, preferring death by the bite of an asp to being paraded through Roman streets as a vanquished oriental sensation by the triumphant victor.[1] Antonius and Cleopatra thus escaped Octavian's grasp and eventually transcended the bounds of history to become literary and cinematic icons as one of the world's most famous pairs of "star-cross'd lovers." Their children, however, met quite a different fate: without the protection of their Roman father and their royal mother, the twins, Alexander Helios and Cleopatra Selene, as well as their younger brother, Ptolemy Philadelphus, soon fell into the hands of the Roman invaders.[2] Their elder stepbrothers, Ptolemy XV Kaisar, called "Caesarion," and M. Antonius, called "Antyllus," both in Egypt, were also subjected to Octavian's power, while for their younger brother in Rome, Iullus Antonius, it was only a question of time until he had to face Octavian.[3]

Octavian acted coolly and swiftly: Caesarion, Caesar's alleged son by Cleopatra, and Antyllus, Antonius' eldest by Fulvia, both had to die; they were betrayed by their own tutors and murdered. The lives of Iullus and his younger siblings, however, were spared, and they were transferred to the

---

[1] On Antonius' and Cleopatra's death: Strabo 17.795; Livy, *Per.* 133; frag. 54; Plut. *Ant.* 76–7, 84–6; Flor. 2.21.9–11; Cass. Dio 51.10–14; Oros. 6.19.17–18. On Actium and their end, see Carter 1971: 204–34; Hölbl 1994: 222–7; Whitehorne 1994: 186–96; Clauss 1995: 85–103; Bleicken 1999: 275–96; Kienast 1999: 71–4; Schuller 2006: 123–8.

[2] On Selene, see Stähelin 1921; Macurdy 1932: 224–8; Whitehorne 1994: 197–202; Grenier 2001; Roller 2003: 76–90; Andreae 2006: 73–6. On Helios: Wilcken 1894; Rolley 2006: 165–8. On Philadelphus: Hofmann 1959b.

[3] On Caesarion, see Hofmann 1959a; Schuller 2006: 131–7; Andreae 2006: 61–73; Rolley: 168–75. On Antyllus: Groebe 1894b. On Iullus: Groebe 1894a; *PIR²* A 800; Eck 1996; Hallett 2006a. Antyllus and Caesarion's death: Suet. *Aug.* 17.5; Plut. *Ant.* 81; Cass. Dio 51.6.1–2, 51.15.5; Oros. 6.19.20.

household of the victor's sister Octavia who happened to be Antonius' ex-wife. She took care of the children and raised them with the explicit support of her brother. As *princeps*, the later Augustus took pride in claiming a close and familial relationship with Antonius' children, and it is surprising that Iullus is later even referred to as one of the three closest persons to the *princeps*.[4] Imperial authors such as Plutarch, Suetonius, Velleius Paterculus, and Cassius Dio unanimously describe Augustus as a loving and caring surrogate father to Antonius' orphaned children by Fulvia and Cleopatra.[5]

However, the question of *why* Augustus chose to play the foster-father to Antonius' progeny is not addressed by imperial authors and has not been posed in any scholarly work thus far. In this chapter I will therefore examine the consequences which this peculiar relationship held for a man who not only ruled an aristocratic *domus* but tried to establish a monarchy. To assume that Octavian's care for the children was based on individual emotional bonds to the children of Antonius would be to graft contemporary Western notions of familial relations onto conditions of the first century BCE. Rather, Octavian's behavior is in line with notions of familial obligation toward fatherless children that were culturally specific to this period. Roman society had developed a complex kin system in which certain social arrangements developed that took into account the demographic problem of fatherless children:[6] particular kinsmen were supposed to act as surrogate parents to fatherless children. The moment Octavian put his sister in charge of the children's upbringing he found himself in the position of a mother's brother, an *avunculus*. Individual nephews and uncles were not free to define this particular familial relationship in any way they chose, but rather they did so within strict social standards. By caring and standing up for his sister's children at any cost, that is, by acting as an *avunculus*, a Roman male fulfilled social expectations. Furthermore, he thereby displayed *pietas* and *fides*, thus proving to himself and others that he was a good and worthy *civis*.[7]

By raising Antonius' children the future Augustus exploited these social expectations for his own benefit. He was able to present himself as an impeccable Roman family man while simultaneously keeping potential

---

[4] Plut. *Ant.* 87: Iullus is mentioned after Agrippa and Livia's sons.
[5] Octavian was not on good terms with either Fulvia or Cleopatra. During the Perusinian War, Fulvia rallied the anti-Octavian opposition together with her brother-in-law L. Antonius. Reconciliation between the triumvirs was possible only after her death (Plut. *Ant.* 30; Cass. Dio 48.28.3); cf. Hallett 1977; Fischer 1999: 40–8.
[6] On the demographic background, see Harlow and Laurence 2002: 8–11; Scheidel (this volume).
[7] On these values in the context of Roman familial role playing, see below, 227–30.

opponents to his position in check. By including his former enemy's children in his *domus*, the first *princeps* thus made a clever move to stabilize his position in Roman society. By ostentatiously demonstrating social responsibility for orphaned children, Augustus actually perverted a traditional Roman family strategy, which aimed at offering fatherless children unqualified support, to his own political ends. I will first discuss here the premises of this special familial situation and demonstrate how Antonius' enemy Octavian became *avunculus* Augustus to Antonius' children. Then I will explain Augustus' motives in integrating his enemy's children into his own home, and I will end by examining the limits of Augustus' *avunculus–nepotes* role playing.

FROM ACTIUM TO ROME

The decisive battle of Actium, where Antonius met his match in Octavian's right-hand man, Agrippa, had been preceded by massive propaganda on both sides.[8] Octavian was anxious to avoid the impression that he was going to war against a Roman compatriot, since this would have meant that he was carrying on the Civil War from Pharsalus via Philippi to Actium and Alexandria. He also had to consider that Antonius still had many supporters in Rome, and not everyone was convinced of the necessity of waging war on the former consul.[9] Octavian therefore emphasized Cleopatra's political and military power, representing her as a dangerous threat to Rome and the sole and legitimate reason for inflicting war on Egypt. Antonius, in Octavian's propaganda, was passed off as a love-stricken fool in the hands of the Egyptian queen, who used him only to secure land and power for herself and her children.[10] In this context Antonius' naming of his children by Cleopatra is cited as evidence of their father's folly. His choice of "Selene" and "Helios" was interpreted as an example of his Hellenistic-oriental megalomania.[11]

---

[8] Suet. *Aug.* 69; Plut. *Ant.* 55; Cass. Dio 50.1. Cf. K. Scott 1933; Charlesworth 1933; Kleiner 1992: 364–7; Sumi 2005: 207–13.

[9] Cf. Clauss 1995: 83–4. On the declaration of war, see Reinhold 1982.

[10] Suet. *Aug.* 17.1; Plut. *Ant.* 58, 60; Cass. Dio 49.34.1, 50.3.4–5, 50.5.1–6.1.

[11] The names Selene and Helios are mentioned by Suet. *Calig.* 26.1; Plut. *Ant.* 36; Cass. Dio 50.25.4, 51.21.8; Euseb. *Chron.* p. 163 Helm. Arnaud 1993 suggests that we read the children's *cognomina* in Latin (i.e. *sol* and *luna*), since the change of name would have been addressed to a Roman audience; Antonius thus put himself in the role of *kosmokratōr* and committed sacrilege. There is, however, no record that the Roman people recognized this overture, nor that Antonius' alleged religious improprieties were used against him in Octavian's propaganda. On possible reasons for the children's names, see Tarn 1932; on Cleopatra's children by Roman fathers as a "physical fusion" of Egypt and Rome, see Schuller 2006: 187–8.

Beyond the naming of the children, Octavian held Antonius' political actions in Egypt against him. During a ceremony in the winter of 34 – the so-called "Donations of Alexandria" – Cleopatra was pronounced "Queen of Kings" by the triumvir. Antonius also accepted Caesarion as Caesar's legitimate son and bestowed on him the corresponding title "King of Kings." Furthermore, he apportioned the Eastern world among his and Cleopatra's children in the manner of a Hellenistic king, but by virtue of his triumviral *imperium*: Alexander was given Armenia as well as parts of Media and Parthia that had yet to be conquered; Ptolemy received possessions in Syria and Cilicia as well as the overlordship of Asia Minor; Cleopatra Selene was granted the Cyrenaica and Libya.[12] Although Antonius' politics in Alexandria were not addressed to a Roman audience but were meant to strengthen his position in the East, the donations led to serious repercussions in Rome since he was distributing parts of the Roman Empire to foreign sovereigns. In consequence, Antonius' favoritism with respect to his Ptolemaic family was turned against him by his triumviral colleague as evidence of his estrangement from the Roman *mos* – which Octavian claimed to represent and protect.[13]

Octavian's propaganda clearly associated Cleopatra Selene and Alexander Helios – born after Antonius and Cleopatra's first encounter at Tarsus[14] – with their mother. Since Cleopatra was not a Roman citizen and so not privileged with *conubium*, the legal right to contract marriage with a Roman citizen, her children by Antonius – as well as her son by Caesar – were considered *peregrini* like herself.[15] Hence, all discussion of a marriage

---

[12] Cass. Dio 49.41, 50.1.5, 51.25; Plut. *Ant.* 54. The donations were granted after Antonius staged a triumphal procession in Alexandria honoring his victory over Artavasdes of Armenia. By transferring this Roman ritual to the East he established Alexandria as a second capital of the Roman Empire; see App. *B Civ.* 5.145; Cass. Dio 49.39–40; Vell. Pat. 2.82; Livy, *Per.* 131; Tac. *Ann.* 2.3; Plut. *Ant.* 50; Plin. *HN* 33.82–3; Strabo 12.532; Jos. *AJ* 15.104. During the ceremony in the *gymnasium* Antonius presented his Ptolemaic family as rulers of the East. Antonius' donations were legal since the senate had voted to ratify all of his acts (App. *B Civ.* 5.75); however, an application was never presented (Cass. Dio 49.41.4). On the donations, see Bengtson 1977: 216–20; Huzar 1978: 196–200; A. Roberts 1988: 274–7; Hölbl 1994: 218–20; P. M. Martin 1995: 180–3; Schrapel 1996.

[13] Cass. Dio 50.24–30, esp. 25–6. Cf. Plut. *Ant.* 55, 58.

[14] The exact birth date of the twins is unknown; they might have been conceived at Tarsus in 41 (Plut. *Ant.* 25; App. *B Civ.* 5.8–9), but their existence is first mentioned in connection with Antonius' return to Cleopatra in 37 (Plut. *Ant.* 36). Ptolemy was born in 36. On their birth dates, see Roller 2003: 77–8.

[15] On *conubium*: Gai. *Inst.* 1.56. Cf. Treggiari 1991a: 43–9. A marriage between Cleopatra and Antonius is mentioned by Plut. *Ant.* 31, *Comp. Dem. Ant.* 1, 4; Suet. *Aug.* 69.2; Sen. *Suas.* 1.6; Livy, *Epit.* 131; Euseb. *Chron.* p. 162 Helm. Cf. Volterra 1978. Crook (1957) points out that Antonius' will was deliberately misconstrued by Octavian to demonstrate Antonius' un-Romanness. Apparently, Antonius named his children with Cleopatra as heirs. This would have been illegal because *peregrini* could not be instituted as *sui heredes*. J. P. Johnson 1978 suggests a *fidei commissum* to solve the legal problem.

between Antonius and Cleopatra is misguided because in terms of Roman civil law their relation was not considered a *iustum matrimonium*. In Octavian's propaganda, Selene, Helios, and Philadelphus represented the external enemy because they were children of the *peregrina* Cleopatra. Since they were conceived at a time when Antonius was still married to Octavia, their existence was moreover an everlasting insult not only to Octavian's sister, whom Plutarch described as the epitome of Roman female virtues, but also to Antonius' legitimate children, Antonia Maior and Minor, who lived with their mother Octavia.[16] Against this background of Antonius' extramarital affairs and illegitimate offspring, Octavian could easily fashion himself as the avenger of his family's honor, one who fulfilled his familial duties just as an exemplary Roman brother and uncle should.[17]

So long as Octavian was waging his propaganda and military campaigns against Antonius and Cleopatra, he was careful not to mention any genealogical connection between his sister's children and Cleopatra's offspring. Rather, Helios, Selene, and little Ptolemy were rhetorically fashioned as the "illegitimate" antagonists to Octavian's "legitimate" nieces, Antonia Maior and Minor. The fact that these children were fathered by the same man and thus were actually part of one formidable "patchwork family" to which Antonius' children by previous marriages and Octavia's children by C. Marcellus all belonged – and to whom even Octavian might claim a familial bond – was not explicitly acknowledged until 29 BCE.[18] In 32, however, Alexander Helios, Cleopatra Selene, and Ptolemy Philadelphus were all cited as evidence of Cleopatra's dangerous influence on Octavian's former triumviral colleague and brother-in-law.

After the fall of Alexandria, the three siblings were taken prisoner and brought to Rome. There they met their half-brother Iullus Antonius, who had stayed with his former stepmother Octavia.[19] Iullus was lucky to be younger than Caesarion and Antyllus, who were not spared by Octavian. During the preparations for war Cleopatra and Antonius had their eldest sons enrolled for military service and thus declared them their supposed successors. Cassius Dio takes this as an explanation for their execution:

---

[16] Plut. *Ant.* 31; 57. Cf. Cass. Dio 50.26.1–2; Plut. *Ant.* 53. Modern opinions of Octavia echo Plutarch: Tarn and Charlesworth 1965: 64–5; Doer 1968–9; Huzar 1985–6: 106; Andreae 2006: 98–102; Schuller 2006: 107–8; 110. On Antonia Maior and Minor: Groebe 1894c and 1894d.

[17] Cass. Dio 50.26.2; Plut. *Ant.* 57; Liv. *Epit.* 132.

[18] Antonius had (at least) seven children by four Roman wives (Fadia, Antonia, Fulvia, and Octavia) and Cleopatra. Cicero mentions children with Fadia who might have died in 44/43 (Cic. *Phil.* 2.3, 3.17, 13.12, *Att.* 16.11.1); cf. Leon 1959; C. P. Johnson 1972–3; Huzar 1985–6.

[19] Plut. *Ant.* 81; Cass. Dio 51.15.5–7. Iullus in Octavia's care: Plut. *Ant.* 54.

As far as the boys were concerned, this enrolment was to bring about their destruction. In the event, Octavian spared neither but treated them as grown men, who had been vested with some semblance of authority.[20]

By having Antyllus and Caesarion killed, Octavian had rid himself of two possible opponents, who in the near future might have rallied discontented "Antonians," and perhaps even displeased "Caesarians," against the new order. In addition, Octavian also eliminated important symbols of the rebellious "Ptolemaeans" in Alexandria. He disregarded any familial bond between himself and his victims and acted strictly according to terms of war. However, various sources suggest that it was not easy for Octavian to disregard the ties of family: even the pro-Augustan Cassius Dio mentions Antyllus' former engagement to Octavian's only daughter Iulia as a possible social obstacle for Octavian.[21] Plutarch likewise tells of a hesitating Octavian who had qualms about killing his adoptive father's alleged son before finally signing Caesarion's death warrant.[22]

Back in Rome, Octavian was granted a triple triumph celebrating his victories in Dalmatia, Actium, and Alexandria. Since Cleopatra's suicide had thwarted Octavian's spectacular plan to show her off in Rome, Helios and Selene were made to stand in for their mother.[23] Even so, Octavian did not do completely without Cleopatra. The subjugation of Egypt was crowned by a tableau of the dead queen surrounded by her children:

Among the items which were carried along was an effigy of the dead Cleopatra lying on a couch, so that in a sense she too, together with the live captives, who included her children Alexander, named the Sun, and Cleopatra, named the Moon, formed a part of the pageant. After this came Octavian …[24]

By virtue of their sobriquets, "Helios" and "Selene," as well as by being benefactors of Antonius' distribution of the East, the children functioned as living evidence of Antonius' delusion. This symbolism had been used by Octavian in his prewar propaganda and was revived again in this procession: now the Ptolemaic "sun" and "moon" were walking in front of a Roman general. If the children in 32 were made rhetorically to represent their mother and personify an anti-Roman threat, they did so visually in 29.

---

[20] Cass. Dio 51.6.1–2 (trans. Scott-Kilvert 1987). After Actium Antonius sent Antyllus as an ambassador to Octavian (Cass. Dio 51.8.4). Although he ultimately failed, Antyllus was apparently old enough to represent his father in an important military mission.

[21] Cass. Dio 51.15.5. Antyllus' engagement to Iulia was part of the arrangements at Tarentum (Cass. Dio 48.54.4; Suet. *Aug.* 63); whether it was ever formally dissolved is not known.

[22] Plut. *Ant.* 81.

[23] Cf. Suet. *Aug.* 17.4; Livy, frag. 54. On the triple triumph, see Gurval 1995: 25–36.

[24] Cass. Dio 51.21.8 (trans. Scott-Kilvert 1987). See also Euseb. *Chron.* p. 163 Helm; *Res gest. div. Aug.* 4.

During the triumph celebrating Actium, Octavian presented his audience with an image of the victorious power of a Roman family standing in stark contrast to a tableau of Ptolemaic family defeat. The *triumphator* was flanked by his thirteen-year-old nephew Marcellus, while his stepson Tiberius rode on his left. Furthermore, in Marcellus' name Octavian extended his triumphal donation to boys under eleven, thus highlighting his nephew's exceptional position.[25] Octavian presented the progeny of his own lineage as a counterpart to that of the vanquished Ptolemaic queen. To achieve this semantically, Selene and Helios had to stand for their mother exclusively; their genealogical bond to Marcellus and Octavian himself had to be denied and thus any connection between victor and vanquished suppressed.

It was common practice to present vanquished kings or queens and their families during triumphal processions. However, after the triumph their fate was usually not the victor's personal responsibility, but the senate's. Usually they were subsequently transported either to the *carcer* Tullianus to be killed – like Vercingetorix after Caesar's triumph, or Tigranes, son of Tigranes the Great, and Aristobulus after Pompey's – or they were provided a guarded rustic retreat where they would spend the rest of their lives in exile – like Perseus after his defeat at the hands of Aemilius Paullus, or Cleopatra's sister, Arsinoe, who was thus spared by Caesar.[26] Of course, Helios, Selene, and Ptolemy did not fall into the same category of defeated enemies such as either Perseus or Vercingetorix, since they were not vanquished rulers but belonged to the larger group of royal captives. Although the fate of the latter was of no great interest to Roman historiographers, it can be assumed that they generally shared exile with their former sovereigns.[27]

Hence, banishment to a guarded exile would have been the standard procedure for Antonius' children. Yet after his triple triumph Octavian did something completely different: in an unprecedented move, he transferred the three children of Antonius and Cleopatra to Octavia's home.[28] It is not known who gave this instruction; some scholars argue that Octavia's generosity and good relationship with Iullus led her to decide to raise her

---

[25] Cf. Suet. *Tib.* 6.4; Cass. Dio 51.21.3; cf. Suet. *Aug.* 41.2. See Sumi 2005: 217–18.

[26] Vercingetorix's death: Cass. Dio 43.19.4. Pompey's triumph: Plut. *Pomp.* 45; App. *Mith.* 17.117; Cass. Dio 37.6.2. Paullus' triumph: Plut. *Aem.* 32–7. Caesar's treatment of Arsinoe: Cass. Dio 43.19.2–4.

[27] Perseus' children were also presented during Paullus' procession; their youthful innocence moved the Romans to tears, so it can be assumed that it was not customary to kill children. Later, the young Macedonians shared their father's exile; two died young, and one ended up as a scribe for the local authority (Plut. *Aem.* 33, 37). He obviously neither participated in an elite lifestyle nor kept his status as a member of the royal Antigonid house.

[28] Suet. *Aug.* 17.5; Plut. *Ant.* 87; Cass. Dio 51.15.6.

ex-husband's children together with her own.[29] While we may speculate about Octavia's role in the matter, the crucial point is whatever she did, she acted within the boundaries of her brother's consent. Although Octavia as a widow was legally independent, her household was part of her brother's greater *domus*.[30] It is therefore not convincing to assume that Octavia invited her ex-husband's children to stay without the knowledge or consent of her brother. Not only must Octavian have consented to the children's upbringing by Octavia, but, as I will argue here, he should be regarded as the author of this decision, directing Octavia to integrate Antonius' children into his own *domus*.[31] Furthermore, he adopted the role of an *avunculus* and acted as a surrogate father. In order to accomplish this, Selene, Helios, and Ptolemy's public images had to be made over completely: they no longer served as projections of victory over oriental aggression and decadence but were turned into respected members of the Augustan household as step-nephews and stepniece to the First Man of Rome.

The triumphal procession was also a turning point for the personal situation of Iullus Antonius. He was conspicuously not part of the triumph: since Octavian was officially celebrating a victory over the last Hellenistic monarch, the fact that the defeated general at Actium had been a Roman consul had to be carefully glossed over. Thus Antonius' only surviving legitimate Roman son would not march before the victorious Octavian. But Iullus suffered humiliation in a different way: all monuments commemorating his father had been removed and the day of Antonius' birth cursed. It was even forbidden for members of the *gens* Antonia to use the *praenomen* Marcus ever again.[32] Apart from the *damnatio memoriae*, Iullus also suffered the consequences of the confiscation of his father's property, which must have occurred during Antonius' lifetime. It is not clear what measures were taken to expropriate the property of the former triumvir. Was it confiscated in connection with his designation as a *hostis publicus*, or did the Roman senate simply ratify a "plain" confiscation of Antonius'

---

[29] Cf. Wilcken 1894: 1442; Groebe 1894a: 2584; Vittinghoff 1936: 26; Huzar 1978: 230; Kleiner 2005: 33–4; Andreae 2006: 100; Schäfer 2006: 248. A. Roberts (1988: 358) stresses Octavia's "abiding love for Antonius." No mentioning of Octavian's reasons: Macurdy 1932: 224; Grant 1972: 230; Whitehorne 1994: 198; Fischer 1999: 106; Kienast 1999: 73; Bleicken 1999: 292.

[30] See the following section below.

[31] Luther (2006: 215) praises Augustus' decision to raise Antonius' children as a noble act of acknowledging their aristocratic parentage and does not suspect any ulterior motives. Furthermore, Luther unconvincingly envisions a melancholic Octavian at Actium, not wholeheartedly celebrating his victory over Antonius, but instead contemplating his dysfunctional family.

[32] Cass. Dio 51.19.3; cf. Plut. *Cic.* 49, *Ant.* 86. See Babcock 1962 on the dating of the *damnatio memoriae*.

goods in Rome after war had been declared on Cleopatra?[33] Regardless of the particular context, for Iullus as well as for his half-sisters, Antonia Maior and Minor, this act stripped them entirely of their inheritance. All of their father's possessions had been confiscated and obviously transmitted to the victorious Octavian.[34] Iullus, however, did not live the life of an isolated orphan. Like his Ptolemaic half-siblings, he moved into Octavian's *domus* and was raised by his former stepmother Octavia.

With his move to welcome Antonius' dispossessed children into his home, Octavian reduced the senate's condemnation of Antonius to an absurdity. As part of Octavian's *domus*, the children re-entered Roman society at the highest social stratum because they were now physically, and thus personally, close to the *princeps*.

AUGUSTUS AS *AVUNCULUS*: A ROLE DESCRIPTION

After her divorce from Antonius, Octavia never remarried. She is mentioned as part of her brother's *domus*; however, it is unknown whether she lived in the same building as he.[35] Under her roof, though, she assembled nine children of whom only five were her own. In addition to Marcellus, Marcella Minor and Maior, conceived during her marriage with C. Marcellus, she cared for her daughters by Antonius as well as his children by Fulvia and Cleopatra. Ancient authors describe her as a paragon of motherhood and praise her especially for her gentleness towards her rivals' progeny.[36]

During the reign of her brother, her home developed into a center of intellectual and literary life: Octavia welcomed Vitruvius, Nestor, and

---

[33] The acts which the senate passed against Antonius are handed down to us ambiguously. On the one hand, since Octavian was anxious about waging war on a Roman citizen, he might have hesitated to declare Antonius a *hostis* (Cass. Dio 50.4.3, 50.26.3); on the other hand, the declaration is supported by Suetonius (Suet. *Aug.* 17.2). Usually such a declaration was accompanied by expropriation in order to withdraw financial support and hence social status from the "enemy." Both acts needed to be ratified separately, therefore dispossession without condemnation is possible; cf. the actions against Dolabella in 43 (Cic. *Phil.* 11.6.15, *Fam.* 10.20.4). On Antonius' declaration as *hostis*: Jal 1963: 59; on its date: Ungern-Sternberg 1970: 116, n. 153; on the *damnatio memoriae*: Vittinghoff 1936: 21–2, 26–7. On Octavian's disposal of Antonius' former belongings, see the following section. Only Iullus and the Antoniae were Antonius' *sui heredes*, since Selene, Helios, and Ptolemy were considered *peregrini* and as such they had no legal claim on their father's property; cf. Crook 1957; J. P. Johnson 1978.

[34] Cass. Dio 51.15.7, 53.27.5.

[35] Octavia is mentioned as part of the *aulē Augustou* (M. Aur. *Med.* 8.1; cf. Suet. *Aug.* 73). She probably occupied a building associated with the *domus palatina* of her brother. On Augustus' court, see Winterling 1999: 48–56. On *domus* and *familia*, see Saller 1984 and 1994: 88–95; on the *domus Augusta* in particular: Corbier 2001: 166–78; Moreau 2005.

[36] Plut. *Ant.* 57, 87; Prop. 3.18.14; Jer. *Adv. Iovinian.* 1.46 (Migne, *PL* 23.288) = Sen. frag. 76; cf. Val. Max. 9.15.2. See Watson 1995: 197–206.

Athenodorus of Tarsus, as well as Virgil and Crinagoras of Mytilene at her house.[37] The children apparently benefited from the intellectual atmosphere and all of them seem to have enjoyed an excellent education. Some of them even served as sources of inspiration for a few of Crinagoras' epigrams.[38] There is no evidence that Octavia made any distinctions between the upbringing of her own children and her stepchildren, or discriminated against Iullus and his Egyptian siblings. Quite to the contrary, it must be assumed that she treated them as kin and as equal to her own children, in line with Augustus' public self-image as an impeccable family man about whom Suetonius would later write:

> But he spared the rest of the offspring of Antonius and the queen [Cleopatra], and afterwards maintained and reared them according to their several positions, as carefully as if they were his own kin.[39]

Augustus must be understood as the main force behind the decision to raise and promote his enemies' children. Furthermore, he did not just tacitly accept the new addition to his *domus* but acted as surrogate father socially as well as legally. With Antonius' death, Iullus and the Antoniae lost their *paterfamilias* and became *sui iuris*. Since all of them were still under age a *tutor* was needed to represent them legally.[40] Usually a *tutor* was announced by the father in his will. There is no record as to whether Antonius left instructions for concrete arrangements – but then again, his will was never executed.[41] If tutelary appointments were not made in a will, the next male agnate (or sometimes a more distant relative of the same *gens*) acted as *tutor legitimus*.[42] However, there is no evidence that any member of the *gens* Antonia acted as either *tutor* or surrogate parent of Antonius' children or even claimed this position. Instead, Augustus assumed the legal role of the children's *tutor*, even though he was only cognatically (as opposed to agnatically, the more important relation in Roman law) related to the

---

[37] See Singer 1944: 123–9; Hemelrijk 1999: 104–9.
[38] Nestor taught Marcellus (Strabo 14.5.15); the grammarian L. Crassicius instructed Iullus (Suet. *Gram.* 18.3). Crinagoras wrote epigrams on Marcellus (Diehl. *Anth. Lyr. Graec.* 6.161), Antonia (ibid. 6.244; 9.239), and Selene (ibid. 9.235).
[39] Suet. *Aug.* 17.5 (trans. Rolfe 1914). The ancient sources give no hint of Augustus' motivation. Roller (2003: 83, n. 42) suggests that Augustus cared for the young Ptolemies because he felt obliged to honor Pompey's promise to protect the lineage of Ptolemy XII Auletes. Roller further argues that Augustus even thought to return one of the children to their mother's throne but then somehow simply forgot about the matter. Since there is no source proving Augustus' fidelity to Pompeian promises and considering his precautions in governing Egypt, Roller's thesis has to be rejected.
[40] For more on guardianship, see the Introduction (13–18) and Golden (this volume): 44–6.
[41] Cf. Cass. Dio 50.3.3–5; Plut. *Ant.* 58; Suet. *Aug.* 17.1.
[42] Gai. *Inst.* 1.149, 155–6, 164; *Inst. Iust.* 1.15 pr.–1, 1.16.7.

Antoniae, and managed their financial and legal affairs.[43] In doing so, Augustus prevented any other Roman male from legally attaching himself to Antonius' children and thus from asserting legal claims on their behalf. In addition, Augustus occupied the socially important role of *avunculus* to Antonius' progeny.

In his important study on Roman familial relations, Maurizio Bettini was the first to show that a certain mode of conduct was expected to exist between a Roman and his collateral kin.[44] Side relatives such as the father's brother (*patruus*), or the matrilineal uncle and aunt (*avunculus* and *mater-tera*), were supposed to fulfill certain obligations toward their siblings' offspring. In the case of the *avunculus*, he was obliged to defend his nephews and nieces and to maintain an ostentatiously affectionate relationship with them, even though the *avunculus* was not agnatically related to his sister's children. Consequently, a male legally outside the *familia* interfered in the concerns of a different patrilineally structured kin-group – and this interference was expected of him.[45] Avuncular care therefore must not be confused with the duties and responsibilities of a *tutor*, who was a legal necessity for fatherless children under age and was often related agnatically to the children.

The relationship between a Roman and his kin was not determined and characterized by individual sympathy but was defined socially. Acting as an *avunculus* is therefore best described in terms of role behavior.[46] The acceptance of one's role was important for one's individual positioning in

---

[43] Cass. Dio 51.15.7.
[44] Bettini 1992: 13–132. Bremmer 1976 and 1983 argues that Indo-European societies have generally developed an affectionate relationship between uncle and nephew that includes fostering in the extended family. On Bremmer, see Golden (this volume). Bettini's studies have been criticized by Saller (1997), who argues against Bettini's structuralist approach (which objections do not concern my argument), as well as against the relevance of the cognate kin group by insisting on the *domus* as the heart of the family: since many Roman families would have been fragmented owing to high mortality rates, Saller argues that it would have been impossible for such role-specific behavior to develop. Although this might have been the case for an individual family, it did not have impact on society as a whole. Roman society developed an understanding of acting as a *persona*, i.e. according to certain socially defined role expectations; see Fuhrmann 1979; J. Martin 2002b: 157–8. There is ample evidence that Roman society also developed familial role behavior; see, e.g., Bannon 1997; Harders 2006. See also Bettini 2002; J. Martin 2002a: 15; and Harders 2006: 26–7 on Saller. Studies in medieval and early modern history focus on the importance of familial role behavior to construct super-domestic networks; see, e.g., Severidt 2002; Ruppel 2006; and generally Segalen 1990: 282–7; Mitterauer 2003: 165–354.
[45] On the structural importance of the wife's brother: Lévi-Strauss 1967: 61–3. On the *avunculus*: Bettini 1992: 51–79. Avuncular behavior originates from the accentuated brother–sister tie that structures the Roman kin system; see Harders 2005 and 2006: 337–44. On the impact of cognates on Roman society: J. Martin 2002a: 13–17.
[46] On Roman role behavior: Fuhrmann 1979; J. Martin 1997: 12–13.

Roman society. Martin points out that acting according to certain role expectations can be seen as "dispositive" of Roman society.[47] In contrast to Greek society, in which a different concept of the person, centering on a strong individual identity, had developed, Roman society did not praise spontaneous and individual actions, but rather reliability and submission to the needs of the *res publica*.[48] Hence, a Roman was not true to himself, but true to his *persona*, his social role. Therefore Roman society can be described as a "mask-to-mask-society," characterized by a "high degree of predictability"[49] of individual actions – thus echoing one of Rome's main virtues, *fides*.

To act according to the expectations of specific roles was not restricted to certain social-political positions or offices, for example acting as a senator or magistrate,[50] but was intertwined with – in modern terms – "private," domestic behavior.[51] In fulfilling familial role expectations every Roman male was able to present himself as a responsible family man as well as a respectable *civis* because his domestic conduct revealed his general reliability as well as his *pietas*. The immanent political meaning of *pietas* is pointed out by Cicero, who equates familial and political *pietas*: "*pietas* is the feeling which renders kind offices and loving service to one's kin and country."[52] Since it was possible to derive civic qualities from domestic behavior, it can be assumed that Roman citizens were pressured to meet such public expectations all the time. It is therefore not surprising that Augustus, the First Man in Rome, took care to play the part of the family man irreproachably as all eyes were trained on him.[53]

There is considerable evidence of exemplary avuncular behavior among the elite of Republican Rome that illustrates the kind of tradition that Augustus took up by adopting the role of an *avunculus*. To outline traditional avuncular behavior, I will concentrate on the kin group of M. Livius Drusus (tribune in 91 BCE), in which a number of exemplary avuncular activities can be observed. Apparently, every generation of this family had its

---

[47] J. Martin 2002b: 158.

[48] On the Greek concept of the person, see J. Martin 1997: 6–12.

[49] "Hohe Erwartbarkeit": J. Martin 1997: 13. See also J. Martin 2002b: 158.

[50] On the regimentations of senatorial behavior, see Baltrusch 1988: 7–27. On social control, see J. Martin 2002b.

[51] On the problematic opposition of public and private, see Winterling 2005.

[52] Cic. *Inv. rhet.* 2.161: *pietas, per quam sanguine coniunctis patriaeque benivolum officium et diligens tribuitur cultus* (trans. Hubbell 1960). Cf. Cic. *Off.* 2.13.46, *Rep.* 6.16, *Planc.* 3, 96. Acting according to certain familial roles was recognized and praised by the Roman public; deviant behavior, however, was censured. See Treggiari 2005 on Cicero's use of role expectations in his judicial speeches and Harders 2005: 68–70 on Scipio Aemilianus' ostentatious role-play.

[53] Augustus as head of the *domus*: Suet. *Aug.* 64–6; 72–6. On Augustus' self-fashioning through his household, see Milnor 2005: 83–93.

ideal uncle, starting with Drusus himself: Drusus' sister Livia had first been married to Q. Servilius Caepio, with whom she had two children. After divorcing Caepio, Livia married M. Porcius Cato, a grandson of the famous Cato the Censor. Unfortunately Cato died young and left his widow with another son and daughter. Livia did not stay in her late husband's *domus* but turned to her brother who willingly opened his home to his sister and all her children and acted as surrogate father to them. Drusus thus occupied a familial position which rivaled, or at least encroached upon, that of the close male agnates of his nephews and nieces: although Servilia and Caepio's father was still alive, and although the *patruus* of Porcia and the young Cato was there to care for them, yet it was the *avunculus* who brought up Livia's fatherless children.[54] Drusus' conduct was praised by his contemporaries as well as by subsequent generations. His nephew, Cato the Younger, took pride in referring to his *avunculus* Drusus even late in life, and his upbringing in Drusus' *domus* forms a substantial part of Cato's biography.[55]

In the next generation, Cato carried on in the tradition of exemplary avuncular behavior. He is mentioned as a surrogate father to his fatherless nephew M. Iunius Brutus. Cato was the most important role model for young Brutus – his mother Servilia's second husband, D. Iunius Silanus, had no influence on young Brutus' education. Even Cato's strained relations with Servilia, who had a lasting affair with Cato's archenemy Caesar, did not change his avuncular dedication.[56] As an adult, Brutus deployed all of his *auctoritas* to support his sister's children and tried to secure their inheritance as well as their social status after their father, M. Aemilius Lepidus, had been declared *hostis publicus*. Although Lepidus was not dead, his status as an enemy of the state had, in some sense, more serious consequences for his children: his citizenship was withdrawn and his property confiscated.[57] Brutus would not tolerate these social and financial consequences for his "fatherless" nephews. His pleas to Cicero illustrate the obligations an *avunculus* felt towards his sister's children:

---

[54] Plut. *Cat. Min.* 1; Val. Max. 3.1.2. Cf. Harders 2006: 143–7. See also Augustus' alleged last wish to be appreciated for his ability and his efforts to fulfill role expectations: Suet. *Aug.* 99.1.

[55] Drusus as *avunculus* to Cato: Cic. *Mil.* 16; Val. Max. 3.1.2; Plut. *Cat. Min.* 1–2; [Aur. Vict.] *De vir. ill.* 80.1. Drusus is even referred to as a *magnus avunculus* to his nephew Cato's own nephew Brutus (Cic. *Brut.* 222).

[56] Cato as *avunculus* to Brutus: Cic. *Brut.* 119; Plut. *Brut.* 2; [Aur. Vict.] *De vir. ill.* 82.1. Cf. Harders 2006: 170–6. Servilia's affair with Caesar: Cic. *Att.* 2.24.3; Suet. *Caes.* 50.2; Plut. *Cat. Min.* 24; *Brut.* 5.

[57] Lepidus as *hostis*: Cic. *Ad Brut.* 15.2; *Fam.* 12.10.1; Livy, *Epit.* 119; Vell. Pat. 2.64.4; App. *B Civ.* 3.96. On his declaration as *hostis publicus*: Vittinghoff 1936: 9–18, 23–7; Jal 1963: 55–61; Ungern-Sternberg 1970: 116–20.

I beg and beseech you, Cicero … appealing to our close friendship and your kindness to me, to forget that my sister's children are the sons of Lepidus, and to consider that I have succeeded to the place of their father … I cannot do enough for my sister's children to satisfy my affection or duty (*voluntas mea aut officium*) … or what can I promise my mother and sister and these children, if Brutus being their *avunculus* has no weight with you and the senate against the fact of Lepidus being their father?[58]

Brutus thus refers to his role of *avunculus* to Lepidus' sons as an *officium* which he cannot deny them, and makes demands of Cicero's cooperation as their surrogate father.

Acting as *avunculus* here – similar to Augustus' case later – was not tied to a circumscribed familial constellation: Cato and Brutus were only half-brothers to the mothers of their nephews, and thus neither Cato and Servilia nor Brutus and Iunia belonged to the same agnate group. Furthermore, allusions to typical avuncular behavior or the conduct of other familial roles such as that of a *patruus* are made without reference to a concrete familial situation or constellation. Mentioning a familial position alone sufficed to evoke a certain pattern of behavior which became proverbial, like the objurgatory manner of a *patruus*.[59] In addition, certain actions could be explained by crediting avuncular mildness. After L. Caesar had given his speech in favor of his nephew Marcus Antonius, Cicero urged the senate to stand firm and to declare Antonius a *hostis publicus*, reminding his fellow senators not to act "avuncularly" in this case: "He is an *avunculus*; but are you also *avunculi*?"[60]

Since Augustus was Octavia's brother, he was formally the *avunculus* of Antonia Maior and Minor; to Iullus, Selene, Helios, and Ptolemy he was neither agnate nor cognate. As they were all fathered by Antonius, Cleopatra's offspring as well as Fulvia's son were half-siblings of Octavia's daughters. This complicated familial situation nevertheless provided Augustus with the framework to claim avuncular relationships with all of them by extending his familial bonds from his nieces to their half-siblings. Simultaneously, he forced them to accept the social roles of nephew and niece toward him in return.

In which ways did Augustus act as an *avunculus* to Antonius' children? It seems that he was subtly combining various elements of possible avuncular behaviors toward Iullus and his siblings. Since Augustus, much like Drusus

[58] Cic. *Ad Brut.* 13.1 (trans. Shuckburgh 1899–1904). Cf. Bettini 1992: 59–60. Cf. Bernstein (this volume) on Pliny the Elder as surrogate father to his nephew Pliny the Younger.
[59] See Cic. *Cael.* 25; Pers. *Sat.* 1.8–11; Catull. 74, 78. Cf. Bettini 1992: 26–50; Hickson 1993.
[60] Cic. *Phil.* 8.2.

before him, opened his house to the fatherless children and made them part of his *domus*, it must be assumed that he was responsible for their education, while Octavia oversaw their physical well-being. Suetonius mentions that Augustus took it upon himself to teach his daughter and granddaughters to spin and weave as well as teaching his grandchildren to read, write, and swim.[61] Whether he did the same for the children in his sister's household is not specifically mentioned, but it is clear that Augustus ostentatiously presented himself as a man who took the education of his youngest family members very seriously. Furthermore, of the known teachers of Marcellus and Iullus, Athenodorus and Nestor of Tarsus were also dispatched on diplomatic missions on behalf of the *princeps*.[62] Because of Augustus' professional relations with the Greek philosophers, it is plausible that *he* engaged them to teach his nephews, rather than Octavia. There is strong evidence in Suetonius that Augustus was proud to provide Cleopatra's children with an upbringing adequate to their station as Ptolemaic princess and princes.[63] In accepting responsibility for the children's education and upbringing, Augustus echoed the behavior of M. Porcius Cato, who took over the education of his fatherless nephew Brutus.

Similar to Brutus' concerns about his nephew's inheritance, Augustus also managed the finances of Iullus and the Antoniae. As mentioned above, he had already taken possession of Antonius' estate. Antonius' legal heirs, Iullus and the Antoniae, had no claim on their inheritance owing to their father's dispossession – which put Augustus in the position of a benefactor able to restore some part of their fortune:

To his nieces, the daughters whom Octavia had had by Antonius and had reared, he assigned money from their father's estate. He also ordered Antonius' freedmen to give at once to Iullus, the son of Antonius and Fulvia, everything which by law they would have been required to bequeath him at their death.[64]

As the children grew older, Augustus displayed further avuncular responsibility. He must be understood as the main force behind Selene's marriage to Juba of Mauretania. While Plutarch indeed mentions Octavia as the marriage broker in this affair, Cassius Dio names Augustus as the initiator of the marriage.[65] Dio's argument is the more plausible since a marriage

---

[61] Suet. *Aug.* 64.2–13. See also Singer 1944: 112–13.

[62] Strabo 14.5.14; Lucian, *Macr.* 21. Cf. Bowersock 1965: 38–9; Kienast 1999: 467–8.

[63] Suet. *Aug.* 17.5.   [64] Cass. Dio 51.15.7 (trans. Cary 1960).

[65] Plut. *Ant.* 87; Cass. Dio 51.15.6. See Singer 1944: 111. For a different view, see Watson 1995: 202–3. Crinagoras commemorated this marriage (Diehl. *Anth. Lyr. Graec.* 9.235; see Braund 1984), it can be dated after 19 BCE; cf. Grenier 2001: 101; Roller 2003: 86–9.

between a member of the *domus Augusta* and one of Rome's most trusted lieges is clearly one of strategic importance, implicating two ruling families, so only Augustus could have arranged and approved it, while Octavia would have had no say in what amounted to foreign policy.[66] At the time when Juba married Selene, he was enthroned as the ruler of his father's kingdom. Augustus' former *contubernalis* was thus elevated from vassal-king to bridegroom of the emperor's stepniece, binding Juba politically as well as quasi-familially to Augustus. Selene's marriage to Juba thus served an exogamic policy of the *princeps*. The fact that Selene was unrelated to Augustus by blood or law or that Antonius was her father did not matter: the familial contract between Juba and Augustus worked because Juba married an esteemed member of the *domus Augusta*, the precious foster niece of Augustus himself.

During the Republic it was not unusual for a marriageable girl's uncle to have a hand in choosing her potential bridegroom. Cato the Younger is again an example of an *avunculus* who scrupulously chose his nephew-in-law: he rejected the offer of Pompey because he did not want to be bound to his political opponent by kinship. T. Pomponius Atticus, on the other hand, demonstrated how an *avunculus* could choose his nephew's future wife – against even the wishes of the boy as well as of his father, Q. Tullius Cicero.[67] The avuncular involvement can be explained by Roman familial strategies to cross-link one's family group with as many other family units as possible, thus creating a large cognatic network.[68] Since the *avunculus* felt responsible for his sister's children, he must have had a considerable interest in his future nephew-in-law, whose family group would then be connected to him by marriage. Augustus followed these traditional matrimonial strategies by, on the one hand, aiming to interlink himself and his family with the Roman aristocracy by marriage to assure his own position. On the other hand, he also followed endogamic strategies to build a dynasty within his own bloodline, thus securing succession by increasing the legitimacy of the chosen heir. As Augustus had only one child of his own, he had to revert to his sister's progeny, Livia's sons, and even Antonius' children in order to multiply his possibilities of connecting other families through intermarriage. The "marry-go-round" devised by the first *princeps* is so complex that modern

---

[66] Cf. Suet. *Aug.* 48.1, who describes Augustus' policy of encouraging the intermarrying of allied kings in order to establish *adfinitas*. Juba's marriage to Selene is extraordinary because he did not marry a foreign royal bride, but a member of the Augustan household; the principle, however, is the same.

[67] Cato and Pompey: Plut. *Cat. Min.* 30; *Pomp.* 44. Atticus and Q. Cicero: Cic. *Att.* 13.50.2, 13.58.1, 15.22.2; Nep. *Att.* 10.2–4.

[68] Cf. J. Martin 1993: 159–61; Harders 2006: 55–65.

scholars find it difficult to represent it in a family tree that depicts all the ramifications.[69]

While Selene's marriage to Juba increased Augustus' power by exogamy, Augustus used Antonius' progeny to build up a dynastic lineage. The marriage between Antonia Minor and Livia's son Drusus is well known,[70] but Antonia's half-brother Iullus was also made to serve endogamic purposes. He married his former stepsister Marcella Maior after her divorce from Agrippa. Through this marriage, Augustus bound Iullus even closer to himself and turned his stepnephew into an *adfinis*. Iullus thus ascended within the hierarchy of the dynasty as his children by Marcella would have been related by blood to the *princeps* – in other words, potential heirs to the throne.[71]

Iullus' elevated position within Augustus' household is also demonstrated by his political career. The *princeps* gave Iullus a hand up in order to assure his stepnephew's success in the *cursus honorum*. Thus, Iullus was elected into office long before "his year": he bypassed the standard age qualifications and became praetor approximately six years earlier than usual in 13 BCE; only three years later he was elected consul and later received Asia as a province to govern.[72] Interferences with the *leges annales* are known only for members of the *domus Augusta*. The *princeps* himself had to ask the senate for his relatives to be released from the age qualifications. In Iullus' case this procedure is not documented, nevertheless it must be assumed that Augustus facilitated his career much as he did for Marcellus, Tiberius, Drusus, Germanicus, and C. and L. Caesar, for all of whom there is evidence.[73] Iullus was singled out by this special imperial protection as a highly valued member of the Augustan household. Furthermore, during his praetorship, Iullus was able to demonstrate his gratitude to the *princeps* by hosting magnificent chariot races and

---

[69]   On Augustus' marriage alliances: Syme 1939: 421–3; Corbier 1995. On his endogamic policy: Severy 2003: 62–7.

[70]   Val. Max. 4.3.3; Suet. *Calig.* 1.1, 15.2, 23.2, *Claud.* 1.1; Jos. *AJ* 18.6.6. The elder Antonia was married off to L. Domitius Ahenobarbus, thus linking the *domus Augusta* to one of the last remaining old patrician families.

[71]   Cf. Vell. Pat. 2.100.4: *etiam matrimonio sororis suae filiae in artissimam adfinitatem receperat* – "He [*sc.* Augustus] had admitted him to the closest ties of relationship through a marriage with his sister's daughter" (trans. Shipley 1961). See also Plut. *Ant.* 87; Tac. *Ann.* 4.44.

[72]   Cass. Dio 54.26.2; Vell. Pat. 2.100.4; Jos. *AJ* 16.6.7. According to Cassius Dio (52.20.2), Maecenas proposed lowering the age qualification for the praetorship from forty to thirty years of age in 29 BCE. The scenario described by Dio, however, is almost certainly his own fabrication and we have no reliable information as to the actual context and year in which this change was ultimately made. Since Velleius (2.100.4) stresses Augustus' personal involvement in Iullus' career, Iullus is likely to have not been subject to the traditional "Republican" age limits. On Iullus' government of Asia, see Atkinson 1958: 327.

[73]   See Kienast 1999: 156. On Marcellus, Tiberius, and Drusus: Cass. Dio 53.28.3, 54.10.4, 56.28.1; on C. and L. Caesar: *Res gest. div. Aug.* 14; Germanicus: Suet. *Calig.* 1.1.

wild beast shows.[74] The Roman audience was thus presented with Antonius'
son as loyal nephew and subject, presiding over games in honor of his father's
erstwhile enemy. As a distinguished member of the *domus Augusta*, Iullus is
probably also portrayed on the *Ara Pacis*. This is not the place to engage in a
detailed archaeological discussion about the identifications of the different
members of Augustus' large family on this complex monument; nevertheless
it seems at least plausible that Iullus was placed somewhere in the large
procession displayed on the friezes.[75] Plutarch's comment that Iullus had a
very close relationship to Augustus would thus be visually confirmed.

When Iullus' stepmother and mother-in-law, Octavia, died in 11 or 9 BCE,
Augustus arranged a state funeral for his sister. After the *princeps* himself and
Antonia Minor's husband Drusus delivered the *laudationes*, Octavia's body
was carried in the funeral procession by her sons-in-law.[76] Cassius Dio's
record of the *pompa* does not specify Octavia's sons-in-law, but it must be
assumed that, next to Drusus, L. Domitius Ahenobarbus, and M. Valerius
Messala, Iullus was part of the procession and was thus once more declared an
important member of the *domus Augusta*.

Of all of Antonius' children Iullus occupied a special position, especially
because in contrast to Cleopatra's children, he was a Roman male citizen
and thus, in Roman terms, the only legitimate successor to his father and
head of the family. This meant that Augustus was able to patronize Iullus
politically – a favor he could not extend to Iullus' peregrine half-brothers.
Through the imperial-avuncular promotion of Iullus, the *princeps* was able
to show his magnanimity and prove his *pietas* to the Roman plebs as well as
to the remaining aristocracy. Although the day-to-day relationship between
Augustus and Iullus Antonius and Cleopatra's children cannot be reconstructed from the surviving sources, it generally seems to have been the
embodiment of traditional Roman family life –at least insofar as the leading
character, Augustus, behaved exactly as an *avunculus* should.

AUGUSTUS AS AN IMPERIAL FAMILY MAN

Even at first glance the image of a loving and caring *avunculus* Augustus,
who pursued no ulterior motives when putting on that role, seems too
good to be true. Beyond his instrumental use of the children in creating
endogamic and exogamic networks, what else did Augustus gain by playing

---

[74] Cass. Dio 54.26.2.   [75] See the suggestions made by Rose 1997: 103–4; Hallett 2006a: 155.
[76] Cass. Dio 54.35.4–5. According to Dio, Octavia died in 11; according to Suetonius, in the year 10/9
        (Suet. *Aug.* 61.2; see also Livy, *Per.* 140; *Cons. ad Liv.* 69–70). On Octavia's death: Singer 1944: 131–3.

surrogate father to Iullus and his half-siblings? And did he always behave like the perfect uncle, even if that meant that he subordinated his own personal interests, as the *avunculus* L. Caesar did when he defended his nephew Antonius against the senate?

As the man who propagated the concept of *res publica restituta*, Augustus had to conform to the expectations of the Roman public in terms of his role as a family man.[77] Concerning Iullus Antonius and his siblings, Augustus adopted the social role of *avunculus* and, by virtue of that decision, he was compelled to play the role exemplarily – the fact that formally he was only something like a step-*avunculus* to Antonius' children by Fulvia and Cleopatra did not alter public expectations. On the other hand, letting Antonius' and Cleopatra's children live was a danger to his own position. After all, he was a monarch who could not allow his archenemies' children to avenge their parents' fate. An adult Iullus Antonius could very possibly have been in the position to offer a place of refuge for Augustus' critics and even an alternative to his rule. Certainly, Augustus was in no way forced to act as he did. Without any ado, he could have imprisoned Cleopatra's children and sent Iullus into a guarded exile. By treating Selene, Helios, Ptolemy, and Iullus as kin, however, he turned the formerly hostile relationship – as presented during the triumph – into a familial one, choosing to advertise his relation to the children through the roles of *avunculus* and *nepotes*. Apart from the children themselves, the most important audiences for this role-play were the Roman aristocracy and the *plebs Romana*.

First of all, by integrating Antonius' children into his household, Augustus extended a gesture toward those parts of the Roman aristocracy that were still loyal to Antonius. Although as Octavian he had had some of Antonius' officers executed after the battle of Actium, the new Augustus could not eliminate every "Antonian," and so often let mercy prevail – especially after his return to Rome and his declaration of *res publica restituta*.[78] The necessary integration of Antonius' followers into the new Augustan aristocracy is thus paralleled by Augustus' integration of Antonius' children into his own house-hold and may be interpreted as a subtle offer of amnesty. While Antyllus was killed in Alexandria, his younger brother prospered as the stepnephew of the *princeps*. By caring like an *avunculus* for Iullus, Augustus committed an act of grace that he also extended to some of the "Antonian" members of the Roman

---

[77] During his reign Augustus tried particularly to restore family morals, for example by his marriage legislation, cf. Severy 2003: 44–56. Furthermore, the *princeps* used the domestic sphere to characterize himself as an impeccable *civis*. Milnor (2005: 93) suggests the term "politicized domesticity."

[78] Cass. Dio 51.2.4–3.1; Vell. Pat. 2.86.2–3. Cf. Syme 1939: 299–300.

aristocracy and highlighted his own desire for a new beginning – thus stabilizing his position in Rome.

Concerning the fate of Alexander Helios and Ptolemy Philadelphus, scholarship so far has argued that if they were not killed immediately after the triumph,[79] they must have died young because of the foreign Roman climate.[80] The possibility, however, that both Ptolemaic princes died a natural death and did not grow up cannot be ruled out completely.[81] Contrary to both positions, I will argue that the lack of record about their fate does not necessarily imply that they died young at all; rather, the context of Augustus' ostentatiously assumed role as an *avunculus* to his other nieces and nephews suggests that both might have survived to adulthood, but in the golden cage of Augustus' household for political reasons.

Roller argues that Helios and Philadelphus must have died young because otherwise they would have been promoted politically and married off to serve Augustus' dynastic purposes like Selene and Iullus.[82] Roller's argument, however, is not convincing: Augustus could not further any political career of the brothers because, unlike Iullus, they were not Roman aristocrats who were able to run the *cursus honorum*, but Ptolemaic princes. Also, sending them on any diplomatic mission to the East would always have meant providing them with ways to contact faithful Ptolemaic supporters and so claim their mother's kingdom. Marrying the princes to loyal foreign brides would have been equally risky: while their sister Selene was taken care of by the loyal Juba, it was far more difficult to find a foreign bride, preferably with a capable and long-living father-in-law who was loyal and powerful enough to keep Cleopatra's sons in check. It is therefore not surprising that Augustus neither promoted Helios and Philadelphus nor arranged marriages for them; it is far more plausible to assume that the princes led a comfortable life in Augustus' household.[83] Again, by integrating Cleopatra's sons into his *domus*, Augustus kept any anti-Augustan opposition in Alexandria in check. The sight of Cleopatra's children presented in triumph and then integrated into the victor's household "might have shattered the hope of any supporters they

---

[79] Murder is insinuated by Syme (1939: 300) and taken for granted by P. M. Martin (1995: 249).

[80] So Roller 2003: 84.

[81] Dio mentions in the context of Selene's wedding to Juba that her brothers were spared out of consideration to the bridal couple (Cass. Dio 51.15.6); the reason why their lives should be endangered in 20/19, nine years after their arrival in Rome, Dio does not mention. Roller 2003: 82, n. 40 therefore suggests that Dio is guilty of anachronism and confuses the situation in 30 with that in 20/19. In any event, our knowledge of the brothers' fate remains thin.

[82] Cf. Roller 2003: 84, n. 47.

[83] See also Meiklejohn 1934: 193–4; Whitehorne 1994: 198. It is therefore not convincing to assume that Alexander and Philadelphus followed their sister to Mauretania; for a different view, see Grant 1972: 231.

might have had."[84] By transferring the legitimate and direct heirs to Cleopatra to Rome, Augustus put a hold on any attempt to turn the Roman province of Egypt into a Hellenistic kingdom again, since any contender in Alexandria would have had difficulties in legitimizing his claim to the throne while Cleopatra's sons were still alive – although out of reach. Augustus' care for Cleopatra's sons might therefore be characterized as an overwhelming familial embrace that suffocated any resistance and possible attempts to avenge their parent's fate.

In the long run, by acting as an exemplary family man Augustus demonstrated *pietas* and thus the excellence of his character, which extended even to the social responsibility he assumed with respect to orphaned children – even if they were fathered by his enemy. The Roman people were thus made to perceive Augustus as a good *civis* who honored the *mos maiorum*. Similar to other arrangements – for example the Augustan laws on adultery and marriage – Augustus was able to build upon Roman traditions and could stress his strict conformity to them.[85] His conduct toward Antonius' children was therefore part of Augustus' self-fashioning as an ideal Roman and simultaneously helped to stabilize his position of power within Roman society and even his position as the conqueror of Ptolemaic Egypt.

DEVIANT *AVUNCULUS* – REBELLIOUS *NEPOTES*

While Augustus had to meet certain expectations in adoption of the role of *avunculus*, Iullus and his half-siblings likewise had to accept their parents' enemy as their uncle, extending their quasi-familial loyalty to Augustus. As *nepotes* to Augustus, their behavior was guided by social norms as well. Of all people, it was their father who had offered an example of how a nephew's deviant conduct toward an *avunculus* was socially censured: after Antonius had proscribed his uncle L. Caesar, he had to suffer the public reprimands of his mother as well as the scorn of the public and was cited by later historians as the primary example of an ungrateful nephew.[86]

How difficult this role-play must have been for Augustus and Antonius' children is shown by the fact that there are a number of instances in which Augustus deviated from the avuncular role in crucial ways. As mentioned above, he restored to Iullus and the Antoniae part of their paternal inheritance,

---

[84] Meiklejohn 1934: 194.
[85] For Augustus' own assessment, see *Res gest. div. Aug.* 8. On the Augustan marriage laws, see Mette-Dittmann 1991.
[86] Vell. Pat. 2.67.2; App. *B civ.* 4.37; Plut. *Ant.* 20; Cass. Dio 47.6.3; [Aur. Vict.] *De vir. ill.* 85.3.

but was careful not to include Antonius' property on the Palatine. Instead, after Actium Augustus bestowed Antonius' former residence on his friends Agrippa and Messalla. Antonius' children thus lost all claims to their former home, and Augustus obviously did not stand in to defend their rights.[87] Rather, his move to give the *domus* away to the leading commander of Actium added to his new nephew and nieces' humiliation as Agrippa occupied Antonius' very own home – a symbolic gesture to remind the public once more of Antonius' thorough military defeat. In addition, the donation to Agrippa and Messalla prevented Iullus from reviving the *domus* of his father and holding up an Antonian tradition or establishing his own house as distinct from that of the *princeps*. He had no choice but to remain a dependent member of the *domus Augusta*.

Another instance in which Augustus deviated from that which would be expected of him as Iullus' *avunculus* was his refusal to offer him a military command even as he promoted Iullus' political career. Unlike Tiberius and Germanicus, who did command armies under Augustus, Antonius' son apparently could not be trusted with such an office. Iullus was denied the opportunity to become a military leader; the possibility that he could try to usurp Augustus' position through military power was thus minimized.

Much like Augustus in his role as *avunculus*, Antonius' children also had difficulties in conforming to the roles of the loyal niece and nephew and in certain ways were unwilling to do so. After her marriage to Juba, Cleopatra Selene presented herself as the queen of Mauretania with distinct Egyptian reminiscences and thereby subtly demonstrated her claim to her mother's throne. While Juba proved his loyalty to Rome by choosing the Latin title REX IUBA ("KING JUBA") for the legend on his coins, his wife had her coins minted with the Greek title of ΚΛΕΟΠΑΤΡΑ ΒΑΣΙΛΙΣΣΑ ("QUEEN CLEOPATRA") and added images such as the crocodile and the Hellenistic diadem, unmistakable symbols of her ancestry.[88] Selene also emphasized her Ptolemaic heritage by giving her son the dynastic name Ptolemy.[89]

While Selene symbolically resisted her integration into the Augustan order and claimed her mother's heritage, her half-brother Iullus finally plotted against his *avunculus* in spite of Augustus' demonstrative affection, protection, and support. In 2 BCE he was found – among others – to be closely

---

[87] Cass. Dio 53.27.5. After the house burned down in 25, Agrippa moved into Augustus' house while Messalla was paid off. Antonius' former *domus* was not restored.

[88] On Selene's coinage: Grenier 2001; Roller 2003: 90.

[89] On Ptolemy of Mauretania: Hofmann 1959c.

entangled with the *princeps'* only daughter, Iulia. The reputed lovers were separated and condemned: Iulia was exiled; Iullus was forced to commit suicide.[90] The advances of this group of young aristocrats toward Iulia are likely to have been a veritable conspiracy with Iullus as its leader, rather than simply an evening's entertainment of a debauched clique of aristocratic paramours.[91] As Antonius' son, Iullus had the requisite prestige (on his mother's side he was related to C. Gracchus, on his father's to the *gens Iulia*),[92] motive (revenge for his father and mother), aristocratic grandeur, and perhaps talent to establish a serious alternative to Augustus. His actual plans are not known; Syme presumes that Iullus "may have aspired to the place of Tiberius as stepfather of the princes," but regardless his scheme failed.[93]

Iullus' plotting against his uncle shows that Augustus' meticulous familial integration had backfired. However, even on the brink of a *coup d'état*, the *princeps* was still able to exploit the social expectations of the relationship between nephew and *avunculus* for his own purposes. Publicly, he showcased his socially legitimate disappointment at his nephew's ungrateful behavior after he had extended all forms of avuncular love toward him:

> Iullus Antonius, who had been a remarkable example of Caesar's clemency, only to become the violator of his household, avenged with his own hand the crime he had committed. After the defeat of Marcus Antonius, his father, Augustus had not only granted him his life, but after honoring him with the priesthood, the praetorship, the consulship, and the governorship of provinces, had admitted him to the closest ties of relationship through a marriage with his sister's daughter.[94]

Despite the ultimate fates of Cleopatra's children and Iullus Antonius, Augustus' adaptation of the social role of *avunculus* proved to be a clever move to serve the power politics of Rome's first *princeps*.

CONCLUSION

Augustus' treatment of Antonius' children brilliantly demonstrates Roman strategies to cope with the demographic problem of fatherless children. Growing up without parents did not mean growing up alone, because

---

[90] Vell. Pat. 2.100.4; Sen. *De brevitate* 4.6; Plin. *HN* 7.149; Tac. *Ann.* 1.10; 3.18; 4.44; Cass. Dio 55.10.15. Cf. Suet. *Aug.* 65.

[91] On the conspiracy: Syme 1939: 426–7 and 1984: 924–34; Eck 1996; Kienast 1999: 134, 169; Dettenhofer 2000: 176–9; Fantham 2006: 85–9. For a different view, see Severy 2003: 180–4.

[92] On the dynastic implications of Iullus' unusual *praenomen* which recalled his Julian ancestry, see Hallett 2006a: 157. Antonius and Fulvia thus marked their claim as pretenders to Caesar's succession.

[93] Syme 1939: 427.   [94] Vell. Pat. 2.100.4 (trans. Shipley 1961). See also Tac. *Ann.* 3.18.1.

Roman society had developed a familial role system in which a surrogate father, if necessary, was provided. The social expectations that shaped the role of the Roman *avunculus* defined him as a surrogate father who had to take care of fatherless children within his cognate kin. By taking over this specific social responsibility, a Roman was able to prove his *pietas* and *fides* – which meant that under the watchful eyes of Roman society, a Roman *avunculus* could hardly refuse to carry out his familial duties if he wanted to be perceived as an honorable and trustworthy Roman *civis*.

In the case of Augustus' assumed role as *avunculus* toward Antonius' and Cleopatra's children, the importance of this specific structure within the Roman kinship system is particularly well illustrated because of the first *princeps'* exploitation of its mechanisms for his own benefit. In extending his avuncular responsibility to his nieces Antonia Maior and Minor's half-siblings, he adopted the social role of *avunculus* to Marcus Antonius' other children by Fulvia and Cleopatra. Augustus thus established a quasi-familial bond with the children and integrated them into his household. By playing the part of *avunculus* he demonstrated not only his *pietas* but also his *clementia* to the fatherless children of his enemy. Integrating the children in his *domus* was also the best way to control them. Iullus was prevented from presiding over his own house, because his integration into another *domus* and his new role as the *princeps'* nephew meant dependence on Augustus. Cleopatra's children were likewise kept in the golden cage of Augustus' household, thus unable to assume their natural roles as leaders of a potential pro-Ptolemaic opposition in Alexandria.

As surrogate father to Antonius' children, Augustus succeeded in stabilizing and augmenting his own political position by displaying the façade of a responsible and respectable family man who demonstrated exemplary care for the fatherless children in his sister's household. In so doing, however, he actually perverted the values connected with the avuncular role by completely subordinating them to his personal interests. Thus Augustus' relationship to Antonius' children can be cited as an example of the paradoxical situation of the first *princeps*, who was obliged, on the one hand, to act as any other normal Roman aristocrat in order for his rule to be accepted, but who needed, on the other, to massage the social norms of the Republic in order to stabilize his *de facto* autarchy.

CHAPTER 13

Cui parens non erat maximus quisque et vetustissimus pro parente: *paternal surrogates in imperial Roman literature*

Neil W. Bernstein

INTRODUCTION: BEREAVEMENT AND SELF-PRESENTATION

Despite its relatively high incidence,[1] fatherlessness presented a social challenge to young aristocratic Roman men who aspired to a political career. Roman society placed great emphasis on the authority wielded by a father, the emulation of his example by his sons, and the political and social connections granted through membership in a high-status family. Upper-class Roman literary sources generally represent youth as an unstable age, in need of careful guidance. Pliny the Younger, for example, observes that the son of Corellia Hispulla, an *adulescens*, needs "not only a teacher but also a guardian and a master at this slippery period of life."[2] In addition to the prejudice that might potentially be focused upon the young man without a guardian, a fatherless man could also find himself without the important links of patronage or *suffragium* that were essential at the beginning of an imperial Roman career. The social disadvantages affecting legitimately born children bereaved of their fathers at an early age naturally differ

---

My thanks to Judith Hallett, Sabine Hübner, Ilaria Marchesi, Francis Newton, and Yi-Ting Wang for many helpful comments, suggestions, and stimuli.

[1] Demographic simulations of Roman marriage, fertility, and life-expectancy patterns suggest that by the age of twenty roughly one-third of upper-class men could expect to have lost their fathers. Richard Saller's microsimulation predicts a 38 percent incidence of fatherlessness for "senatorial" men before the age of twenty; see Saller 1994: 64. In the present volume (p. 36, above) Walter Scheidel examines criticism of Saller's arguments and concludes that "Saller's projections are fairly robust." See also the review of ancient demographic data in the Introduction to the present volume.

[2] *Cui in hoc lubrico aetatis non praeceptor modo sed custos etiam rectorque quaerendus est* (*Ep.* 3.3.4). Sherwin-White (1968: 212) estimates that Corellia's son was about fourteen years old. In attempting to excuse Caelius' behavior as youthful indiscretion, Cicero appeals to the "many slippery paths of adolescence" (*multas vias adulescentiae lubricas, Cael.* 41), while Tacitus explains that thanks to his corrupt mother's exile, the younger Papinius was protected "during the slippery period of youth" (*lubricum iuventae, Ann.* 6.49) from being forced into suicide like his older brother. See Eyben 1993: 19–24.

considerably from those affecting the illegitimate, though in comparison with other societies ancient Rome was remarkably free of prejudice against the illegitimate.[3] While servile or freedmen "child-minders" might provide instructive and (potentially) psychologically stabilizing companionship for a fatherless young man,[4] of necessity they could not provide the social benefits that came from a publicly visible association with an older upper-class man.

Some upper-class young men of the early imperial period chose to negotiate the social challenges of fatherlessness by associating themselves with paternal surrogates who had no familial connection to them. In this chapter I examine the rhetorical strategies used by two fatherless members of the imperial Roman elite to assert the legitimacy of their political aspirations. I shall first examine Statius, *Silvae* 5.2, a lengthy encomiastic poem addressed to Crispinus, a young fatherless man who took up an early appointment as *tribunus militum*. I next turn to several letters of the younger Pliny in which he considers his relationships both with the older men who supported his early career and the younger men whom he hopes to serve as patron, political supporter, and instructive example. Esther Goody's studies of shared parenthood in West African states provide valuable parallels to the practices discussed in this paper. According to Goody, fosterage by non-relatives regularly occurs in complex hierarchical states that, like ancient Rome,

---

[3] On illegitimate children in Roman society, see Beltrami 1998; in Roman Egypt, see Malouta in the present volume; on the relative lack of Roman prejudice against the illegitimate, see Rawson 1989: esp. 10–18. On illegitimacy in Greek culture, see Ebbott 2003; Ogden 1996 and his chapter in the present volume.

[4] Keith Bradley has identified the frequent experience of bereavement, coupled with high rates of divorce and remarriage, as factors contributing to the "dislocation" experienced by children in the Roman family; see Bradley 1991a: 125–55. The high incidence of these "dislocating" events, as indicated by the demographic data, should advise against attributing a specific predictive value to any individual child's experience of bereavement. Both Bradley and Suzanne Dixon have emphasized two factors that might mitigate the psychological experience of bereavement. These include (a) the presence of "child-minders" attached to the aristocratic child, who provided a form of stability in the child's life by accompanying him or her, in spite of various changes in household composition, through childhood into adulthood and beyond; and (b) the communal orientation of the Roman family, in which other members of the *familia* willingly served as parental surrogates. See Bradley 1991a: 138; Rawson 1991b: 23. As Dixon observes: "Anthropological proponents of cultural relativism have … succeeded in demonstrating that it is not damaging to a young child to be cared for by a variety of people if the arrangements are embedded in a social structure and therefore perceived as normal and accompanied by the kind of emotional and other supports associated with kin-based care" (1999: 220). These considerations should properly invalidate attempts to psychoanalyze Roman politicians; such as, e.g., Frost 1997, who endeavors to relate the younger Cato's political program to the psychological needs for control and intimacy putatively created by his orphanhood. My focus in this chapter will accordingly be not on irrecoverable psychological states, but on the means of public presentation chosen by aristocratic fatherless men.

feature market economies, occupational differentiation, and the practice of clientelage. These forms of fosterage, however, are not undertaken solely as the response to the loss of a parent. Rather, living parents willingly forgo "immediate benefit from their children's assistance in order that the children shall have the most advantageous position possible in the social system as adults."[5] Fosterage provides opportunities for training in a marketable skill (apprentice fosterage) or for securing patronage from powerful individuals (alliance fosterage). A further parallel to the practices discussed in this paper can be seen in the fact that West African fosterers do not formally adopt their charges: "rather, it is older children who are sent off, and it is their training and sponsorship into adult roles which is being delegated to others."[6] Goody accordingly divides the parental role into multiple components, including "biological, nurturance, training, sponsorship, [and] jural."[7] The focus in this chapter is primarily on the components of "training" and "sponsorship" necessary to negotiate the complexities of a Roman political career, though the elder Pliny's testamentary adoption of the younger Pliny provides "jural" aspects as well. In each man's case, paternal surrogates perform some of the overlapping roles attributed to the absent father, providing important social connections and enabling the fatherless young man to counter charges of immaturity and inexperience.

CRISPINUS, THE YOUNG MAN FULL OF PROMISE

Silvae 5.2 is an encomium of Crispinus upon the occasion of his appointment as *tribunus militum* at the unexpectedly early age of sixteen.[8] Crispinus is one of only five addressees of senatorial rank in the collection, and he is further distinguished by his patrician pedigree. Crispinus' father, Vettius Bolanus, was suffect consul, governor of Britain, and proconsul of Asia.[9] Though Bolanus transmitted a distinguished political legacy to his son, Statius also acknowledges that his early death left his son open to the potential criticism that could be levelled at irresponsible youth. Crispinus' appointment as *tribunus militum* two years earlier than expected and the

---

[5] See Goody 1988: 275. [6] Goody 1988: 271. [7] See Goody 1999.

[8] See Bernstein 2007, from which some arguments below have been adapted; see also Zeiner 2005: 201–9; Hardie 1983: 146–51. Citations of the *Silvae* are taken from Courtney 1990. Geoffrey Nathan's discussion (this volume) of Claudian's encomium of Stilicho, the guardian of a fatherless emperor, complements my discussion of Statius' encomium of Crispinus, the fatherless young man who flourishes under the emperor's guardianship.

[9] *PIR* V.323. White (1973: 282) conjectures that he was adlected into the patriciate as a reward for denying Vitellius reinforcements during the war of 68–9 CE.

conviction of his mother on a charge of poisoning furnish further potential sources of disapproval. Crispinus' chosen career as an advocate and military officer also left him particularly vulnerable to criticism of his inexperience. Young advocates could provoke the resentment of their seniors, while young military officers were criticized for their perceived lack of discipline.[10] Rather than tactfully omit mention of these potential sources of disapproval, Statius chooses to address each directly. This section accordingly focuses attention on Statius' account of Crispinus' fatherlessness and its effects within the broader context of the poet's defense of his subject's character. In Statius' adroit presentation, fatherlessness becomes merely one of many challenges that Crispinus has successfully overcome.

Statius employs two major rhetorical strategies to address the challenge of Crispinus' fatherlessness: praise of his virtuous disposition and enumeration of the paternal surrogates who will guide, educate, and support the young man. The poet acknowledges the absence of a father as guide and mentor as potentially hazardous for any young man yet argues that Crispinus possesses particular intellectual and emotional gifts that protect him from such dangers:

And now you prepare for a journey, making ready for departure at no sluggish pace. Not yet have the signs of strong manhood crept over your cheeks and your life's course is still to be determined. Your father is not by your side; for he died, swallowed by the cruel Fates and leaving two children without a guardian. He did not even strip boyhood's purple from your tender arms and clothe your shoulders in white. Who has not been corrupted by youth uncurbed and the hastened freedom of a new toga, as when a tree ignorant of the pruning hook rears up leaves and exhales its fruit in foliage? But in your heart were Pierian concerns, and modesty, and character taught to make its own law. Then came blithe probity, a tranquil brow, elegance fearing luxury's borderline, family affection dispensed in all its forms: to yield to your coeval brother, admire your father, and to forgive your unhappy mother.[11]

---

[10] Criticism of young advocates: e.g. Quint. *Inst.* 12.6.2; Plin. *Ep.* 2.14.2–4; Eyben 1993: 74–6; of young officers, e.g. Tac. *Agr.* 5.2; Plin. *Ep.* 8.14.4–7; Eyben 1993: 50–1.

[11]
iamque adeo moliris iter nec deside passu
ire paras. nondum validae tibi signa iuventae
inrepsere genis et adhuc tenor integer aevi,
nec genitor iuxta; fatis namque haustus iniquis
occidit et geminam prolem sine praeside linquens;   65
nec saltem teneris ostrum puerile lacertis
exuit albentique umeros induxit amictu.
quem non corrupit pubes effrena novaeque
libertas properata togae? ceu nescia falcis
silva comas tollit fructumque exspirat in umbras.   70
at tibi Pieriae tenero sub pectore curae
et pudor et docti legem sibi dicere mores;
tunc hilaris probitas et frons tranquilla nitorque

The young man's array of virtues includes his poetic interests, his *pudor*, self-control, *probitas*, calm, elegance coupled with moderation, and his *pietas*. Elsewhere in the *Silvae* Statius commonly applies the majority of these praise *topoi* to adult men. Crispinus' possession of these qualities thereby associates him with mature individuals, in particular friends of Statius such as Pollius Felix and Atedius Melior whose portraits are more fully developed across multiple poems of the collection.[12]

Yet even as he details Crispinus' virtues and announces the young man's departure for his first significant career assignment, Statius begins to address the implications of the young man's fatherlessness. Along with his brother, Crispinus was left "without a guardian" (*sine praeside*, 65). His father neither appointed a *tutor* for his immature son nor survived to witness the most important transition in the young man's life, the assumption of the *toga virilis* (66–7).[13] The narrator employs a metaphor from the natural world to conclude his description of the hazards implicit in Crispinus' bereaved state. To leave a young man's natural development improperly tended invites criticism. A fatherless young man is like a tree that has not been pruned back and thus may fail to produce fruit (69–70).[14] Elsewhere in the *Silvae* Statius

> luxuriae confine timens pietasque per omnes
> dispensata modos; aequaevo cedere fratri   75
> mirarique patrem miseraeque ignoscere matri   (*Silv.* 5.2.61–76).

Translation adapted from Shackleton Bailey 2003.

[12] Pollius Felix: poetic concerns (*Silv.* 2.2.112), philosophical calm and self-control (2.2.121–32). Atedius Melior: elegance coupled with moderation (2.3.70–1), *pietas* (2.1.96). *Probitas*, however, is a quality associated elsewhere in the *Silvae* only with women and younger men, such as Violentilla (1.2.12), Glaucias (2.1.40), Claudia (3.5.17, 67), Priscilla (5.1.117, 154). *Pudor* is often attributed to the same types of individual (Violentilla, 1.2.36; Glaucias, 2.1.40; Philetus, 2.6.48; Priscilla, 5.1.65) but can also be associated with mature men (Domitian, 4.1.10; Statius and/or his father, 5.3.218).

[13] Zeiner (2005: 202–3) suggests that Crispinus' father died when his son was over the age of fourteen. A *tutor* was no longer legally required for young men who had reached this age, though they could still seek advice from a *curator*. In Zeiner's view, Statius would not have knowingly exposed Crispinus' father, Bolanus, to the social criticism that would otherwise have been implied in a charge of insufficient attention to his children's welfare. Rather, "Statius implies … that Crispinus' maturity allowed him to manage his own financial and personal affairs without the help of a *tutor* or *curator*" (203). Saller (1994: 181–203) provides a full discussion of the social obligations implied in the guardianship of Roman children; see also the review of Roman guardianship in the Introduction to the present volume. In contrast to Zeiner, White (1973: 282–4) suggests that Bolanus may have named Crispinus' mother as his *substitutus pupillaris*, which in turn may have provided her with a motive for attempted murder to secure his share of the inheritance; and Crispinus' family may have moved up the date of his assumption of the *toga virilis* following the murder attempt.

[14] The *topos* recurs, e.g. in the criticism of neglectful fathers at [Plut.] *De liberis educandis* 2e (trans. Babbitt 1956): "What trees if they are neglected do not grow crooked and prove unfruitful? Yet if they receive right culture, they become fruitful, and bring their fruit to maturity" (Ποῖα δὲ δένδρα οὐκ ὀλιγωρηθέντα μὲν στρεβλὰ φύεται καὶ ἄκαρτα καθίσταται, τυχόντα δ᾽ ὀρθῆς παιδαγωγίας ἔγκαρπα γίγνεται καὶ τελεσφόρα;). See Bloomer 2006: 86.

typically refers to productive human intervention in the natural world as a form of praise of his addressees.[15] In *Silvae* 2.2, for example, the beauty, serenity, and productivity of the landscape dominated by Pollius Felix all serve as reflections of his ethical qualities,[16] while the river Vulturnus recounts the productive results of the construction of the *via Domitiana* in *Silvae* 4.3.[17] In his lament for Glaucias (*Silvae* 2.1), furthermore, the narrator uses the example of grafting as support for his argument that Atedius Melior's fosterage of the young freedman was in fact superior to the natural parenthood provided by other fathers: "I have seen branches grafted on to a different tree rise higher than their own."[18] The description of the sterile disorder that may result from a father's failure to "prune back" a young man's growth sharply contrasts with the typically positive account in the *Silvae* of the productive outcome of human intervention in the natural world. By calling attention to Crispinus' virtues, Statius confirms that his young *laudandus* has successfully avoided the hazards of instability and sterility that potentially threaten fatherless young men.

The second rhetorical strategy employed by Statius in order to address Crispinus' fatherlessness is to associate him with a number of older men who perform various functions as actual, potential, and figurative paternal surrogates. I briefly list them before proceeding to a more detailed discussion of the actual and potential surrogates. Crispinus' actual paternal surrogates include Statius and the emperor Domitian. The emperor serves in important aspects as Crispinus' primary paternal surrogate, using his legal authority to resolve conflict in the young man's family. Were Crispinus to travel to Britain, he would encounter potential paternal surrogates. The narrator claims that one of his father's adoring former subjects would gladly serve as his preceptor and recall aspects of Bolanus' governorship to him. Finally, like the other addressees of the *Silvae*, Statius' Crispinus inhabits a world made explicable through mythological comparisons and populated by mythological figures.[19] The gods themselves are suborned to serve as figurative surrogates for the fatherless young man.

The emperor Domitian performs the most significant surrogate role by intervening directly in Crispinus' family affairs. Before the occasion of

---

[15] In general, see Pavlovskis 1973.
[16] See Newlands 2002: 164–74; Nisbet 1978.
[17] *Silv.* 4.3.72–94; see Smolenaars 2006; for a reading of the negative aspects of human intervention in this poem, see Newlands 2002: 284–325.
[18] *Vidi ego transertos alieno in robore ramos | altius ire suis, Silv.* 2.1.101–2. For fuller discussion, see Bernstein 2005.
[19] On mythological speakers in the *Silvae*, see K. M. Coleman 1999; on mythological comparisons, see Szelest 1972; on both subjects, see Newlands 2002: *passim.*

Silvae 5.2, Crispinus' mother had been charged with the attempted poisoning of her son, which she would presumably not have dared had Bolanus been alive.[20] According to Statius, our only source of evidence, Domitian himself had passed judgment in the case and the mother was executed. By discharging a judiciary role, the emperor performs a function comparable to that of the *paterfamilias*, who was expected to convene a *consilium* in order to resolve intrafamilial disputes.[21] As mentioned above, Statius notes that Crispinus was left without a guardian (*sine praeside*) upon his father's death. By serving the emperor Domitian in his first appointment, however, Crispinus acquires a greater *praes* than any his father could have appointed. In the conclusion of the poem, the narrator addresses Crispinus with the following praise: "Happy are you who already now take your oath under the great guardian (*sub praeside*)!"[22] By presenting Domitian as the judge who resolves Crispinus' familial difficulties and the guardian who serves as the *praes* otherwise lacking upon his father's death, *Silvae* 5.2 counters any suggestions of scandal arising from Crispinus' fatherlessness and familial conflict.

The emperor's role as judge and *praes* is complemented by the participation of several other individuals as preceptors for Crispinus. Some of these figures occupy figuratively paternal roles. In proposing to educate Crispinus through reference to his father's example, Statius aligns himself and his *laudandus* with a famous father–son pair, Aeneas and his son Ascanius:

Learn, boy (for you need not seek the beautiful love of courage from an unrelated preceptor; let the praise of your relatives nurture your spirit. Let the Decii and the returning Camilli be taught to others), learn of your father ...[23]

In the *Aeneid* Aeneas similarly instructs Ascanius to recall the examples of his family members, in particular his father and maternal uncle, as inspiration for his own conduct.[24] The passage of *Silvae* 5.2 evokes this scene of the *Aeneid* both in its opening phrase (*disce, puer*) and in its similar situation of a preceptor's presenting the example of a father as inspiration to a son. Statius

---

[20] White (1973: 282–4) suggests that the desire to secure Crispinus' share of his inheritance may have been the motive for his mother's murder attempt. His older brother may have already inherited: according to White, *aequaevo ... fratri* (*Silv.* 5.2.75) implies that they are members of the same generation, not twins.

[21] For the family *consilium*, see Treggiari 1991a: 264–75; Dixon 1992: 47.

[22] *Felix qui magno iam nunc sub praeside iuras* (*Silv.* 5.2.176).

[23]
    disce, puer (nec enim externo monitore petendus
    virtutis tibi pulcher amor: cognata ministret
    laus animos. aliis Decii reducesque Camilli
    monstrentur), tu disce patrem ...   (*Silv.* 5.2.51–4).

[24] Verg. *Aen.* 12.435–40. Aeneas adapts Hector's similar prayer for his son Astyanax (Hom. *Il.* 6.476–81). See Petrini 1997: 106–8.

presumes to serve as Crispinus' preceptor and educate him in the manner of Aeneas instructing his son Ascanius. Yet he cleverly permits the young man to appear as if he has already outstripped his teacher. Crispinus praises the emperor's *pietas* in passing the negative judgment against his mother (*Silv.* 5.2.84–94), a contrast with the attitude assumed by Statius' narrator, who vituperates Crispinus' mother.[25] The contrast that Statius constructs between the attitudes assumed by his narrator and his addressee Crispinus, coupled with the narrator's eventual rhetorical capitulation and praise of Crispinus' forgiving attitude toward his mother (*Silv.* 5.2.97), further supports the poem's argument that the young man has no need of guardians because he has already begun to surpass the wisdom of his preceptors.

Silvae 5.2 introduces a further series of preceptors who supplement the surrogate roles performed by Domitian and the narrator by exhorting Crispinus to emulate his father, by shielding him from criticism and attesting to his maturity. Should Crispinus travel to Britain, where his father once served as governor, Statius imagines that an anonymous Caledonian subject would also take up the preceptor's task of relating Bolanus' deeds:

> Then an elderly inhabitant of that harsh land shall tell you: "Here your father was accustomed to dispense justice … He himself put on this cuirass when battle called, this one he stripped from a British king." Just so Phoenix told Pyrrhus about Achilles, a man unknown to him, as he prepared to make successful wars against the Trojans.[26]

Where the narrator's preceptorial role is compared to a father's (Aeneas instructing Ascanius), the Caledonian's role is compared to a surrogate father's. In the comparison that concludes this section, Statius compares Crispinus' hearing about his father from the Caledonian to the fatherless Pyrrhus' hearing about his dead father, Achilles, from his paternal surrogate, Phoenix.[27] Domitian, Statius, the Caledonian, and even divine preceptors[28]

---

[25] *Silv.* 5.2.77–82. Nauta (2002: 307) criticizes Statius for his tactlessness in alluding to the affair at such length and suggests that Crispinus needed the poet's help in stressing his favor with the emperor. By contrast, Zeiner (2005: 203–4) observes the encomiastic function of the parallel that Statius draws between the emperor, who exhibits *pietas* toward the entire world, and Crispinus who exhibits it toward his mother's memory.

[26]
           cum tibi longaevus referet trucis incola terrae:
           "hic suetus dare iura parens …
                 … hunc ipse vocantibus armis
           induit, hunc regi rapuit thoraca Britanno,"
           qualiter in Teucros victricia bella paranti
           ignotum Pyrrho Phoenix narrabit Achillem.   (*Silv.* 5.2.143–4, 148–51)

[27] *Silv.* 5.2.150–1. [Plut.] *De lib. educ.* 4b again provides a parallel: the ideal pedagogue should serve his charge as Phoenix served Achilles.

[28] Mars, Minerva, Castor, and Quirinus educate Crispinus in warfare (*Silv.* 5.2.128–31).

perform the educational role that Bolanus, had he lived, would otherwise have fulfilled for his son.

In her recent study of the *Silvae* Noelle Zeiner has detailed the numerous rhetorical strategies through which Statius performs his characteristic role of "licensed spokesperson" for his patrons and addressees.[29] On her reading, *Silvae* 5.2 is a work of encomiastic advocacy for Crispinus, which singles out his particular forms of distinction (youth and descent) for praise even as it justifies his precocious career ambitions. This section has examined how *Silvae* 5.2 approaches the subject of Crispinus' fatherlessness within the context of praise of the young man's numerous distinctions. Statius begins by praising the virtues of Crispinus' character, which enable him to avoid the hazards that beset fatherless young men. He next furnishes him with a series of paternal surrogates who fulfill many of the functions that Bolanus would have otherwise discharged, such as resolving family conflict and educating his son through example. The poem appeals both to the authority of the emperor as judge and *praeses* and to that of its poet as preceptor outstripped by his precocious student. Through this carefully calculated strategy of presenting his addressee, Statius addresses fatherlessness as one potential challenge to Crispinus' public image, among others such as his precocity and his mother's criminal prosecution. The promising young man, according to his encomiast's admiring narrative, successfully overcomes each challenge.

PLINY THE YOUNGER, THE "ANELLO CONNETTIVO" LINKING THE OLDER GENERATION WITH THE YOUNGER

Where Statius offers an encomium of a young man who has not yet fulfilled his considerable promise, the younger Pliny's collection of *Letters* includes a series of retrospective accounts detailing aspects of his highly successful career. Pliny's *Letters* record the transmission of jural identity by paternal surrogates, their provision of political support, and the exemplary behavior enacted by the surrogates and emulated by their figurative descendant. The letters provide examples of these activities as performed both by the paternal surrogates who supported Pliny's own early career and by Pliny himself in his role as a paternal surrogate for select members of the next generation. This section examines how these carefully presented autobiographical narratives are linked conceptually to two of Pliny's commentaries on the

---

[29] See Zeiner 2005: 45–74.

political situation of his own day.[30] These include his account of the "restoration of liberty" (*reducta libertas*) to the Senate in Letter 8.14 and his praise of Trajan as the ideal adoptee in the *Panegyricus* (chs. 7–11). In Pliny's work, surrogacy serves as a governing paradigm both for the author's personal experience and for ideal imperial governance.[31]

Though never directly mentioning his biological father, who died when he was still a minor,[32] Pliny credits a series of paternal surrogates with advancing his early progress through the ranks of the imperial bureaucracy. These men include Verginius Rufus, his *tutor* (*Ep.* 2.1.8); his maternal uncle, the elder Pliny, who adopted him by testament after his death in 79 (*Ep.* 5.8.5); Cornutus, an older colleague whom Pliny "followed as a teacher and honored as a father"; and Corellius Rufus, whom he treats as a figurative father in his account of the older man's death (*Ep.* 1.12).[33] Pliny praises Verginius for offering support that went far beyond the limited legal obligations of a *tutor*. He concludes his encomium by noting that the senior statesman, who lacked a son of his own, used him as a symbolically filial representative instead. In instructing Pliny to serve as his representative in making his excuses to a senatorial committee, Verginius remarks: "Even if I had a son, I would still entrust this to you."[34]

While Pliny represents men such as Verginius Rufus and Corellius Rufus as political supporters, exemplary models, and moral instructors, he also takes pains to declare his independence from them. He distances himself from them so as not to let their greater *auctoritas* appear to overwhelm him.[35] This process is the reverse of his treatment of the elder Pliny. Pliny honors his maternal uncle and adoptive father as his *domesticum exemplum* (*Ep.* 5.8.4). Yet as consular, friend of Trajan, and author of the *Panegyricus*, the younger Pliny surpasses the elder Pliny in social rank, literary achievement, and mode

---

[30] For Pliny's *Letters* as autobiographical narratives, see (among many others) Henderson 2002a: 43–153; Shelton 1987.

[31] As Henderson (2002a: 149) observes, the relation between a paternal surrogate (dynastic, private, and figurative) and his fictive kin serves a paradigmatic function for Pliny, recurring in a number of contexts throughout his corpus: " 'Trajan adopted by old Nerva' … is replicated by 'Pliny "adopted" by Verginius and Spurinna, then adopted by uncle C. Plinius Secundus.' " See further Bernstein 2008.

[32] Sherwin-White (1968: 70) observes that Pliny's father must have died before his son was fourteen, as Verginius Rufus was appointed as Pliny's *tutor legitimus* (cf. *Ep.* 2.1.8). Geoffrey Nathan's chapter in the present volume provides suggestive parallels. Both Stilicho and Symmachus assumed the duties of guardianship for the fatherless Honorius and Boethius respectively. In the *Consolation of Philosophy*, as discussed by Nathan, Boethius praises his fosterer and father-in-law, Symmachus, for his superlative performance of surrogate paternity, though in less specific and extensive terms than Pliny.

[33] *Cum sequerer ut magistrum, ut parentem vererer* (*Ep.* 5.14.5). For the death of Corellius, see Hoffer 1999: 141–59.

[34] *Etiam si filium haberem, tibi mandarem* (*Ep.* 2.1.9).   [35] See Hoffer 1999: 155–6.

of life.[36] Rather than imitate the elder Pliny, the younger Pliny in fact makes his own selection of preferential models from the successful men of the older generation. The rhetoric of fictive kinship frames his self-presentation as the figurative son of the men who once supported his early political career.

Having profited from the support of these members of the older generation, Pliny in turn attempts to serve as a patron, political supporter, and instructive model to people in the younger generation. Roberto Gazich has accordingly described Pliny as the "anello connettivo" linking the older generation with the younger.[37] The beneficiaries of Pliny's patronage and instruction include Junius Avitus, whom Pliny instructs on the etiquette of *amicitia* (*Ep.* 2.6); Genialis (*Ep.* 8.13), whom Pliny commends for studying his speeches; Fuscus Salinator and Ummidius Quadratus, who "look to [Pliny] as a guide, as a teacher";[38] and numerous other younger individuals for whom Pliny stands in as a surrogate parent.[39] Some of Pliny's beneficiaries are known to have been fatherless (such as the children of Arulenus Rusticus, who was executed by Domitian in 93),[40] and there is no reason to assume that the demographic incidence of fatherlessness as indicated by Saller's microsimulation affected Pliny's circle any differently from any other sample of upper-class Romans. Yet in almost all cases, whether benefiting a fatherless child or one with an intact family, Pliny indicates that he is serving in a supplementary parental role. In Goody's terms, he shares the work of sponsorship and training with other parents and surrogates rather than attempting to exclusively control the parental role. He observes throughout his letter to Junius Mauricus (*Ep.* 2.18), for example, that he searches for a *tutor* for the children of Arulenus Rusticus only at the direction of their uncle Mauricus, who is now responsible for them after his brother's execution. He similarly describes himself to Quintilianus "as if another father of this girl of ours" (*tamquam parens alter puellae nostrae*, *Ep.* 6.32.2) when giving 50,000 sesterces to Quintilianus' daughter. Pliny's indications that he has no child of his own (expressed most pointedly in his

[36] As Cova 2001 has shown, the younger Pliny explicitly signals Verginius' *tranquillitas* and Vestricius Spurinna's *otium* as better models for his own life than the elder Pliny's ceaseless *vigilia* and *studia*. See also Henderson 2002a: 69–102.

[37] Gazich 2003: 132.

[38] *Ipsi me ut rectorem, ut magistrum intuebantur* (*Ep.* 6.11.2); Pliny in turn serves them "as an exemplar" (*quasi exemplar*, *Ep.* 6.11.3). For Pliny's role as an instructive figure, see Gazich 2003; Guillemin 1929: 32–40; Gerini 1894: 172–82.

[39] Henderson (2002b: 218) observes Pliny's use of the "metaphor of the 'extended family'" in his patronage of Romatius Firmus (*Ep.* 1.19). Hoffer (1999: 93–110) discusses Pliny's role as the symbolic "father" of Comum in the context of a system of imperial patronage that discouraged child-rearing among the upper classes.

[40] See Sherwin-White 1968: 95.

letters on Calpurnia's miscarriages, *Epp.* 8.10 and 8.11) present an implicit incentive for him to serve in the role of a paternal surrogate. He can trust more certainly in the young men whom he supports to carry on his legacy than a child of his own who may never materialize. Given his advanced age (in Roman terms) at the time of publication of the final books of *Letters*, he would not in any event have been able to observe a child of his own growing to maturity.[41]

In his collection of letters Pliny uses the rhetoric of surrogate paternity to present himself as the figurative son of the older men who supported his earlier political career. He presents an educational theory in Letter 8.14 that legitimates both the benefits that he received from these paternal surrogates and his own efforts to instruct young men. This letter presents an important contrast between the present day, the Flavian period, and previous eras of Roman history.[42] Pliny claims that, in contrast to the debased era of his young manhood, when according to him military discipline was lax and the senate was "fearful and tongueless" (*curiam trepidam et elinguem, Ep.* 8.14.8), upper-class young men once had models of military and political excellence to observe and from whom to learn. They learned their craft by watching their fathers perform as soldiers and senators. If they were fatherless at that age, like Pliny and a significant percentage of the Roman upper class, then they watched another respected older man:

There was the tradition in former times that we learned from our elders not only with our ears but also with our eyes. Thereby we would have the principles on which we would soon act and which we would pass on in turn to our descendants. Thus young men received instruction initially through military service, so that, by obeying, they would become accustomed to command others; while following, to lead as commanders. While seeking offices as candidates, they stood outside the doors of the senate house and were spectators of public debate before they were participants. Each man's father served as his teacher, or some older and more distinguished man would stand in for the man who did not have a father.[43]

[41] Sherwin-White (1968: 41) places the publication of Books 8 and 9 in 107/8, when Pliny was forty-five or forty-six at the youngest. His birth date is deduced from his claim that he had passed his seventeenth birthday at the time of the eruption of Vesuvius in August, 79 (*Ep.* 6.20.5). While Pliny's hopes of fathering children at his age were entirely reasonable, his chances of living to see a son reach maturity were not high. Frier's life table for the Roman Empire suggests a life expectancy of fifteen years for a man aged forty-five, with a 17 percent chance of dying before the age of fifty; see Parkin 1992: 144. In the event, Pliny would die childless in Bithynia.
[42] See Gazich 2003: 127–31; Beutel 2000: 179–83, 258–62; Gazich 1992: 149–50.
[43] *Erat autem antiquitus institutum, ut a maioribus natu non auribus modo verum etiam oculis disceremus, quae facienda mox ipsi ac per vices quasdam tradenda minoribus haberemus. inde adulescentuli statim castrensibus stipendiis imbuebantur ut imperare parendo, duces agere dum sequuntur adsuescerent; inde honores petituri adsistebant curiae foribus, et consilii publici spectatores ante quam consortes erant. suus cuique parens pro magistro, aut cui parens non erat maximus quisque et vetustissimus pro parente (Ep. 8.14.4–6).*

Pliny's account does not specify exactly when in the past (*antiquitus*) one should imagine that this idealized era of virtuous soldiering and independent politics occurred. What comes through clearly instead is the important contrast, elaborated at far greater length in the *Panegyricus*, between the terrified and passive Domitianic senate and the newly liberated senate attempting to get its bearings in the era of *reducta libertas* under Trajan.[44] The interest of this letter for the present argument lies in its representation of an idealized educational tradition performed in part by paternal surrogates. Through his description of a model of education in which paternal surrogates as well as biological fathers may participate, Pliny implicitly authorizes his efforts both to honor his early supporters and to serve as a patron and exemplary model to other men's children. He thereby guides the reader's reception of his earlier representations of his own development as a fatherless statesman and author who benefited from the training and sponsorship of paternal surrogates.

Pliny's idealization of the educational tradition of prior times in Letter 8.14, summed up through the claim that each man observed his father or found a respected surrogate to serve as his teacher, draws on a lengthy Roman literary tradition of nominating the father as the ideal educator. Roman literary tradition privileges the relationship between father and son as the ideal context for moral and political pedagogy. The father who writes literature for the instruction of his son represents his paternal and didactic authority as coextensive. In this tradition, filial emulation of a good father represents the best means of forming another good man. Yet fathers such as Cato the Elder who served as the personal educators of their own children were in fact exceptional. In practice, the Roman upper-class young man was far more likely to receive his education from child-minders, pedagogues, and various professional instructors.[45] Roman didactic authors nevertheless lay claim to the traditional authority of the *paterfamilias* and assimilate it to their role as public educators. Such authority can appear to be biologically based when appealed to by writers such as the elder Cato, Cicero, and the elder Seneca, who dedicated their didactic works to living sons.[46] The most famous *dictum* that the elder Cato produced for his son's benefit regards

---

[44] See Beutel 2000: 179–83, 258–62.

[45] As Bloomer (2006: 72–3) emphatically states: "The idea that a father of the elite class would educate his own son was almost nonsensical … The performance of such [educational] tasks by delegated agents, while partly functional and efficient, also advertised the status of the owner, the man who does not have to work." See also Bonner 1977. For the elder Cato as the educator of his children, see Plut. *Cat. Mai.* 20. Pliny praises Genialis for studying his speeches with his father (*Ep.* 8.13).

[46] LeMoine 1991 traces the theme from the elder Cato through the Church Fathers.

the character of the orator, as quoted by the elder Seneca: "What then did that man [Cato] say? 'An orator, Marcus my son, is a good man skilled in speaking.'"[47] Seneca uses Cato's *dictum* to frame the contrast between his sons, good men who will be good orators, and the depraved orators of his own day who claim other people's sayings as their own and prove through their effeminate behavior that they are hardly men (*Controv.* 1. *praef.* 6–10). Though Cicero dedicated a greater number of his philosophical works to non-relatives, he addressed the *Partitiones oratoriae* and the *De officiis* to his son Marcus.[48] Pliny appears to reassert this tradition in a letter that envisions an ideal past in which fathers preferentially served as their sons' teachers. He adds the important detail, however, that senior, unrelated men may substitute as educators for the fatherless.[49]

Though the *Panegyricus* focuses on a different social context from the personal letters, the imperial regime rather than Pliny's circle of aristocratic friends, Pliny nevertheless activates similar themes of parental surrogacy. The contrast that Pliny briefly presents in Letter 8.14 between the constrained era of Domitian and the liberated era of Trajan resurfaces as one of the dominant conceptual oppositions that structures the *Panegyricus*. The model of surrogate parenthood that he presents in Letter 8.14 can therefore be read in the additional context of dynastic surrogacy, also a major theme of the *Panegyricus*. The Julio-Claudians had practiced intrafamilial adoption, while the Flavian emperors Titus and Domitian had succeeded their biological father, Vespasian. Galba adopted Piso, an unrelated person, at the beginning of the war of 68–9, but Otho's coup precluded his establishment of a stable succession.[50] Nerva's adoption of Trajan therefore had a conceptual precedent in Galba's choice of successor, but Trajan's peaceful accession and stable regime – which, three years into his reign, form the subjects of Pliny's effusive praise – were without imperial parallel. The peaceful transition of power to an adopted yet unrelated emperor represented a new dynastic strategy which would be employed successfully throughout the rest of the century.

In the *Panegyricus* Pliny praises Nerva for his choice to adopt Trajan and makes no direct mention of Trajan's biological father. Nerva's adoption of

---

[47] *Ille ergo vir quid ait? "Orator est, Marce fili, vir bonus dicendi peritus,"* Sen. *Controv.* 1. *praef.* 9, 10. The elder Cato addressed advice to his son on a number of topics, including rhetoric, medicine, and agriculture. See Sen. *Controv.* 1. *praef.* 9; Plin. *HN* 29.14; Serv. *ad Verg. Geo.* 1.46; Jordan 1860: 77–80.

[48] As Dyck (1996: 12) observes, the latter work in particular was "deeply embedded in the father–son relation. It was meant as a call to order, an emphatic reminder of his responsibilities to himself, his family, and his society."

[49] Quintilian also observes that the educator may also stand *in loco parentis* (*Inst.* 2.9.1, 12.11.5).

[50] Tac. *Hist.* 1.12–19; Suet. *Galb.* 17; Plut. *Galb.* 23; Cassius Dio 64.5; *CIL* VI.2051.

his successor is represented as the most significant and praiseworthy event of his brief reign, as well as its fitting climax:

Your prayers were heard, but only so long as this served the interests of that august and venerable ruler; for the gods claimed him to take his place in the heavens, thinking that nothing merely mortal should follow his godlike and immortal act and that the honor proper to a noble deed was for this deed to be the last of its author, who should then be deified at once so that one day posterity might wonder whether he was already god when his last deed was done. Thus his highest claim to be the Father of his country was his being father to you; and this was his greatest glory and renown: once he had had ample proof that the Empire rested securely on your shoulders he left the world to you and you to the world, beloved and regretted by all for that very act of foresight intended to ensure that there need be no regrets.[51]

By relating Nerva's role as *publicus parens* to his surrogate paternity of Trajan, Pliny recapitulates on a grander level the image presented in the personal letters of the surrogate parent as patron, educator, and benefactor. The childless Pliny presumes to benefit unrelated young men, just as his own paternal surrogates had benefited him in his early career. By the same token, Nerva's virtuous act of paternal surrogacy enables him to benefit the entire Roman people.[52] The emphasis on Nerva's surrogacy of Trajan as opposed to direct paternity also enables Pliny to present Trajan as a paradoxical figure containing aspects of divinity and humanity.[53] The quasi-divine emperor, who will become fully divine upon his death, is neither limited by his physical inheritance from his biological father nor his dynastic inheritance from his political successor. Trajan acquires jural identity and political legitimacy from his predecessor, Nerva, yet distances himself from his paternal surrogate and eventually supersedes him through a more successful imperial career. In these respects, Trajan performs the same exchange with Nerva as Pliny with some of his paternal surrogates, in particular the elder Pliny. The *Panegyricus*' representation of surrogacy may therefore be read as conceptually coextensive with that of the personal letters.

---

[51] *Audita sunt tua vota, sed in quantum optimo illi et sanctissimo seni utile fuit, quem di ideo caelo vindicauerunt, ne quid post illud divinum et immortale factum mortale faceret: deberi quippe maximo operi hanc venerationem, ut novissimum esset, auctoremque eius statim consecrandum, ut quandoque inter posteros quaereretur, an illud iam deus fecisset. Ita ille nullo magis nomine publicus parens, quam quia tuus. Ingens gloria ingensque fama: cum abunde expertus esset, quam bene umeris tuis sederet imperium, tibi terras te terris reliquit, eo ipso carus omnibus ac desiderandus, quod prospexerat ne desideraretur* (*Pan.* 10.4–6). Translation adapted from Radice 1969.
[52] For the Roman emperor as the figuratively paternal benefactor of the people, see T. R. Stevenson 1992.
[53] On the antithesis between Trajan's humanity and divinity in the *Panegyricus*, see Rees 2001: especially 162–4.

CONCLUSION

Rather than sinking into obscurity, the fatherless men studied in this paper increase their social and political capital by forming multiple relationships with paternal surrogates. The success enjoyed by Crispinus and Pliny, however, should not obscure the fact that fatherlessness may have posed a significant obstacle to those unable to form adequate relationships with paternal surrogates. The goal of this study has not been to generalize these men's experiences, to represent them as typical of an upper-class Roman norm, but rather to indicate how each chose to address his fatherlessness within the context of a calculated strategy of literary self-presentation. In this respect, Geoffrey Nathan's chapter in the present volume complements this one, as many of the rhetorical strategies examined in this chapter will recur in literary representations of surrogacy among the late antique Christian elite.

In *Silvae* 5.2 the favor of the emperor Domitian grants incontestable legitimacy to Crispinus' precocious political career, while Crispinus' outstripping of his preceptor Statius indicates that he is already a fully mature individual without need of guardianship. The poem also serves as an imperial encomium, honoring the emperor for his role in resolving familial disputes and restoring *pietas* to the world. In Pliny's *Letters*, Verginius Rufus, Corellius Rufus, and the elder Pliny serve as political mentors and literary models for the younger Pliny that surpass those offered by his unmentioned biological father. Pliny in turn increases his own *auctoritas* by offering himself as an exemplary model to young men of the succeeding generation, even those whose fathers are still living. Pliny's claims that the paternal surrogate can serve as an educator and public benefactor gain further point when read in the contexts of *reducta libertas* in Letter 8.14 and of Nerva's dynastic adoption of the emperor Trajan in the *Panegyricus*. Across Pliny's works the theme of paternal surrogacy permits him to account for the successes both of his own career and of the new imperial regime. Statius and Pliny represent interaction with paternal surrogates as offering opportunities unavailable in a biological relationship. In each case, surrogate paternity transcends biological paternity and permits the young man to overcome the challenges of bereavement. Nor are the interests of the paternal surrogate himself forgotten. Both Statius' account of serving as preceptor for Crispinus and Pliny's accounts of the transmission of patronage, instruction, and political and economic support across three generations show how serving as a paternal surrogate can add to the surrogate's social and cultural capital.

CHAPTER 14

The education of orphans: a reassessment of the evidence of Libanius

Raffaella Cribiore

> How should I rate my orphan state? I would have been so glad to see my father in his old age, but I know this for certain, that if my father had reached a ripe old age, I would now be engaged upon a different life path.

So says Libanius in the first part of his *Autobiography* (*Or.* 1.6), in which he attempted to appraise the positive and negative influence of certain events on his life.[1] The loss of his father when he was an eleven-year-old boy apparently was not a catastrophe that shattered his life. The sophist's regret at being deprived of the comfort of a fatherly presence was counterbalanced by his realization that the event had unforeseen positive consequences. His father would not have allowed him the many years of study he enjoyed but instead would have prevented his academic career and made sure that he engaged in local politics, the law courts, or the imperial administration. Paradoxically, therefore, his personal loss allowed Libanius a degree of freedom from parental control that permitted him to follow his calling.

Libanius' orations, and particularly the narrative of his life, reveal circumstances that might temper the harshness of an orphan state and which allowed him to become an acclaimed sophist and teacher in fourth-century Antioch.[2] The letters of Libanius, too, introduce to the reader many of the students who attended his school of rhetoric – almost 200 young men, of

---

[1] For the text of Libanius, see Förster 1903–27. Translations of his orations appear in Norman 1965; 1969–77; and 1992, and translations of his letters in Bradbury 2004 and Cribiore 2007a, 233–321. Fortune is the subject of *Or.* 1.1–155, composed as a complete oration with a guiding theme. The rest of this speech (156–285) is an ensemble of memoirs that was appended in a disorderly fashion after Libanius' death. The people appearing in this chapter are identified either according to the prosopography of Seeck 1906 or according to the listing in *PLRE* I. Seeck listed those who appear in Libanius' letters with their names followed by Roman numerals. Most of the students and members of their families need to be cited according to this prosopography because they were not of such a status as to be included in *PLRE*. The names of those who are included in the latter prosopography are followed by Arabic numbers.

[2] He was born in 314 CE and died *c.* 393 CE. On Libanius as teacher of rhetoric, see most recently Cribiore 2007a.

257

whom 134 can be placed in a period of fifteen school years.[3] Many of these
letters are sent to students' fathers and address their concerns regarding
their sons' academic progress and behavior. In late antiquity fathers closely
controlled their sons' education and apparently determined its duration,
sometimes withdrawing the young men from school so that they might
embark on economically advantageous careers. But the fact that at least a
quarter of the students of Libanius appear to have lost their fathers before or
during their attendance at his school[4] shows the effect on late antique
society of high mortality and comparatively late male marriage. These
data are in full agreement with what one would expect from demographic
tables if one takes into account that it is quite likely that the orphan state of
some students escapes us.[5] Libanius did not dwell on every student's life
story but mentioned most of them in passing. Libanius' writings, therefore,
offer strong test cases for the issue I am considering, that is, the influence of
an orphan state on advanced education. Bearing in mind the sophist's own
experience, it is possible to evaluate the factors that affected the education of
the fatherless young men who figure in his writings. A recent, thorough study
of the condition of widows and orphans in the Roman period considered the
works of Libanius among other late antique evidence. Krause concluded that
orphans had great difficulty in paying for their studies and that fatherless
boys at the age of fourteen or fifteen (that is, at the start of their education in
rhetoric) were underrepresented among the sophist's students because of the
obstacles they encountered.[6] In this chapter I revisit the orations and letters of
Libanius to see if Krause's conclusions can be fully validated.

The data derived from Libanius' writings pertain to individuals who
belonged to the upper levels of society and could afford an education in
rhetoric.[7] Though we do not know precisely the cost of higher education,
the general consensus based on the ancient sources is that teachers derived a
large part of their income from their pupils' tuition and gifts. Financial
compensation of teachers and the maintenance of students who lived away

---

[3] See Petit 1956: 60–1. These are students who attended in the periods 354–65 and 388–93.
[4] See the table of orphan students in Petit 1956: 138, which is incomplete. To these one should add
Eusebius xx; Iamblichus 2; the sons of Hestiaeus; the brother of Philoxenus, Thalassius 2 (*Ep.* 330);
John Chrysostom, and Basil the Great.
[5] Cf. Scheidel (this volume). Since Libanius often alludes in passing to his students without enlarging on
their lives, it is possible that even more orphans attended his classes.
[6] See Krause 1994–5: III, 182–3. Some students joined the school at a younger age, as for example the
fifteen-year-old in *Or.* 34.3, who was already capable of declaiming at that age and must have entered
the school quite young.
[7] On the attitudes of the elite classes toward education, see Watts 2006: 6–19.

from home were often a burden on their families.[8] Besides a few sons of teachers or of minor decurions,[9] the vast majority of Libanius' students came from propertied classes with traditions of culture and education. Libanius taught not only pagan but also some Christian youths, but his letters disclose the religion of an addressee very rarely. This is not a hindrance to my study because, as Nathan argues in this volume, Christianity per se had a limited impact on support for elite children.

The legal issues regarding orphans are known already.[10] When a father died without officially nominating a *tutor* for his son who was still a minor (that is, younger than fourteen years old), close male kin (older brothers, uncles, and grandfathers) might become guardians of an orphan or, in the absence of suitable male guardians in the family, a magistrate could choose one or more guardians (ἐπίτροποι). On reaching the age of fourteen, boys were free of legal authority, yet sometimes curators were appointed to help young men younger than twenty-five to administer their properties.[11] Mothers were not always trusted with the property of a fatherless child, especially if they remarried; if they decided not to marry again, they could act as legal guardians of their children.[12]

Though Libanius does not explicitly say so, this appears to have been the role of his mother, who did not remarry and chose to be "everything" (τὰ πάντα) for her children. According to her son, "she feared the baseness of guardians and the inevitable necessity to go to court" that arose from their excesses.[13] This apparently indulgent woman provided for Libanius' schooling but was far from stern in his first years when he was a lazy, "sleeping" student. Nor did she interfere when Libanius became enamored of rhetoric at the age of fifteen and dedicated all his time to this passion. Yet, it is notable that years later when he declared his intention to leave Antioch to continue his studies in Athens, his loving and protective mother strongly opposed this wish, even though her powers were by then greatly curtailed. Unable to deter him, she turned to her brothers to prevent him from

[8] See Cribiore 2007a: 183–91.
[9] See, e.g., the son of the unimportant decurion (*curialis*) Cratinus, *Ep.* 93 and Silvanus, the son of the teacher Gaudentius *Ep.* 87 and *Or.* 38.
[10] See Saller 1994: 181–200.
[11] Such curators were called κουράτωρ or κηδεμών in the legal sources. Libanius was not particularly inclined to use legal terms in a proper way. He never used the first term and employed the suggestive word κηδεμών to indicate various functions, most often that of a pedagogue (see, e.g., *Epp.* 41 and 456).
[12] See Evans Grubbs 2002: 236–60 and especially 254–7. On the customs and laws regulating widows who remarried, see also Krause 1994–5: III, 157–91.
[13] See *Or.* 1.4. As a rule, Libanius uses the term ἐπίτροπος to indicate an orphan's guardian (e.g. *Epp.* 1172 and 1273). Only once (*Ep.* 319) does he employ this word to indicate overseers of land.

leaving, and their intervention was decisive. His older uncle told the young man to give up because he would never give his consent. It was only after this disapproving uncle died that Libanius was allowed to leave. His younger uncle in fact was on his side and persuaded his resisting mother.[14] The mother of Letoius, a student of Libanius, might also have had the same legal responsibility as a *tutor*.[15] This woman, who elicited the sophist's admiration because of her determination not to remarry even though she had only one child, wished to enroll her son in the school in Antioch and accompanied him on the long and difficult journey from Armenia to make sure that he had a smooth start. The letters concerning this student, however, show that she also relied on an uncle and a family friend who were involved in protecting and helping the family. They tried "to aid an orphan and not turn him over to those who wish to plunder him."[16] The evidence from Libanius apparently indicates that the authority of an uncle over a youth depended on his status, culture, and closeness to the sophist. If a maternal uncle was better positioned than a paternal one, he took control of the situation in protecting the young man and making sure that he was accepted in the school of Antioch.

The above cases exemplify the troubles encountered by widows in antiquity when they chose to maintain better control over their children by not remarrying. They had to rely on a circle of relatives and friends, provided these people were trustworthy. John Chrysostom, who belonged to a well-off family in which his father died after his birth and his young mother did not remarry, remarked that young widows had to discourage the claims of some relatives on their children's patrimony. They also found it difficult to maintain control over their households and to be obeyed by slaves.[17] Libanius confirms that the death of the head of the family might provide an opportunity for base slaves to harm the interests of the dead master's survivors.[18] Women who had lost their husbands supposedly had some trouble retaining a strong influence over pedagogues as well. As a rule, pedagogues assisted wealthy students *in loco parentis*. They represented the family, and their functions consisted of supervision of their wards' moral behavior and study habits and of practical help with academic difficulties

---

[14] *Or.* 1.11–13: his uncle told the tearful mother that the separation would not be of long duration and that education in Athens would bear much fruit. Both uncles, in any case, did not have legal power over young Libanius.

[15] Letoius iv. In this case we have to suppose that Letoius was not yet fourteen years old.

[16] See Libanius, *Ep.* 285 and 104. It is impossible to know if this uncle was paternal or maternal.

[17] Jo. Chrys. *De sacerdotio* 1.5 (Migne, *PG* 48.624); cf. Clark 1993: 61.

[18] *Or.* 18.290.

and health problems.[19] According to Libanius, their authority seems to have derived mainly from the student's father, who supervised in order to ensure that the process of education functioned well. Widows, who struggled to maintain mastery of their households, had limited power over them. When Libanius was studying in Antioch, people marveled at his self-control and serious engagement with grammar and rhetoric, to the point that some approached his uncles to offer their daughters to him in matrimony.[20] Libanius did not accept but agreed that he had been "incorruptible, and not because of the fearful vigilance of a pedagogue." He remarked that a pedagogue was powerless since he was an orphan, and Fortune had helped him with her providence.[21] Whereas the authority of an orphaned youth's pedagogue was generally impaired because he was unable to rely on a father's support, there were exceptions to the rule. Thus Libanius related the example of an attendant who had been able to become an orphan boy's guardian (ἐπίτροπος) and who was such a solicitous caregiver that his ward was not conscious of being bereft of a father.[22]

The assistance of an extended, caring family and especially the supervision of grandfathers and uncles contributed greatly to an orphan's success.[23] Bernstein in this volume shows the impact of paternal surrogates in assuring the success of some prominent orphans in the western Roman Empire. The larger evidence that Libanius offers for the Eastern world refers to surrogate parents within the family. Libanius sent two letters to the grandfather of a student who bore the name Libanius in his honor. The old man had brought young Libanius to school in lieu of the youth's father, Antiochus, who had attended the same school but was now dead.[24] The death of this father might have slowed down his son's application, since Libanius remarked that "albeit late, finally" he had this student.[25] Antiochus, who "should have lived to bring his son to us, just as an athlete brings his son to the same trainer," is an important presence in these letters. The sophist rejoiced at the physical resemblance between father and son (they had the same face and

---

[19] See Cribiore 2001: 47–50.
[20] *Or.* 1.12. Of course we have no way of testing the veracity of his report.
[21] We are in the dark about the status of pedagogues of orphans. They apparently continued their services, but it is unclear to whom they had to respond.
[22] *Or.* 58.11. We do not know how old this boy was but he must have been under fourteen years of age because Libanius uses the expression "lawful guardian."
[23] Krause 1994–5: III, 49–77. Cf. in this volume Harders on the role of Augustus as uncle in raising Anthony's children.
[24] *Epp.* 1020 and 1034.
[25] Yet this expression is not unique. The sophist was always impatient to receive the scions of the best families.

voice!) and confessed that he often had the impression that Antiochus himself was at the school, telling him about his child "the sort of things that a father says about his son." But it is the conduct of the grandfather that attracts attention since he stepped fully into the role as primary caregiver. He kept up a correspondence with his grandson, communicated with Libanius by letter, and sent him a large quantity of wine as compensation for or in appreciation of his services. The sophist highly esteemed his writing style, which far from being weak and uninspired (as the old man feared) showed "a man in his prime," and he strongly encouraged him to continue writing to his grandson. Young Libanius was learning to compose well-wrought, rhetorical letters by being exposed to the letters of the ancient writers and could benefit from the masterful letters of his grandfather as well.[26]

The chances of a father's outliving his adult son were naturally less than the opposite. Only one other grandfather who was involved in his grandson's education emerges from Libanius' correspondence.[27] Usually uncles (on both the mother's and the father's side) assisted widows in the upbringing of their children. The evidence provided by the family of the wealthy Agesilaus of Ancyra in Galatia permits us to see the various mechanisms set into motion when the head of the family died before his time.[28] Before Libanius started to teach in Antioch he had met Agesilaus in Galatia. Since Agesilaus wanted to make sure that both of his sons, Strategius and Albanius, learned rhetoric with the sophist, he personally took them to Antioch in 355, where they soon were numbered among Libanius' favorite students in spite of their short attendance. Strategius, who may have been exposed to rhetoric before, remained in Antioch for only one year, but his irreproachable performance allowed Libanius to consider him one of his "sons." In writing a letter of recommendation for him,[29] the sophist remarked to the addressee:

You will surely not be cross with me because I call a student this. He was one of the many who studied with me but was one of the few above reproach, and yet, he was always with me, studying and sharing my table, the afternoon work, and all the other things that befit a young man who is trusted because of his character.

---

[26] On practicing epistolary skills at the school of the grammarian, see Cribiore 2001: 215–19; and on writing letters in rhetorical school, see Cribiore 2007a: 169–73.
[27] The grandfather of the student Diophantus was also interested in his education when the boy's father was still alive, cf. *Epp.* 465 and 601 from the years 355 to 357. It is possible, however, that the latter was dead when Libanius sent the grandfather a last letter (*Ep.* 766) in the year 362.
[28] On the letters that regard the various members of this family, see Festugière 1959: 153–9.
[29] *Ep.* 287.2. The addressee was then the governor of Armenia and Strategius wanted to have a position.

Albanius, the younger brother, would have liked to continue his studies beyond the two years he was allowed to with Libanius and in fact showed great promise of becoming a scholar. His brief training in rhetoric permitted him to produce work that aroused the admiration of an eminent rhetor, particularly when he delivered a panegyric on Domitius Modestus, the powerful *comes orientis* (Count of the East) who was stationed in Antioch.[30] Libanius nurtured the hope that the boy would follow his example and embark on an academic career, but in vain. Parents considered some training in rhetoric useful, but often found the lengthy training necessary to become a sophist superfluous and counterproductive. Early involvement in practical activities and employment in the administration were more desirable even when financial need was not an issue. The death of a father might complicate the scenario. When Albanius' father died, his mother was responsible for pulling him out of school. She did not have the legal power to do it, but her son responded to emotional pressure, "her crying and begging."[31] Albanius entered public service and became part of the retinue of the governor of Galatia as a rhetor: by 363 he was already wealthy in his own right.[32]

A few years later Libanius again dealt with the same powerful family and confronted the educational needs of an orphan one more time. The sister of Strategius and Albanius was married and had a son, Eusebius, whom Libanius had held in his arms as a baby when he passed through Galatia years before.[33] Being part of such a family, this boy was destined to become a student of the sophist. When his father died in 364, Eusebius' maternal uncles brought him to Antioch to introduce him to their former teacher.[34] They would have probably done so even had his father been alive, since Libanius does not seem to have been well acquainted with his old students' brother-in-law. But in addition to the welcome visit, Libanius also received a letter of recommendation from the boy's paternal uncle, who did not know the sophist but made sure to exhort him to take care of Eusebius.[35] One more letter, from a former teacher of rhetoric, to whom Libanius responded with impeccable *savoir faire*, completed this student's application.[36] Not so many people were involved when other students applied to the school in Antioch because letters from their fathers were deemed

---

[30] Modestus 2. [31] *Ep.* 1444.2.
[32] See *Ep.* 834, sent to this governor. Since the sophist was always afraid of critics who suggested that he had very few successful students, he encouraged the governor to be very stern with Albanius and other young men who were his former students and not to let them slacken.
[33] The youth was Eusebius xx; his father was Eusebius xix.
[34] See *Ep.* 1240.
[35] See *Ep.* 1241, sent to Olympius viii where Libanius reminded him of all his debts toward the family.
[36] See *Ep.* 1242. Androcles, a local sophist from Ancyra, had given the rudiments of the art to the boy.

sufficient,[37] and thus one might conclude that the application of an orphan set into motion a longer chain of contacts. Yet, besides that, the loss of his father apparently had no repercussions on Eusebius' education.

Was this student an exception? Other young men who lost their fathers before embarking on higher studies or at the beginning of their attendance do not seem to have encountered excessive difficulty in acquiring an education.[38] Students who belonged to wealthy families had at their disposal an effective support system according to which surviving members of the family endeavored to help them pursue the education which their rank demanded. The world of rhetoric was a man's world. Some women who came from prominent families with traditions of paideia attended the school of the grammarian (the second stage of education) but did not have access to a rhetorical school, which served the needs of those destined for public life. Thus the women to whom Libanius wrote are few and are exceptional in their achievements.[39] Unlike fathers, therefore, mothers did not directly approach the sophist with letters of recommendation for their sons, yet they could facilitate their acceptance, and their voices reached Libanius in other ways. Widows were active behind the scenes in soliciting the help of relatives and friends and expressing through them their concerns for Libanius to hear and heed.

A family that figures prominently in Libanius' correspondence, for example, is that of the poet and rhetor Acacius, who lived in Cilicia. His son and son-in-law attended Libanius' school.[40] In 358 a third member of the family joined them, the orphan Philoxenus, and the sophist wrote to Acacius, "I trust that Philoxenus, too, will do what is worthy of the family."[41] When he sent his friend a report of the boy's progress at the end of the following school year,

[37] On letters of application to Libanius' school, see Cribiore 2007a: 112–17.
[38] A list of these students includes (besides Libanius iv and Eusebius xx): the orphan of *Or.* 34.3; Calycius (*Ep.* 26); Chrysogonus (*Ep.* 1273); the nephew of Demetrius (*Ep.* 23); Dionysius (*Ep.* 426); the grandson of Megethius (*Ep.* 1101); the sons of Hestiaeus (*Ep.* 144); Philoxenus (*Ep.* 26) and his brother (*Ep.* 148); the sons of Urbitius (*Ep.* 1160); Basil the Great, John Chrysostom, and Libanius himself. We do not know whether other students who are simply referred to as orphans were in this condition when they started to attend or lost their fathers later; see, e.g., Dianius (*Ep.* 376); Eusebius 25 (*Ep.* 885) who was adopted by his paternal uncle; Julianus xv (who lost his mother during schooling and his father before); Parnasius (*Ep.* 912). The evidence above shows that relatively young orphans are amply present among Libanius' students, contrary to what Krause (1994–5: III, 183) maintained.
[39] See, e.g., Alexandra the wife of his friend Seleucus (*Ep.* 734), who was the daughter and sister of grammarians, had an excellent education, and exchanged books with Libanius. Women of this sort who could feel at ease in writing to such a prominent sophist were very rare. Cf. the vast majority of the women who sent letters in Greco-Roman Egypt in Bagnall and Cribiore 2006. On women who appear in Libanius' works, cf. Schouler 1985.
[40] Acacius 7; his son was Titianus, and Calycius married his daughter.
[41] See *Ep.* 26.2. It is unclear how Acacius was related to this boy.

Libanius reiterated that Philoxenus had been "worthy of your family in all respects": his academic progress was entirely satisfactory and his behavior was impeccable even though Acacius had warned the teacher that the boy liked to fight.[42] Another letter indicates that Philoxenus' mother operated in the background and tried to secure the goodwill of other people in order to encourage Libanius to pay special attention to her son and to know how he was doing in school. This woman's brother, who had been a fellow student of Libanius in Athens, was the most suitable person on whom she could rely for news, but apparently Libanius' uncle was another source of information for her, since she was on friendly terms with his wife.[43] Thus Philoxenus' mother succeeded in her intent to communicate, albeit indirectly, with the teacher. Libanius in fact enjoined her brother to inform her that "god willing, her son will be such as to satisfy her: he has a willing disposition and a capable nature." He sent another indirect message to her when Philoxenus' brother had also become a student and, after a vacation at home, this widow tried to keep both boys in Cilicia: after all, her relative Acacius was a superb rhetor who was willing at times to teach his own son and the two orphans.[44] Since this mother used the pretext that the weather in Cilicia was better than in Antioch, Libanius wrote stiffly to Acacius: "tell the mother of the two boys that it is summer here too, and a moderate wind blows." Acacius was often traveling to Antioch to be in contact with Libanius so that it was the maternal uncle of Philoxenus who received his excellent final report of progress after two years of attendance.[45]

Other examples of students who enjoyed the support of caring relatives and whose mothers were still alive[46] confirm that families felt the responsibility to help orphans secure some higher education. The life story of Libanius himself is exemplary in this respect. Exceptions to this social convention need to be considered with care. Thus the orphan nephew of the renowned sophist and governor Demetrius of Tarsus apparently encountered such financial difficulties in pursuing his education in Antioch that Libanius had to plead with members of his family on his behalf.[47] It is unnecessary, however, to infer from this example that orphans had particular trouble in financing their studies.[48] A correct reading of the situation revealed by the letters concerning this youth must take into account that he had run away from his relatives,

---

[42] According to *Ep.* 60, Acacius had said jokingly that the boy might be useful to Libanius by participating on his side in the fist fights that were apparently common between students of rival sophists; see, e.g., Eunap. 9.1.6.483–9.2.21.485 and Himer. *Or.* 4.9 and 19.

[43] See *Ep.* 45 written to Ecdicius ii, the maternal uncle of the boy.

[44] See *Ep.* 148 written to Acacius.   [45] See *Ep.* 147 of the year 359/60.

[46] It is likely that these women had not remarried.   [47] Demetrius 2. *Epp.* 23 and 24.

[48] Krause (1994–5: III, 182) uses this as an example of the economic straits orphans encountered when they wished to study rhetoric.

who would have preferred that he pursue his studies in his own country. In spite of Libanius' remark on the nobility of the young man's search for rhetoric ("he ran away from you in noble flight, the only kind of flight that is praiseworthy"), the family and the mother of this young man were probably justified in their anger and failure to provide financial support.[49] Libanius, who had a weakness for studious boys, also had a vested interest in wishing to keep this student with him.

Boys who had lost both mother and father or whose mothers remarried, however, might require a wider network of support in order to attain their educational goals. A rich dossier of letters in Libanius' correspondence concerns a student by the name of Dionysius, who studied rhetoric in spite of being destitute.[50] When his father was murdered by robbers, Dionysius ran away, lost all his property at home, and was in dire straits. Meanwhile his mother and her new husband apparently lived in luxury.[51] All this notwithstanding, Dionysius succeeded in acquiring an education that lasted many years under the guidance of Libanius, was offered good positions, composed a masterly panegyric of a governor, and was able to write elegant, rhetorical letters that made his teacher rejoice. Most importantly, he gained back all his land with the help of the rhetoric he had learned, increasing the good reputation of the sophist.[52] Many factors contributed to the success of this orphan who had started with every possible disadvantage. Libanius solicited the help of a donor, possibly a governor, who offered the boy economic support by regularly providing goods from his properties.[53] When this subsidy was interrupted, the sophist wrote a masterful letter to get it restored without offending the eminent supporter. Another wealthy young man, moreover, came to the rescue of this fellow student. Libanius wrote to a governor that Julianus "took in this young man, shared his funds with him, and made many people think that they were brothers. One was so wealthy that both could have the benefit of it."[54]

---

[49] Orphans, moreover, were not the only students in financial difficulties, see, e.g., Themistius 2 who studied with Libanius and later became governor of Lycia; his father did not give him money for books, *Ep.* 428.

[50] See *Epp.* 319, 426, 837, 1168–9, 1237–8, 1470, and 1501.

[51] There is no way of knowing why Dionysius ran away and whether the new husband of his mother was responsible for his troubles.

[52] Several letters of Libanius concern an accusation of rape or abduction that was brought against this young man, years after he left school. Since our knowledge of this affair and of Dionysius' motivations is limited, it is useless to speculate on the importance of his past on this matter. In any case, with the help of Libanius who enlisted the aid of several governors Dionysius was acquitted.

[53] *Ep.* 319 refers to a sort of scholarship with which Procopius 1, possibly governor of Cilicia, funded the boy's studies.

[54] See *Ep.* 1169, Julianus xv. We have to surmise, moreover, that Libanius exempted Dionysius from tuition. Such exemption was not exceptional. On Libanius' policy toward tuition, see Cribiore 2007a: 183–8.

One reason for the generous conduct of Julianus might be that he personally understood Dionysius' plight since he also was fatherless. Toward the end of his studies, moreover, he had to return home because his mother was murdered. Libanius wrote to the governor in charge of administering justice, saying that Julianus "should have gone home to see his mother for other reasons so that she might enjoy her son's excellence in her old age. But now he is going to shed tears on her tomb, mourning the woman who bore him both because she is dead and because of the way she died."[55] In any case, the loss of his father at the start of or during his schooling did not hamper this youth's academic progress at all. Julianus was a brilliant pupil. Libanius called him "the head of the chorus," that is, the most competent of all his students (κορυφαῖος). This title referred to a prestigious position, reserved for very few, that apparently existed in Athens and probably in other schools.[56] After leaving Antioch, Julianus continued to conduct himself in a commendable way, so that a year later his teacher congratulated him on the honors he had received from his native city.[57]

Painting the portrait of a very diligent orphan in a letter of recommendation, Libanius remarked on the "self-control and discipline of his everyday life, for anyone who is so attached to books keeps out of trouble."[58] The painstaking study of rhetoric helped young men fulfill the expectations of their families and status; gave them mastery of oral and written language; and also inculcated in them such precious qualities as hard work and tenacity. The latter two orphans do not provide the only examples of success among Libanius' students. The sophist wrote to a governor that Chrysogonus from Phoenicia "was left an orphan, but suffered a greater misfortune than being an orphan, that is, dishonest guardians, who made themselves masters of his property and suffered that he would go hungry."[59] His attendance at the school in Antioch, albeit not very long, allowed this student to oppose in court the people who had prevailed over him, recouping his possessions. Libanius continued to offer assistance in order that he become an advocate in the retinue of governors. The acquisition of some rhetorical skills not only gave young men the actual power to overcome their misfortunes but also secured the invaluable help of their teacher, who tirelessly pleaded on their behalf with eminent men. Besides the obvious affection Libanius felt for his students, their success in life increased his reputation.

[55] *Ep.* 835 to Entrechius 1.   [56] Cf. Eunap. 9.2.7, 483.
[57] See *Ep.* 1130.3, Julianus' city celebrated his return.
[58] Cf. *Ep.* 666; on the peerless Faustinus, see below.
[59] Chrysogonus 2, see *Epp.* 1273 and 1208, a letter to another governor. This student may have lost both parents.

According to tradition, a full course of rhetoric (which Libanius himself
had followed) included learning both the theory of issues (στάσις), which
imparted a mastery of arguments, and the theory of the parts of speech. This
thorough training, which took many years, was the only one that truly
satisfied Libanius as an educator. He spoke generically of the necessity for
students to learn "the whole" and never openly admitted that they could
succeed with less. Students who were willing to dedicate so much time to
the art, however, were rare. In the sophist's late years, one orphan, another
Eusebius, again aroused his hope that a student would follow in his foot-
steps.[60] Eusebius had been adopted by his dead father's brother. He was
entangled in an obscure legal affair and lost much of his wealth in spite of his
uncle's and mother's support. Difficulties, however, did not keep him from
higher education. On the contrary: he was the student who attended
Libanius' school for the longest time. His commitment and inborn qualities
convinced his teacher that an academic career was perfect for him. He was
the head of the chorus (κορυφαῖος) and had the responsibility of teaching
in emergencies, for example when Libanius was ill. Eusebius' family, however, had different plans even though he became an orator of the first
quality. Civic service could bring a young man a good reputation, and
Libanius tried to help his former student undertake a burden commensurate
with his possessions. But Eusebius aimed higher and wished to be adlected
into the Senate of Constantinople, a choice his teacher disapproved of
because it might force him into great expenditures while diminishing his
influence at home.[61] Libanius had witnessed the accomplishments and hard
work of an influential senator, Domninus, who left an impoverished son at
his death.[62] Yet against his better judgment Libanius assisted Eusebius by
appealing to friends and acquaintances.

So far I have considered cases of orphans who abandoned rhetoric after a
short training and of others whose loss did not prevent them from attending
Libanius' classes for many years. A correct understanding of the average
attendance of students in the school of Antioch is necessary to avoid the risk
of misrepresenting the actual educational prospects of orphans by over-
rating the impact of their status on schooling. A few of Libanius' students
prolonged their attendance for up to five years (or more), but the majority
limited it to two or three years. The reasons why a young man quit his

[60] Eusebius 25; letters that concern him are 884–7.
[61] On the duties of members of the Great Senate, see Jones 1964: 1, 523–62. Libanius, however, approved
of his students belonging to city councils and undertaking liturgies on behalf of their communities.
[62] Domninus 2; see *Epp.* 952–3; this youth was a student of Libanius.

studies were many.[63] Parents might hear rumors about the school and withdraw their sons;[64] fathers might take up new positions and change their residence;[65] or students might be forced to withdraw because of poor health.[66] But the chief reason why students in the fourth century were satisfied with just a few years of rhetorical education was that the discipline had lost some of its prestige. A relatively brief training was sufficient for success in the law courts as a "literary" advocate or as a prerequisite before moving on to the training in Latin and Roman law that made a young man more competitive on the job market.[67]

A father's death, therefore, was only one of the causes that might force a youth to interrupt his education, even when he had dedication and a predisposition to the art. One of these gifted students, for example, was Faustinus, whom Libanius called "the best of the Pisidians and of our students."[68] He did not share the nonchalant attitude of those of his schoolmates who dedicated much of their time to the theater, mimes, and chariot races but "were asleep" in class. He was so dedicated that Libanius anticipated that in time he would even surpass his teachers in ability. Yet, when his father died, Faustinus had to withdraw to tend to his patrimony and used his rhetorical knowledge in the law courts. His family could not adequately support him because his surviving grandfather was weak and "had yielded to old age." Faustinus had become the head of the family and could not afford to stay away from his home country.

A more distressing predicament compelled another student, Eudocius, to withdraw upon the death of his father Caesarius.[69] This notable from Armenia had enlisted the aid of several people to have his sons accepted. Since he had enrolled them first in another school, thereby incurring Libanius' displeasure,[70] he feared lest the sophist reject them or not give them the attention they needed. Thus a family friend and the governor of Armenia (in addition to Caesarius himself) had pleaded on behalf of Eudocius and his younger brother.[71] In his stiff responses to the recommenders, Libanius also

[63] On this, cf. Cribiore 2007a: 174–83 and 191–4 and Cribiore 2007b.
[64] See, e.g., *Epp.* 32, 41, and 129.   [65] See *Ep.* 1250.   [66] See *Epp.* 1245 and 1371.
[67] On rhetoric's rival studies (Latin and Roman law), see Liebeschuetz 1972: 242–55; on the actual relevance of rhetoric, see Heath 2004: 277–331. Cf. Libanius, *Epp.* 117, 653, 1394, and especially *Or.* 57 against his former student Severus, who quit after little more than a year to become a successful advocate.
[68] See *Ep.* 666.
[69] Eudocius i; his father was Caesarius ii and his brother was Caesarius iii.
[70] The school in question must have been in Antioch, too, with one of Libanius' rivals. Libanius would not feel offended by attendance in an Armenian school.
[71] See *Epp.* 248–50.

pointed to an added reason for acceptance, the fact that an uncle of these students had gone to school with him: bonds of friendship formed during schooling were long-lasting.[72] All the efforts of this father to foster his children's education, however, came to a halt when he died a few years later, and his older son had to leave rhetoric to take the reins of the household.

City councils were always on the lookout for people of curial status who might be eligible for civic service. Their attempts to compel orphaned students of curial status to undertake liturgies were sometimes obviously misguided when the children were still minors, as in the case of the diligent sons of the decurion Urbicius, who were too young to be pulled out of school.[73] Eudocius, though, did not have the legitimate excuse of his age. Like the orphaned son of the Domninus mentioned above,[74] he was trapped and was burdened with a heavy liturgy. Yet an appeal to his foster father and teacher brought the desired results. Libanius intervened with Maximus, the governor of Armenia, who came to the rescue.[75] The sophist acknowledged the assistance by responding: "They say that Eudocius grieves for his father only a little, and that you are the reason for this, because you diminished his feelings of bereavement with many great deeds." When confronted with an unbearable liturgy, an impoverished orphan would sometimes literally run away. The mother of Dianius begged him to return to her and his city from Antioch, but while he did not want to disobey her and cared for his country, he was frightened "because of the necessity of undertaking liturgies, poor as he was." This time Libanius apparently did not have recourse to the usual authorities but pleaded with the philosopher Themistius to help this youth who was going to Constantinople to see him.[76] The philosopher was most qualified to help in this difficult situation, because he had power at court, was a teacher himself, and apparently regarded Libanius' students as his own.

Libanius declared in an oration that some orphans used their condition as an excuse for laziness, but those who had authentic "love" (ἔρως) for paideia found a way to achieve it and continued to "drink at the springs of

---

[72] To somewhat maintain his professorial authority, he also added that these students deserved to be admitted because of their talent. He apparently later also accepted Caesarius' son-in-law, *Ep.* 254.

[73] *Epp.* 1163 and 1172; see Petit 1956: 141.

[74] The son of Domninus was entrapped with a liturgy that his father owed to Constantinople.

[75] Maximus 19. *Ep.* 645 shows that the despondent Eudocius wrote timidly to his teacher to test the ground; *Ep.* 646 attests to the help he received from the governor through Libanius' mediation and the long letter he sent the sophist with regard to that. From *Ep.* 814 it appears that Eudocius was finally relieved from his duty.

[76] *Ep.* 376 to Themistius 1. The sophist told him among other things that Dianius had memorized many of the latter's discourses.

the Muses" with no other concerns.[77] This statement, which was influenced by the overall argument of the speech in question, is not entirely realistic and fair, particularly when the death of the head of the household threatened its financial ruin. And yet it should not be entirely discounted. A talented young man with a passion for rhetoric and born in an elite household had a strong ally against life's misfortune: Libanius himself who acted as surrogate father. The equivalence of teacher and father, which sometimes occurs in literature and particularly in writers of late antiquity, is far more than a cliché in his work.[78] Whereas Libanius considered all good students his sons because he nourished their talent for rhetoric, those who lost their fathers even more clearly fulfilled his need to beget real children of the intellect.

Returning now to the initial question that Libanius posed about himself, what can we conclude about the orphan state of his students? Was the education of these young men seriously compromised by this important loss? The evidence is large enough to warrant some general conclusions. It shows that other factors such as wealth and a supportive family were crucial in assuring that a young man entered school and remained on the right track. Undoubtedly the loss of a father might have repercussions on schooling, since it might delay his application or force him to withdraw from school to take care of the family's possessions or to undertake grievous financial burdens. Orphans, though, were not the only young men who were forced to make those choices and who had to shoulder responsibilities that were part of an adult life.[79] Most orphans of the upper class were able to acquire some rhetorical education in spite of some difficulties. A strong, close family where uncles and more rarely grandfathers took the place of the departed parent and a prosperous financial situation were the real determiners of success. Whereas a father's death might occasionally have a drastic effect on length of studies, the crucial factors that helped a young man go to and stay in school were family support, ability to pay for costly studies, lack of urgent need to earn a living, and personal motivation and talent.

---

[77] See *Or.* 55.14.
[78] See Cribiore 2007a: 138–41. Cf., e.g., *Epp.* 59, 300, 634, 782, 1071, and 1538. The image of a teacher as the father of a student (a father as important as the natural father) appears before late antiquity but in this period in particular is used to describe pedagogic relationships, see Kaster 1988: 67–9. Cf. Himer. *Or.* 9.30 and 24.20 and Eunap. 483. Libanius, moreover, was not an entirely happy natural father, which can partly explain his affection for his students. His son Cimon, who died at a relatively young age, was born of his relation with a woman of low condition so that the sophist had to wage many battles to be able to recognize him as legitimate.
[79] Sooner or later an individual of curial status had to undertake civil service that might increase his standing before his fellow citizens.

The information derived from Libanius, therefore, is generally optimistic with regard to orphans obtaining some higher education. It shows that a father's loss did not compromise irremediably a young man's chance to function in the future at the highest echelons of society. It is crucial, however, to keep in view that this evidence refers to elite social strata. The few impoverished but talented orphans who obtained the sophist's personal assistance were also born into elite families that had fallen into disgrace. As a rule, the relatives who acted as surrogate fathers were members of privileged milieus who felt responsible for the success of one of their own.

CHAPTER 15

"Woe to those making widows their prey and robbing the fatherless": Christian ideals and the obligations of stepfathers in late antiquity

Geoffrey Nathan

When Augustine of Hippo wrote of his own father some twenty years after his death, he recalled him with something less than unqualified filial piety.[1] Although always a "momma's boy," the rhetor-turned-cleric's descriptions of his father were less than complimentary: he described Patricius as foul-tempered, uxorious, and spiritually weak. Indeed, his father's death merits hardly a comment in his autobiography; although his eventual conversion to Christianity did somewhat redeem him in his son's eyes. Augustine's was perhaps a unique opinion, insofar as he actually expressed such ambiguity, but the fact that for a good part of his minority, he grew up without a father was by no means unusual. As studies by Richard Saller, Brent Shaw, and several here in this volume have indicated, the phenomenon of fatherless households in ancient Rome was tied strongly to general marriage practices, resulting age differentiation in spouses, and of course mortality rates.[2]

These trends did not significantly change in late antiquity.[3] We have numerous examples of children growing up in households where the father was either deceased or simply absent for such extended periods of time that their children might as well have been fatherless. Nor did this appear to be a class or ethnically based situation. Theodosius II's minority was dominated and heavily regulated by his formidable elder sister, Pulcheria. The Ostrogothic king Theodoric's grandson and successor, Athalaric, grew up largely under the tutelage of his mother, Amalasuintha. Augustine, who, as

I would like to thank Sabine R. Hübner and David M. Ratzan for help in this project, but especially all my students in History 3110, a seminar on the Roman family, held at the University of New South Wales in First Session, 2007. They brought up many useful questions and observations directly relevant to this topic, and I would like to dedicate this essay to them.

[1] August *Conf.* 1–2, *passim*.
[2] Saller 1987; Saller and Shaw 1984; Shaw 1987; and Scheidel (this volume).
[3] See Nathan 2000.

mentioned above, lost his father in his teenage years, was from a curial family in the provincial backwater of Thagaste in North Africa. And St. Epiphanius of Pavia was an orphan from a family so humble that his normally grandiloquent biographer Ennodius passes over his origins with uncharacteristic brevity.[4] Of course, we have no real quantitative analysis on the rates of fatherless households, but it was clearly common enough to merit discussion in various genres of literature, most notably in legal and religious writings.[5]

The purpose of this study is to look at the role of father surrogacy in late antiquity, a particularly useful exercise since the place of Christianity grew significantly throughout the Empire and beyond – a religion whose founder spoke of special treatment for orphans and widows. Such special treatment became something not only focused upon by theologians but also institutionalized in early Christian communities – Sigismund notes that the pluralization of family structures was a key component in this broadening understanding of community responsibility. Surrogacy could come in many forms: sometimes the role of the father was taken by a family member (often, as we have seen, by mothers);[6] sometimes by an individual who had an obligation in some form to a minor or his family; and sometimes the Church itself took responsibility for raising an orphan.

Therefore, by way of introduction, a discussion of the Christian ideas surrounding the fatherless will serve as a useful background before considering the practice of surrogacy itself in late antiquity. I will focus on three figures who were rendered fatherless while still young: the Emperor Honorius (r. 395–423); a young fifth-century North African bishop, Antoninus; and the sixth-century aristocrat and scholar, Boethius (c. 480 – c. 525). What we will find is that although there were a number of differences in their respective experiences, they also shared similarities that manifested themselves in certain discernible patterns.

Stepfathers (*vitrici*) in the Classical world in theory had few or no legal rights over their partner's children. In the unlikely event that a woman's former husband was still alive and yet their children lived with her, they would of course remain legally under his *potestas*. Nor would a new husband gain control of his wife's children, were she a widow. Since he possessed no blood relationship – cognatic or agnatic – his legal authority would be nonexistent. In practical terms, however, the ability to influence and control stepchildren was not uncommon, and often new wives acceded to the

---

[4] Enn. *Vita Epiphanii* 1–2.   [5] See Scheidel (this volume): 95–9.
[6] See Hübner and Ratzan (this volume): 17–18; Hübner (this volume): 67–9, 73.

demands of their spouses.[7] A man of high social station, after all, could provide the connections to ensure his stepchildren's future.[8] The purpose, however, of remarriage was often pragmatic, especially outside the aristocratic world: male protection and material support for the *heres* until he (or she) reached adulthood. Although they rarely served as formal guardians, stepfathers were nevertheless expected to protect their stepchildren and could play a crucial role in their security and well-being.

On the other hand, having no parents did not necessarily mean a child – at least among Rome's elite – would be left to fend for himself. "Growing up without parents," as Ann-Cathrin Harders noted earlier in this volume, "did not mean growing up alone."[9] Family, stepparents, or family friends might all fill the gap. We have seen in this volume numerous examples of more distant kin taking up the onus of raising a child, to a point that certain distant relations were characterized by the Romans themselves into certain taxonomic patterns of motherhood and fatherhood, as well as masculinity and femininity.[10]

And even beyond the realm of the family, Romans in the imperial period did try to deal with the problems of orphaned children in creative, if not entirely successful ways. The *alimenta* system set up by the second-century emperors and by a number of cities (mostly in Italy) was an open acknowledgment of the fact that the government had some responsibility to impoverished minors of the Empire.[11] The distribution of funds, most famously attested to by an inscription in the small city of Veleia in southern Italy, indicates the scale of these projects: 50,000 sesterces were distributed to poor (citizen) children in one year alone.[12] Private philanthropy of this sort existed as well: Publius Licinius Papirianus, for example, donated 1.3 million sesterces to support five hundred boys and girls annually from the *colonia* of Cirta Sicca in Numidia.[13] Many of these children were not orphaned, but it is not difficult to assume that a great many were.[14] These public systems of support remained intact until finally ended by Diocletian

---

[7] See Gray-Fow 1988 as an illustration of how extensive the influence of a *vitricus* could be. See Hübner (this volume) for a discussion of remarriage and stepfathers.

[8] Cf. J. Coleman 1988 (noted in the Introduction to this volume: 8).

[9] Harders (this volume): 239.

[10] See Bettini 1991: 1–105. Saller (1997) demurs on this point, but Bettini (2002) replies.

[11] Although Susan Holman (2001) has argued persuasively that the *alimenta* system (along with grain distributions) were initiated to strengthen the community more than care for the poor. Note that the editors of this volume take a somewhat different view of the system. See the Introduction, n. 48.

[12] *CIL* xi.1147 (*ILS* 6675). See Criniti 1991.

[13] *CIL* viii.1641 (*ILS* 6818).

[14] Note that Scheidel's numbers above suggest that, on average, a third of children would be fatherless by the age of fifteen: 32; 36.

almost two centuries later. Protecting inheritances from the unscrupulous and greedy was, of course, another component of imperial care. Jurists wrote copious legislation providing protection for those minors *sui iuris* (under their own legal power), especially from those *tutores* ostensibly responsible for their wards' well-being.[15] In sum, the imperial government presumed a certain paternalism in trying to ensure that underage citizens made it to adulthood and in easing the process of succession.

At much the same time, an alternative and much smaller system of support and paternalism was developing in the Christian communities that increasingly dotted the cities of the Mediterranean in the second and third centuries. They drew a strong sense of caring for orphans from the religion's Jewish roots.[16] The book of *Exodus* in particular explicitly orders support and care for the fatherless (22:22, and this was considered a special responsibility of Israel's kings. The prophets, too, had exhorted Jews to look after orphans, since it was believed that God himself was especially concerned for their well-being.[17] The New Testament took up the interest in *agapē* (unselfish love) and urged Christians to support both the widowed and those left without a father.[18] This fell into a larger Christian mission to minister to the poor (both in life and in spirit), where poverty was not only a blessing of sorts but also a model of faith: Paul wrote significantly of Jesus' self-impoverishment for the bettering of all humanity.[19]

Part of this interest, of course, was reflected in the ways that Christians saw themselves as part of an "adopted" family: Paul had also spoken of the adoption (*huiothesia*) of God through Christ.[20] But the tangible product of such an ideology was a system of material assistance in the early Church for its poorer members, with special attention and consideration for widows and orphaned children. Early on, this help seemed generalized in feasts (also called *agapai*) for the whole Christian community.[21] More concretely, the establishment of the diaconate, open initially to both men and women, was a special ministerial office created within the Church hierarchy specifically (though not exclusively) to collect and distribute alms to the poor. Much of that charity was focused on the most marginalized members of the Christian community: the widowed and orphaned – although it was a system of support, as Marcus Sigismund has already noted, about which we know

---

[15] *E.g.* Gai. *Inst.* 1.142–99. See Kaser 1975.   [16] See Sigismund (this volume).
[17] Jer. 5:28 and Ezek. 22:7.   [18] John 14:18 and Jas. 1:27.
[19] 2 Cor. 8:9; cf. Phil. 2:5–8.   [20] Rom. 8:15, 23; 9:4.
[21] Acts 6; 20:7, 11; 2 Pet. 2:13; Ignatius, *Ep.* 8; Tert. *Apol.* 39. It is not entirely clear what the specifics of the meal were, but they were clearly separate from Eucharistic meals; Hippolytus, *Trad. ap.* 26.

relatively little.[22] Indeed, some scholars have suggested that the degree of that support probably was minimal and temporary.[23] Nevertheless, the Heavenly Father would fill the role of the deceased earthly father through the Church's support.

This raises the question of who were considered orphans; as this volume has shown, it is not always clear from ancient sources whether the term referred to a minor who had lost one parent (usually a father) or both. The classical and koine Greek term, *orphanos*, could mean parentless or fatherless (indeed, *orphanos* in modern Greek can still mean fatherless).[24] The Latin term, *orbus*, has a similar dichotomous meaning (*orphanus* is post-classical and is drawn from Greek sources). The Christian use of the word is equally fuzzy, although the Jewish tradition seems to imply that it refers generally to those without fathers: "We are orphans and fatherless, our mothers are as widows."[25] That widows and orphans were traditionally grouped together implies a connection between the two (*orbitas* could mean the state of orphanhood or widowhood). Probably parentless and fatherless could be used interchangeably, although given the demography of marriage and mortality rates, it would not be hard to conclude that orphan in the Christian context more often referred to the latter.

That said, the history of the early Church is one in which the responsibilities to orphans were loudly proclaimed. One of the most common components of that charity, apart from material assistance, was finding prospective adoptive or surrogate fathers. The rationale for this activity was manifold: the Christian father provided practical material support, he offered an example for his adoptee to follow, and of course he provided important moral guidance especially in religious belief.[26] Given the Church's intolerance in matters of exposing children, too, the responsibility for finding proper surrogate parents seems to have fallen increasingly to the Church as well. Indeed, the emperor Constantine's laws concerning the loss of *potestas* for fathers who exposed their children may have been a reflection of the impact of Christianity's centrality in these matters.[27] On his father's martyrdom, for example, Origen was given over to a pious and wealthy woman in the Christian community to be raised.[28] Members of the clergy may have acted as facilitators or perhaps established more formal procedures.

---

[22] Sigismund (this volume).   [23] Notably Krause 1994–5.   [24] Liddell and Scott 1968: 1257–8.
[25] Lam. 5:3. See Sigismund (this volume): 86, n. 12.   [26] T. S. Miller 2003: 65, 140–2, 145.
[27] In particular, *Cod. Theod.* 5.9.1 and 11.27.1, although there are similar provisions for the sale of infants and children. See, however, Evans Grubbs 1987: 187–212 for a different take on these laws. Cf. Evans Grubbs 1995: Appendix 1:5 (p. 345).
[28] Euseb. *Hist. eccl.* 7:2.

The earliest complete canons from the Council of Elvira (305 or 306) do not provide any clues, but the *Apostolic Constitutions* (based on the early third-century *Didascalia*) indicates that bishops ought to provide orphan boys with training in a useful trade (presumably from a Christian foster father) and to care for orphan girls until they marry (also apparently finding suitable husbands).[29]

By the fourth and fifth centuries, with the recognition and patronage of Christianity by the imperial government, the notions of Christian responsibility entered a new stage. The traditional source of income for the Church – voluntary giving and endowments in the form of rents suddenly became supplemented by large land grants from both the government and an increasingly Christianized aristocracy (that we see our first laws in fifth-century Italy banning simony – the sale of clerical offices – suggests that there were also other sources!).[30] Specialized institutions were able to develop, including poorhouses (*ptōchotropheia*), hospitals (*hospitii/xenoi*) and, of course, orphanages (*orphanotropheia*).[31] The orphanage was a clear acceptance that the idea of the Church's acting as a surrogate parent had become formalized and institutionalized. Indeed, the title of *orphanotrophus* (the official who ran the orphanage) was interpreted specifically as a foster father.[32] And, of course, the *oblatio*, or the donation of an underage child to a monastery, became a common enough practice that by the sixth century Benedict had to spell out specific instructions for their care in his monastic rule.[33] The establishment of these institutions, combined with some important legal changes in the reign of Justinian I, radically changed the status of children who lacked fathers or parents and goes beyond the scope of this chapter.[34]

The early Church, in sum, took an active and material interest in seeing to the care of its younger and often parentless members. As John Boswell noted twenty years ago, Christians saw themselves as God's *alumni*, so that they became familiar with the importance of surrogacy both literally and

---

[29] *Ap. Const.* 4:2. Whether this also included the provision of a dowry is unclear. A much later hagiographical tradition has St. Nicholas providing three girls with gold for dowry; Jacobus de Voragine, *Legenda Aurea, Vita Nich.* 2.

[30] Hall 2000: 740.

[31] On later philanthropy in the East, Constantelos 1968: esp. 241–56.

[32] See Venantius Fortunatus, *Vita S. Martini* 2.405; *Cod. Iust.* 1.3.32, 41. The classical term, *orphanophylax*, referred to an Athenian official who cared for children whose fathers died in war; Xen. *Vect.* 2.7.

[33] Benedict, *Regulae.* 22, 30, 37, 59. On oblation, see Boswell 1988: 228–55.

[34] See most recently, T. S. Miller 2003. Cf. Boswell 1988.

figuratively.[35] The impact of this interest, or lack thereof, in specific cases is what shall occupy much of our interest here.

Before discussing three examples from the late antique West, let me preface my observations by noting certain aspects regarding the nature of the sources themselves. In the cases of Honorius and Boethius we are dealing primarily with material that is the product of a highly stylized literary tradition. As such, obscure vocabulary and syntax, mythological and historical references, classical poetic and prose motifs, and other literary conceits abound.[36] They thus must be viewed almost solely as rhetorically pregnant representations of family and interfamilial dynamics. As Neil Bernstein has noted earlier, *topoi* employed in describing the nature and function of paternal surrogacy were no exception.[37] To say, then, that the relationships described in the surviving sources are idealized would be to mouth a truism; rather we can speak of these sources in terms of degrees of verisimilitude. Certainly in the case of Augustine's barebones report of Antoninus' early life, we can speak of something less than an elaborately (and consciously?) fictive construction; in Claudian's description of Honorius' marriage to Maria, on the other hand, we cannot. Thus, I have specifically chosen these three examples as, in my opinion, best reflecting the range of literary representation and genres.

With that caveat in mind, let us turn now to the first of our fatherless children: the emperor Honorius. When his father Theodosius I died in 395, Honorius acceded to the Western Empire at ten or eleven years of age. His mother, Aelia Flavia Flacilla, had died in 386, and his stepmother, Galla, had died the year before the boy came to the throne. He was thus completely and fully an orphan. But near his death, Theodosius had asked his most favored general, Flavius Stilicho, to act as a protector (*epitropos*) of his younger son, while the emperor traveled back to Constantinople.[38] While this term tended to be used more in an administrative sense than an adoptive one, Stilicho used this "duty" to lay claim to a guardianship over the young emperor – and proceeded to act as the de facto ruler of the West until his fall and execution in 408.

The political rise and fall of Stilicho is not at issue here, nor in fact is the actual nature of the relationship between the general and his puppet emperor. Just as Augustus acted as the loving *avunculus* to Marcus Antonius' children

---

[35] Boswell 1988: 178.
[36] Although some have argued for the originality of Claudian's work in particular; M. Roberts 1989: 1–3, *passim*.
[37] Bernstein (this volume): 245–6.
[38] Zos. 4.59; cf. Oros. 7.37.1 and Eunap. frag. 62. Note, however, that Orosius uses the word *cura*, a word traditionally associated with a *tutor*'s role.

for his own political interests,[39] Stilicho sought primarily to strengthen his own power by forging connections to the Theodosian line. He married Theodosius' niece, Serena, and engaged his daughters to Honorius. But Stilicho's plans were an unquestionable failure. As Kenneth Holum humorously noted, "Stilicho employed his western protégé to stud with Maria … but Honorius failed even in this function."[40] Despite the fact that Stilicho arranged two marriages for the emperor to his daughters, Maria (who died in 408) and Thermantia, no issue ensued from either marriage. After Stilicho's death, the latter was sent packing to live with her mother in Rome.[41] And of course, these machinations did not save him from his political and literal demise. The true nature of the relationship between the young emperor and the general cannot really be determined, but certainly it was not ideal.

That said, Stilicho had as court poet and chief propagandist Claudian Claudianus, a writer of considerable and prolific talent. For twelve years he promoted the wisdom, responsibility, and talents of the emperor's protector, frequently in the context of his role as surrogate father to the young emperor. In a series of poems concerning the imperial family, without ever directly being called a stepfather or adoptive father, Stilicho is largely portrayed as such. It began, if we are to believe the poet, with Theodosius himself asking Stilicho to take care of his two sons, and enjoining upon him this *cura* as his son-in-law (presumably Theodosius adopted his niece, Serena) and kinsman.[42] And its nature was carefully characterized as a father's role: in a later panegyric celebrating the general's consulship of 400, for example, Honorius is described as possessing a restless filial devotion, *trepida pietate*, for Stilicho.[43] Indeed, Claudian goes so far as to say that the general was a truer father than Theodosius ever was![44]

Given that Stilicho actively advertised his position as one that bordered on foster parent, what was the nature of that relationship? The need for practical, material support would not have been an issue of significance. Nevertheless, the general care of his ward ranked highly among the general's responsibilities. This included protecting Honorius from all physical harm. Stilicho is described as a shield (*clipeus*) so strong that the young man did not even mourn his own father.[45] And as a surrogate father, Stilicho trains the young man for his responsibilities as an adult. That included the rules of

---

[39] Harders (this volume).   [40] Holum 1982: 49.
[41] On Maria's death and Honorius' remarriage, see Zos. 5.28.1. On Thermantia's repudiation, Zos. 5.35.3; 37.5. Thermantia died in 415, apparently still married to Honorius, *Chronicon Paschale*, s.a. 415.
[42] Claud. *Panegyricus de tertio consulatu Honorii* 151–8.
[43] Claud. *De consulatu Stilichonis* 1.117.   [44] Claud. *Stil.* 3.122.   [45] Claud. *Stil.* 2.62–5.

statecraft, the responsibilities to his people, and the need to honor the desires of his departed father.[46]

A second and apparently key aspect of his fatherly duties lay in Stilicho's choosing a bride for his stepson. Claudian chronicled and commemorated the marriage of the emperor Honorius to Maria in an *Epithalamium* in considerable detail, although it clearly bore no relation to reality.[47] His use of mythological motifs and *topoi* served not only to accentuate the drama, but also to highlight certain ideals. The thoughts and actions of his characters – they are too stylized to call them historical persons – must thus be viewed and interpreted with care. Nevertheless, the poem focuses on notions of what constituted proper courting, betrothal, and marriage. By extension, it reflects the ideals of the marriage within the broader context of the desires of two families and their respective *patres*.

Claudian describes a union forged by Love, but cognizant of the niceties of family honor and respect. Claudian's readers are first made privy to the love-struck thoughts of the young emperor. Honorius is a man impatient to be married: already, before marriage, he calls Stilicho father-in-law (*socer*).[48] He arranges to send betrothal gifts of great value and antiquity.[49] His pursuit of Maria has been honorable and proper through Stilicho's choice of bride. Honorius has not forced himself upon any married woman: "I have not broken violently the bonds of a woman to her husband."[50] And as emperor and *sui iuris*, he has even sent representatives of high rank to Stilicho as agents to petition for the marriage, paying proper respect to the father and his family.[51]

But Claudian also emphasizes that the marriage was wanted by his now dead father, and with Stilicho fulfilling an old promise to his former master. It was Theodosius who had given his niece and adopted daughter, Serena, to Stilicho to wed, so Maria is owed in return: "pay the interest of my father owed to me, return to the golden palace his kindred."[52] Indeed, Stilicho himself is aware of this responsibility: the general's troops speak directly to the *genius* of Theodosius, informing the long-departed emperor that his

[46] Claud. *Stil.* 2.66–78. Interestingly, Claudian continues (2.78–99) by saying that this is what Stilicho attempted to do with Honorius' elder brother, Arcadius, and to save him from self-interested and worthless ministers.

[47] For more on Claudian, see Cameron 1970 and Schanz, Hosius, and Krüger 1920: 3–32. The poet also wrote *Fescennia de nuptiis Honori Augusti*.

[48] Claud. *Epith. de nup. Hon. Aug.* 20–1.

[49] *Epith.* 10–13. A necklace supposedly worn by Livia and other empresses is the prized gift.

[50] *Epith.* 28: *non rapio praeceps alienae foedera taedae.*   [51] *Epith.* 32–3.

[52] *Epith.* 37–8: *faenus mihi solve paternum, redde suos aulae.* The implication, of course, is that Maria is worth even more than Serena because she was the daughter of both Serena *and* Stilicho.

servant's debt and duty to his old master has been repaid.[53] Moreover, Serena had cared for Honorius when he was just a boy and was thus effectively her foster child. As such, Claudian reasons that it is right and proper to marry Maria, since it is assumed that such children should marry their adopted siblings: "Why not return a daughter to an adopted son?"[54] Respect for family honor and a father's wishes are preserved.

The poem has no description of the actual wedding, but it climaxes with the celebration after the wedding. The guest of honor is, unsurprisingly, Stilicho. Although the protector of his ward and the Empire, Stilicho has for this occasion hung up his war mantle, and Rome's soldiers have dressed in white and anointed themselves with fragrant spices. They toast not the bride and groom, but the bride's father. Hailed as the happiest of fathers (*fortunatissime patrum*), it is the wedding party's greatest hope that Stilicho's own son Eucherius shall surpass his father and Thermantia, his second daughter, shall make as good a match as Maria.[55] Claudian thus draws a parallel between son and foster son. But even more significant are the two fathers, Stilicho and the departed Theodosius, and their respective roles as the prime movers in their respective children's marriages. In that sense, Stilicho is acting as father, foster father, and father-in-law all rolled into one. As Claudian summarized in a much less well-known piece: "Stilicho is both father-in-law and father."[56]

Finally, there is a strong commitment by Stilicho not only to serve Honorius – he was (in theory) emperor, after all – but also to serve as an important advisor to his ward once he reached his majority. Throughout the panegyric on Stilicho's consulship, Claudian is at great pains to show the general as a protector and confidante of an emperor who was quickly approaching his majority. He is a "confidence in war, an advisor in peace."[57] Indeed, a measure of his success at teaching Honorius was that the emperor achieved enough wisdom to listen sagely to the advice of his protector, as well as that of the senate and people of Rome.[58] This introduces a novel element into the role of the surrogate father that was not emphasized in the Classical period: the notion of a certain onus of moral and ethical education. Indeed, in one poem praising Stilicho's wife, Serena, Claudian notes one of

---

[53] *Epith.* 300–5.
[54] *Epith.* 44: *quid iuveni natam non reddis alumno?* The jurist Gaius seems to imply that this was a relatively common event (1.60). See now Hübner 2007.
[55] *Epith.* 295–341.
[56] *Fescinnina de nuptiis Honorii Augusti* 3.12: *Stilicho socer est, pater est Stilicho.*
[57] *Stil.* 3.122–3: *fiducia belli, | pacis consilium.*   [58] *Stil.* 3.1115–19.

her principal roles was to aid her husband in precisely this task.[59] The key of inculcating a certain set of values, however, is also seen in the context of its utility. Stilicho's advice and guidance would serve the emperor well when he took the reins of power in his own right.

What is of course missing in these many references to Stilicho's relationship with Honorius is any reference to Christian ideals concerning parenthood, especially interesting given this last issue of moral education.[60] The faith of neither man can be in doubt, but specific Christian ideals, beliefs, and practices are almost wholly absent when describing the nature of the relationship. Given that most of our information comes from the classicizing works of Claudian, this is hardly surprising, but this point is important to keep in mind when we look at our next two *orphani*.

Our second fatherless figure of interest was a young bishop who briefly ministered to the rural North African *castellum* of Fussala, some seventy kilometers from Hippo Regius. We know considerably less about Antoninus than we do about Honorius; we have only two letters that mention him from his mentor and later detractor, Augustine of Hippo.[61] Indeed, had not a controversy surrounding his episcopacy occurred, we probably would not have known of him at all. His situation as bishop proved to be problematic – he apparently embezzled Church funds and trod clumsily and heavily over a community that had only recently eschewed the schismatic movement of Donatism (which had, among other things, rejected the established clerical hierarchy in favor of its own) – and it resulted in two councils (the second being appointed by Pope Boniface) to hear the charges against him.[62] Significantly, his story is not only one of his own personal failings, but of Augustine's as well.

The first of Augustine's letters, Letter 209, addressed to Pope Celestinus, offers few details about Antoninus. We learn that he had been brought up in a monastery under Augustine's direction from a very young age (*parvula aetate*), and that he had been appointed in haste to the bishopric of Fussala since he had knowledge of the Punic language (which was still apparently being spoken in the more rural regions of Roman North Africa).[63] Little more is said about his background, although it is clear from the tone of the letter that Augustine had had high hopes for the young man, who had served only as a *lector* prior to his accession to the episcopate. Augustine admits to his own poor judgment in putting this young man in such an

---

[59] *Carm. min.* 39 (39): *laus Serenae.*
[60] For Christian notions of childrearing, Nathan 2000: ch. 6 *passim.*
[61] August. *Epp.* 209 and 20*.   [62] For a good summary, see Chadwick 1983.   [63] August. *Ep.* 209.3.

important role. The bishop describes Antoninus as his *filium in Christo*, hardly an endorsement of his role as a foster father, as this was a stock phrase of Christian address. But he had a real liking for the young man – "I honestly cared about him" – that was clearly not feigned.[64] So much was clear in the fact that he gave such a young man so important an office.

The second letter, Letter 20*, however, gives us a little more information about Antoninus' background and early life, as well as Augustine's relationship with the younger cleric. It turns out that Antoninus was not completely orphaned, for when he arrived with his mother in Hippo (probably from the North African hinterland) as a young child, Augustine discovered that the boy's father was in fact very much alive. Moreover, he implies that mother and father were still married. To make matters worse, she was living with another man, and out of wedlock. This *vitricus*, as the bishop calls him, was completely unacceptable, especially since the woman petitioned the local church for help in their extreme poverty.[65] As a condition for aid, Augustine insisted that the relationship end. As an added incentive, he agreed to take all three into the care of the Church: the unnamed stepfather (who soon died) and Antoninus into a monastery; the woman into a hospice for widows and elderly women: "and so because of this, in God's mercy, they all came under our care."[66]

The tale up to this point is worth considering. Not only did Augustine take responsibility for raising Antoninus, but he did so for reasons that were not strictly based on this family's need. There was a keen awareness of the impropriety of the "stepfather's" status – that he was neither financially nor morally (nor perhaps legally) entitled to raise his mate's son. Augustine here inserts himself through the Church as fulfilling the proper parental authority, with sufficient resources and ethical standing to rear him correctly. The bishop's insistence that the improper relationship end is consistent with what he saw as his moral responsibility, but placing such a condition on a truly destitute family seems to run counter to the practical responsibility of the Church to its poorer parishioners. We know nothing about the manner in which this precondition was taken initially, but Augustine's insistence was successful. We have, then, an important distinction between only a nominally Christian and proper surrogate fatherhood and one wholly inappropriate.

---

[64] August. *Ep.* 209.9: *sinceram habeo caritatem*. Cf. Frend 1983.
[65] August. *Ep.* 20*.2; cf. Frend 1983.
[66] August. *Ep.* 20*.2: *ac per hoc omnes in Dei misericordia sub cura nostra esse coeperunt.*

What is of equal interest is Antoninus' life once he entered the monastery. The practical matters of his material well-being were of course addressed and the dire state of his poverty was brought to an end. Probably he still had contact with his mother, since she lived to an old age. But in addition to being fed, clothed, and housed, Augustine saw in the boy considerable talent. Like other boys in the institution, he was given formal education. Not only was the youth versed in the Punic language, but he was sufficiently gifted intellectually that by his late teens he was ordained as a *lector* (reader) in Hippo's church: the bishop noted that he stood out among his fellow "*consortes*" in the monastery. He was well praised by his abbot, too. The young man's education seems to have gone beyond the standard. The matter of care and training for Antoninus – and one consistent with his talents – was thus an important part of Christian care as well, just as with our other orphans.

We must wonder, too, whether Augustine's affection for the young man may have had an emotional dimension associated with the loss of his own son, Adeodatus. Like Antoninus, the bishop's long-departed son had a considerable intelligence of his own, one described by his father as vast.[67] Whatever the nature of his personal feelings, so impressed was Augustine that when an appointment for a rural episcopacy fell through, he quickly accepted the suggestion of investing Antoninus as bishop. The now-grown orphan had never held a priesthood, although that was not necessarily an impediment: Ambrose, Augustine's mentor, for example, had never been ordained in any order before he assumed the see of Milan. But Antoninus was only twenty years of age, quite young to be placed in a position of such authority. The parishioners in his diocese at rural Fussala had been ones who had recently left the Donatist camp to rejoin the Catholic fold.[68] This was thus an appointment that called for diplomacy and delicacy.

Antoninus possessed neither. In a very short time he had alienated most of the populace, largely made up of *coloni*, the proto-serfs of late antiquity. They so objected to his highhanded oversight and his apparent financial indiscretions and misuse of Church funds that they threatened to leave en masse to another community and leveled a number of charges against their bishop. Augustine's initial inquiry found that many of the accusations had substance and the younger man was chastened. Antoninus appealed to the Pope, who set up his own inquiry and apparently upheld many of the bishop of Hippo's original findings. We never find out what happened to Antoninus after this issue was laid to rest, although it seems as if he had to be

---

[67] August. *De beata vita* 6.   [68] Augustine actually uses the word *catholicus*: *Ep.* 209:2.

removed at last from his see, if not from his station.[69] Whatever his fate, it is clear that Augustine still had an abiding concern and feeling of responsibility for his errant ward even after all that had happened. He ends his letter by saying how much these events had wounded him personally.[70]

The tale of Antoninus is interesting not only because Augustine and the Church actively fulfilled the role of the "good" surrogate father, but also because it is essentially a tale of failure on the elder bishop's part. It might go too far to say that the young man was Augustine's protégé, but certainly the closeness he felt for him went beyond the practical support given by the Church. He had understood his duty clearly, but he was sufficiently blinded by the younger man's skills that he let his own biases and affection overpower both Christian traditions regarding the investiture of bishops and a father's clear understanding of his son's readiness to take his place in society. Augustine in both letters notes that it was *his* failing and responsibility that things went so terribly wrong and blames himself for Antoninus' opportunity to cause so much grief. The bishop of Hippo in his enthusiasm overlooked the common sense of a Christian father and the duties of a responsible cleric. In sum, in the case of his de facto ward, Augustine had undermined the directives of his office and his faith.

Our last *orphanus* was the sixth-century consul, scholar, and philosopher, Anicius Manlius Severinus Boethius. His father, probably a notable political figure in the 480s, died while Boethius was still a child.[71] He would grow up to play a prominent role in the Roman senate and serve King Theodoric before falling foul of some obscure political scandal that led to his arrest and eventual execution in 524 or 525.[72] As a child of the aristocracy and in fact a member of the most aristocratic of Roman *gentes*, the Anicii, like Honorius he received a well-cared-for upbringing in the absence of his father.

We know little specifically about Boethius' childhood, except that he was raised in an aristocratic house in the city of Rome itself.[73] The *desolatum* of losing his father (nothing is said about his mother, but since he was subsequently raised in a foster home, we can presume that she was also deceased) was balanced against the blessing of being brought up in one of the most important families in Rome – "*summi viri.*" Although we are given no definitive statement as to that family, the facts of his subsequent personal and public life point to the house of Q. Aurelius Memmius Symmachus.

[69] See Munbier 1983.   [70] August. *Ep.* 20*.32.
[71] Martindale (*PLRE* II: 232–3) argues that Flavius Manlius Boethius (cos. 487) was his father. Cf. Chadwick 1981: 5. Martindale suggests that Boethius was seven or eight at the death of his father. Marenbon (2003: 8) suggests a date of around 476 for his birth, making him an orphan at twelve.
[72] The date of his death is uncertain; see Chadwick 1981: 55.   [73] Boethius, *De cons. phil.* 2.3.5–7.

Indeed, Chadwick and others take for granted that Boethius was raised in his household.[74] The specific nature of that relationship is unclear – it may have been a formal guardianship or it could have been something more informal. If the former, much of his subsequent life makes sense.

Like his great-grandfather of almost identical name,[75] Symmachus was one of the leading senatorial and intellectual luminaries of his day. At some point in the second decade of the sixth century, he served as President of the Senate (*caput senatus*).[76] Not only did he engage in the sorts of extensive literary activities common among late-Roman aristocrats – notably editing older classical works and composing a seven-book history of Rome – but he also extended his classicism to devoting a significant portion of his personal wealth to restoring Rome's more famous public buildings.[77] And significantly, he appears to have patronized important thinkers of the day, apparently including the Neoplatonic Christian polymath, Dionysus Exiguus.[78]

If we accept the likelihood of Symmachus' role as foster father, the life of Boethius comes into sharper focus. Like that of Honorius, his rearing is described by the aristocrat as a *cura*, articulating once again the resonances of the legal responsibilities of a Roman *tutor* or *curator* respectively.[79] And like Honorius and Antoninus, under Symmachus' tutelage Boethius was trained for the career that he would pursue. From early on in his life, he was versed in classical literature, including – rarely for this age – the Greek canon. Also unusual was his interest in philosophy as an adult: in addition to his best-known work, *The Consolation of Philosophy* (a primarily Neoplatonic exercise), he wrote a commentary on Cicero's *Topica* and translated Porphyry's commentary of Aristotle's *Categories* from Greek into Latin. Perhaps more ambitiously, Boethius planned to translate with commentary most of the Aristotelian and Platonic canon into Latin – a project unrealized due to his political downfall.[80]

Boethius' literary activities not only reveal superlative training as a youth, but also the specific interests of the elder senator. Raffaella Cribiore has already described the potential dangers of being orphaned with specific reference to education (and the ways to avoid that!), and certainly, without

---

[74] Chadwick 1981; cf. Marenbon (2003: 8) concurs.
[75] Q. Aurelius Symmachus, one of the famous pagan aristocratic holdouts against Christianity in the late fourth century, was a poet, rhetorician, and editor of classical Roman texts; cf. *PLRE* I: 865–70.
[76] Anon. Valesianus 15.92. On the date, *PLRE* II: 1045.
[77] Cassiodorus (*Var.* 4.51) notes his work in restoring the theatre of Pompey, but also refers to other unspecified works carried out.
[78] Cass. *De div. lectionibus* c. 23.
[79] Boethius, *De cons. phil.* 2.3.5: *… summorum te virorum cura suscepit.*   [80] Marenbon 2003: 17–20.

stepfathers or a strong familial support system, learning might be delayed.[81] Symmachus seems to have been involved in Boethius' education and the things he studied. Symmachus was versed in Greek and had served as Theodoric's envoy to Constantinople on at least one occasion. His erudition in Greek was in fact profound enough that the Constantinopolitan grammarian Priscian dedicated several works to him. He also was interested in philosophy – so much so that his reputation in this regard extended even to the East.[82] His sponsorship of Greek-speakers in Italy, too, suggests that he saw the traditional aristocratic virtue of bilingualism as an important component of Boethius' upbringing. But Greek philosophy was a somewhat unusual discipline for Westerners to pursue. Since Symmachus' reputation for erudition was matched by that of his ward, it is clear that the aristocratic foster father had prepared the orphan well. [83]

Boethius' education and training led to a distinguished, if not entirely happy, political career. In addition to assuming traditional senatorial offices, including the consulship in 510, he was eventually made a *patricius* – the highest possible status for a member of the imperial aristocracy. Significantly, too, he served under King Theodoric as the highly influential *magister officiorum* until his arrest in 523. He had sufficient political clout that he had his two underage sons both named consul in 522. Had he not run afoul of a supposed plot against Theodoric, he probably would have become the leading senator in the West.

Of equal practicality, like Stilicho, Symmachus found Boethius a suitable wife and, unsurprisingly, from within his own house. As the father of at least three daughters, he gave in marriage his eldest, Rusticiana, to Boethius when they both came of age. In his semi-autobiographical work, *The Consolation of Philosophy*, Boethius not only expresses great respect for his wife, but the goddess Philosophy admits that his happiness has only been truly diminished by his wife's absence. By all accounts, it was a harmonious and productive marriage: they had two sons in quick order. As an act of filial piety, one of his two sons was christened Flavius Symmachus. Rusticiana's devotion to her husband was such that the Goths accused her many years later of desecrating statues of Theodoric in revenge for the execution of her husband and father.[84] And, of course, Boethius himself describes her in traditionally glowing terms, praising her modesty (*modestia*), chastity

---

[81] Cribiore (this volume).   [82] Procop. *Goth.* 1.1.32.
[83] On Symmachus' erudition, see Ennodius, *Paraenesis didascalica Ambrosio et Beato*, p. 408; on Boethius', see Cass. *Libellus* (Th. Mommsen, *MGH[AA]* 7.5–6 [1894]).
[84] Procop. *Goth.* 3.20.29–31.

(*pudicitia*), and decency (*pudor*). Indeed, as a reflection of his gratitude, and as a measure of his praise, he goes so far as to say that Rusticiana was a female version of her father![85]

The suitability of the match was therefore a reflection of Symmachus' duties as a foster parent and on *his* suitability for that role. That is best articulated by Boethius' praise for Symmachus in the passage immediately preceding his discussion of his wife and children. His praise is that of a son's: Philosophy calls the elder man wise and strong and concerned for Boethius' well-being, even more than his own. He also praises Symmachus for being upright morally and his closest of friends.[86] Just as the fifth-century Gallic poet Paulinus of Pella said a father should be a friend and advisor to his son, so, too, does Boethius seem to cast his father-in-law in such a light.[87]

Many fathers did try to instill more than fear of the whip and disinheritance into their offspring. Paulinus' father, for example, had tried to act as a resource for his son, advising him on management of his properties, and was presented as a model for good behavior.[88] Sidonius Apollinaris' good-humored criticism of a fictional reprobate, to cite another example, was framed as a commendation to his son for avoiding the company of evil men.[89] And the fourth-century Symmachus had made it a point to tutor his own son in grammar, rhetoric, and oratory, intimating involvement and concern.[90] These fathers seemed to have had the best interest of their sons at heart and provided practical advice for their betterment. These examples are furthermore distinguished partially because of their concern for worldly affairs. The religious world and Christian concerns again seem to be curiously absent.[91]

And, of course, that best interest extended to protection of sons to the best of a father's ability. In the case of Boethius, his arrest apparently sparked sufficient controversy that Theodoric feared Symmachus' political opposition – and indeed Boethius seems to suggest that he was involved in trying to free his son-in-law.[92] This was also sufficient grounds to have

[85] Boethius, *De cons. phil.* 2.4.6. [86] Boethius, *De cons. phil.* 1.4.40.
[87] Paulinus of Pella, *Eucharisticon* 229–44. [88] Paul. Pella, *Euch.* 229–32. [89] Sid. Apoll. *Ep.* 3.13.
[90] Symmachus (*Ep.* 4.20) mentions that he started to relearn Greek with his son. *Epp.* 6.51, 6.61, and 8.38 also mention his involvement in the younger Symmachus' education.
[91] Of course, it should not be overlooked that Boethius wrote four major treatises on Christian theology, mostly supporting the Trinitarian view of Chalcedonian Christians. It is clearly the most definitive evidence that he was raised an orthodox Christian and participated in the patristic tradition of Christological debates. But he remained a layman, led a secular life, and there is little indication that Symmachus himself was any great pursuer of Christian learning: the only oblique suggestion comes in Ennodius, *Paraenesis didascalica Ambrosio et Beato* 410, where the bishop asked the senator for his assessment of his work stylistically.
[92] Boethius, *De cons. phil* 2.4.4–5.

the elderly senator arrested and subsequently put to death.[93] In sum, Symmachus went so far as to die in order to protect his foster son and son-in-law.

The tale of Boethius as a foster son, then, bears similarities to his earlier counterparts, but what do these three orphans collectively say about the nature of surrogate fatherhood in late antiquity and for the relationship between foster parent and foster child?

First, that surrogate fatherhood was clearly conceived within the traditional rubric of fatherhood. The requirements, responsibilities, and pretensions of a "real" father, quite apart from any specific actions, found articulation in the words with which they were described. The rhetorical resonances of filial piety, of responsibility in the wake of loss, and the continued sense of fatherly affection and responsibility into adulthood were themes that can be traced in the stories of all three orphans. Even the term, *cura*, which had a distinctively legal flavor, could also be seen in terms of the duties of a parent: Sidonius Apollinaris writing to his wife, for example, had called their daughter their *cura communis*.[94] Halfway between a father and a guardian, the surrogate father – whether as an individual or in the corporate entity of the Church – was largely consistent with the traditional models of the Classical age.

We should not neglect how the Church absorbed and redeployed the main roles of stepfathers. Once monasteries started to accept "donated" children – and it appears to have been something that began as early as the early fourth century[95] – the apparatus of the Church assumed the functions of foster fathers. True, there could be other reasons for placing a child under the Church's care not solely associated with a child's well-being. Parents could "pledge" children – especially daughters – to the Church as a means of improving their own standing in the Christian community. It might also relieve families of certain financial obligations in raising children, including issues of dowries and inheritance. Illegitimacy offered a third issue. And, of course, defective or deformed children might be placed in monasteries instead of abandoning them.[96] But religious houses provided economic

[93] Anon. Valesianus 15.92.   [94] Sid. Apoll. *Ep.* 5.16.5.
[95] Some early oblates included Paphnutius, Daniel the Stylite, and Gregory of Nazianzus. It is significant, however, that we have no Western examples until the early fifth century.
[96] These are issues brought up in some of the chapters above: for financial concerns, including those associated with the sex of a child, Sigismund and Hübner; on illegitimacy, Ogden, Golden, and Malouta. Significantly, no one has looked at the issue of defect, perhaps a tacit understanding that those who were physically unfit would be exposed without hope of being raised. On the issue of exposure, see Arjava 1996: 81, n. 12; cf. T. S. Miller 2003: 141–74; W. V. Harris 1994.

and material support, they created a *domus* that offered emotional links to a new "family," and they created a social milieu by means of which an orphan might find access to office and responsibility that in other circumstances might be denied them. Throughout this volume, these sorts of responsibilities have formed our core understanding of foster or surrogate fathers.

Secondly, much as Harders and Bernstein have argued, the relationship between surrogate father and child was reflexive: children raised by surrogate fathers were supposed to take on the qualities and the interests of these "fathers." In the case of Honorius, Claudian walked a rhetorically fine line: he had to exhort the emperor to embrace fully the characteristics of Stilicho to become, in effect, a "Stilicho-in-training," while at the same time still implicitly acknowledging the general's superiority. For Boethius, his career and noble death were a vindication of the learning, career, and philosophical predisposition of Symmachus. He not only reflected the character of Symmachus in his life and career, but also in fact surpassed it – another way to conceptualize his success as a surrogate father. And for Antoninus, those qualities and interests were not only seen in his career, but also in his troubles when he was raised to the episcopate. His shortcomings and failures were a reflection of Augustine's own.

This reflexivity moreover displayed something new that had not really been articulated before, namely that there was an onus upon the surrogate parent to instill morals into his ward and for the child to take on those moral qualities. It is not simply that they were raised to succeed or replace their parents or surrogate parents – an idea that of course existed long before late antiquity. Nor was morality per se a new component in the makeup of a "successful" adult; that too had a long historical pedigree. It was the suggestion that the moral values inculcated in a child were now a part of that process of succession. In the case of Honorius, Claudian tries to demonstrate how that moral guidance by Stilicho affected the development of the emperor. In the case of Boethius, he himself notes this moral reflexivity.

Finally, and perhaps most intriguingly, the role of Christianity rested only incidentally upon these responsibilities. In the case of our two aristocratic orphans, there seems to be no application of its concerns at all, and in the case of Antoninus, imperfectly applied both in his youth and as a young adult. Not only is there barely any discussion of Christian ideas surrounding surrogate fatherhood, but also more broadly there is little in the works of the Western patristic writers to suggest that fathers were responsible for the religious upbringing of their children.[97] Indeed, as I have argued elsewhere, mothers had a more significant place in the Christian tradition of imbuing their children with their moral and religious education.[98] And so much is evident from the cases of Honorius and Boethius.

This leads us to an intriguing question, and one which requires more study, about whether the moral dimension placed in the foster-father/foster-child relationship was catalyzed by Christian belief. At this point, it is too early to say definitively. If a newly emphasized component of child-rearing in late antiquity was religious/moral education, then perhaps there is a Christian dimension to this aspect of surrogate fatherhood as well. Perhaps.

But if we can see here a tenuous connection to Christianity, we must ask finally why Christianity did not have a more visible impact on the way this relationship was expressed. This is a particularly significant question, since early and late antique Christian writers did place value on the special status of orphaned children. One must be cautious in this regard. Certainly one can argue for the significance of the practical aspects of foster-parenthood as being universal: providing protection, shelter, and material goods to ensure an orphan's survival. We can also point to important cultural concerns, especially among the aristocracy, as to maintaining status, wealth, and ensuring the proper political career. But I would also argue that these goals were not inconsistent with Christian concerns. Physical help, education (or training), the need for a suitable spouse, and successful adulthood were all foci of Christian interest as well. Any inculcation of religious ideals and exhortations to lead a Christian life must thus be weighed against these interests when fatherless children navigated the treacherous waters from childhood to adult. One late antique senator wrote that for children to find pleasure in the process of education and growing up, a father must become a child again.[99] The responsible foster father, like a biological father, took that trip with his de facto child.

---

[97] Jerome makes one reference to a husband's responsibility for religious activity in *Ep*. 66 (cf. more extensively Paulinus of Nola, *Ep*. 13), but it is addressed to a man who had recently lost his wife and had no children. Pammachius, the addressee in both letters, was known for his charitable works. Cf. Palladius, *Historia Lausiaca*. 62.

[98] Nathan 2000: 143–6.   [99] Symmachus, *Ep*. 3.20.

Bibliography

Abbreviated references to scholarly journals follow the conventions of *L'année philologique*.

Aarde, A. G. van (1999) "Fatherlessness in first-century Mediterranean culture: the historical Jesus seen from the perspective of cross-cultural anthropology and cultural psychology," *Hervormde Teologiese Studies* 55: 97–119.
  (2001) *Fatherless in Galilee: Jesus Child of God*. Harrisburg, PA.
  (2002) "Jesus as fatherless child," in *The Social Setting of Jesus and the Gospels*, ed. E. Stegemann, B. J. Manila, and G. Theissen. Minneapolis: 65–84.
Abel, P. F.-M. (1949) *Les Livres des Maccabées*. Paris.
Africa, T. W. (1978) "The mask of an assassin: a psychohistorical study of M. Junius Brutus," *Journal of Interdisciplinary History* 8: 599–626.
Alden, M. J. (1996) "Genealogy as paradigm: the example of Bellerophon," *Hermes* 124: 257–63.
Alföldy, A. (1976) "*Redeunt saturnia regna* – Zum Gottesgnadentum des Sulla," *Chiron* 6: 143–58.
Alston, R. (2002) *The City in Roman and Byzantine Egypt*. London.
Amato, P. R. (1994) "The implications of research on children in stepfamilies," in *Stepfamilies: Who Benefits? Who Does Not?*, ed. J. Dunn and A. Booth. Hillsdale, NJ: 81–8.
  (2004) "Tension between institutional and individual views of marriage," *Journal of Marriage and Family* 66: 959–65.
  (2007) *Alone Together: How Marriage in America Is Changing*. Cambridge, MA.
Amato, P. R., and J. M. Sobolewski (2004) "The effects of divorce on fathers and children. Nonresidential fathers and stepfathers," in Lamb (2004): 341–67.
Ameis, K. F., and C. Hentze (1965) *Homers Ilias für den Schulgebrauch. Zweiter Band, Viertes Heft, Gesang XXII–XXIV*. 4th edn. Leipzig and Berlin.
Andersen, O. (1978) *Die Diomedesgestalt in der Ilias* (Symbolae Osloenses Suppl. 25). Oslo, Bergen, and Tromsø.
Anderson, G. (2000) *Fairytale in the Ancient World*. London and New York.
Andreae, B. (2006) "Kleopatra und die historischen Persönlichkeiten in ihrem Umkreis," in *Kleopatra und die Caesaren. Eine Ausstellung des Bucerius Kunst Forums 28. Oktober 2006 bis 4. Februar 2007*, ed. B. Andreae. Munich: 48–125.
Andrews, A. (1961) "Philochorus on phratries," *JHS* 81: 1–15.

Angel, R., and J. L. Angel (1993) *Painful Inheritance: Health and the New Generation of Fatherless Families*. Madison.

Arjava, A. (1996) *Women and Law in Late Antiquity*. Oxford and New York.

(1997) "The guardianship of women in Roman Egypt," in *Akten des 21. Internationalen Papyrologenkongresses, Berlin 13.–19.8.1995*, ed. B. Kramer, W. Luppe, H. Mähler, and G. Pöthke. Stuttgart and Leipzig: 25–30.

(1998) "Paternal power in late antiquity," *JRS* 88: 147–65.

Arnaud, P. (1993) "Alexandre-Helios et Cléopâtre-Sélènè. Origine et postérité romaines d'un couple cosmique," in *Marc Antoine. Son idéologie et sa descendance. Actes du colloque organisé à Lyon le jeudi 28 juin 1990*, ed. E. Cizek. Lyon: 127–41.

Atkinson, K. M. T. (1958) "The governors of the province Asia in the reign of Augustus," *Historia* 7: 300–30.

Austin, N. (1999) "Anger and disease in Homer's *Iliad*," in *Euphrosyne: Studies in Ancient Epic and its Legacy in Honor of Dimitris N. Maronitis*, ed. J. N. Kazazis and A. Rengakos. Stuttgart: 11–49.

Avery, H. C. (1998) "Achilles' third father," *Hermes* 126: 389–97.

Baab, O. J. (1962) "Fatherless," *The Interpreter's Dictionary of the Bible*, vol II, ed. G. A. Buttrick. New York: 245–6.

Babbitt, F. C. (1956) *Plutarch: Moralia*. London.

Babcock, C. L. (1962) "Dio and Plutarch on the *damnatio* of Antonius," *CPh* 57: 30–2.

Badian, E. (1970) *L. Cornelius Sulla. The Deadly Reformer*. Sydney.

(1996a) "Cornelia (1)," *OCD*. 3rd edn.: 392.

(1996b) "Sempronius Gracchus, Gaius" and "Sempronius Gracchus (3), Tiberius," *OCD*. 3rd edn.: 1384–5.

Badian, E., C. B. Pelling, and T. Heath (1996) "Sulpicius Rufus, Servius," *OCD*. 3rd edn.: 1455.

Bagnall, R. S. (1991) "Freedmen and freedwomen with fathers?," *JJP* 21: 7–8.

(1993) *Egypt in Late Antiquity*. Princeton.

Bagnall, R. S., and R. Cribiore (2006) *Women's Letters from Ancient Egypt 300 BC–AD 800*. Ann Arbor, MI.

Bagnall, R. S., and P. Derow (2004) *The Hellenistic Period: Historical Sources in Translation*. Malden, MA, and Oxford.

Bagnall, R. S., and B. W. Frier (2006) *The Demography of Roman Egypt*. 2nd edn. Cambridge and New York.

Bagnall, R. S., B. W. Frier, and I. C. Rutherford (1997) *The Census Register P.Oxy. 984*. Brussels.

Balcer, J. M. (1987) *Herodotus and Bisitun. Problems in Ancient Persian Historiography*. Stuttgart.

Balla, P. (2003) *The Child–Parent Relationship in the New Testament and its Enviroments*. Tübingen.

Balland, A. (1981) *Fouilles de Xanthos VII. Inscriptions d'époque impériale du Létôon*. Paris.

Balsdon, J. V. P. D. (1951) "Sulla Felix," *JRS* 41: 1–10.

Baltrusch, E. (1988) *Regimen morum: Die Reglementierung des Privatlebens der Senatoren und Ritter in der römischen Republik und frühen Kaiserzeit.* Munich.

(2002) "Auf dem Weg zum Prinzipat: Die Entwicklung der republikanischen Herrschaftspolitik von Sulla bis Pompeius (88–62 v. Chr.)," in *Res publica reperta. Zur Verfassung und Gesellschaft der römischen Republik und des frühen Prinzipats. FS J. Bleicken*, ed. J. Spielvogel. Stuttgart: 245–62.

Bannon, C. J. (1997) *The Brothers of Romulus: Fraternal Pietas in Roman Law, Literature and Society.* Princeton.

Barden Dowling, M. (2000) "The clemency of Sulla," *Historia* 49: 303–40.

Barton, St. V. (1998) "Living as families in the light of the New Testament," *Interpretation* 52: 130–44.

Bauer, J. B. (1995) *Die Polykarpbriefe* (Kommentar zu den Apostolischen Vätern 5). Göttingen.

Bauer, W., and H. Paulsen (1985) *Die Briefe des Ignatius von Antiochia und der Polykarpbrief* (Handbuch zum Neuen Testament 18). Tübingen.

Baumgartner, W. (ed.) (1974) *Hebräisches und aramäisches Lexikon zum Alten Testament.* Leiden.

Beasley-Murray, G. R. (1999) *John* (World Biblical Commentary 36). 2nd edn. Nashville.

Beaucamp, J. (1985) "Le veuvage dans les papyrus byzantins," *Pallas* 32: 149–57.

(1990–2) *Le statut de la femme à Byzance (4e–7e siècle),* vol. i. *Le droit impérial;* vol. ii: *Les pratiques sociales.* Paris.

Beentjes, P. C. (1998) "'Sei den Waisen wie ein Vater und den Witwen wie ein Gatte.' Ein kleiner Kommentar zu Ben Sira 4,1–10," in *Der Einzelne und seine Gemeinschaft bei Ben Sira*, ed. R. Egger-Wenzel and I. Kramer. Berlin and New York: 51–64.

Behr, H. (1993) *Die Selbstdarstellung Sullas. Ein aristokratischer Politiker zwischen persönlichem Führungsanspruch und Standessolidarität.* Frankfurt.

Beltrami, L. (1998) *Il sangue degli antenati: stirpe, adulterio e figli senza padre nella cultura romana.* Bari.

Bengtson, H. (1977) *Marcus Antonius: Triumvir und Herrscher des Orients.* Munich.

Benigno, F. (1989) "The southern Italian family in the early modern period: a discussion of co-residential patterns," *Continuity and Change* 4: 165–94.

Bennett, H. V. (2002) *Injustice Made Legal. Deuteronomic Law and the Plight of Widows, Strangers and Orphans in Ancient Israel.* Grand Rapids, MI and Cambridge.

Bensel, K. (2005) "Die Melchisedek-Typologie in Hebräer 7,1–28. Ihre Beziehung zu kontemporären Melchisedek-Traditionen und den Prinzipien jüdischer Schriftexegese." Diss. Heverlee, Leuven.

Bernstein, N. W. (2005) "Mourning the *puer delicatus*: status inconsistency and the ethical value of fostering in Statius, *Silvae* 2.1," *AJPh* 126: 257–80.

(2007) "Fashioning Crispinus through his ancestors: epic models in Statius, *Silvae* 5.2," *Arethusa* 40.2: 183–96.

(2008) "Each man's father served as his teacher: constructing relatedness in Pliny's letters," *Classical Antiquity* 27: 202–30.

Bettini, M. (1991) *Anthropology and Roman Culture. Kinship, Time, Images of the Soul*, trans. J. Van Sickle. Baltimore and London.

(1992) *Familie und Verwandtschaft im antiken Rom*. Frankfurt am Main and New York.

(2002) "The Metamorphosis of 'texts' into 'sources' in Roman social history. Some examples from Richard Saller's 'Roman Kinship: Structure and Sentiment'," *QS* 56: 199–226.

Beutel, F. (2000) *Vergangenheit als Politik: neue Aspekte im Werk des jüngeren Plinius*. Frankfurt am Main.

Beyer, K. (1984) *Die aramäischen Texte vom Toten Meer*. Göttingen.

Biblarz, T. J., and G. Gottainer (2000) "Family structure and children's success: a comparison of widowed and divorced single-mother families," *Journal of Marriage and Family* 62: 533–48.

Binder, G. (1964) *Die Aussetzung des Königskindes. Kyros und Romulus*. Meisenheim am Glan.

Blankenhorn, D. (1995) *Fatherless America: Confronting our Most Urgent Social Problem*. New York.

(2007) *The Future of Marriage*. New York.

Bleicken, J. (1999) *Augustus: Eine Biographie*. Berlin.

Bloomer, W. M. (2006) "The technology of child production: eugenics and eulogics in the *de liberis educandis*," *Arethusa* 39: 71–99.

Boak, A. E. R. (1955) "The population of Roman and Byzantine Karanis," *Historia* 4: 157–62.

Böckler, A. (2000) *Gott als Vater im Alten Testament: Traditionsgeschichtliche Untersuchungen zur Entstehung und Entwicklung eines Gottesbildes*. Gütersloh.

Bohm, C. (1989) *Imitatio Alexandri im Hellenismus. Untersuchungen zum politischen Nachwirken Alexanders des Großen in hoch- und späthellenistischen Monarchien*. Munich.

Bonner, S. F. (1977) *Education in Ancient Rome: From the Elder Cato to the Younger Pliny*. Berkeley.

Borkowski, A., and P. du Plessis (2005) *Textbook on Roman Law*. 3rd edn. Oxford.

Boswell, J. (1988) *The Kindness of Strangers. The Abandonment of Children in Western Europe from Late Antiquity to the Renaissance*. New York.

Bourriot, F. (1976) *Recherches sur la nature du genos. Étude d'histoire sociale athénienne. Périodes archaïque et classique*. Lille.

Bowersock, G. W. (1965) *Augustus and the Greek World*. Oxford.

Bowman, A. K. (1986) *Egypt after the Pharaohs, 332 BC–AD 642*. London.

Bowman, A. K., and D. W. Rathbone (1992) "Cities and administration in Roman Egypt," *JRS* 82: 107–27.

Bradbury, S. (2004) *Selected Letters of Libanius from the Age of Constantius and Julian*. Liverpool.

Bradley, K. R. (1985) "Child labour in the Roman world," *Historical Reflections/ Réflexions Historiques* 12: 311–30.

(1987) *Slaves and Masters in the Roman Empire*. New York.

(1991a) *Discovering the Roman Family: Studies in Roman Social History*. New York.

(1991b) "Remarriage and the structure of the upper-class Roman family," in Rawson (1991a) Oxford, and New York: 79–98.

Bradshaw, J., C. Stimson, C. Skinner, and J. Williams (1999) *Absent Fathers?* London and New York.

Bramlett, M. D., and W. D. Mosher (2002) "Cohabitation, marriage, divorce and remarriage in the United States," *Vital Health Statistics* 23 (22) (National Center for Health Statistics).

Braund, D. (1984) "*Anth. Pal.* 9. 235: Juba II, Cleopatra Selene and the course of the Nile," *CQ* 34: 175–8.

Bremmer, J. N. (1976) "Avunculate and fosterage," *Journal of Indo-European Studies* 4: 65–78.

(1983) "The importance of the maternal uncle and grandfather in archaic and classical Greece and early Byzantium," *ZPE* 50: 173–86.

(1995) "Pauper or patroness. The widow in the early Christian church," in *Between Poverty and the Pyre. Moments in the History of Widowhood*, ed. J. Bremmer and L. van den Bosch, London and New York: 31–57.

(1999) "Fosterage, kinship and the circulation of children in ancient Greece," *Dialogos* 6: 1–20.

Brennan, T. C. (1992) "Sulla's career in the nineties: some reconsiderations," *Chiron* 22: 103–58.

Brenner, A. (1986) "Female social behaviour: two descriptive patterns within the 'birth of the hero' paradigm," *VT* 36: 257–73.

Briant, P. (1996) *Histoire de l'empire perse de Cyrus à Alexandre*. Paris.

Bridenthal, R. (1982) "The family: the view from a room of her own," in *Rethinking the Family: Some Feminist Questions*, ed. B. Thorne and M. Yalom. New York: 225–39.

Bringmann, K. (2002) *Geschichte der römischen Republik. Von den Anfängen bis Augustus*. Munich.

Brown, P. G. McC. (1990) "Plots and prostitutes in Greek New Comedy," *Papers of the Leeds International Latin Seminar* 6: 241–66.

Brown, S. (2004) "Family structure and child well-being: the significance of parental cohabitation," *Journal of Marriage and Family* 66: 351–67.

Brox, N. (1991) *Der Hirt des Hermas* (Kommentar zu den Apostolischen Vätern 7). Göttingen.

Bundesministerium für Familie, Senioren, Frauen und Jugend (ed.) (2003) *Die Familie im Spiegel amtlicher Statistik. Lebensformen, Familienstrukturen, wirtschaftliche Situation der Familien und familiendemographische Entwicklung in Deutschland*. Berlin.

Buraselis, K. (1996) "Stray notes on Roman names in Greek documents," in *Roman Onomastics in the Greek East: Social and Political Aspects. Proceedings of the International Colloquium on Roman Onomastics, Athens, 7–9 September 1993*, ed. A. D. Rizakis. Athens: 55–63.

Burnett, A. P. (2005) *Pindar's Songs for Young Athletes of Aigina*. Oxford.

Buszard, B. (2005) "The decline of Roman statesmanship in Plutarch's *Pyrrhus-Marius*," *CQ* 55: 481–97.

Butler, H. E. (1909) *The Apologia and Florida of Apuleius of Madaura*. Oxford.

Butrica, J. (1993) "Lygdamus, nephew of Messalla," *LCM* 19.4: 51–3.

Cagniart, P. F. (1989) "L. Cornelius Sulla's quarrel with C. Marius at the time of the Germanic invasion (104–101 BC)," *Athenaeum* 67: 139–49.

Calder, W. M. (1930) "Adoption and inheritance in Galatia," *JThS* 31: 372–4.

Calderini, A. (1953) "Apatores," *Aegyptus* 33: 358–69.

Cameron, A. (1970) *Claudian*. Oxford.

Candau Morón (2000) "Plutarch's Lysander and Sulla: integrated characters in Roman historical perspective," *AJPh* 121: 453–78.

Cantarella, E. (2003) "Fathers and sons in Rome," *CW* 96: 281–98.

Caplan, H. (1954) *Rhetorica ad Herennium*. Cambridge, MA.

Carcopino. J. (1929) "Séance du 30 janvier," *BSAF*: 84–6.

Carey, C. (1992) *Apollodorus. Against Neaira. [Demosthenes] 59*. Warminster.

Carney, E. D. (2000) *Women and Monarchy in Macedonia*. Norman.

Carpenter, R. (1945) "The identity of the ruler," *AJA* 49: 353–7.

Carpenter, T. (1986) *Dionysian Imagery in Archaic Greek Art*. Oxford.

Carter, J. M. (1971) *The Battle of Actium: The Rise and Triumph of Augustus Caesar*. London.

Cartledge, P. (2001) *Spartan Reflections*. London.

Cary, E. (ed.) (1960) *Dio Cassius: Roman History VI, Books 51–55*. London.

Casey, J. (1989) *The History of the Family*. Oxford and New York.

Chadwick, H. (1981) *Boethius. The Consolation of Music, Logic, Theology and Philosophy*. Oxford.

(1983) "The new letters of St. Augustine," *JThS*, n.s. 34: 440–5.

Chantraine, P. (1984) *Dictionnaire étymologique de la langue grecque: histoire des mots*. Paris.

Charlesworth, M. P. (1933) "Some fragments of the propaganda of Mark Antonius," *CQ* 27: 172–7.

Cherlin, A. J. (1992) *Marriage, Divorce, Remarriage*. Cambridge, MA.

Cherry, D. (1996) "Intestacy and the Roman poor," *RHD* 64: 155–72.

Chiusi, T. J. (1994) "Zur Vormundschaft der Mutter," *Zeitschrift der Savigny-Stiftung für Rechtsgeschichte, Romanische Abteilung* III: 155–96.

(2005) "Babatha vs. the guardians of her son: a struggle for guardianship – legal and practical aspects of *P. Yadin* 12–15, 27," in *Law in the Documents of the Judaean Desert*, ed. R. Katzoff and D. M. Schaps. Leiden and Boston: 105–32.

Christ, K. (2002) *Sulla. Eine römische Karriere*. Munich.

Clark, G. (1993) *Women in Late Antiquity: Pagan and Christian Lifestyles*. Oxford.

Clarysse, W., and D. J. Thompson (2006) *Counting the People in Hellenistic Egypt*. New York.

Clauss, M. (1995) *Kleopatra*. Munich.

Coale, A. J., and P. Demeny (1983) *Regional Model Life Tables and Stable Populations*. 2nd edn. New York and London.

Cohen, S. J. D. (ed.) (1993) *The Jewish Family in Antiquity*. Atlanta.

Cohn, M. (1920) "Jüdisches Waisenrecht," *Zeitschrift für Vergleichende Rechtswissenschaft* 37: 417–45.

Coleman, J. (1988) "Social capital in the creation of human capital," *American Journal of Sociology* 94: 95–120.

Coleman, K. M. (1999) "Mythological figures as spokespersons in Statius' *Silvae*," in *Im Spiegel des Mythos: Bilderwelt und Lebenswelt/Lo specchio del mito: immaginario e realtà*, ed. F. de Angelis and S. Muth. Wiesbaden: 67–80.

Coleman, M., and L. H. Ganong (2004) *Stepfamily Relationships: Development, Dynamics, and Interventions*. New York.

Collier, J., M. Z. Rosaldo, and S. Yanagisako (1992) "Is there a family? New anthropological views," in *Rethinking the Family: Some Feminist Questions*, ed. B. Thorne and M. Yalom. 2nd edn. Boston: 31–48.

Constantelos, D. J. (1968) *Byzantine Philanthropy and Social Welfare*. New Brunswick, NJ.

Corbier, M. (1991) "Divorce and adoption as familial strategies," in Rawson (1991a): 47–78.

  (1995) "Male power and legitimacy through women: the *domus Augusta* under the Julio-Claudians," in *Women in Antiquity. New Assessments*, ed. R. Hawley and B. Levick. London and New York: 178–93.

  (ed.) (1999) *Adoption et fosterage*. Paris.

  (2001) "Maiestas Domus Augustae (i)," in *Varia Epigraphica. Atti del Colloquio Internazionale di Epigrafia. Bertinoro, 8–10 giugno 2000*, ed. G. Angeli Bertinelli and A. Donati. Faenza: 155–99.

Corcy-Debray, S. (2001) *Jérôme Carcopino. Un Historien à Vichy*. Paris.

Courtney, E. (ed.) (1990) *P. Papini Stati Silvae*. Oxford.

  (1999) *Archaic Latin Prose*. Atlanta.

Cova, P. V. (2001) "Plinio il Giovane contro Plinio il Vecchio," *BStudLat* 31: 55–67.

Cox, C. A. (1988) "Sibling relationships in classical Athens: brother–sister ties," *Journal of Family History* 13: 377–95.

  (1998) *Household Interests. Property, Marriage Strategies, and Family Dynamics in Ancient Athens*. Princeton.

Craddock, F. E. B. (1998) "The Letter to the Hebrews" (New Interpreter's Bible, Vol. xii). Nashville: 1–173.

Crawford, M. H. (1983) *Roman Republican Coinage*. 2nd edn. Cambridge.

Cribiore, R. (2001) *Gymnastics of the Mind: Greek Education in Hellenistic and Roman Egypt*. Princeton.

  (2007a) *The School of Libanius in Late Antique Antioch*. Princeton.

  (2007b) "Lucian, Libanius, and the short road to rhetoric," *GRBS* 47: 71–86.

Criniti, N. (1991) *La Tabula Alimentaria di Veleia. Introduzione storica, edizione critica, traduzione, indice onomastici e toponomici, bibliografia veleiate* (Fonti e Studi, serie prima xiv). Parma.

Crook, J. A. (1957) "A legal point about Mark Antonius' will," *JRS* 47: 36–8.

  (1967) *Law and Life of Rome*. London.

Crotty, K. (1994) *The Poetics of Supplication: Homer's Iliad and Odyssey*. Ithaca and London.

Crowder, K., and J. Teachman (2004) "Do residential conditions explain the relationship between living arrangements and adolescent behavior," *Journal of Marriage and Family* 66: 721–38.

Dagron, G. (ed. and trans.) (1978) *Vie et miracles de sainte Thecle: texte grec, traduction et commentaire* (Subsidia Hagiographica 62). Brussels.

Daly, M. (1996) "Violence against stepchildren," *Current Directions in Psychological Science* 5: 77–81.

(2001) "An assessment of some proposed exceptions to the phenomenon of nepotistic discrimination against stepchildren," *Annales Zoologici Fennici* 38: 287–96.

Daly, M., and M. Wilson (1994) "Some differential attributes of lethal assaults on small children by stepfathers versus genetic fathers," *Ethology and Sociobiology* 15: 207–17.

(1999) *The Truth about Cinderella. A Darwinian View of Parental Love.* New Haven and London.

Daniels, C. R. (ed.) (1998) *Lost Fathers: The Politics of Fatherlessness in America.* New York.

Daube, D. (1966) *Roman Law: Linguistic, Social and Philosophical Aspects.* Edinburgh.

Davies, J. K. (1971) *Athenian Propertied Families 600–300 BC.* Oxford.

Davis, J. K. (1977) *People of the Mediterranean: An Essay in Comparative Social Anthropology.* London.

De Filippi, M. (1980) "Subvenire pupillis," *Labeo* 26: 61–73.

De Ligt, L. (2004) "Poverty and demography: the case of the Gracchan land reforms," *Mnemosyne* 57: 725–57.

De Regt, A. (2004) "Children in the 20th-century family economy: from co-providers to consumers," *The History of the Family* 9: 371–84.

Delcourt, M. (1957) *Héphaistos, ou la légende du magicien.* Liège.

Denis, H., B. Desjardins, and J. Légaré (1997) "Effect of family rupture and recomposition on the children of New France," *The History of the Family* 2: 277–93.

Derks, H. (1995) "A note on *homogalaktes* in Aristotle's *Politika*," *DHA* 21.2: 27–40.

DeSilva, D. A. (2000) *Perseverance in Gratitude. A Socio-Rhetorical Commentary on the Epistle "To the Hebrews."* Grand Rapids, MI, and Cambridge.

Detienne, M., and J.-P. Vernant (1978) *Cunning Intelligence in Greek Culture and Society.* Hassocks. (Translation of *Les ruses d'intelligence: la métis des grecs.* Paris, 1974.)

Dettenhofer, M. H. (2000) *Herrschaft und Widerstand im augusteischen Prinzipat: Die Konkurrenz zwischen* res publica *und* domus augusta. Stuttgart.

Dixon, S. (1984) "Infirmitas sexus: womanly weakness in Roman law," *RHD* 52: 343–71.

(1988) *The Roman Mother.* London.

(1992) *The Roman Family.* Baltimore.

(1997) "Conflict in the Roman family," in Rawson and Weaver (1997): 149–68.

(1999) "The circulation of children in Roman society," in Corbier (1999): 217–30.

(2001) *Reading Roman Women.* London.

Dobesch, G. (2004) "Caesar und der Hellenismus," in *Diorthoseis. Beiträge zur Geschichte des Hellenismus und zum Nachleben Alexanders des Großen,* ed. R. Kinsky. Munich and Leipzig: 108–252.

Doer, B. (1968–9) "Octavia. Eine außergewöhnliche Frau des alten Rom," *Altertum* 14/15: 20–31.

Domsgen, M. (2006) "Familie ist, wo man nicht rausgeworfen wird. Zur Bedeutung der Familie für die Theologie – Überlegungen aus religionspädagogischer Perspektive," *ThLZ* 131: 467–86.

Downey, D. B., J. W. Ainsworth-Darnell, and M. Dufur (1998) "Sex of parent and youths' well-being in single-parent households," *Journal of Marriage and the Family* 60: 878–93.

Duncan-Jones, R. (1982) *The Economy of the Roman Empire: Quantitative Studies*. 2nd edn. Cambridge and New York.

Dupâquier, J., E. Hélin, P. Laslett, M. Livi-Bacci, and S. Sogner (eds.) (1981) *Marriage and Remarriage in Populations of the Past*, London, New York, Toronto, Sydney, and San Francisco.

Dyck, A. R. (1996) *A Commentary on Cicero, De Officiis*. Ann Arbor, MI.

Ebbott, M. (2003) *Imagining Illegitimacy in Classical Greek Literature*. Lanham, MD.

Eck, W. (1996) "Antonius [II 1] Iullus," *Der neue Pauly*, vol. I: 814.

Eckey, W. (2004) *Das Lukasevangelium*, vol. I. Neukirchen-Vluyn.

Eder, W. (1997) "C. Sulla Felix, L.," *Der neue Pauly*, vol. III: 186–90.

Ellis, W. M. (1994) *Ptolemy of Egypt*. London and New York.

Eltrop, B. (1996) *Denn solchen gehört das Himmelsreich. Kinder im Matthäusevangelium. Eine feministisch-sozialgeschichtliche Untersuchung*. Stuttgart.

Erbse, H. (1961) "Betrachtungen über das 5. Buch der Ilias," *RhM* 104: 156–89.

Erdmann, E. (1972) *Die Rolle des Heeres in der Zeit von Marius bis Caesar. Militärische und politische Probleme einer Berufsarmee*. Neustadt a.d. Aisch.

Erhard, R., and H. Janig (2003) *Folgen von Vaterentbehrung. Eine Literaturstudie*. Vienna and Klagenfurt.

Ernout, A., and A. Meillet (1960) *Dictionnaire étymologique de la langue latine: histoire des mots*. 4th edn. Paris.

Evans, E. C. (1941) "The study of physiognomy in the second century AD," *TAPhA* 71: 96–108.

Evans, J. K. (1985) "The cult of the dead in ancient Rome and modern China: a comparative analysis," *Journal of the Hong Kong Branch of the Royal Asiatic Society* 25: 119–51.

(1991) *War, Women, and Children in Ancient Rome*. London and New York.

Evans, R. J. (1994) *Gaius Marius. A Political Biography*. Pretoria.

Evans Grubbs, J. (1987) "*Munitia coniugia*: the emperor Constantine's legislation on marriage and the family." Diss. Stanford.

(1995) *Law and Family in Late Antiquity*. Oxford.

(2002) *Women and the Law in the Roman Empire: A Sourcebook on Marriage, Divorce, and Widowhood*. London and New York.

Eyben, E. (1991) "Fathers and sons," in Rawson (1991a): 114–43.

(1993) *Restless Youth in Ancient Rome*. New York.

Fadinger, V. (2002) "Sulla als *imperator felix* und 'Epaphroditos' (= 'Liebling der Aphrodite')," in *Widerstand – Anpassung – Integration: Die griechische Staatenwelt und Rom. FS Deininger*, ed. N. Ehrhardt and L.-M. Günther. Stuttgart: 155–88.

Fantham, E. (2006) *Julia Augusti: The Emperor's Daughter.* London and New York.

Farrell. J. (2001) *Latin Language and Latin Culture: From Ancient to Modern Times.* Cambridge.

Fears, J. R. (1974) "Cyrus as a stoic exemplum of the just monarch," *AJPh* 95: 265–7.

(1975) "The coinage of Q. Cornificus and augural symbolism on late republican *denarii*," *Historia* 24: 592–602.

(1981) "The theology of victory at Rome: approaches and problems," *ANRW* II.17.2, ed. W. Haase. Berlin: 736–826.

Felson, N. (1999) "Paradigms of paternity: fathers, sons, and athletic/sexual prowess in Homer's *Odyssey*," in *Euphrosyne. Studies in Ancient Epic and its Legacy in Honor of Dimitris N. Maronitis*, ed. J. K. Kazakis and A. Rengakos. Stuttgart: 89–98.

(2002) "*Threptra* and invincible hands: the father–son relationship in *Iliad* 24," *Arethusa* 35: 35–50.

Felson-Rubin, N. (1994) *Regarding Penelope. From Character to Poetics.* Princeton.

Fensham, F. C. (1962) "Widow, orphan, and the poor in ancient near Eastern legal and wisdom literature," *Journal of Near Eastern Studies* 21: 129–39.

Festugière, A. J. (1959) *Antioche païenne et chrétienne.* Paris.

Feucht, E. (1995) *Das Kind im alten Ägypten: Die Stellung des Kindes in Familie und Gesellschaft nach altägyptischen Texten und Darstellungen.* Frankfurt and New York.

Fields, J. (2003) "Children's living arrangements and characteristics: March 2002," *Current Population Reports* P20–547. (Census Bureau).

Fineberg, S. (1999) "Blind rage and eccentric vision in *Iliad* 6," *TAPhA* 129: 13–41.

Finlay, R. A. (1980) "Patroklos, Achilleus and Peleus: fathers and sons in the *Iliad*," *CW* 73: 267–73.

Finley, M. I. (1979) *The World of Odysseus.* 2nd edn. New York.

Finn, R. D. (2006) *Almsgiving in the Later Roman Empire: Christian Promotion and Practice (313–450).* Oxford.

Fischer, R. A. (1999) *Fulvia und Octavia: Die beiden Ehefrauen des Marcus Antonius in den politischen Kämpfen der Umbruchszeit zwischen Republik und Prinzipat.* Berlin.

Flemberg, J. (1991) *Venus Armata. Studien zur bewaffneten Aphrodite in der griechisch-römischen Kunst.* Stockholm.

Flower, M. (2000) "Alexander the Great and Panhellenism," in *Alexander the Great in Fact and Fiction*, ed. A. B. Bosworth and E. J. Baynham. Oxford: 96–135.

Fontenrose, J. (1978) *The Delphic Oracle.* Berkeley.

Förster, R. (1903–27) *Libanius, Opera.* 12 vols. Leipzig (repr. Hildesheim 1963).

Foster, G. (2000) "The capacity of the extended family safety net for orphans in Africa," *Psychology, Health and Medicine* 5: 55–62.

Foster, G., C. Mafuka, R. Drew, S. Mashumba, and S. Kambeu (1997) "Perceptions of children and community members concerning the circumstances of orphans in rural Zimbabwe," *AIDS Care* 9: 391–405.

France, R. T. (2002) *The Gospel of Mark.* Grand Rapids, MI, and Cambridge.

French, V. (1999) "Aristophanes' doting dads: adult male knowledge of young children," *Text and Tradition: Studies in Greek History & Historiography in Honor of Mortimer Chambers*, ed. R. Mellor and L. A. Tritle. Claremont, CA: 163–81.

Frend, W. C. (1983) "Fussala, Augustine's crisis of credibility," *Les Lettres de saint Augustin découvertes par Johann Divjak*. Paris: 251–65.

Friedlander, D., B. S. Okun, and S. Segal (1999) "The demographic transition then and now: processes, perspectives, and analyses," *Journal of Family History* 24: 493–533.

Frier, B. W. (1969) "Sulla's priesthood," *Arethusa* 2: 187–99.

(1971) "Sulla's propaganda: the collapse of the Cinnan republic," *AJPh* 92: 585–604.

Frost, B.-P. (1997) "An interpretation of Plutarch's Cato the Younger," *HPTh* 18: 1–23.

Fuhrmann, M. (1979) "Persona, ein römischer Rollenbegriff," in *Identität*, ed. O. Marquard and K. Stierle. Munich: 83–106.

Funke, S. (2000) *Aiakidenmythos und epeirotisches Königtum. Der Weg einer hellen-ischen Monarchie.* Stuttgart.

Gabrielsen, V. (1997) *The Naval Aristocracy of Hellenistic Rhodes.* Aarhus.

Gaisser, J. H. (1969) "Adaptation of traditional material in the Glaucus-Diomedes episode," *TAPhA* 100: 165–76.

Gallant, T. W. (1991) *Risk and Survival in Ancient Greece: Reconstructing the Rural Domestic Economy.* Stanford.

Gantz, T. (1993) *Early Greek Myth: A Guide to Literary and Artistic Sources.* Baltimore and London.

Gardner, J. F. (1986) *Women in Roman Law and Society.* London and Sydney.

(1993) *Being a Roman Citizen.* London.

(1997) "Legal stumbling-blocks for lower-class families in Rome," in Rawson and Weaver (1997): 35–54.

(1998) *Family and Familia in Roman Law and Life.* Oxford.

Garland, R. (1990) *The Greek Way of Life.* Ithaca, NY.

Gazich, R. (1992) "Retorica dell'ostensione nelle Lettere di Plinio," in *Letterature latina dell'Italia settentrionale: cinque studi*, ed. P. V. Cova, R. Gazich, G. E. Manzoni, and G. Melzani. Milan: 141–95.

(2003) "Retorica dell'esemplarità nelle Lettere di Plinio," in *Plinius der Jüngere und seine Zeit*, ed. L. Castagna and E. Lefèvre. München: 123–41.

Gerber, C. (2005) *Paulus und seine "Kinder": Studien zur Beziehungsmetaphorik der paulinischen Briefe* (Beihefte zur Zeitschrift für die neutestamentliche Wissenschaft 136). Berlin and New York.

Geremek, H. (1969) *Karanis, communauté rurale de l'Égypte romaine au IIe–IIIe siècle de notre ère.* Warsaw.

Gerini, G. B. (1894) *Le dottrine pedagogiche di M. Tullio Cicerone, L. Anneo Seneca, M. Fabio Quintiliano e Plinio il Giovine; precedute da uno studio sulla educazione presso i Romani.* Turin.

Gesenius, W. (1995) *Hebräisches und aramäisches Handwörterbuch über das Alte Testament*, ed. R. Meyer and H. Donner. 18th edn. Berlin.

Gilbert, C. D. (1973) "Marius and *fortuna*," *CQ* 23: 104–7.

Gnilka, J. (1986) *Das Matthäusevangelium. Erster Teil.* Freiburg.

Goitein, S. D. (1967–93) *A Mediterranean Society: The Jewish Communities of the Arab World as Portrayed in the Documents of the Cairo Geniza.* 6 vols. Berkeley, CA.

Golden, M. (1981) "Demography and the exposure of girls at Athens," *Phoenix* 35: 316–31.

    (1990) *Children and Childhood in Classical Athens.* Baltimore.

    (2000) "A decade of demography," in *Polis and Politics. Studies in Ancient Greek History Presented to Mogens Herman Hansen on his Sixtieth Birthday, August 20, 2000,* ed. P. Flensted-Jensen, T. H. Nielsen, and L. Rubinstein. Copenhagen: 23–40.

Goody, E. (1982) *Parenthood and Social Reproduction. Fostering and Occupational Roles in West Africa.* Cambridge.

    (1988) "Parental strategies: calculation or sentiment? Fostering practices among West Africans," in *Interest and Emotion: Essays on the Study of Family and Kinship,* ed. D. W. Sabean and H. Medick. Cambridge: 266–77.

    (1999) "Sharing and transferring components of parenthood: the West African case," in Corbier (1999): 369–88.

Gourmelen, L. (2005) *Kékrops, le Roi-Serpent. Imaginaire athénien, représentations de l'humain et de l'animalité en Grèce ancienne.* Paris.

Gradenwitz, O. (1903) "Zwei Bankanweisungen aus den Berliner Papyri," *APF* 2: 96–116.

Graham, L. K. (1998) "Pastoral care of diverse families," *Interpretation* 52: 161–77.

Grant, M. (1972) *Cleopatra.* London.

Gräβer, E. (1993) *An die Hebräer,* vol. II: *Hebr. 7.1–10.18.* Zurich and Düsseldorf.

Gray-Fow, M. J. G. (1988a) "A stepfather's gift: L. Marcius Philippus and Octavian," *G&R* 35: 184–99.

    (1988b) "The wicked stepmother in Roman literature and history: an evaluation," *Latomus* 47: 741–57.

Green, P. (1982) *Ovid: The Erotic Poems.* New York.

Greene, T. (1963) *The Descent from Heaven: A Study in Epic Continuity.* New Haven and London.

Grelot, P. (1994) *Dieu, le père de Jésus-Christ.* Paris.

Grenier, J.-C. (2001) "Cléopâtre Séléné reine de Maurétanie. Souvenirs d'une princesse," in *Vbique amici. Mélanges offerts à Jean-Marie Lassère,* ed. C. Hamdoune. Montpellier: 101–16.

Griffin, J. (1980) *Homer on Life and Death.* Oxford.

Grimm, J., and W. Grimm (eds.) (1922) "Waise," in *Deutsches Wörterbuch von Jacob Grimm und Wilhelm Grimm,* vol. XIII, ed. K. von Bahder. Leipzig: 1043–53.

Griswold, R. L. (1993) *Fatherhood in America: A History.* New York.

Groebe, P. (1894a) "Iullus Antonius Nr. 22," *RE* I.2: 2583–4.

    (1894b) "M. Antonius Nr. 32," *RE* I.2: 2614.

    (1894c) "Antonia maior Nr. 113," *RE* I.2: 2640.

    (1894d) "Antonia minor Nr. 114," *RE* I.2: 2640.

Gruen, E. S. (1966) "The Dolabellae and Sulla," *AJPh* 87: 385–99.

Grunwald, M. (1922) "Jüdische Waisenfürsorge in alter und neuer Zeit," *Mitteilungen der Gesellschaft für Jüdische Volkskunde (N.F.)* 23: 3–29.

Guillemin, A. M. (1929) *Pline et la vie littéraire de son temps*. Paris.

Gullickson, A., and E. Hammel (2004) "Kinship structures and survival: maternal mortality on the Croatian-Bosnian border, 1750–1898," *Population Studies* 58: 145–59.

Günther, L.-M. (1993) "Witwen in der griechische Antike – zwischen oikos und polis," *Historia* 42: 308–25.

Gupta, S., P. J. Smock, and W. D. Manning (2004) "Moving out: transition to nonresidence among resident fathers in the US, 1968–1997," *Journal of Marriage and Family* 66: 627–38.

Gurval, R. A. (1995) *Actium and Augustus: The Politics and Emotions of Civil War*. Ann Arbor, MI.

Habermann, W. (1998) "Zur chronologischen Verteilung der papyrologischen Zeugnisse," *ZPE* 122: 144–60.

Hall, G. S. (2000) "The organization of the church," in *The Cambridge Ancient History*, vol. XIV: *Late Antiquity. Empire and Successors AD 425–600*, ed. A. Cameron, B. Ward-Perkins, and M. Whitby. Cambridge: 731–44.

Hallett, J. P. (1977) "Perusinae glandes and the changing image of Augustus," *AJAH* 2: 151–71.

(1984) *Fathers and Daughters in Roman Society: Women and the Elite Family*. Princeton.

(1996) "The political backdrop of Plautus' *Casina*," in *Transitions to Empire: Essays in Greco-Roman History, 340–146 BC, in Honor of E. Badian*, ed. R. W. Wallace and M. Harris. Norman: 409–38.

(2002a) "Cornelia," in *Women Writing Latin: From Roman Antiquity to Early Modern Europe*, vol. I: *Women Writing Latin in Roman Antiquity, Late Antiquity, and the Early Christian Era*, ed. L. J. Churchill, P. R. Brown, and J. E. Jeffrey. New York and London: 18–39.

(2002b) "The eleven elegies of the Augustan elegist Sulpicia," in *Women Writing Latin: From Roman Antiquity to Early Modern Europe*, vol. I: *Women Writing Latin in Roman Antiquity, Late Antiquity, and the Early Christian Era*, ed. L. J. Churchill, P. R. Brown, and J. E. Jeffrey. New York and London: 45–65.

(2004) "Matriot Games: Cornelia, mother of the Gracchi, and the forging of family-oriented political values," in *Women's Influence on Culture in Antiquity*, ed. F. McHardy and E. Marshall. New York and London: 26–39.

(2006a) "Fulvia, mother of Iullus Antonius: new approaches to the sources on Iulia's adultery at Rome," *Helios* 33.2: 149–64.

(2006b) "Introduction: Cornelia and her maternal legacy," in *Roman Mothers*, (ed.) J. P. Hallett. Special issue of *Helios* 33.2: 119–47.

(2006c) "Sulpicia and her *fama*: an intertextual approach to recovering her Latin literary image," *CW* 100.1: 37–42.

Hamel, D. (2003) *Trying Neaira. The True Story of a Courtesan's Scandalous Life in Ancient Greece*. New Haven.

Hammond, N. G. L. (1990) "Royal pages, personal pages and boys trained in the Macedonian manner during the period of the Temenid monarchy," *Historia* 39: 261–90.

Hansen, M. H. (1986) *Demography and Democracy: The Number of Athenian Citizens in the Fourth Century BC*. Herning.

Hanson, A. E. (2000) "Widows too young in their widowhood," in *I, Claudia*, vol. II: *Women in Roman Art and Society*, ed. D. E. E. Kleiner and S. B. Matheson. Austin: 149–65.

(2005) "The widow Babatha and the poor orphan boy," in *Law in the Documents of the Judaean Desert*, ed. R. Katzoff and D. Schaps. Leiden: 85–103.

Harders, A.-C. (2005) "Zwischen Kooperation und Repräsentation. Bruder-Schwester-Beziehungen in der römischen Republik und im frühen Prinzipat (2. Jh. v. Chr. – 1. Jh. n. Chr.)," *Historical Social Research* 30: 61–79.

(2006) *Suavissima Soror. Bruder–Schwester-Beziehungen in der römischen Republik*. PhD thesis University of Freiburg, forthcoming in *Vestigia* 60. Munich.

Hardie, A. (1983) *Statius and the* Silvae: *Poets, Patrons and Epideixis in the Graeco-Roman World*. Liverpool.

Harlow, M., and R. Laurence (2002) *Growing Up and Growing Old in Ancient Rome. A Life Course Approach*. London and New York.

Harries, B. (1993) "'Strange meeting': Diomedes and Glaucus in *Iliad* 6," *G&R* 40: 133–46.

Harris, E. (2004) "Notes on a lead letter from the Athenian Agora," *HSPh* 102: 157–70.

Harris, W. V. (1986) "The Roman father's power of life and death," in *Studies in Roman Law in Memory of A. Arthur Schiller*, ed. R. S. Bagnall and W. V. Harris. Leiden: 81–96.

(1994) "Child-exposure in the Roman empire," *JRS* 84: 1–22.

(1999) "Demography, geography and the sources of Roman slaves," *JRS* 89: 62–75.

Harrison, A. R. W. (1968–71) *The Law of Athens*. 2 vols. Oxford.

Hartmann, E. (2000) "Bastards in Classical Athens," in *Double Standards in the Ancient and Medieval World*, ed. K. Pollmann. Göttingen: 43–54.

Hasler, V. (1966) "Waise," *Biblisch-Historisches Handwörterbuch*, vol. III, ed. B. Reicke and L. Rost. Göttingen: 2133.

Heath, M. (2004) *Menander: A Rhetor in Context*. Oxford.

Heckel, W. (1992) *The Marshals of Alexander's Empire*. London and New York.

Heftner, H. (2006) *Von den Gracchen bis Sulla. Die römische Republik am Scheideweg 133–78 v. Chr.* Regensburg.

Heinrichs, J. (1987) "'Asiens König.' Die Inschriften des Kyrosgrabs und das achaimenidische Reichsverständnis," in *Zu Alexander d. Gr. FS G. Wirth*, vol. I, ed. W. Will and J. Heinrichs. Amsterdam: 487–540.

(2003) "Quinar," *Reallexikon der germanischen Altertumskunde*, vol. XXIV, ed. H. Beck *et al.* 2nd edn. Berlin and New York: 32–5.

Hemelrijk, E. A. (1999) *Matrona Docta. Educated Women in the Roman Élite from Cornelia to Julia Domna*. London and New York.

Henderson, J. (2002a) *Pliny's Statue: The Letters, Self-Portraiture & Classical Art.* Exeter.

(2002b) "Funding homegrown talent: Pliny *Letters* 1.19," *G&R* 49: 212–26.

Herlihy, D., and C. Klapisch-Zuber (1985) *Tuscans and their Families: A Study of the Florentine Catasto of 1427.* New Haven and London.

Heubeck, A., S. West, and J. B. Hainsworth (1988) *Homer's Odyssey. A Commentary*, vol. 1. Oxford.

Heuveline, P., and J. M. Timberlake (2004) "The role of cohabitation in family formation: the United States in comparative perspective," *Journal of Marriage and Family* 66: 1214–30.

Hewlett, B. S. (1991) *Intimate Fathers. The Nature and Context of Aka Pygmy Paternal Infant Care.* Ann Arbor, MI.

Heymann, J., A. Earle, D. Rajaraman, C. Miller, and K. Bogen (2007) "Extended family caring for children orphaned by AIDS: balancing essential work and caregiving in a High HIV Prevalence Nation," *AIDS Care* 19: 337–45.

Hickson, F. V. (1993) "*Patruus*: paragon or pervert? The case of a literary split personality," *SyllClass* 4: 21–6.

Higbie, C. (2002) "Diomedes' genealogy and ancient criticism," *Arethusa* 35: 173–88.

Hinard, F. (1985) *Sylla.* Paris.

Hinds, S. (1987) "The poetess and the reader: further steps toward Sulpicia," *Hermathena* 143: 29–46.

Hobson, D. (1983) "Women as property owners in Roman Egypt," *TAPhA* 113: 311–21.

Hoffer, S. E. (1999) *The Anxieties of Pliny the Younger.* Atlanta.

Hofferth, S., and K. G. Anderson (2003) "Are all dads equal? Biology vs. marriage as basis for paternal investment," *Journal of Marriage and Family* 65: 213–32.

Hoffmann, J. P., and R. A. Johnson (1998) "A national portrait of family structure and adolescent drug use," *Journal of Marriage and the Family* 60: 633–45.

Hofmann, M. (1959a) "Ptolemaios XV. Kaisar Nr. 37," *RE* XXIII.2: 1760–1.

(1959b) "Ptolemaios Philadelphos Nr. 38," *RE* XXIII.2: 1761.

(1959c) "Ptolemaios von Mauretanien Nr. 62," *RE* XXIII.2: 1768–87.

Hölbl, G. (1994) *Geschichte des Ptolemäerreiches. Politik, Ideologie und religiöse Kultur von Alexander dem Großen bis zur römischen Eroberung.* Darmstadt.

Hölkeskamp, K.-J. (2000) "Lucius Cornelius Sulla – Revolutionär und restaurativer Reformer," in *Von Romulus zu Augustus*, ed. K.-J. Hölkeskamp and E. Stein-Hölkeskamp. Munich: 199–218.

(2004) *Senatus Populusque Romanus. Die politische Kultur der Republik – Dimensionen und Deutungen.* Stuttgart.

Holman, Susan (2001) *The Hungry are Dying. Beggars and Bishops in Roman Cappadocia.* Oxford.

Hölscher, T. (1984) *Staatsdenkmal und Publikum. Vom Untergang der Republik bis zur Festigung des Kaisertums in Rom.* Konstanz.

Hölscher, U. (1967) "Die Atridensage in der Odyssee," in *Festschrift für Richard Alewyn*, ed. H. Singer and B. von Wiese. Cologne and Graz: 1–16.

Holum, K. (1982) *Theodosian Empresses.* Berkeley.

Holzberg, N. (1999) "Four poets and a poetess or portrait of the poet as a young man? Thoughts on Book 3 of the *Corpus Tibullianum*," *CJ* 94: 169–91.

Homoth-Kuhs, C. (2005) *Phylakes und Phylakon-Steuer im griechisch-römischen Ägypten* (APF Beiheft 17). Munich and Leipzig.

Hopkins, K. (1966) "On the probable age structure of the Roman population," *Population Studies* 20: 245–64.

Horkheimer, M. (1982) "Authority and the family," *Critical Theory: Selected Essays*, trans. M. J. O'Connell. New York: 47–128.

Horn, W. F., D. Blankenhorn, and M. B. Pearlstein. (1999) *The Fatherhood Movement: A Call to Action*. Lanham, MD.

Horsfall, N. (1987) "The 'letter' of Cornelia: yet more problems," *Athenaeum* 65: 231–4.

(1989) *Cornelius Nepos: A Selection including the Lives of Cato and Atticus*. Oxford.

Hubbard, T. (2004–5) "The invention of Sulpicia," *CJ* 100.2: 177–94.

Hubbell, H. M. (ed.) (1960) *Cicero: De inventione*. London.

Hübner, S. R. (2007) "'Brother–sister marriage' in Roman Egypt: a curiosity of humankind or a widespread family strategy?," *JRS* 97: 21–49.

Humbert, M. (1972) "Le remariage à Rome. Étude d'histoire juridique et sociale," *Università di Roma. Pubblicazioni dell' Istituto di Diritto romano e dei Diritti dell' Oriente mediterraneo* 44, Milan.

Humphreys, S. C. (1974) "The *nothoi* of Kynosarges," *JHS* 94: 88–95.

Hunter, S. S. (2003) *Black Death: AIDS in Africa*. New York.

Hunter, V. J. (1989a) "The Athenian widow and her kin," *Journal of Family History* 14: 291–311.

(1989b) "Women's authority in classical Athens: the example of Kleobule and her son," *EMC* 33 (n.s. 8): 39–48.

Huttner, U. (1995) "Marcus Antonius und Herakles," in *Rom und der griechische Osten. FS. H. H. Schmitt*, ed. C. Schubert and K. Brodersen. Stuttgart: 103–12.

Huys, M. (1995) *The Tale of the Hero Who Was Exposed at Birth in Euripidean Tragedy: A Study of Motifs*. Leuven.

Huzar, E. G. (1978) *Mark Antonius. A Biography*. London, Sydney, and Dover.

(1985/6) "Marc Antonius. Marriages vs. careers," *CJ* 81: 97–111.

Ingalls, W. (2002) "Demography and dowries: perspectives on female infanticide in classical Greece," *Phoenix* 56: 246–54.

Jal, P. (1963) "*Hostis* (*publicus*) dans la littérature latine de la fin de la république," *REA* 65: 53–79.

Jameson, M. H. (1986) "Labda, Lambda, Labdakos" in *Corinthiaca: Studies in Honor of Darrell A. Amyx*, ed. M. A. Del Chiaro and W. R. Briers. Columbia, MO: 3–11.

Janko, R. (1992) *The Iliad: A Commentary*, vol. iv: *Books 13–16*. Cambridge.

Jensen, A.-M., and L. McKee (2003) *Children and the Changing Family: Between Transformation and Negotiation*. New York.

Johnson, C. P. (1972–3) "Marc Antonius – man of five families," *Journal of the Society for Ancient Numismatics* 4: 21–2, 24.

Johnson, J. P. (1978) "The authenticity and validity of Antonius' will," *AC* 47: 494–503.

Jones, A. H. M. (1964) *The Later Roman Empire 284–602*. 3 vols. Oxford.

Jordan, H. (1860) *M. Catonis praeter librum De re rustica quae extant*. Leipzig.

Kämmerer, T. (1994) "Zur sozialen Stellung der Frau in Emar und Ekalte," *Ugarit-Forschungen, Internationales Jahrbuch für die Altertumskunde Syrien-Palästinas* 26: 169–208.

Kapparis, K. (1994) "Was *atimia* for debts to the state inherited through women?," *RIDA* 41: 113–24.

(1999) *Apollodoros. Against Neaira [D. 59.]*. Berlin.

(2002) *Abortion in the Ancient World*. London.

Karabélias, E. (1982) "La situation successorale de la fille unique dans la koinè juridique hellénistique," *Symposion*: 223–34.

Kaser, M. (1971) *Das römische Privatrecht* (Handbuch der Altertumswissenschaft x.3.3.1). 2nd edn. Munich.

(1975) "Der Inhalt der *Patria Potestas*," *Zeitschrift der Savigny-Stiftung für Rechtsgeschichte, Romanische Abteilung* 58: 62–87.

Kaster, R. A. (1988) *Guardians of Language: The Grammarian and Society in Late Antiquity*. Berkeley.

Katz, B. R. (1982) "Notes on Sulla's ancestors," *LCM* 7.10: 148–9.

Katz, M. A. (1993) "Buphonia and goring ox: homicide, animal sacrifice and judicial process," in *Nomodeiktes. Greek Studies in Honor of Martin Ostwald*, ed. M. Rosen and J. Farrell. Ann Arbor, MI: 155–78.

Katz, M. M., and M. J. Konner (1981) "The role of the father: an anthropological perspective," in *The Role of the Father in Child Development*, ed. M. E. Lamb. 2nd edn. New York: 155–86.

Kawerau, G., and A. Rehm (eds.) (1914) *Milet*, vol. 1.3: *Das Delphinion in Milet*. Berlin.

Keaveney, A. (1984) "Who were the Sullani?," *Klio* 66: 114–50.

(2005) *Sulla, the Last Republican*. 2nd edn. London.

Keener, C. S. (2003) *The Gospel of John. A Commentary*, vol. ii. Peabody, MA.

Keith, A. (2006) "Critical trends in interpreting Sulpicia," *CW* 100: 3–10.

Kertzer, D. I. (1989) "The joint family household revisited: demographic constraints and household complexity in the European past," *Journal of Family History* 14: 1–15.

Kienast, D. (1999) *Augustus. Prinzeps und Monarch*. 3rd edn. Darmstadt.

Kierdorf, W. (1980) *Laudatio Funebris: Interpretation und Untersuchung zur Entwicklung der Römischen Leichenrede*. Meisenheim am Glan.

Kim, J. (2000) *The Pity of Achilles: Oral Style and the Unity of the Iliad*. Lanham, MD.

Kindstrand, J. F. (1990) "A collection of apophthegmata in an Oxford manuscript," in *Greek and Latin Studies in Memory of Cajus Fabricius*. Studia Graeca et Latina Gothoburgensia 54, ed. S.-T. Teodorsson. Gothenberg: 141–53.

Kirk, G. S. (1983) "The *Iliad*: the style of Books 5 and 6," in *Aspects of the Epic*, ed. T. Winnifrith, P. Murray, and K. W. Gransden, London: 16–31.

(1990) *The Iliad: A Commentary,* vol. ii: *Books 5–8*. Cambridge.

Klapisch-Zuber, C. (ed.) (1985) *Women, Family, and Ritual in Renaissance Italy.* Chicago.

Kleiner, D. E. E. (1992) "Politics and gender in the pictorial propaganda of Antonius and Octavian," *EMC* 11: 357–67.

(2005) *Cleopatra and Rome.* Cambridge, MA, and London.

Knoester, C., and D. L. Haynie (2005) "Community context, social integration into family, and youth violence," *Journal of Marriage and Family* 67: 767–80.

Kouliakiotis, E. (2006) *Genese und Metamorphosen des Alexandermythos im Spiegel der griechischen nicht-historiographischen Überlieferung bis zum 3. Jh. n. Chr.* Konstanz.

Krause, J.-U. (1994–5) *Witwen und Waisen im römischen Reich.* 4 vols. Munich.

(2002) "Waisen," *Der neue Pauly*, vol. XII.2: 378–80.

Kreider, R., and J. Fields (2005) "Living arrangements of children: 2001," *Current Population Reports* P70–104. (Census Bureau).

Kubitschek, W. (1929) "*Spurius, spurii filius, sine patre filius* und *spurius*," *WS* 47: 130–43.

Kuhrt, A. (1995) *The Ancient Near East c. 3000–330 BC*, vol. 1. London and New York.

(2003) "Making history: Sargon of Agad and Cyrus the Great of Persia," in: *Achaemenid History XIII: A Persian Perspective*, ed. W. Henkelman and A. Kuhrt. Leiden: 347–61.

Kullmann, W. (1984) "Oral poetry theory and neoanalysis in Homeric research," *GRBS* 25: 207–23.

(1992) "Vergangenheit und Zukunft in der Ilias," in *Homerische Motive. Beiträge zur Entstehung, Eigenart und Wirkung von Ilias und Odyssee*, ed. R. J. Müller. Stuttgart: 219–42. (Originally published in *Poetica* 2 (1968): 15–37.)

(2002a) "Die Darstellung verborgener Gedanken in der antiken Literatur," in *Realität, Imagination und Theorie. Kleine Schriften zu Epos und Tragödie in der Antike*, ed. A. Rengakos. Stuttgart: 177–205.

(2002b) "Nachlese zur Neoanalyse," in *Realität, Imagination und Theorie. Kleine Schriften zu Epos und Tragödie in der Antike*, ed. A. Rengakos. Stuttgart: 162–76.

Kurylowicz, M. (1983) "Adoption on the evidence of the papyri," *JJP* 19: 61–75.

Lacey, W. K. (1986) "Patria Potestas," in *The Family in Ancient Rome: New Perspectives*, ed. B. Rawson. Ithaca: 121–44.

Lamb, M. E. (ed.) (1987) *The Father's Role: Cross-cultural Perspectives.* Hillsdale, NJ.

(2000) "The history of research on father involvement: an overview," *Marriage and Family Review* 29: 23–42.

(ed.) (2004) *The Role of the Father in Child Development.* 4th edn. Hoboken, NJ.

Lamb, M. E., and C. Lewis (2004) "The development and significance of father–child relationships in two-parent families," in Lamb (2004): 272–306.

Lamb, M. E., and C. S. Tamis-Lemonda (2004) "The role of the father. An introduction," in Lamb (2004): 1–31.

Lambert, S. D. (1993) *The Phratries of Attica.* Ann Arbor, MI.

Lamberton, R. (1997) "Homer in antiquity," in *A New Companion to Homer*, ed. I. Morris and B. Powell. Leiden: 33–54.

Lambrinoudakis, B. K. (1971) Μηροτράφης. Μελέτη περὶ τῆς γονιμοποιοῦ τρώσεως ἡ δεσμεύσεως τοῦ ποδὸς ἐν τῇ ἀρχαίᾳ ἑλληνικῇ μυθολογίᾳ. Athens.

Lang, B. (2001) "Waise," *Neues Bibel-Lexikon*, vol. III, ed. M. Görg and B. Lang. Zurich: 1056.

Lansford, J. E., R. Ceballo, A. Abbey, and A. J. Stewart (2001) "Does family structure matter? A comparison of adoptive, two-parent biological, single-mother, stepfather, and stepmother households," *Journal of Marriage and Family* 63: 840–51.

Lape, S. (2004) *Reproducing Athens. Menander's Comedy, Democratic Culture, and the Hellenistic City*. Princeton.

Laslett, P. (1977) *Family Life and Illicit Love in Earlier Generations*. Cambridge.

Laslett, P., K. Oosterveen, and R. M. Smith (eds.) (1980) *Bastardy and its Comparative History*. Oxford.

Lattimore, R. (1951) *The Iliad of Homer*. Chicago.
  (1965) *The Odyssey of Homer*. New York.

Lee, M. O. (1979) *Fathers and Sons in Virgil's* Aeneid: Tum Genitor Natum. Albany, NY.

Légaré, J., and J.-F. Naud (2001) "The dynamics of household structure in the event of the father's death. Québec City in the 18th century," *History of the Family* 6: 519–29.

Lelis, A., W. A. Percy, and B. C. Verstraete (2003) *The Age of Marriage in Ancient Rome*. Lewiston, NY.

LeMoine, F. J. (1991) "Parental gifts: father–son dedications and dialogues in Roman didactic literature," *ICS* 16: 337–66.

Leon, E. F. (1959) "One Roman's family," *CB* 35: 61–5.

Lerman, R., and E. Sorenson (2000) "Father involvement with their nonmarital children: patterns, determinants, and the effects on their earnings," *Marriage and Family Review* 29: 137–58.

Letzner, W. (2000) *Lucius Cornelius Sulla. Versuch einer Biographie*. Münster.

Lévi-Strauss, C. (1967) "Die Strukturanalyse in der Sprachwissenschaft und in der Anthropologie," in *Strukturale Anthropologie*, ed. C. Lévi-Strauss. Frankfurt: 43–67.

Levy, J. (1963) *Wörterbuch über die Talmudim und Midraschim*, vols. I–II. Darmstadt (repr. of the 2nd edn. Berlin and Vienna, 1924).

Lewis, A. (1970) "Instructions for appointing a guardian," *BASP* 7: 116–18.

Lewis, N. (1982) *The Compulsory Public Services of Roman Egypt*. Florence.

Lewis, R. G. (1991) "Sulla's autobiography: scope and economy," *Athenaeum* 79: 509–19.

Liddell, H., and R. Scott (1968) *A Greek–English Lexicon*, rev. H. S. Jones and R. McKenzie. Oxford.

Liebeschuetz, J. H. W. G. (1972) *Antioch: City and Imperial Administration in the Later Roman Empire*. Oxford.

Link, S. (1998) "Zur Aussetzung neugeborener Kinder in Sparta," *Tyche* 13: 153–64.
Lintott, A. (1999) *The Constitution of the Roman Republic.* Oxford.
Lipsius, J. H., M. H. E. Meier, and G. F. Schömann *et al.* (1905) *Das attische Recht und Rechtsverfahren mit Benutzung des attischen Processes.* Leipzig.
Lona, H. E. (1998) *Der erste Clemensbrief.* Göttingen.
Lotze, D. (1981) "Zwischen Politen und Metöken: Passivbürger im klassischen Athen?," *Klio* 63: 159–78.
Lovano, M. (2002) *The Age of Cinna: Crucible of the Republican Rome.* Stuttgart.
Luck, U. (1993) *Das Evangelium nach Matthäus* (Züricher Bibelkommentare NT 1). Zurich.
Luther, A. (2006) "Die Töchter Marc Antons, die 'zwei Stimmen' in Vergils *Aeneis* und die politische Propaganda des Augustus," in *Frauen und Geschlechter 1. Bilder – Rollen – Realitäten in den Texten antiker Autoren der Kaiserzeit,* ed. C. Ulf and R. Rollinger. Vienna, Cologne, and Weimar: 209–20.
Luz, U. (1997) *Das Evangelium nach Matthäus.* Zurich and Düsseldorf.
Lynn-George, M. (1996) "Structures of care in the *Iliad,*" *CQ* 46: 1–26.
MacDowell, D. M. (1986) *The Law in Classical Athens.* Ithaca, NY.
Mackay, C. S. (2000) "Sulla and the monuments: studies in his public persona," *Historia* 49: 161–210.
Macleod, C. W. (1982) *Homer, Iliad, Book XXIV.* Cambridge.
Macurdy, G. H. (1932) *Hellenistic Queens: A Study of Woman-power in Macedonia, Seleucid Syria, and Ptolemaic Egypt.* Baltimore.
Madden, J. A., and A. Keaveney (1993) "Sulla père and Mithridates," *CPh* 88: 138–41.
Maftei, M. (1976) *Antike Diskussionen über die Episode von Glaucus und Diomedes im VI. Buch der Ilias.* Beiträge zur klassischen Philologie 74. Meisenheim am Glan.
Maier, G. (2004) *Der Brief des Jakobus.* Wuppertal and Giessen.
Malouta, M. (2007) "The terminology of fatherlessness in Roman Egypt: ἀπάτωρ and χρηματίζων μητρός," *Proceedings of the XXIV International Congress of Papyrology, Helsinki, 2004*: 615–24.
(forthcoming 2008) "The life and lot of fatherless individuals as attested in the papyri," in *Law and Society in Greek, Roman and Byzantine Egypt. An Introduction to the Sources,* ed. J. Keenan, J. G. Manning, and U. Yiftach. Cambridge.
Mankell, H. (2005) *Before the Frost,* trans. E. Segerberg. New York.
Marenbon, J. (2003) *Boethius.* Oxford.
Marsiglio, W., P. R. Amato, R. D. Day, and M. E. Lamb (2000) "Scholarship on fatherhood in the 1990s and beyond," *Journal of Marriage and the Family* 62: 1173–91.
Marsman, H. J. (2003) *Women in Ugarit and Israel: Their Social and Religious Position in the Context of the Ancient Near East.* Leiden and Boston.
Martin, D. (1996) "The construction of the ancient family: methodological considerations," *JRS* 86: 40–60.

Martin, J. (1984) "Zur Stellung des Vaters in antiken Gesellschaften," in *Historische Anthropologie: Der Mensch in der Geschichte*, ed. M. Erbe and H. Süssmuth. Göttingen: 84–109.

(1993) "Zur Anthropologie von Heiratsregeln und Besitzübertragung. 10 Jahre nach den Goody-Thesen," *Historische Anthropologie* 1: 149–62.

(1997) "Zwei Alte Geschichten. Vergleichende historisch-anthropologische Betrachtungen zu Griechenland und Rom," *Saeculum* 48: 1–20.

(2002a) "Familie, Verwandtschaft und Staat in der römischen Republik," in *Res Publica Reperta. Zur Verfassung und Gesellschaft der römischen Republik und des frühen Prinzipats. Festschrift für Jochen Bleicken zum 75. Geburtstag*, ed. J. Spielvogel. Stuttgart: 13–24.

(2002b) "Formen sozialer Kontrolle im republikanischen Rom," in *Demokratie, Recht und soziale Kontrolle im Klassischen Athen*, ed. D. Cohen. Munich: 155–72.

Martin, P. M. (1995) *Antoine et Cléopâtre: La fin d'une rêve*. Brussels.

Matussek, M. (1998) *Die vaterlose Gesellschaft: Überfällige Anmerkungen zum Geschlechterkampf*. Reinbek.

(1999) *Die vaterlose Gesellschaft – Briefe, Berichte, Essays*. Reinbek.

(2006) *Die vaterlose Gesellschaft. Eine Polemik gegen die Abschaffung der Familie*. Frankfurt am Main.

McGinn, T. A. J. (1999) "Widows, orphans and social history," *JRA* 12: 617–32.

McLanahan, S., and G. D. Sandefur (1994) *Growing Up with a Single Parent: What Hurts, What Helps*. Cambridge, MA.

McLanahan, S., and M. S. Carlson (2004) "Fathers in fragile families," in Lamb (2004): 368–96.

Meiggs, R., and D. Lewis (1969) *A Selection of Greek Historical Inscriptions*. Oxford.

Meiklejohn, K. W. (1934) "Alexander Helios and Caesarion," *JRS* 24: 191–5.

Merkelbach, R. (1984) *Mithras*. Königstein.

Merriam, C. U. (2002) "Storm warning: Ascanius' appearances in the *Aeneid*," *Latomus* 61: 852–60.

Mette-Dittmann, A. (1991) *Die Ehegesetze des Augustus: Eine Untersuchung im Rahmen der Gesellschaftspolitik des Princeps*. Stuttgart.

Michel, A. (2006) "Gewalt gegen Kinder im Alten Israel," in *"Schaffe mir Kinder …" Beiträge zur Kindheit im Alten Israel und seinen Nachbarkulturen*, ed. A. Kunz-Lübcke and R. Lux. Leipzig: 137–63.

Miller, S. G. (1978) *The Prytaneion. Its Function and Architectural Form*. Berkeley and Los Angeles.

Miller, T. S. (2003) *The Orphans of Byzantium: Child Welfare in the Christian Empire*. Washington, DC.

Mills, S. (2000) "Achilles, Patroclus and parental care in some Homeric similes," *G&R* 47: 3–18.

Milnor, K. (2005) *Gender, Domesticity, and the Age of Augustus: Inventing Private Life*. Oxford.

Mingazzini, P. (1926) "Inscrizioni Urbane Inedite," *BCAR Anno LIII*: 229–30.

Mitscherlich, A. (1963) *Auf dem Weg zur vaterlosen Gesellschaft: Ideen zur Sozialpsychologie.* Munich.

  (1993) *Society without the Father: A Contribution to Social Psychology.* New York.

Mitteis, L. (1912) *Grundzüge und Chrestomathie der Papyruskunde: Zweiter Band: juristischer Teil, Zweite Hälfte: Chrestomathie.* Leipzig and Berlin.

Mitterauer, M. (2003) "Mittelalter," in *Geschichte der Familie*, ed. A. Gestrich, J.-U. Krause, and M. Mitterauer. Stuttgart: 160–363.

Montevecchi, O. (1981) "Una donna 'prostatis' del figlio minorenne in un papiro del Iia," *Aegyptus* 61: 103–15 (= O. Montevecchi, *Scripta Selecta*, ed. S. Daris. Milan, 1998: 273–85).

Moreau, P. (2005) "La *Domus Augusta* et les formations de parenté à Rome," *CCG* 16: 7–23.

Most, G. W. (1985) *The Measures of Praise. Structure and Function in Pindar's Second Pythian and Seventh Nemean Odes.* Göttingen.

Moxnes, H. (1997) "What is family? Problems in constructing early Christian families," in *Constructing Early Christian Families. Family as Social Reality and Metaphor*, ed. H. Moxnes. London and New York: 13–41.

Mrozek, S. (1973) "Zu der kaiserlichen und privaten Kinderfürsorge in Italien des 2. und 3. Jhs.," *Klio* 55: 281–4.

Müller, S. (2002) "Marius vor Vercellae," *Die Zinnfigur* 7: 208.

  (2006) "Alexander der Große als neuer Achilles. Die panhellenische und makedonische Repräsentation des Persienkrieges in den Medien der königlichen Propaganda," in *Zeichen des Krieges in Literatur, Film und den Medien II: Ideologisierungen und Entideologisierungen*, ed. S. Jäger and C. Petersen. Kiel: 263–94.

Munbier, C. (1983) "La question des appels à Rome d'après Lettre 20*," *Les Lettres de saint Augustin découvertes par Johann Divjak.* Paris: 287–99.

Murnaghan, S. (1992) "Maternity and mortality in Homeric poetry," *Cl. Ant.* 11: 242–64.

Mussner, Fr. (1964) *Der Jakobusbrief* (Herders theologischer Kommentar zum Neuen Testament 13.1). Freiburg.

Nathan, G. S. (2000) *The Family in Late Antiquity. The Rise of Christianity and the Endurance of Tradition.* London and New York.

Nauta, R. R. (2002) *Poetry for Patrons: Literary Communication in the Age of Domitian.* Leiden.

Neils, J., and J. H. Oakley (eds.) (2003) *Coming of Age in Ancient Greece: Images of Childhood from the Classical Past.* New Haven.

Neudorfer, H.-W. (2004) *Der erste Brief des Paulus an Timotheus.* Wuppertal and Giessen.

Nevett, L. C. (1999) *House and Society in the Ancient Greek World.* Cambridge and New York.

Newlands, C. E. (2002) *Statius' Silvae and the Poetics of Empire.* Cambridge.

Nicholas, B., and S. M. Treggiari (1996) "*Patria potestas*," *OCD.* 3rd edn.: 1122–3.

Nielsen, H. S. (1999) "Quasi-kin, quasi-adoption and the Roman family," in Corbier (1999): 249–61.

Nisbet, R. G. M. (1978) "*Felicitas* at Surrentum (Statius, *Silvae* II.2)," *JRS* 65: 1–11.

Nobus, D. (2003) "Spectres of fatherlessness: social and clinical implications of a modern scourge," *The Discourse of Sociological Practice* 5: 5–15.

Nolland, J. (1989) *Luke 1–9:20*. World Biblical Commentary 35A. Dallas, TX.
 (2005) *The Gospel of Matthew*. Grand Rapids, MI, and Cambridge.

Norman, A. F. (1965) *Libanius' Autobiography (Oration I)*. London.
 (1969–77) *Libanius, Selected Works*. 2 vols. Cambridge, MA.
 (1992) *Libanius: Autobiography and Selected Letters*. 2 vols. Cambridge, MA.

Norrback, A. (2001) *The Fatherless and the Widow in the Deuteronomic Covenant*. Åbo.

Noy, D. (1991) "The wicked stepmothers in Roman society and imagination," *Journal of Family History* 16: 345–61.

O'Brien, M. (2004) "Social science and public policy perspectives on fatherhood in the European Union," in Lamb (2004): 121–45.

Ogden, D. (1995) "Women and bastardy in ancient Greece," in *The Greek World*, ed. A. Powell. London: 219–44.
 (1996) *Greek Bastardy in the Classical and Hellenistic Periods*. Oxford and New York.
 (1997a) *The Crooked Kings of Ancient Greece*. London.
 (1997b) "Rape, adultery and the protection of bloodlines in classical Athens," in *Rape in Antiquity*, ed. S. Deacy and K. F. Pierce. London: 25–41.
 (1999) *Polygamy, Prostitutes and Death. The Hellenistic Dynasties*. London.
 (2002) "Controlling women's dress: *gynaikonomoi*," in *Women's Dress in the Ancient Greek World*, ed. L. J. Llewellyn-Jones. London: 203–26.

Olsen, L. A. (1999) *La femme et l'enfant dans les unions illégitimes à Rome. L'évolution du droit jusqu' au début de l'Empire*. Bern.

Omitowoju, R. (2002) *Rape and the Politics of Consent in Classical Athens*. Cambridge.

Osiek, C. (1996) "The family in early Christianity. Family values revisited," *Catholic Biblical Quarterly* 58: 1–24.

Osiek, C., and D. L. Balch (1997) *Families in the New Testament World. Households and House Churches. The Family, Religion and Culture*. Louisville, KY.

Parker, H. (1994) "Sulpicia, the *auctor de Sulpicia* and the authorship of 3.9 and 3.11 of the *Corpus Tibullianum*," *Helios* 21: 39–62.
 (2006) "Catullua and the *Amicus Catulli*: the text of a learned talk," *CW* 100: 17–29.

Parker, R. C. T. (1987) "Myths of early Athens," in *Interpretations of Greek Mythology*, ed. J. N. Bremmer. London and Sydney: 187–214.
 (1996) *Athenian Religion. A History*. Oxford.

Parkes, P. (2003) "Fostering fealty: a comparative analysis of tributary allegiances of adoptive kinship," *CSSH* 45: 741–82.
 (2004) "Fosterage, kinship and legend: when milk was thicker than blood?," *CSSH* 46: 587–615.
 (2006) "Celtic fosterage: adoptive kinship and clientage in north-west Europe," *CSSH* 48: 359–95.

Parkin, T. G. (1992) *Demography and Roman Society.* Baltimore and London.

(1997) "Out of sight, out of mind: elderly members of the Roman family," in Rawson and Weaver (1997): 123–48.

(2003) *Old Age in the Roman World. A Cultural and Social History.* Baltimore.

Pasley, K., and S. L. Braver (2004) "Measuring father involvement in divorced, nonresident fathers," in *Conceptualizing and Measuring Father Involvement,* ed. R. D. Day and M. E. Lamb. Mahwah, NJ: 217–40.

Patterson, C. B. (1990) "Those Athenian bastards," *Cl. Ant.* 9: 40–73.

(1994) "The case against Neaera and the public ideology of the Athenian family," in *Athenian Identity and Civic Ideology,* ed. A. L. Boegehold and A. C. Scafuro. Baltimore: 199–216.

(1998) *The Family in Greek History.* Cambridge, MA, and London.

Pavlovskis, Z. (1973) *Man in an Artificial Landscape. The Marvels of Civilization in Imperial Roman Literature.* Leiden.

(1996) "Valerius Messalla Corvinus, Marcus," *OCD.* 3rd edn.: 1580.

Perdue, L. G. (1997) "The Israelite and early Jewish family: summary and conclusions," in *Families in Ancient Israel. The Family, Religion, and Culture,* ed. L. G. Perdue, J. Blenkinsopp, J. J. Collins, and C. Meyers. Louisville, KY: 163–222.

Petit, P. (1956) *Les étudiants de Libanius.* Paris.

Petrini, M. (1997) *The Child and the Hero: Coming of Age in Catullus and Vergil.* Ann Arbor, MI.

Phang, S. E. (2001) *The Marriage of Roman Soldiers (13 BC–AD 235): Law and Family in the Imperial Army.* Leiden and Boston.

(2002) "The families of Roman soldiers (first and second centuries AD): Culture, law, and practice," *Journal of Family History* 27: 352–73.

Philipps, E. J. (1976) "Catiline's conspiracy," *Historia* 25: 441–8.

Pleck, E. H. (2004) "Two dimensions of fatherhood. A history of the good Dad – bad Dad complex," in Lamb (2004): 32–57.

Pomeroy, S. B. (1997) *Families in Classical and Hellenistic Greece: Representations and Realities.* Oxford and New York.

Pong, S.-L., J. Dronkers, and G. Hampden-Thompson (2003) "Family policies and children's school achievement in single- versus two-parent families," *Journal of Marriage and Family* 65: 681–99.

Pope John Paul II (1982) "Apostolic Exhortation Familiaris consortio, no. 19," *Acta Apostolicae Sedis* 74: 101–2.

Popenoe, D. (1996) *Life without Father: Compelling New Evidence that Fatherhood and Marriage Are Indispensable for the Good of Children and Society.* New York.

Powell, A. (2001) *Athens and Sparta. Constructing Greek Social and Political History from 478 BC.* 2nd edn. London.

Pratt, L. (2007) "The parental ethos of the *Iliad,*" in *Constructions of Childhood in Ancient Greece and Italy,* ed. A. Cohen and J. B. Rutter. Princeton: 25–40.

Prostmeier, F. R. (1999) *Der Barnabasbrief* (Kommentar zu den Apostolischen Vätern 8). Göttingen.

Purvis, S. (1998) "A Question of Families," *Interpretation* 52: 145–60.

Rabel, R. (1997) *Plot and Point of View in the Iliad*. Ann Arbor, MI.

Radice, B. (1969) *Pliny: Letters and Panegyricus*. Cambridge, MA.

Ramage, E. S. (1991) "Sulla's propaganda," *Klio* 73: 93–121.

Rank, O. (1909) *Der Mythos der Geburt des Helden. Versuch einer psychologischen Mythendeutung*. Leipzig and Vienna.

Rathbone, D. W. (1990) "Villages, land and population," *PCPhS* 216: 103–42.

Rawson, B. (1986) "The Roman family," in *The Family in Ancient Rome: New Perspectives*, ed. B. Rawson. Ithaca, NY: 1–57.

(1989) "*Spurii* and the Roman view of illegitimacy," *Antichthon* 23: 10–41.

(ed.) (1991a) *Marriage, Divorce, and Children in Ancient Rome*. Oxford.

(1991b) "Adult–child relationships in Roman society," in Rawson (1991a): 7–30.

(2003) *Children and Childhood in Roman Italy*. Oxford and New York.

Rawson, B., and P. R. C. Weaver (eds.) (1997) *The Roman Family in Italy: Status, Sentiment, Space*. Canberra, New York, and Oxford.

Reams, L. E. (1984) "Sulla's alleged early poverty and Roman rent," *AJA* 9: 158–74.

(1987) "The strange case of Sulla's brother," *CQ* 82: 301–5.

Redfield, J. (1975) *Nature and Culture in the* Iliad: *The Tragedy of Hector*. Chicago and London.

Rees, R. (2001) "To be and not to be: Pliny's paradoxical Trajan," *BICS* 45: 149–68.

Reher, D. S., and F. González-Quiñones (2003) "Do parents really matter? Child health and development in Spain during the demographic transition," *Population Studies* 57: 63–75.

Reichardt, T. (2003) *Recht und Rationalität im frühen Griechenland*. Würzburg.

Reinhold, M. (1982) "The declaration of war against Cleopatra," *CJ* 77: 97–103.

Renkema, J. (1995) "Does Hebrew *YTWM* really mean 'fatherless'?," *VT* 45: 119–21.

Richardson, N. (1993) *The Iliad. A Commentary*, vol. VI: *Books 21–24*. Cambridge.

Ringgren, H. (1982) "Jatom," *Theologisches Wörterbuch zum Alten Testament*, vol. III, ed. G. J. Botterweck and H. Ringgren. Stuttgart: 1075–9.

Roberts, A. (1988) *Mark Antonius: His Life and Times*. Upton-upon-Severn.

Roberts, M. (1989) *The Jewelled Style. Poetry and Poetics in Late Antiquity*. Ithaca, NY.

Roessel, D. (1990) "The significance of the name Cerinthus in the poems of Sulpicia," *TAPhA* 120: 243–50.

Rolfe, J. C. (ed.) (1914) *Suetonius*, vol. 1. London.

Roller, D. W. (2003) *The World of Juba II and Cleopatra Selene: Royal Scholarship on Rome's African Frontier*. New York and London.

Rolley, C. (2006) "Kleopatras Kinder," in *Kleopatra und die Caesaren. Eine Ausstellung des Bucerius Kunst Forums 28. Oktober 2006 bis 4. Februar 2007*, ed. B. Andreae. Munich: 164–75.

Roloff, J. (1988) *Der erste Brief an Timotheus* (Evangelisch-Katholischer Kommentar zum Neuen Testament 15). Neukirchen-Vluyn.

Rose, C. B. (1997) *Dynastic Commemoration and Imperial Portraiture in the Julio-Claudian Period*. Cambridge.

Rosenstein, N. S. (2004) *Rome at War. Farms, Families and Death in the Middle Republic*. Chapel Hill and London.

Rousselle, R. (2001) "'If it is a girl, cast it out:' infanticide/exposure in ancient Greece," *Journal of Psychohistory* 28: 303–33.

Roux, G. (1963) "Kypselé: ou avait-on caché le petit Kypselos?," *REA* 65: 279–89.

Rowland Jr., R. J. (1966) "Numismatic propaganda under Cinna," *TAPhA* 97: 407–19.

Rowlandson, J. (1998) *Women and Society in Roman Egypt: A Sourcebook*. Cambridge.

Rubinstein, L. (1993) *Adoption in IV. Century Athens*. Copenhagen.
(1999) "Adoption in Classical Athens," in Corbier (1999): 45–62.

Ruppel, S. (2006) *Verbündete Rivalen. Geschwisterbeziehungen im Hochadel des 17. Jahrhunderts*. Cologne.

Ruschenbusch, E. (1966) Σώλωνος νόμοι: *Die Fragmente des solonischen Gesetzeswerkes mit einer Text- und Überlieferungsgeschichte*. Wiesbaden.

Russell, D. A. (1966) "On reading Plutarch's *Lives*," *G&R* 13: 139–54.

Rutherford, R. B. (1982) "Tragic form and feeling in the *Iliad*," *JHS* 102: 145–60.

Sallares, R. (2002) *Malaria and Rome: A History of Malaria in Ancient Italy*. Oxford.

Saller, R. P. (1984) "*Familia, domus*, and the Roman conception of the family," *Phoenix* 38: 336–55.
(1987) "Men's age at marriage and its consequences in the Roman family," *CPh* 82: 21–34.
(1991) "Roman heirship strategies: in principle and in practice," *The Family in Italy from Antiquity to the Present*, ed. D. I. Kertzer and R. P. Saller. New Haven: 26–47.
(1994) *Patriarchy, Property and Death in the Roman Family*. Cambridge.
(1997) "Roman kinship. Structure and sentiment," in Rawson and Weaver (1997): 7–34.

Saller, R. P., and B. Shaw (1984) "Tombstones and Roman family relations in the Principate: civilians, soldiers and slaves," *JRS* 74: 124–56.

Sauer, G. (2000) *Jesus Sirach/Ben Sira*. Göttingen.

Saunders, T. J. (1970) *Plato. The Laws*. New York.

Schäfer, C. (2006) *Kleopatra*. Darmstadt.

Schanz, M., C. Hosius, and G. Krüger (1920) *Geschichte der römischen Literatur bis zum Gesetzgebungswerk des Kaisers Justinian: Die Literatur des 5. und 6. Jahrhunderts* (Handbuch der Altertumswissenschaft VIII.4.2). 4th edn. Munich.

Schaps, D. M. (1979) *Economic Rights of Women in Ancient Greece*. Edinburgh.

Scheidel, W. (ed.) (1991a) *Marriage, Divorce, and Children in Ancient Rome*. Oxford.
(1991b) "Adult–child relationships in Roman society," in Rawson (1991a): 7–30.
(1996) *Measuring Sex, Age and Death in the Roman Empire: Explorations in Ancient Demography*. Ann Arbor, MI.
(1997) "Quantifying the sources of slaves in the early Roman empire," *JRS* 87: 156–69.
(1999) "Emperors, aristocrats and the Grim Reaper: towards a demographic profile of the Roman élite," *CQ* 49: 254–81.

(2001a) *Death on the Nile: Disease and the Demography of Roman Egypt*. Leiden and Boston.

(2001b) *Debating Roman Demography*. Leiden and Boston.

(2001c) "Roman age structure: evidence and models," *JRS* 91: 1–26.

(2007a) "Marriage, family, and survival in the Roman imperial army: Demographic aspects," in *A Companion to the Roman Army*, ed. P. Erdkamp. Malden, MA: 417–34.

(2007b) "Roman funerary commemoration and the age at first marriage," *CPh* 102: 389–402.

Schlosser, J., G. Vanoni, F. Avemaria, and E.-M. Faber (2001) "Vaterschaft Gottes," *Lexikon für Theologie und Kirche*, vol. x, ed. W. Kaspar *et al*. 3rd edn. Freiburg: 544–8.

Schmidt, A. (ed.) (1985) *Gesammelte Schriften: Max Horkheimer*, vol. iii: *Schriften 1931–1936*, ed. A. Schmidt and G. Schmidt Nörr. Frankfurt am Main.

Schmitt, H. H. (2005) "Herrscherlegenden," in *Lexikon des Hellenismus*, ed. H. H. Schmitt and E. Vogt. 3rd edn. Wiesbaden: 452–4.

Schnackenburg, R. (2001) *Das Johannesevangelium. Dritter Teil*. Freiburg, Basel, and Vienna.

Schnapp-Gourbeillon, A. (1982) "Le lion et le loup: Diomédie et dolonie dans l'Iliade," *QS* 15: 45–77.

Schödel, W. R. (1990) *Die Briefe des Ignatius von Antiochien: Ein Kommentar*. Munich.

Scholz, P. (2003) "Sullas *Commentarii* – eine literarische Rechtfertigung," in *Formen römischer Geschichtsschreibung von den Anfängen bis Livius*, ed. U. Eigler, U. Gotter, N. Luraghi, and U. Walter. Darmstadt: 172–95.

Schouler, B. (1985) "Hommages de Libanios aux femmes de son temps," *Pallas* 32: 123–48.

Schrapel, T. (1996) *Das Reich der Kleopatra: Quellenkritische Untersuchungen zu den "Landschenkungen" Mark Antons*. Trier.

Schuller, W. (2006) *Kleopatra. Königin in drei Kulturen: Eine Biographie*. Reinbek.

Schulthess, O. (1886) *Vormundschaft nach attischem Recht*. Freiburg.

Schüngel-Straumann, H. (2000) *Tobit*. Freiburg, Basel, and Vienna.

Schürmann, H. (2001) *Das Lukasevangelium. Erster Teil*. Freiburg, Basel, and Vienna (repr. of 1984).

Schüssler-Fiorenza, E. (1983) *In Memory of Her. A Feminist Theological Reconstruction of Christian Origins*. London.

Scodel, R. (1992) "The wits of Glaucus," *TAPhA* 122: 73–84.

Scott, E. (2001) "Killing the female? Archaeological narratives of infanticide," in *Gender and the Archaeology of Death*, ed. B. Arnold and N. L. Wicker. Walnut Creek, CA: 3–21.

Scott, K. (1933) "The political propaganda of 44–30 BC," *Memoirs of the American Academy in Rome* 11: 7–50.

Scott, S. P. (trans.) (1932) *The Civil Code*. 17 vols. Cincinnati.

Scott-Kilvert, I. (ed.) (1987) *Cassius Dio: The Roman History, the Reign of Augustus*. London.

Seeck, O. (1906) *Die Briefe des Libanius*. Leipzig.

Seesemann, H. (1954) "Orphanos," *Theologisches Wörterbuch zum Alten Testament*, vol. v, ed. G. J. Botterweck and H. Ringgren. Stuttgart: 486–8.

Segalen, M. (1990) *Die Familie. Geschichte, Soziologie, Anthropologie*. Frankfurt am Main, New York, and Paris.

Seltzer, J. A. (2000) "Families formed outside of marriage," *Journal of Marriage and the Family* 62: 1247–68.

(2004) "Cohabitation in the United States and Britain: demography, kinship, and the future," *Journal of Marriage and Family* 66: 921–28.

Severidt, E. (2002) *Familie, Verwandtschaft und Karriere bei den Gonzaga. Struktur und Funktion von Familie und Verwandtschaft bei den Gonzaga und ihren deutschen Verwandten (1444–1519)*. Leinfelden-Echterdingen.

Severy, B. (2003) *Augustus and the Family at the Birth of the Roman Empire*. New York and London.

Shackleton Bailey, D. R. (2003) *Statius: Silvae*. Cambridge, MA.

Shapiro, H. A. (2003) "Fathers and sons, men and boys," in Neils and Oakley (2003): 85–111.

Sharp, M. (1999) "The village of Theadelphia in the Fayum: land and population in the second century," in *Agriculture in Egypt: From Pharaonic to Modern Times (Proceedings of the British Academy 96)*, ed. A. K. Bowman and E. Rogan. Oxford: 159–92.

Shaw, B. D. (1984) "Latin funerary epigraphy and family life in the Later Roman Empire," *Historia* 33: 457–97.

(1987) "The age of Roman girls at marriage: some reconsiderations," *JRS* 77: 30–46.

(1996) "Seasons of death: aspects of mortality in Imperial Rome," *JRS* 86: 100–38.

(2001) "Raising and killing children: two Roman myths," *Mnemosyne* 54: 33–77.

Shelton, J.-A. (1987) "Pliny's Letter 3.11. Rhetoric and autobiography," *C&M* 38: 121–39.

Sherwin-White, A. N. (1968) *The Letters of Pliny*. Oxford.

Shields, C. (1992) *The Republic of Love*. Mississauga, ON.

Shipley, F. W. (ed.) (1961) *Velleius Paterculus, Compendium of Roman History*. London.

Shuckburgh, E. (ed.) (1899–1904) *The Letters of Cicero*. 4 vols. London.

Silverstein, L. B., and C. F. Auerbach (1999) "Deconstructing the essential father," *American Psychologist* 54: 397–407.

Simmons, T., and M. O'Connell (2003) "Married-couple and unmarried-partner households: 2000," *Census 2000 Special Reports* CENSR-5. (Census Bureau).

Singer, M. W. (1944) "Octavia Minor, sister of Augustus: an historical and bio-graphical study." PhD thesis Duke University.

Skoie, M. (2002) *Reading Sulpicia: Commentaries 1475–1990*. Oxford.

Slater, N. W. (1993) "Theozotides on adopted sons (Lysias *fr.* 6)," *Scholia* 2: 81–5.

Smock, P. J. (2000) "Cohabitation in the United States: an appraisal of research themes, findings, and implications," *Annual Review of Sociology* 26: 1–20.

Smolenaars, J. J. L. (2006) "Ideology and poetics along the *via Domitiana*: Statius *Silv.* 4.3," in *Flavian Poetry*, ed. R. R. Nauta, H.-J. van Dam, and J. J. L. Smolenaars. Leiden: 223–44.

Sourvinou-Inwood, C. (1979) *Theseus as Son and Stepson. A Tentative Illustration of the Greek Mythological Mentality.* London.

Stacey, J. (1998) "Dada-ism in the 1990s: getting past the baby talk about father-lessness," in *Lost Fathers: The Politics of Fatherlessness in America*, ed. C. R. Daniels. New York: 51–83.

(2003) "Queer like us," in *All our Families: New Policies for a New Century: A Report of the Berkeley Family Forum*, ed. M. A. Mason, A. S. Skolnick and S. D. Sugarman. New York.

Stähelin, F. (1921) "Kleopatra Selene Nr. 23," *RE* xi.1: 784–5.

Stegemann, W. (1980) "Lasset die Kinder zu mir kommen. Sozialgeschichtliche Aspekte des Kinderevangeliums," in *Traditionen der Befreiung*, vol. 1, ed. W. Schottroff and W. Stegemann. Munich and Berlin: 114–44.

Steinwenter, A. (1955) *Das Recht der koptischen Urkunden* (Handbuch der Altertumswissenschaft x.4.2). Munich.

Stevenson, J. (2005) *Women Latin Poets: Language, Gender, and Authority from Antiquity to the Eighteenth Century.* Oxford.

Stevenson, T. R. (1992) "The ideal benefactor and the father analogy in Greek and Roman thought," *CQ* 42: 421–36.

Stolz, H. E., B. K. Barber, and J. A. Olsen (2005), "Toward disentangling fathering and mothering: an assessment of relative importance," *Journal of Marriage and Family* 67: 1076–92.

Strasburger, H. (1990) *Zum antiken Gesellschaftsideal*, ed. W. Schmitthenner and R. Zoepffel. Hildesheim and New York. (Originally published in *Abh. der Heidelberger Akademie der Wissenschaften, phil.-hist. Kl.* 4. Heidelberg 1976.)

Strauss, B. S. (1993) *Fathers and Sons in Athens: Ideology and Society in the Era of the Peloponnesian War.* Princeton.

Strohschein, L. (2005) "Parental divorce and child mental health trajectories," *Journal of Marriage and Family* 67: 286–300.

Strotmann, A. (1991) *"Mein Vater bist du!" Zur Bedeutung der Väter in kanononi-schen und nichtkanonischen Schriften.* Frankfurt am Main.

Stroud, R. S. (1971) "Greek inscriptions: Theozotides and the Athenian orphans," *Hesperia* 40: 280–301.

Sumi, G. S. (2002) "Spectacles and Sulla's public image," *Historia* 51: 414–32.

(2005) *Ceremony and Power: Performing Politics in Rome between Republic and Empire.* Ann Arbor, MI.

Swain, S. C. R. (1989) "Plutarch's *de fortuna romanorum*," *CQ* 39: 504–16.

(1990) "Hellenic culture and the Roman heroes of Plutarch," *JHS* 110: 126–45.

Syme, R. (1939) *The Roman Revolution.* Oxford.

(1960) "Bastards in the Roman aristocracy," *Proceedings of the American Philosophical Society* 104: 323–7 (reprinted in R. Syme [1979] *Roman Papers*, vol. ii, ed. A. R. Birley. Oxford: 510–17).

(1962) *The Roman Revolution.* 4th edn. Oxford.

(1964) *Sallust*. Berkeley.

(1981) "A Roman orator mislaid," *CQ* 31: 421–7.

(1984) "The crisis of 2 BC," in R. Syme, *Roman Papers*, vol. III, ed. A. R. Birley. Oxford: 912–36.

Szelest, H. (1972) "Mythologie und ihre Rolle in den *Silvae* des Statius," *Eos* 60: 309–17.

Taplin, O. (1992) *Homeric Soundings: The Shaping of the* Iliad. Oxford.

Tarn, W. W. (1932) "Alexander Helios and the Golden Age," *JRS* 22: 135–60.

Tarn, W. W., and M. P Charlesworth (1965) *Octavian, Antonius and Cleopatra.* Cambridge.

Tasker, F. L., and S. Golombok (1997) *Growing Up in a Lesbian Family: Effects on Child Development.* New York.

Taubenschlag, R. (1955) *The Law of Graeco-Roman Egypt in the Light of the Papyri, 332 BC – 640 AD.* 2nd edn. Warsaw.

(1959) *Opera Minora*, vol. II. Warsaw.

Thomas, Y. (1986) "À Rome, pères citoyens et cité des pères II siècle avant J.C. – IIè siècle apres J.C.," in *Histoire de la famille*, vol. I, ed. A. Burguière and P. Beillevaire. Paris: 195–229.

(1996) "Rom: Väter als Bürger in einer Stadt der Väter," in *Geschichte der Familie,* vol. I: *Altertum,* ed. A. Burgière, Ch. Klapisch-Zuber, M. Segalen, and F. Zonabend. Frankfurt am Main: 277–326.

Thommen, L. (2000) "Gaius Marius – oder: Der Anfang vom Ende der Republik," in *Von Romulus zu Augustus*, ed. K.-J. Hölkeskamp and E. Stein-Hölkeskamp. Munich: 187–98.

Traill, D. (1989) "Gold armor for bronze and Homer's use of compensatory TIMH," *CPh* 84: 301–5.

Treggiari, S. (1991a) *Roman Marriage. Iusti Coniuges from the Time of Cicero to the Time of Ulpian.* Oxford.

(1991b) "Divorce Roman style: how easy and how frequent was it?," in Rawson (1991a): 31–46.

(1993) "Review of M. Bettini (1991) *Anthropology and Roman Culture. Kinship, Time, Images of the Soul* (trans. John van Sickle). Baltimore," *Phoenix* 47: 274–6.

(2005) "Putting the family across: Cicero on natural affection," in *The Roman Family in the Empire. Rome, Italy and Beyond*, ed. M. George. Oxford: 9–35.

Trevett, J. C. (1992) *Apollodorus, Son of Pasion.* Oxford.

Trowell, J., and A. Etchegoyen (2002) *The Importance of Fathers: A Psychoanalytic Re-evaluation.* Hove and New York.

Tsirpanlis, E. C. (1966) "Patronymics in Homer," *Platon* 18: 241–56.

Tyrrell, W. M., and F. S. Brown (1991) *Athenian Myths and Institutions. Words in Action.* New York.

Ulf, C. (1990) *Die homerische Gesellschaft. Materialien zur analytischen Beschreibung und historischen Lokalisierung.* Munich.

Ungern-Sternberg, J. v. (1970) *Untersuchungen zum spätrepublikanischen Notstandsrecht. Senatusconsultum ultimum und hostis-Erklärung.* Munich.

Uzzi, J. D. (2005) *Children in the Visual Arts of Imperial Rome*. Cambridge.

Van Bremen, R. (1996) *The Limits of Participation: Women and Civic Life in the Greek East in the Hellenistic and Roman Periods*. Amsterdam.

Van Dam, R. (2003) *Families and Friends in Late Roman Cappadocia*. Philadelphia.

Van Minnen, P. (1994) "House-to-house enquiries: an interdisciplinary approach to Roman Karanis," *ZPE* 100: 227–51.

   (1998) "Did ancient women learn a trade outside the home? A note on *SB* xviii 13305," *ZPE* 123: 201–3.

Van Poppel, F. (2000) "Children in one-parent families: survival as an indicator of the role of parents," *Journal of Family History* 25: 269–90.

Vatin, C. (1970) *Recherches sur le mariage et la condition de la femme mariée à l'époque hellénistique*. Paris.

Vernant, J.-P. (1982) "From Oedipus to Periander: lameness, tyranny and incest in legend and history," *Arethusa* 15: 19–38 (translation of "Le tyran boiteux: d'Oedipe à Périandre," *Le Temps de la Réflexion* 2 [1981]: 235–55).

Veyne, P. (1978) "La famille et l'amour sous le Haut-Empire romain," *Annales ESC* 33: 35–63.

Vidal-Naquet, P. (1981a) "The Black Hunter and the origin of the Athenian *ephebeia*," in *Myth, Religion and Society. Structuralist Essays by M. Detienne, J.-P. Vernant and P. Vidal-Naquet*, ed. R. L. Gordon. Cambridge: 147–62. (Originally published in *PCPhS* 14 [1968]: 49–64, translation of "Le Chasseur Noir et l'origine de l'éphébie athénienne," *Annales ESC* 23 [1968]: 947–64.)

   (1981b) "Slavery and the rule of women in tradition, myth and utopia," in *Myth, Religion and Society. Structuralist Essays by M. Detienne, J.-P. Vernant and P. Vidal-Naquet*, ed. R. L. Gordon. Cambridge: 187–200.

Vittinghoff, F. (1936) *Der Staatsfeind in der römischen Kaiserzeit. Untersuchungen zur "damnatio memoriae,"* Munich.

Volk, K. (2006) "Von Findel-, Waisen-, verkauften und deportierten Kindern. Notizen aus Babylonien und Assyrien," in *"Schaffe mir Kinder …" Beiträge zur Kindheit im Alten Israel und seinen Nachbarkulturen*, ed. A. Kunz-Lübcke and R. Lux. Leipzig: 47–87.

Volkmann, H. (1958) *Sullas Marsch auf Rom*. Munich.

Volterra, E. (1978) "Ancora sul matrimonio di Antonio con Cleopatra," in *Festschrift für Werner Flume zum 70. Geburtstag: 12. September 1978*, ed. H. H. Jakobs, B. Knobbe-Keuk, E. Picker, and J. Wilhelm. Cologne: 205–12.

Wade, M. (1968) *The French-Canadians, 1760–1967*. Toronto.

Wahl, H. M. (1999) "Ester, das adoptierte Waisenkind. Zur Adoption im Alten Testament," *Biblica* 80: 78–99.

Watson P. A. (1989) "Filiaster: *privignus* or 'illegitimate child'?," *CQ* 39: 536–48.

   (1995) *Ancient Stepmothers: Myth, Misogyny and Reality*. Leiden, New York, and Cologne.

   (1996) "Sulpicia (1)," *OCD*. 3rd edn.: 1454.

Watts, E. J. (2006) *City and School in Late Antique Athens and Alexandria*. Berkeley.

Weaver, P. R. C. (1997) "Children of Junian Latins," in Rawson and Weaver (1997): 55–72.

Weber, M. (1972) *Wirtschaft und Gesellschaft. Grundriss der verstehenden Soziologie.* 5th edn. Tübingen.

Weiler, I. (1980) "Zum Schicksal der Witwen und Waisen bei den Völkern der Alten Welt. Materialien für eine vergleichende Geschichtswissenschaft," *Saeculum* 31: 157–93.

Wengst, K. (2001) *Das Johannesevangelium. 2. Teilband.* (Theologischer Kommentar zum NT 4.2). Stuttgart.

Werner, V. (1995) *Quantum bello optimus, tantum pace pessimus. Studien zum Mariusbild in der antiken Geschichtsschreibung.* Bonn.

West, M. L. (1978) *Hesiod Works & Days.* Oxford.
    (1997) *The East Face of Helicon: West Asiatic Elements in Greek Poetry and Myth.* Oxford and New York.

White, P. (1973) "Notes on two Statian prosopa," *CPh* 68: 279–84.

Whitehead, D. (1977) *The Ideology of the Athenian Metic.* Cambridge.

Whitehorne, J. (1994) *Cleopatras.* London.

Whitman, C. (1958) *Homer and the Heroic Tradition.* New York.

Wiedemann, T. E. J. (1989) *Adults and Children in the Roman Empire.* London.

Wiesehöfer, J. (1994) *Die "dunklen Jahrhunderte" der Persis. Untersuchungen zu Geschichte und Kultur von Fars in frühhellenistischer Zeit.* Munich.
    (2004) "Daiukku, Deiokes und die medische Reichsbildung," in *Deiokes, König der Meder. Eine Herodot-Episode in ihren Kontexten,* ed. M. Meier, B. Patzek, U. Walter, and J. Wiesehöfer. Wiesbaden: 15–26.
    (2005) *Das antike Persien von 550 v. Chr. bis 650 n. Chr.* 3rd edn. Düsseldorf.

Wilcken, U. (1894) "Alexandros Nr. 28," *RE* I: 1441–2.

Wilfong, T. G. (2002) *Women of Jeme: Lives in a Coptic Town in Late Antique Egypt. New Texts from Ancient Cultures.* Ann Arbor, MI.

Winterling, A. (1999) *Aula Caesaris: Studien zur Institutionalisierung des römischen Kaiserhofes in der Zeit von Augustus bis Commodus (31 v. Chr. – 192 n. Chr.).* Munich.
    (2005) "'Öffentlich' und 'privat' im kaiserzeitlichen Rom," in *Gegenwärtige Antike – antike Gegenwarten. Kolloquium zum 60. Geburtstag von Rolf Rilinger,* ed. T. Schmitt, W. Schmitz, and A. Winterling. Munich: 223–44.

Wirth, G. (1993) *Der Weg in die Vergessenheit. Zum Schicksal des antiken Alexanderbildes.* Vienna.

Wiseman, T. P. (1974) "Legendary genealogies in late-republican Rome," *G&R* 21: 153–64.

Wöhrle, G. (1999) *Telemachs Reise. Väter und Söhne in Ilias und Odyssee oder ein Beitrag zur Männlichkeitsideologie in den homerischen Epen.* Göttingen.

Wolff, H.-J. (1944) "Marriage law and family organisation in ancient Athens: a study of the interrelation of public and private law in the Greek city," *Traditio* 2: 43–95.
    (1945) "The background of the postclassical legislation on illegitimacy" *Seminar* 3: 21–45.
    (1978) *Das Recht der griechischen Papyri Ägyptens in der Zeit der Ptolemäer und des Prinzipats,* vol. II: *Organisation und Kontrolle des privaten Rechtsverkehrs* (Handbuch der Altertumswissenschaft x.5.2). Munich.

(2002) *Das Recht der griechischen Papyri Ägyptens in der Zeit der Ptolemäer und des Prinzipats,* vol. I: *Bedingungen und Triebkräfte der Rechtsentwicklung* (Handbuch der Altertumswissenschaft x.5.1), ed. H. -A. Rupprecht. Munich.

Woods, R. (1993) "On the historical relationship between infant and adult mortality," *Population Studies* 47: 195–219.

(2007) "Ancient and early modern mortality: experience and understanding," *Economic History Review* 60: 373–99.

Wosnik, B. (1963) *Untersuchungen zur Geschichte Sullas.* Würzburg.

Yarbrough, O. L. (1995) "Parents and children in the letters of Paul," in *The Social World of the First Christians (FS W. A. Meeks)*, ed. L. M. White and O. L. Yarbrough. Augsburg, MN: 126–41.

Yiftach-Firanko, U. (2006) "Spouses in wills: a diachronic survey (III BC – IV AD)," *JJP* 36: 153–66.

Youtie, H. C. (1973) *Scriptiunculae*, vol. I. Amsterdam.

(1975) "ΑΠΑΤΟΡΕΣ: law vs. custom in Roman Egypt," in *Le monde grec: pensée, litterature, histoire, documents: hommage à Claire Préaux*, ed. J. Bingen. Brussels: 723–40 (repr. in H. C. Youtie [1981] *Scriptiunculae Posteriores*, vol. I. Brussels and Bonn: 179–201).

Zeiner, N. K. (2005) *Nothing Ordinary Here: Statius as Creator of Distinction in the Silvae.* New York.

Index

A note on Roman names: we have listed Romans of the Republican and early imperial periods by their common anglicized name instead of by *nomen*, e.g. "Cicero (M. Tullius Cicero)," "Pliny the Younger (G. Plinius Caecilius Secundus)." Romans for whom there is no such common name are listed by the name most commonly found in the text, e.g. "Crispinus (Vettius Crispinus, son of M. Vettius Bolanus)." While such a system inevitably does some violence to Roman naming conventions and is not strictly consistent, it does follow the usage by the various authors of this book and should thus make the index easier to use for most readers.

fatherlessness
 ancient causes of 9, 44, 120, 121
 and biology 5, 246, 250, 253, 255, 256
 and criminal behavior 6, 266
 definition of 5–13, 19–21, 25–8, 86, 120, 277
 and dislocation 58, 61, 73, 242
 and economic consequences of 8, 10, 52–5, 61,
  62, 64, 76–7, 80, 95, 142, 165, 170, 221, 223,
  229, 258, 265–6; *see also* debt; poverty
 and memory 144, 146, 148–50, 154, 157–9, 175,
  179, 224, 225, 248
 and modern debate 3, 5–8, 27, 101, 105–6
 and opportunity 19, 23, 24, 25, 44, 58, 141, 159,
  161, 190–1, 195–216, 256, 257, 286
 poetic representation of 141–60, 162–74, 243–9
 and politics *see* politics
 and psychological consequences 43, 58–60, 61,
  79, 97, 99, 118, 141, 142–3, 147–8, 150, 152–4,
  155, 157–61, 171, 179, 241, 242, 257
 rates of 5–7, 8–10, 33–6, 55–7, 106
 and rhetoric 23, 146–50, 151, 152, 157, 195–216,
  243–9, 252
 and social identity 85, 99, 142, 147, 165, 169–72,
  195–216
 and social status 13, 20–1, 77, 119, 131, 141, 229
 virtual 12, 19–21, 97, 105–19, 120–38, 143, 169,
  171, 174; *see also apatōr*, illegitimacy
 and war *see* war
 see also father-absence; fathers; orphans
fathers
 ancient fathers, scholarship on 4, 61, 64, 142
 authority of 47, 64, 76–7, 149, 159, 161, 175,
  176, 257
 biological ("natural") 5, 6, 100, 105, 252
 divine 51, 83, 116–17, 144–5
 economic responsibilities of 62, 64, 108, 169
 and education 10, 77, 175, 201, 231, 252, 258,
  261, 265, 271, 287–8
 and emotional relationship to children 10, 59,
  112, 142, 143, 144, 145, 175, 177
 and guardians 15, 17, 169, 173; *see also*
  guardianship
 modern fathers, scholarship on 3
 and paternity *see* paternity
 poetic representations of 22–3, 142, 147, 159–61,
  175, 178, 217, 246–9; *see also* poetry
 and protection 36, 40, 87, 151, 168
 and rivalry with sons 147, 148, 149, 160; *see also*
  sons
 as role models 22, 43, 143, 147–50, 157,
  159–60, 161, 176, 178, 179, 182–4, 190, 191,
  229, 241–3
 as social mediators 10, 62, 150, 172, 178, 190,
  201, 241–3
 see also fathering

fathers-in-law 53, 281, 282; *see also* household;
 marriage
fides 240
fosterage 48–51, 97, 107, 145, 201, 209–15, 227,
 242, 246, 278, 282, 286–90; *see also* surrogate
 fathers
foundlings 47, 195; *see also alumni/ae*
freedmen 125, 189, 195, 199, 202
friends 142, 175, 230, 260, 270; *see also* networks
Fulvia (wife of M. Antonius) 217, 218, 225, 230,
 233, 235, 239
funerals 179, 182, 189, 234

Gellius (Aulus Gellius) 183
gender 10, 15, 16, 44, 45, 87, 91, 123, 181–2, 191, 278
genos 107, 113–14; *see also* family, Greek; household
Glaucus 157, 158–9
gnēsios 20, 107, 108, 110, 112, 116, 174; *see also*
 illegitimacy
God/gods 83, 87–8, 90, 98, 116–17, 143–4, 161,
 173–4, 180, 181, 182, 276, 278; *see also* religion;
 and names of individual gods
godparents 48
Goody, Esther 59, 242, 251
Gracchus, G. Sempronius 177, 179–82, 184–5, 239
Gracchus, T. Sempronius 179, 180, 181, 184
grandchildren 220; *see also* grandparents
grandparents 6, 51, 130, 169
 grandfathers, maternal 169
 grandfathers, paternal 36, 51, 145, 151, 156, 157,
  160, 169, 178, 259, 261–2, 269, 271
 grandmothers 90
 great-grandparents 131
 see also grandchildren
grief *see* bereavement
guardianship 13–18, 36–7, 40, 44–6, 49, 81, 89, 91,
 93, 226, 290
 Greek 14–15, 44, 65–6, 73, 170
 and mothers *see* mothers
 Roman 15–18, 45, 62, 64, 67, 73–4, 76, 245, 247,
  259, 261, 267
 of women 16, 54, 74, 185, 186, 191; *see also*
  epiklēros; *kyrios*
 see also cura; *pupilli/ae*; *epitropos*; *tutor*; *curator*

half-siblings 65, 66, 72, 81, 112, 116, 217, 221,
 225–6, 230, 234, 235, 238; *see also* siblings
head of household *see* household, head of
Hector 42, 142, 155, 162, 163–8
Helen 168, 172
Hephaestus 117, 153
Hera 51, 116–17, 173
Heracles 51, 65, 108, 116, 144, 197, 198, 213, 214
Hermas, the Shepherd of 95
Hermione 168